SOCRATES ON TRIAL

Socrates on Trial

Thomas C. Brickhouse and Nicholas D. Smith

CLARENDON PRESS • OXFORD

*This book has been printed digitally and produced in a standard specification
in order to ensure its continuing availability*

OXFORD
UNIVERSITY PRESS

Great Clarendon Street, Oxford OX2 6DP
Oxford University Press is a department of the University of Oxford.
It furthers the University's objective of excellence in research, scholarship,
and education by publishing worldwide in
Oxford New York

Auckland Bangkok Buenos Aires Cape Town Chennai
Dar es Salaam Delhi Hong Kong Istanbul Karachi Kolkata
Kuala Lumpur Madrid Melbourne Mexico City Mumbai Nairobi
São Paulo Shanghai Singapore Taipei Tokyo Toronto
with an associated company in Berlin

Oxford is a registered trade mark of Oxford University Press
in the UK and in certain other countries

Published in the United States
by Oxford University Press Inc., New York

ISBN 0-19-823938-6

ὅσα μὲν γὰρ ἐφ᾽ ἡμῶν γέγονεν, εἰκότως ἂν ταῖς δόξαις ταῖς ἡμετέραις αὐτῶν διακρίνοιμεν, περὶ δὲ τῶν οὕτω παλαιῶν προσήκει τοῖς κατ᾽ ἐκεῖνον τὸν χρόνον εὖ φρονήσασιν ὁμονοοῦντας ἡμᾶς φαίνεσθαι.

(Isocrates, *Helen* 22)

For things that happen in our own time, it is proper to judge in accordance with our own beliefs; but as regards things so long ago, it is proper for us to show our judgment to be in agreement with sensible men alive at that time.

PREFACE

In the years we have worked together on Socratic philosophy in general, and on Plato's *Apology* in particular, we have become increasingly suspicious of two of the most common tendencies in the modern interpretation of Plato's early dialogues: first, the rejection of individual arguments, or even whole works, on the supposition that they reflect merely Socratic irony, haughtiness, or arrogance; and, secondly, the neglect, especially on the part of professional philosophers, of the historical contexts of the arguments—the very contexts, that is, in which Plato's intended audience would have interpreted them. In this book we attempt to provide a detailed interpretation of Plato's *Apology* that resists such shortcomings. Although we shall argue for our interpretative tendency in Section 1.5, we shall assume that any textually sound interpretation that brings a serious point to light, *ceteris paribus*, should be given preference over one that portrays Socrates merely as boasting, jesting, or inviting his own condemnation. Furthermore, we shall attempt at least to outline aspects of the relevant legal, cultural, or historical environment that we believe illuminate the meaning of Socrates' words. This does not reflect a presupposition on our part about the historical accuracy of Plato's portrayal (though we shall discuss this issue in Section 1.1.2), for Plato's ancient readers would have the relevant background information in mind as they read his *Apology*, even if they expected its substance to be fiction. We do not expect that those scholars who disagree fundamentally with the interpretive principles that guide our approach will be won over by our arguments. But we do hope to show at least that our assumptions do not ever force us into inconsistency or into disregarding or violating the most plausible reading of the text. To the extent that we have succeeded, we recommend our methods and assumptions to others. To the extent that we have failed, we invite our readers to educate us, so that we may better understand the man and the work whose appeal has so long captivated us.

One conclusion we have drawn from our investigation is certain to disappoint some readers. Socrates is revered by many as a kind of idealized philosophic martyr. The image of the philosopher in court as commanding and haughty, yet entirely relaxed, witty, and controlled, is indeed a very appealing one. It is hard to resist being drawn to a man who can so casually and fearlessly put himself above those whom he knows will succeed in taking his life unjustly. The image of Socrates we present is at least to some degree less romantically compelling, for on our view his haughtiness and wittiness in the courtroom have been exaggerated, and the real story of the *Apology* is that, constrained and propelled by the moral principles according to which he had lived and for which he would die, Plato's Socrates sincerely tried to win his release, and failed. But we recommend to our readers something also worthy of admiration, if somewhat less dramatically so: a man who steadfastly maintains his moral principles even when confronted by those who, he is convinced, are totally ignorant of their value, and even when he believes that only by abandoning those principles could he save himself from an unjust death. In a sense, then, we substitute one ideal portrait of Socrates for another: as we see him, Plato's Socrates is a man of superlative strength of character and constancy of commitment, who continues to practice his 'mission' at a time when other responses might prove to be more emotionally satisfying. But the very adherence to his principles we attribute to Socrates also forbade him from enjoying what might otherwise have mitigated the hopelessness of his predicament: he could not, on our view, receive the gratification that haughty defiance of his judges might have brought him.

Whenever possible, we have employed abbreviations for names and works in our notes in the same form as those given in *The Oxford Classical Dictionary*, and where those provided a choice, we have used the shortest versions (for example D. L. for Diogenes Laertius instead of the alternative, Diog. Laert., and Diod. for Diodorus Siculus instead of Diod. Sic.). We believe our other abbreviations will be self-explanatory. All dates given, unless otherwise noted, are BC. Whenever we had three or fewer ancient texts to offer as evidence for our claims, we added the citations in parentheses, unless some commentary was needed in addition. References to modern work are always given in the notes.

In the notes we have referred to works cited simply by their author's names, followed, when necessary, by the number corresponding to that work given in the bibliography, and the relevant page numbers, though works not specifically on Socrates or Plato's *Apology* that are cited only once may be given a complete bibliographical reference when cited in a note and omitted from the bibliography. For the bibliography, we have found it useful to give a separate list of abbreviations for periodicals cited. These may be found immediately following the bibliography.

The passages cited from Plato are those of the Oxford Classical Texts, using the standard form of citation—Stephanus page, letter, and line numbers. On the spelling of Greek proper names, we have usually employed the more familiar Latinized versions, especially for names that are widely recognized in that form. Hence we refer to Plato, and not Platon, Socrates and not Sokrates, Crito and not Kriton, and so on. Whenever direct transliteration of names seemed acceptable to us, however, we employed it in favor of Latinization. When we refer frequently to important Greek words, we first list the Greek and then give a direct transliteration, which we use consistently thereafter. In such cases, we have always avoided Latinization; this will be especially noticeable in our use of 'ai' in favour of 'ae' in certain words (such as '*daimonion*'), and our representing upsilon with 'u' and never with 'y' (as in '*psuche*'), and omicron with 'o' and never with 'u' (as in '*elenchos*'). For Greek words or phrases not used frequently, we cite only the original Greek with a translation to English. Unless otherwise noted, any translations appearing in this book are our own.

ACKNOWLEDGEMENTS

We are indebted to many people and institutions for their various contributions to our work on this project. Charles M. Reed has helped us in the interpretation of historical material and in assisting us overcome a number of infelicities in our diction. Mogens Herman Hansen and Peter Krentz have also provided us with assistance in historical matters. A sizeable number of friends, journal editors, commentators at conferences, and audiences have been kind enough to read parts of this project; David Halperin, James Klagge, Richard Kraut, Mark McPherran, Julius Moravcsik, Charles M. Reed, and especially Gregory Vlastos deserve special recognition for their efforts in prompting us to tighten our arguments and abandon at least some of our follies. Halperin, Klagge, Kraut, McPherran, and Moravcsik were also kind enough to read and criticize an entire draft of this book. T. H. Irwin, David Keyt, and Henry Teloh each provided helpful comments on two or more sections. We have also profited enormously from discussions with Alan Code. Various sections of this book were written while one or both of us received funding from the National Endowment for the Humanities; the writing of other parts was supported by grants administered by our own institutions. Nicholas D. Smith owes a special debt to the Center for Programs in the Humanities at VPI & SU in this regard. He also gratefully acknowledges the Departments of Philosophy and Classics and the library systems at the University of California, Berkeley, and at Stanford University for granting him access to their facilities. We owe the most to Gregory Vlastos, whose work has inspired us from the time we were undergraduates, whose support early in our careers was generously provided, and without whose subsequent exhortations, criticisms, and kindnesses (with regard to this work especially) we could never even have attempted such a project as this.

Various sections of this book are revised versions of articles we published elsewhere. Some have undergone substantial changes; in others, the changes are mainly cosmetic. All are at least somewhat changed. We are grateful to the following journals, editors, and publishers for their permission to use these materials.

'The Formal Charges against Socrates', which appeared in the *Journal of the History of Philosophy* 23 (1985), 457-81, has been revised herein as Sections 1.4.3-4, 3.1.1-4, and 3.1.6.

'Irony, Arrogance, and Sincerity in Plato's *Apology*', which appeared in *New Essays on Socrates*, ed. by E. Kelly, University Press of America (Lanham, New York, and London) 1984, 29-46, has been revised herein as Sections 1.5.1-3 and 5.1.1-2.

'Socrates' First Remarks to the Jury in Plato's *Apology of Socrates*', which appeared in the *Classical Journal* 81 (1986), 289-98, has been revised herein as Sections 2.1.1-4.

'Socrates' Evil Associates and the Motivation for His Trial and Condemnation', which appeared in *Proceedings of the Boston Area Colloquium in Ancient Philosophy* vol. III, ed. J. Cleary, University Press of America (Lanham, New York, and London) 1987, has been revised herein as Sections 2.4.1-5 and 4.1.1.

'The Origin of Socrates' Mission', which appeared in the *Journal of the History of Ideas* 44 (1983), 657-66, has been revised herein as Sections 2.5.1-5.

'The Paradox of Socratic Ignorance in Plato's *Apology*', which appeared in the *History of Philosophy Quarterly* 1 (1984), 125-31, has been revised herein as Sections 2.6.1-5.

'Socrates and Obedience to the Law', which appeared in *Apeiron* 18 (1984) 10-17, has been revised herein as Sections 3.3.1-6.

'Socrates' Proposed Penalty in Plato's *Apology*', which appeared in the *Archiv für Geschichte der Philosophie* 64 (1982), 1-18, has been revised herein as Sections 5.2.1-4 and 5.3.1-3.

'"The Divine Sign Did Not Oppose Me": A Problem in Plato's *Apology*', which appeared in The *Canadian Journal of Philosophy* 16 (1986), 511-26, has been revised herein as Sections 5.5.1-7.

CONTENTS

1

PRELIMINARIES

1.1 Some Historical Issues

1.1.1 AUTHORSHIP AND DATING

Given the history of its attribution to Plato, and the evidence provided by stylometric analyses,[1] there is virtually universal agreement among scholars that Plato did indeed write the *Apology* that has come down to us under his name.[2] The actual date of the *Apology*'s composition, however, is a matter of controversy. Neither stylometric analysis nor any of the other techniques used for establishing the chronological order of the dialogues can do more than place the *Apology* within the group of early dialogues.[3]

Nevertheless, many contemporary scholars maintain that Plato's *Apology* was written within the first two or three years following Socrates' trial and execution.[4] No doubt their confidence rests in large part on the assumption that Plato would have chosen to write about the trial when the event was still fresh in his mind. Such an opinion about the probable date of composition, however, is by no means universally held. Hackforth, for example, argues that the Xenophontic version predates Plato's.[5] Inasmuch as the trial took place in 399, and Xenophon did not even return from Asia Minor until 394, Hackforth's view allows for an interval of up to a decade between the actual trial and the composition of Plato's *Apology*. But the

---

[1] The method of stylometry is now over a century old, but the work we take to be definitive is by Leonard Brandwood (2). A summary of Brandwood's results may be found in Brandwood (1), xvi–xviii.

[2] To the best of our knowledge only Ast (474–9) and Zürcher have doubted the authenticity of Plato's *Ap.*

[3] There is now widespread argreement among contemporary Platonists as to which dialogues constitute the 'early period' group. For an excellent discussion and a review of the variety of opinions, see Guthrie (1), vol. 4, 39–72.

[4] See, e.g. J. Adam, xxi; Guthrie (1), vol. 4. 72; Kahn, 307–8; Montuori (5), 85; Wolff, 85. This view is opposed by Chroust ((3), 43), who supposes the *Ap.* to have been written after the *Charm., Prt., Lys., Euthphr.*, and possibly even the *Meno*, though before Xenophon's *Ap.*

[5] Hackforth (2) 8–45. This view is opposed by Chroust (3), 18–19, 39.

arguments advanced by Hackforth and others[6] for the later date of composition, though intriguing, are hardly decisive. Since there is reason to believe that all the early dialogues had been completed prior to Plato's first trip to Syracuse sometime around 387,[7] we can have some confidence that the *Apology* was written at some point during roughly the first decade following Socrates' trial. Any more precise dating of the work is probably impossible.

1.1.2 HISTORICAL ACCURACY

Fortunately, the exact date of composition of the *Apology* is of little consequence to its reader. By contrast, the question of its historical accuracy—of the extent to which it reflects what Socrates actually said at his trial—has traditionally been regarded as being of fundamental importance for our ability to recover a genuinely Socratic, as opposed merely to an early Platonic, philosophy. As we have said, the *Apology* can be confidently placed within a group of early dialogues, works that show not only remarkable stylometric and literary similarities but also close philosophical affinities to one another, with marked contrasts to the philosophical views expounded in Plato's later works. But the *Apology* is atypical in two important respects. First, it is the only work in which Plato makes it clear that he actually witnessed what Socrates said (see 34al and 38b6). Secondly, unlike virtually all of the other early dialogues in which Plato depicts Socrates asking questions of others and saying little about his own views (the *Crito* is also an exception), the *Apology* consists of three Socratic speeches, only the first of which is interrupted (and then only briefly) by a dialogic episode. During these speeches, Socrates makes a number of purportedly autobiographical remarks and articulates a variety of philosophical commitments. For these reasons, those who take the *Apology* to be essentially accurate in tone and substance (if not in every detail) claim that it is especially revealing about the thought of the historical Socrates. When other early dialogues contain the same facts or views contained in the *Apology*, or whatever follows from them, we are told that the material in question is genuinely Socratic. As Gregory Vlastos puts it, 'if this [the essential historical accuracy of the *Apology*] is conceded, our problem of sources is solved in principle. For we may then use the *Apology* as a

---

[6] See, e.g., J. Coulter. 269–303.
[7] See Guthrie (1), vol. 4, 53–4; Montuori (5), 85.

touchstone of the like veracity of the thought and character of Socrates depicted in Plato's other early dialogues.'[8]

The claim that Plato's version of the speech is a reliable source for the thought of the historical Socrates has a great deal of initial plausibility, indeed so much so that many modern scholars have found the claim compelling.[9] Since Plato actually witnessed the trial, the emotionally charged atmosphere 'must have branded those words into his mind', as Vlastos puts it.[10] This is not to say, however, that all who uphold the *Apology*'s historical accuracy would claim it is accurate in every detail. The remarks of Grote are typical. '[Plato's version] is in substance the real defence of Sokrates; reported and, of course, drest up, yet not intentionally transformed, by Plato.'[11] In support of such a conclusion, Taylor adds an observation often quoted with approval by commentators on the *Apology*: 'we must understand that like all circulated versions of celebrated speeches . . . the published speech is supposed to have been "revised" in accordance with the canons of prose writing. Plato has no doubt done for Socrates what men like Demosthenes did for their own speeches before giving them to the world'.[12]

There are other reasons for scepticism as to how much, if anything, can be known about what Socrates actually said before the court. First, as we have seen, there is no hard evidence that the *Apology* was composed a short time after the trial. The more time that passed between the occurrence of the event and Plato's account of it, the more likely it is that the report is inaccurate. Moreover, even if we assume that the *Apology* was written very soon after the trial and, hence, that Plato was quite able to capture accurately both the tone and the substance of what was said, it obviously does not follow that he in fact did so. We must remember that the trial of Socrates was notorious

---

[8] Vlastos (4), 4. A similar view is expressed by M. Nussbaum (2), 233 and n. 1. This view of the primary importance of the *Ap.* to the historical questions is shared even by Montuori, who is extremely sceptical, however, about Plato's accuracy (see esp. (5), 42–53, 60, 243).

[9] For examples of modern commentators who take Plato's Socrates to be essentially faithful to the historical Socrates, see Allen (1), 33–4 and (3), 33–6; Burnet (2), 63–6; Cornford (1), 303; Ehrenberg (1), 373; A. Ferguson, 170; Galli (2), 85; Gomez Robledo, esp. 125 ff.; Grote (2) vol. 1, 281–2; Guthrie (2), 29–35; Horneffer (1); Humbert (2), 30; Kraut (3) 3–4, n. 1; Osborn, 194; Rudberg (2), 107; Vogel (3); Zeller (2) 197–9, n. 1. Their view is supported by Panaitios' assessment, reported by D.L. (2.64).

[10] Vlastos (4), 3–4.

[11] Grote (2), vol. 1, 281.

[12] A. E. Taylor (2), 156.

and spawned a number of 'Socratic defenses',[13] of which only two (of this period) have come down to us, those of Plato and Xenophon. And we know of at least one instance, Polycrates' *Accusation of Socrates*, in which the opposite side of the case is presented.[14] Such evidence, then, at least suggests that the trial and execution of Socrates gave rise to a 'genre' of writings concerned not so much with what was actually said at the trial but with what *could* or *should* have been said on Socrates' behalf by his admirers and what *could* or *should* have been said against him by his detractors.

To defeat such sceptical considerations, some commentators have attempted to supply a motive for Plato's writing of the *Apology*. Consider, for example, Burnet's widely influential argument: 'Now Plato's aim is obviously to defend the memory of his master by setting forth his character and activity in their true light; and, as most of those present [at the trial] must still have been living when the *Apology* was published, he would have defeated his own end if he had given a fictitious account of the attitude of Socrates and the main line of his defence'.[15] Unfortunately, Burnet's way of stating his assumption begs the question as it stands, since whether or not Plato had wished to set forth the character and activity of Socrates 'in their true light' is the very thing at issue. But Vlastos has advanced a similar argument that avoids the defect of Burnet's: 'when Plato was writing the *Apology* he knew that hundreds of those who might read the speech he puts into the mouth of Socrates had heard the historical original. And since his purpose in writing was to clear his master's name and to indict the judges, it would have been most inept to make Socrates talk out of character'.[16]

It is entirely likely that Plato would have wished to clear his master's name for posterity; certainly he was not writing only to provide an unbiased report of the trial for posterity. The degree of distortion that follows from Plato's apologetic intention may be impossible

[13] Xenophon, in the opening lines of his *Apology*, refers to the fact that 'others' have written about what Socrates did, but he mentions no specific authors (see *Ap.* 1). For a complete list of those in addition to Plato and Xenophon who wrote 'Socratic Defenses', see Lesky, 499; Oldfather (2), 204. Aristotle refers in general terms to the Socratic literature at *Rh.* 1417a20 and at *Poet.* 1447b10.

[14] The most detailed reconstruction of Polycrates' accusations is by Chroust (3), esp. 69–100. The ancient sources include Aisch. Rhet. 1.173; Xen., *Mem.* 1.2.9.–61; Isoc., *Bus.* 5; D: L. 2.38–9; Libanius, *Ap.*

[15] Burnet (2), 63–4. Seeskin ((1), 60) cites Burnet's argument with approval.

[16] Vlastos (4), 3.

to identify, however, though on Vlastos's view a patently inaccurate account would surely be discredited by those who had heard the original. But others aver that the *Apology* is essentially a Platonic fiction, an 'obvious idealization of his master'[17] and 'an outspoken piece of propaganda for the life of a philosopher'.[18] The 'fiction theory' holds that the 'Socratic literature' sparked by the trial attempted no accurate representation of Socrates' words or opinions; rather, these works sought only to defend the nobility of philosophy itself, using the moment of the trial only as a way of enhancing their characters' words by fixing them within a provocative and dangerous setting.[19] On this view, the character 'Socrates' speaking before the court is but a literary device by means of which the friends of philosophy could praise it by showing the world the dedicated, principled life that philosophy engenders.

The questions raised by the 'fiction theory' are not only important for one who would use the *Apology* as a historical source; they require fundamental judgments to be made before the text itself may be understood. For example, if Plato's intended (ancient) audience would not be disposed to take his work as a representation of the actual trial, any knowledge that audience had about the trial or its context need not figure importantly in their understanding of the text. Fiction creates a reality of its own, and that reality—if not in itself incoherent—must be understood and evaluated in its own right. It is no criticism of fiction that the events it portrays never really happened, or never happened in the way the fiction portrays them as happening. On the other hand, to the degree that Plato's audience expected historical accuracy, they would have brought to bear in their reading

---

[17] Shorey (3), 33.   [18] Lesky, 520.

[19] The 'fiction theory' has had both ancient and modern proponents, for various reasons. For example, it was advanced by Dion. Hal. in the first century BC (see *Rhet.* 8 and 12), and in more recent times by Adorno; Ast, 474–88; Bonnard, 61; Bruns, 203–23; Chroust (3), 190; Derenne, 158–67; Dupreél; Friedländer, vol. 2, 157–60; Gigon (2); Gomperz (3), 32–43; Kuhn, 135; Lesky, 499; Montuori (5), 140–3, 243; Murray, 174; Norvin, 31; Oldfather (2), 203–11; Raschini, 36; Schanz (1), 74. Maximus of Tyre's story that Socrates was entirely mute at his trial (*Oratio* 3, p. 38, lines 5–18, ed. Hobein) implies clearly that Plato's account is fictional. We are not at all impressed by this evidence, and are also unmoved by the evidence of a genre of 'Socratic' works, whose contents cannot all be historically accurate. The Socratic genre may have begun with serious attempts at historical accuracy, only later to become increasingly prone to embellishment and invention, and thus Plato's *Apology,* which was written quite early relative to other works said to be in this genre, cannot be merely assumed to be as suspect as later 'Socratic writings'.

of the *Apology* a great deal of knowledge about the context of
Socrates' trial. Modern readers cannot reasonably hope to recover the
common knowledge of the ancient readers in full, but we must attempt to recover it as fully as possible if we are to be in anything like
the position Plato could expect his readers to be in as they read his
text, whether or not they took it—or were supposed to take it—as fiction. Our question is this: how much of this knowledge is required for
the best understanding of the text (if there is such a thing)? In what
follows, we shall argue that a number of considerations tell against
the 'fiction theory' and in favor of the 'accuracy theory'; accordingly, in the remainder of the book we shall attempt as much as possible
to call attention to what we know of the context of the trial, thus putting ourselves in the best position possible to understand Plato's
account in the way we believe its intended readers were supposed to
understand it. To some extent our conclusions about the fictional or
non-fictional nature of the *Apology* will remain uncertain, however;
so the emphasis in our interpretation on the context of the trial reflects
an assumption of our method more than a settled criterion of
adequacy in interpretation.

Unfortunately, Plato tells us nothing about his motives in writing
the *Apology*, but Xenophon begins his account by expressing his view
that the last days of Socrates should be remembered and stating that
his purpose in writing is to explain the proud tone (μεγαληγορία/
megalēgoria) characterizing Socrates' speech to the jury. He agrees
other accounts correctly showed that Socrates' speech was indeed
characterized by *megalēgoria*, but complains that other authors have
failed to explain why (Xen. *Ap.* 1). So Xenophon sets out to show
that, on the basis of what he had been told by Hermogenes, Socrates
preferred death to life. Of course, the Xenophontic version disagrees
with the Platonic version in a number of important respects.[20] But
Xenophon's intent in writing his defense of Socrates is clear: he seeks
to provide a historically accurate account of Socrates' *megalēgoria*
(*Ap.* 1); he is not merely defending the life of philosophy. In his account Xenophon refers to various things that Hermogenes told him
Socrates said. If the 'fiction theory' were right, then Xenophon would
knowingly fictionalize these references, thereby impugning Her-

---

[20] Where Xenophon's and Plato's versions disagree, most scholars reasonably take
Plato's to have the greater claim to accuracy, since Xenophon's version is explicitly
based upon second-hand information, whereas Plato was actually at the trial.

mogenes' credibility as a witness, and this *in an explicit effort to pro-vide an accurate explanation of what Socrates did*. Since Xenophon is the only author about whom we have direct evidence concerning his intention in writing a 'Defense', and since the evidence he provides supports the 'accuracy theory', it would appear that all the 'fiction theory' can claim is that the evidence we are thus provided is not decisive.

Adherents to the 'accuracy theory' also argue that had Plato seriously distorted any of the actual events at the trial, his contemporaries would have disputed the inaccuracies of his account. Those inclined to the 'fiction theory' deny this, claiming that no ancient reader would have seen the works of the 'Socratic genre' as attempts at historical accuracy in the first place. Hence the authors of these works would not be concerned about an audience who would dispute the facts of the case. But there is reason to favor the 'accuracy theory' on this issue as well. For one thing, we have no particular reason to suppose that a 'Socratic genre' already existed at the time Plato wrote the *Apology*. Given what we know about the dating of the work, the 'Socratic genre' may have come later—inspired in part by the work we are now trying to interpret. So even if works within this genre were not expected to be accurate, it does not follow that the *Apology* should not be taken as accurate. In addition, we know of at least one instance where an ancient author disputes the authenticity of a work supposedly within this genre *precisely on the ground* that it contains false elements. Diogenes Laertius (2.38) tells us that Favorinus, in the first book of his *Memorabilia*, denies that Polycrates' speech was one of those actually given at the trial because Polycrates mentions the rebuilding of the long walls by Conon, which did not happen until six years after Socrates' death. But none of the surviving ancient reports make such a criticism against Plato's or Xenophon's versions, which would lend at least some support to the idea that neither version makes any blatant historical distortions. And just as Favorinus was concerned with accuracy, we know from reading Diogenes that he, at least, viewed all such works as reporting historical events. And though much of Diogenes' biography is highly dubious, the fact remains that he took seriously all of the evidence he had as attempts to report history. If there was such a genre of fictional idealizations as the 'fiction theory' suggests, then, it was unknown to Favorinus and Diogenes.

Another consideration derives from an argument recently advanced by R. E. Allen.[21] It has long been noticed that Isocrates' *Antidosis* is unmistakably similar to Plato's *Apology* in a number of important respects. And it is clear that in writing the *Antidosis*, a fictional defense of his own life's work as a rhetorician against the prejudices of a hostile public, Isocrates intended to compare his own life with the life of Socrates. But, as Allen points out, it is extremely unlikely that Isocrates meant to compare himself with a fictional Socrates constructed by Plato. It follows, Allen concludes, 'that Isocrates, who was in a position to know, must have supposed that Plato's *Apology* is essentially accurate to the speech Socrates gave'.[22]

An even stronger argument for the essential accuracy of Plato's *Apology* can be made from the evidence provided by Isocrates' *Antidosis*. Given the similarities between the two works (and there are many), Allen apparently assumes that Isocrates actually used Plato's text to form the basis of his own argument. But the texts are not so similar in matters of style and diction as to require that parts of the *Antidosis* were actually drawn from or even modelled on the *Apology*. We know that at the time of the trial Isocrates was a grown man and considered himself a friend of Socrates. It is likely, then, that he would have been thoroughly familiar with what Socrates said either through his own experience or through the accounts of others who were present. But we also know that at the time of the composition of the *Antidosis* Isocrates and Plato were rivals, although there is no reason to think that their disagreements were vehement.[23] Since Isocrates was a rhetorician who prided himself on his ability to compose novel and clever speeches, it is unlikely that he would have used a speech of a rival in the way Allen proposes. It seems more likely that the similarities between the *Apology* and the *Antidosis* are due to both authors' recollections of the same moving historical occurrence. On this way of construing the evidence provided by the *Antidosis*, the similar things implied by both it and the *Apology* about Socrates' trial at least partially confirm the basic accuracy of Plato's version.

A final consideration derives in part from the internal evidence of the *Apology* itself regarding Socrates' principles together with external evidence provided by ancient sources other than Plato regarding Socrates' commitment to those same principles. According to the 'fiction theory', Plato provides us with a picture of what it is to be

---

[21] Allen (3), 33–6. See also Seeskin (1), 55 and n. 1, 68.   [22] Allen (ibid), 35.
[23] See *Phdr*. 278e5–279b3, and Rogers (2), 44.

thoroughly committed to philosophical principles even in the face of death. But on this view the picture is largely the work of Plato's considerable powers of imagination. The proponents of the 'fiction theory' see Plato's Socrates either as courting martyrdom or as utterly indifferent to the legal outcome of the trial. They thus fail to pay due attention both to the implications of the very principles they cite as explaining Plato's account of the trial, and to the evidence available to us that the historical Socrates actually held such principles. Now it is a primary thesis of our book that his principles require Socrates to do everything in his power, consistent with those principles, to gain his acquittal. If we are right, they allow him neither to seek martyrdom nor to scorn the proceedings with indifference. Moreover, there is good independent reason provided by Xenophon and the other writers of this period for thinking that the actual philosopher, Socrates, held these same principles.[24] Since virtually all the ancient reports insist that Socrates was a man who stood rigidly by his principles, the conclusion we should draw from these ancient reports is that Socrates was the sort of man who would have behaved at his trial in the manner that Plato describes. If so, we have an additional reason to think that Plato's version of what was said must bear some resemblance to the words Socrates actually spoke at his trial.

1.1.3 SUMMARY AND CONCLUSIONS CONCERNING THE HISTORICITY ISSUE

Since there is no compelling reason to doubt the basic accuracy of the *Apology* and at least some reason to think it accurate, we conclude (as have most commentators) that more probably than not the Platonic version captures at least the tone and substance of what Socrates actually said in the courtroom. Of course, we cannot have anything like dogmatic confidence that any of the particular points Socrates made were precisely as Plato states them. So we are inclined to believe, for example, that Socrates actually made reference to Chairephon's inquiry at the Delphic sanctuary and that he questioned his prosecutor, Meletus, at the trial, since both events are reported by Plato and

---

[24] Virtually every writer who is well disposed towards Socrates tells us that he was steadfastly committed to his moral principles. Since our concern is only to provide an interpretation of Plato's *Apology*, however, in so far as these principles are cited in the advancement of our following interpretation, we shall attempt only to document reports of them in the work of Plato.

Xenophon. And it is more likely than not that Socrates made reference to his unyielding commitment to virtue, since this, too, is reflected in both ancient versions of his speech, and is moreover a feature of Isocrates' closely related *Antidosis*. But one cannot claim to know that Socrates made any one of the more specific remarks attributed to him in the Platonic version, for any such claim would go far beyond what is warranted from the very slender evidence afforded by the ancient sources. So no commitment to that sort of specificity is intended in the interpretation that follows. But, though we cannot assume accuracy on any given point, we believe that the burden of proof must be borne by those who would deny it, and not by those of us who are inclined to grant it. Naturally, on any issue as difficult as this one, commentators must use special caution, and in the following chapters we claim only to interpret Plato's *Apology*. But we confess that in doing so we take ourselves also to be saying a number of things of significance as regards the character and commitments of the man who actually addressed the Athenian court.[25] And since we do not suppose that the *Apology* is purely a work of fiction whose intended audience did not expect accuracy, we will feel free to employ other historical materials in our interpretation as shedding light on the context in which the work was written—a context that would be well understood by Plato's intended (ancient) audience, but which might be only dimly in the minds of many modern readers.

1.2 The Use of Other Dialogues in Interpreting the *Apology*

1.2.1 THE EARLY DIALOGUES AND CONSISTENCY

If what we have said so far is true, when we can fairly assume that the views Plato's Socrates expresses in the *Apology* are genuinely Socratic, though Plato provides the actual words by which Socrates expresses them. This is, of course, true only if we find no internal or

---

[25] In thinking that evidence warrants only the weak conclusion that there is no good evidence against the 'accuracy theory', and at least some evidence for it, we agree with Allen (3), 35. We are also in sympathy with Kahn, who says, 'Where [Plato's] portrait is unfaithful, we are in no position to correct it. As far as we are concerned, the Socrates of the dialogues *is* the historical Socrates. He is certainly the only one who counts for history of philosophy' (319, his emphasis). Also, Magalhães-Vilhena (3), who says, 'Si le Socrate platonicien n'est pas le Socrate de l'histoire, il est du moins le portrait le plus compréhensif et le plus convaincant qui reste entre nos mains' (223).

external evidence that has at least an equal claim to legitimacy and that contradicts Plato's version. But what of the external evidence provided by Plato himself in other dialogues? Naturally such evidence cannot be employed in the historical debate against those who view the *Apology* as representing Plato's own early thought and not the views of the historical Socrates. But the other early dialogues do offer a variety of situations and arguments in which we see Plato's Socrates in action; and if we may take the *Apology* as at least a roughly accurate portrait of the historical Socrates, then to the extent that the other early dialogues portray him in a compatible way, we can expand our picture of the man accordingly. Similarly, if something in the *Apology* is unclear or ambiguous, and if other early dialogues help in supplying an expanded but consistent picture, we may employ evidence from them to interpret the *Apology*. And if the accounts of Socrates we find in the other early dialogues are to some degree corroborated by still other ancient sources, then the evidence from Plato's other dialogues weighs against those who view all these works as revealing only Plato's own thought.

In any case, the issue is not whether the early dialogues represent Plato's commitments; there can be little doubt that in so far as the early dialogues advance philosophical doctrines they advance views Plato himself believed. The issue is whether they reflect only Platonic views, or whether they reflect commitments Plato gained from his beloved master, Socrates. Since Socrates obviously had an enormous influence on Plato, we may suppose that the latter would extensively represent the views of the former. Since the other early dialogues provide many opportunities for Plato to represent Socratic views, we shall not only freely claim the views contained in other early dialogues as relevant evidence in developing an understanding of the *Apology* as a Platonic work, but we also believe such evidence sheds at least some light on the views and activities of the historical Socrates.

The other early dialogues must nevertheless be used with caution. Commentators have often maintained that the early dialogues contain a number of inconsistencies. We believe that at least some of these alleged inconsistencies are only apparent, and we shall have opportunity in this book to resolve some of these explicitly. But as a matter of principle, it seems to us that if another early dialogue conflicts with the doctrines or portrait of Socrates we find in the *Apology* there is no a priori reason for preferring one source to the other. There are, naturally, a number of ways in which such conflicts might come about: perhaps Socrates was never really clear, and Plato's inconsistency is only an accurate portrait of Socrates' own; perhaps Plato never really understood Socrates and committed the inconsistency in his confusion; perhaps Socrates never addressed the specific issue at all, and Plato erred in trying to work out explicitly what was only implicit in the real Socrates' remarks; or perhaps Plato in one or both instances is self-consciously fictionalizing to suit purposes unique to that work or those works. Such a conflict would not constitute anything like clear evidence for the 'fiction theory', at least without much further argument; it would, however, undercut any attempt to discern the relevant aspect of the historical Socrates.

1.2.2 TRANSITIONAL AND LATER DIALOGUES

A final point must be made on this topic. There are a number of dialogues that are typically seen as transitional, from the period during which Plato's own unique philosophical views were emerging, and still others that are said to be from the middle and later periods of his work, when these views were in full flower or under subsequent revision or elaboration. It is not appropriate here to review either the evidence for such assessments or the many debates about the specific dating of each of the relevant dialogues. In forming the arguments of this book, we shall assume that material taken from any of the supposedly transitional dialogues is intrinsically more suspect as shedding light on any passage in the *Apology* than material taken from early dialogues such as the *Euthyphro* or the *Crito*. Still later dialogues, such as the *Phaedo, Symposium*, or the *Phaedrus*, are on our view nearly worthless in helping us to interpret the *Apology*, except in so far as they supplement or clarify points or issues without adding substantially to them. That is not to say that there is no truth to be found about the historical Socrates in these later dialogues; there may well be. But what is pertinent cannot be well distinguished from what is not, thus throwing all such evidence (or nearly all) into suspense. Of course, where later Platonic work corroborates or even enhances clear and independent evidence from earlier works or other ancient authors, the consistency of these later materials does not detract from the picture we get from the more secure sources, and in fact may often be viewed as a valuable addition to the rest of the evidence.

Three works by Plato raise especially interesting and difficult problems: the *Gorgias*, the *Meno*, and Book I of the *Republic*. Each of these offers portrayals of Socrates that at least initially appear consistent with those of earlier works. But each work contains one or more crucial departures from or additions to the positions we find in the early dialogues: the *Gorgias* in concluding with a 'great myth' (*Grg.* 523a1–526d2), the likes of which can otherwise be found only in what are plainly dialogues of the middle period; the *Meno* in advancing what can only be Plato's own theory of recollection (ἀνάμνησις), according to which all knowledge in this life is recalled from experiences one had at a time prior to one's human existence (*Meno* 85d9–86b4); and the *Republic* with the decidedly un-Socratic political and metaphysical ventures of Books II–X. In fact, many of the interpretations that we shall confront in this book derive from materials gleaned from these works, and though each instance needs to be addressed individually, we must warn here that we will be very sceptical of any claim about the views represented in the *Apology* whose only or best defense can be made by appealing to one or more of these three works. Even where these works offer what appears to be a consistent picture of Socrates, we fear that certain colorations or even corruptions of his views may lurk. Thus, though like others we will employ evidence from these works to add to the evidence derived from earlier works, we will not be convinced by any argument derived strictly or even mainly from these three later works. Each of these three later writings, after all, employs material that apparently coheres with major doctrines of the 'early' dialogues; yet each frequently does so in such a way as to lead to conclusions quite foreign to those doctrines and themes. Such, then, is the taint on the *Gorgias, Meno,* and *Republic* for our purposes.

1.3 Socrates

1.3.1 SOCRATES' PERSONAL LIFE AND APPEARANCE

At *Apology* 17d2–3, Socrates says he is seventy years old.[26] Since the trial was held in 399 BC[27] that would make his year of birth 469 or 470,[28] depending upon whether 399 was the year he became seventy or

---

[26] See also *Cri.* 52e3. D. L. (2.44) agrees but says that some claim Socrates died at 60; see Zeller ((2), 53, n. 1) on this, however.

[27] See D. L. 2.44, where Demetrius of Phalerum and Apollodorus place his death in the first year of the 95th Olympiad (400/399). Zeller ((2), 53, n. 1) reasons that

would have become seventy-one. In earlier years, he had shown himself physically hearty and courageous in war.[29] Doubtless this may have contributed to the interest he aroused in a wide variety of associates and youths, from among the wealthy élite[30] to those of extreme poverty[31] and from among his fellow Athenians[32] as well as among many of foreign birth and citizenship.[33]

Certainly his appeal was not derived from good looks or elegant appearance. His hair had probably been going grey for some time now (Aisch. *Rhet*. 1.49), and he may well have been going bald.[34] His features were, moreover, hardly 'classical': his bulging eyes, thick lips, and blunt nose led both Plato and Xenophon to compare him in looks to a satyr (Pl., *Symp*. 215b4–6, *Tht*. 143e7–9; Xen., *Symp*. 4.19.5) as well as to such other unlovely creatures as sting-rays (Pl., *Meno* 80a4–6) and crabs (Xen., *Symp*. 5). To these we can add an over-large belly (Xen., *Symp*. 2.18) and an awkward, perhaps waddling gait (Pl., *Symp*. 221b1–4). His manner of clothing himself was an unending source of comment by friend and foe alike. His habits of

the trial occurred in April or May of 399 BC and, on the basis of *Phd*. 59d8–e2 and Xen., *Mem*. 4.8.2 (see also *Cri*. 43c9–d1), that Socrates' execution took place in May or June of that year (see also C. Phillipson, 254). On this delay of one month, however, compare D. L. 2.42.

[28] For more on Socrates' dates, see Diod. 14.37.7, who adds that the Athenians subsequently repented of their decision and put Socrates' accusers to death without trial; though most unlikely, similar stories appear in D. L. 2.43.

[29] On Potidaia (431–30 BC), see *Ap*. 28e2, *Symp*. 219e5–220e7; on Delion (424 BC), see *Ap*. 28e3, *Symp*. 220e7–221c1, *La*. 181b1–4; on Amphipolis (422 BC, see *Ap*. 128e2. As to the confidence with which we can maintain these events in Socrates' life, however, it certainly does not help that they are never mentioned by Xenophon, for whom such military distinctions, one would think, would hold special interest. See also the questions raised in Ath. 5.

[30] Lists including such men are offered by Plato at *Ap*. 33d9–34a2 (see also 38b6–7) and *Phd*. 59b6–c3 and Xenophon at *Mem*. 1.2.48. To these we may safely add the notorious Charmides, Critias, and Alcibiades, as well as any number of others who are mentioned throughout the works of Plato and Xenophon.

[31] This fact, among many others, is conveniently overlooked in the unlikely reconstructions of Winspear and Silverberg (see esp. their portrayal of the 'select circle' that surrounded Socrates late in life (55)). But there were at least two such associates: Aischines Socraticus, whose poverty may have been self-imposed (see *Ap*. 33e2; *Phd*. 59b8; D. L. 2.34, 35, 60, 62; 3.36; Sen. *Ben*. 1.8), and Antisthenes (see *Phd*. 59b8; Xen. *Mem*. 2.10; 3.4, 6; 4.2, 6, 44; 6.5, 8; 8.4–6; D. L. 2.31, 36; 6.2). Another may have been Aristeides (see *Tht*. 151a1).

[32] See notes 30 and 31, above.

[33] Plato gives a separate list of these at *Phd*. 59c1–3, to which we should plainly add Phaedo himself. On the spurious Simon and Bruson of Heraclea, whom some would add to lists of 'Socratics', see Zeller (2), 247, nn. 1, 2.

[34] See Ath. 507A ff. This is also suggested by the comparison of Socrates to Silenos, who is typically represented as balding.

going barefooted and wearing the same old cloak were also noted.[35] He may have been unconcerned about bathing as well.[36]

Nor could Socrates' appeal have been enhanced by his financial condition, though a number of facets of his personal life suggest comfortable circumstances in earlier times. For example, in the *Phaedo* (60a2) we learn that Socrates' wife's name is Xanthippe (see also Xen., *Symp.* 2.10; D. L. 2.26),[37] which suggests that she comes from an aristocratic background.[38] This is further supported by the aristocratic names of his eldest and youngest sons, Lamprocles and Menexenus, respectively. The fact that the second of his three sons is named after Socrates' father, Sophroniscus,[39] and not the first, as would be customary, is itself in all likelihood a token of Xanthippe's aristocratic family background.[40] (It is alleged that Socrates had also at some time been married to a certain Myrto, the daughter or granddaughter of Aristeides the Just,[41] which suggests that Socrates had been taken by her family as a man of sufficient station to join it through marriage. This story, however, despite its plausibility given the relative ages of Socrates and his sons,[42] is a matter of sharp dispute among scholars, and since we have nothing to add to what has already been said on either side,[43] we shall not pursue it further here.) Perhaps Socrates' appeal to the family (or families) of his wife (or wives) derived from

[35] *Symp.* 174a3–4, 220a5–b7; Xen. *Mem.* 1.6.2; Ar., *Nub.* 103, 363; D. L. 2.28, 35, 36, 41.

[36] *Symp.* 174a3–5; Ar., *Av.* 1282, 1553, *Nub.* 837; but cp. D. L. 2.25.

[37] See also note 50, below.

[38] From the appearance in it of 'ipp'; see Ar., *Nub.* 64.

[39] Sources for the sons' names: Xen., *Mem.* 2.2.1: D. L. 2.26. On the elder Sophroniscus, see *La.* 180d7, Xen., *Hell.* 1.7.15, and D. L. 2.18, 40; but compare Epiphanius, *Exp. Fid.* 1087A. For more on Socrates' sons see also *Ap.* 34d6–7, 41e2; *Cri.* 45c8–9, 48c3, 54a1–b3; *Phd.* 60a2, 116a7–b2; Arist., *Rh.* 1390b30; Plut. *Cat. Mai.* 20.

[40] See, e.g., Burnet (1), 129; A. E. Taylor (1), 13.

[41] D. L. 2.26; Plut., *Aristeides* 27; Ath. 555D–556A. Winspear and Silverberg refers us to *Phd.* 89A on this point (40, n. 56), but this must be a mistake. Plutarch's version has Socrates take her in to spare her from her poverty, which seems altogther unlikely given her family background.

[42] See A. E. Taylor (1), 15–16.

[43] See, e.g., A. E. Taylor ((1), 15–16), who was inclined to believe that Socrates did have an earlier wife, and Zeller ((2), 62–4, n. 3), who disputes this story and in our opinion makes the better case. Taylor also seems to have changed his mind about this later on: see Taylor (3), where he repeats that the story is chronologically possible, but none the less calls it 'unlikely' (83). A far less plausible case than either of the above is argued by Winspear and Silverberg (40–1), who think Myrto was the *later* wife. Woodbury (2) comes to the same conclusion. Both Bicknell and Fitton insist that Xanthippe never was Socrates' wife, but rather just his mistress; on their view, Myrto was Socrates' only wife.

the fact that his father appears to have been a sculptor, a lucrative craft during the boom in the Athenian economy and construction program of the fifth century (D. L. 2.18). Since sons were ordinarily trained in the crafts of their fathers,[44] Socrates may have had at least the opportunity to become modestly wealthy.[45] Moreover, Socrates' mother's name, Phainarete (Pl., *Tht.* 149a2, *Alc. I* 131e4; D. L. 2.18), is in the aristocratic style,[46] but of the woman herself we know nothing beyond the curious description of her in Plato's *Theaetetus* (149al-2) as a 'burly' (βλοσυρός) midwife. (Perhaps Socrates' notorious physical features derive from her side of the family.)

But Socrates' poverty, at least during the later part of his life, seems certain. In the *Apology* he cites it as evidence for the urgency he feels in his mission in Athens (31c2-3),[47] and this same poverty is reported or represented in the serious works of Xenophon (*Oec.* 2.2, 11.3; *Mem.* 1.2.1), as well as the comedies of Eupolis (*PCG.* V, fr. 386), Ameipsias (*PCG.* V, fr. 9), and of course Aristophanes (*Nub.* 103, 175, 362; *Av.* 1282)[48]. If his poverty was already notorious in 423 BC, when Aristophanes' *Clouds* was first produced, Socrates had been poor for a long while by the time of his trial, whatever the circumstances of his youth had been. It also seems clear that Socrates did not take money for his philosophic pursuits,[49] though he may have accepted gifts of food and wine (D. L. 2.74; Sen., *Ben.* 1.8, 7.24; Quint. Inst. 12.7.9). His carelessness about money must have made him a most difficult and frustrating man to have as one's husband and pro-

---

[44] Timon of Phlius and Duris in D. L. 2.19 say Socrates was so trained. (See also Paus. 1.22.8, 9.35.2.) There is much confusion in these reports, however, (as for example, that he was a slave taken in by Crito, which Winspear and Silverberg absurdly find probable—39-40), and since in addition no word of this training can be found in Plato, Xenophon, or for that matter even Aristophanes, Socrates' alleged training in sculpture must be viewed as at best a matter of speculation. But see Winspear and Silverberg, who (strangely) announce that '[t]here can be no question that in his early years Socrates followed the same useful and, to the Greeks, humble trade as his father' (12).

[45] For other (questionable) testimonial evidence suggesting this, see Demetrius of Phalerum in Plut. *Aristeides* 1; Libanius, *Ap.* 3, 7; D. L. 2.20.

[46] We can infer this from its appearance in the context of Ar. *Ach.* 49.

[47] See also *Ap.* 23b9-c1, 36d4, e1, 37c4, 38b1-5; *Rep.* I, 337d8-10, 338b7.

[48] It should not be forgotten, however, that Socrates fought as a hoplite only a year before the production of the *Clouds*, and hence had the requisite wealth to qualify for that status.

[49] *Ap.* 19d9-e1, 31b5-c3, 33a8-b1; *Euthphr.* 3d8; *Symp.* 219e1-2; Xen., *Mem.* 1.2.5, 1.5.6, 1.6.3, and esp. 1.6.13, where he compares such a thing to prostitution; D, L. 2.27, 31; Sen., *Ben.*5.6.

vider, given the restrictive customs of the day (and Xanthippe's apparently aristocratic background). Perhaps this did lead his much maligned wife to the ill humor and violent emotion with which her name has become associated.[50] Nevertheless, the combined grief and respect for his conversations with his friends depicted in Plato's *Phaedo* (60a3-b1) certainly suggests that Xanthippe's love for her husband existed at his death.

1.3.2 SOCRATES' INTELLECTUAL LIFE

Neither beauty or wealth, then, contributed to Socrates' appeal. It was, rather (as we might have supposed all along), his passion for and unceasing pursuit of philosophy. Plato says Socrates had the standard training in music and gymnastics (*Cri.* 50d8-e1), which would be unremarkable, but he is often also portrayed as having had (early in life, at least) a considerable interest in natural philosophy,[51] though that he had any significant interest in such things later in life as explicitly and emphatically denied in the *Apology* (19c1-d5; see also 23d2-9, 26d1-e2, and *Phdr.* 229c6-230a6), as well as by Xenophon (*Mem.* 1.1.14; 4.7.6) and by Aristotle (*Metaph.* 987b1-2). If there was a scientific period at all it was long over by the time of his influence on these later writers and thus by the time of his trial.[52] More likely Socrates had a less substantial acquaintance with the theories he is supposed to have studied, either through his penchant for conversation with intelligent people in general or through the casual reading of their works.[53] Indeed, we would expect at least this much interest in such things from a man of such manifest commitments to the intellec-

---

[50] This was very likely extremely exaggerated (though perhaps not wholly fabricated) by later commentators. See, e.g., Teles. in Stob., *Flor.* 5.64; Sen., *Constant.* 18.5, *Ep.* 104, 177; Porph. (in Theodoret., *Gr. Affect. Cur.* 12.65); D. L. 2.36-7; Plut., *Cat. Mai.* 20, *Coh. Ira.* 13.461; Ael., *VH* 11.12; Ath. 219. But Plato (*Phd.* 60a2-b1) shows her in no particularly unflattering light, and Xenophon's treatment (in *Mem.* 2.2.7-8, where she is unnamed, and *Symp.* 2.10) hardly approaches the immoderation of later gossips. That Aristophanes did not employ her temper in his comedy cannot be cited in her defense, however, as Socrates was probably not yet (or only just) married to her in 423 BC when the *Nub.* was first produced, though for a provocative speculation on this, see Guthrie (1), vol. 3, 386, n. 3.

[51] *Phd.* 96a6-98b6; Aristeid., *Or.* 45, 21; D. L. 2.19, 45; Ar., *Nub. passim.*

[52] For what we believe are compelling reasons for this, see Lacey, 26-7.

[53] This is all that can be derived from what Plato says in the *Phd.*, for example, and accords as well with what Xenophon says in the *Mem.* That the works of 'learned men' were readily available to anyone is obvious from *Ap.* 26d6-e2.

tual life. He is said to have been more closely associated with
Archelaus, the Athenian disciple of Anaxagoras.[54] This might help to
explain Meletus' clumsy confusion of Socrates with Anaxagoras at
Apology 26d4-5,[55] but it would be astonishing if there had been a
significant influence on Socrates by Archelaus that remained so
undetectable in the testimonies of Plato, Xenophon, and Aristotle.[56]
This is especially the case given other (however playful or exaggerated) claims Socrates makes in Plato's dialogues to have been influenced by a variety of other people, including Prodicus (*Meno* 96d7;
Cra. 384b2-4; and perhaps *Charm.* 163d3-4) and Connus (*Euthyd.*
272c2, 295d3-5; *Menex.* 235e8-236a1), as well as two women,
Aspasia[57] and Diotima (*Symp.* 201d1-212b2). So it is reasonable to
take Meletus' confusion in the *Apology* (and Aristophanes'
caricature in the *Clouds*[58]) for what Socrates says it is, the standard
careless charges made against all philosophers (see *Ap.* 23d4-6), and
to suppose that the substance and style of Socrates' philosophic life
came about without significant prior influence or precursor.

1.3.3 ATHENS IN 399 BC

All through the *Apology* (18a7-e4; 19a8-c5; 20c4-d4; 21b1-2, d1-e4;
22e6-23a3, c7-d2, d9-e3; 24a2-b1; 28a4-8), Socrates reminds the
jurors of the widespread and powerful bias against him, which he
fears will infect them and cause them to condemn him unjustly. Since
he speaks so directly about the sources of this bias as an essential ingredient in his predicament, we can defer extended discussion of it un-

[54] D. L. 2.16, 19; 10.12, and esp. the connection claimed thirteen or fourteen
years before Plato's birth by Ion of Chios, as reported in D. L. 2.23. Also,
Theodoret., *Gr. Affect. Cur.* 12.67, 175; Clem. Al., *Strom.* 302A; Eus., *Praep. Evang.*
10.14.13, 14.15.11; 15.61.11; Cic., *Tusc.* 5.4; Sext. Emp., *Math.* 10.360; Theophr., *Phys.
Opin.* fr. 4. Burnet ((1), 124-5), Guthrie ((1), vol. 2, 239), A. E. Taylor ((1), 6 and (7),
56-8), and Winspear and Silverberg (36-8), among others, report this as well supported
by such evidence. But Zeller ((2), 57-9, n. 3) produces powerful reasons why we should
doubt this connection. Different reasons for doubt are offered by Calder ((2), 85), who
points out that D. L. could be confusing the philosopher Socrates with Socrates
Anagyrasius, a general on the Samos mission. (But see Woodbury (1), 302.)

[55] As C. Phillipson (39) and Burnet ((1), 124-5) suggest.

[56] Some of Archelaus' teachings are indeed referred to in the biographical passage
at *Phd.* 96a6-98b6, but so are those of a wide variety of other earlier thinkers, so
this fact can hardly support the connection.

[57] *Menex.* 235e8-236a1; see also Xen., *Mem.* 2.6.36, *Oec.* 3.14; Ath. 569F,
599A-B (Hermesianax fr. 7.89-94, ed. Powell); scholion on Ar., *Ach.* 526.

[58] See Lacey's remark about this on 26-7.

til later, when we shall examine his actual speeches. But it is appropriate now at least to mention some of the conditions in Athens that may have affected the trial.

It should, for example, not be forgotten that Athens had only just concluded the Peloponnesian War. The effects of this war had been disastrous on her economy and on her political life; factions blamed each other for her defeats, and suspicion and power-mongering were rife.[59] In 411 BC, four hundred members of the oligarchic faction overthrew the democracy for a time, and in 404 BC there was another upheaval, brought about by some of the same men, the so-called Thirty Tyrants. The Thirty added further terror and uncertainty to a situation already fraught with grief and insecurity. In such an atmosphere it is no surprise that Athens should look for those who had corrupted her youth and aroused the gods against her.

Nor is it a surprise that the Athenians looked for the guilty among thinkers like Socrates. After all, by their very nature and regardless of their particular persuasions, such intellectuals challenge established wisdom and tradition. During the classical period there seems to have been a number of prosecutions of intellectuals,[60] the most famous and perhaps earliest of which was the trial of Anaxagoras. Socrates reminds his jurors of this case at *Apology* 26d4–e2, and vigorously distinguishes his own views from those of Anaxagoras. The distinctions between Socrates and the Sophists[61] (with whom he is associated in Aristophanes' *Clouds*, for example) would doubtless have seemed insignificant to those of an anti-intellectual stripe. And Socrates was certainly an intellectual; we need know little else about him to find nothing surprising in his claim that he found in his city great hostility toward himself and his pursuits.

Other aspects of Socrates' life may also have contributed to his con-

[59] An especially pungent description of these phenomena is offered by C. Phillipson (5).

[60] For a representative list of such cases, see Dover (2), 24–54. Dover argues against the authenticity of many of the accounts of such actions, including the one against Anaxagoras (27–32), and the psephism (decree) under which it was said to have been tried. We are unconvinced by at least some of Dover's arguments, however, (on which see page 32, below), and are inclined to believe that Socrates' trial was not unique. See also Diogenes Laertius' claim (at 2.20) that Socrates was the first philosopher to be tried and put to death, which is at least consistent with others (such as Anaxagoras) being tried and banished earlier, and suggests that others were later put to death.

[61] That such hatred could be both ignorant and passionate is shown by the case of Anytus in Plato's *Meno* 91b7–92e6.

demnation. Though in Chapter 2 we shall argue that the putative effects of Socrates' personal associations on the trial have been overstated, it remains true that a number of his associates were men with extremely unsavory reputations at the time Socrates was indicted.[62] Plato's uncle, Charmides, for example, was one of the Thirty, and was recognized as one of Socrates' admirers; Xenophon even tells us that it was Socrates who persuaded Charmides to enter politics (*Mem.* 3.7.1).[63] Even worse, Socrates may also have been linked to Critias, whose iron-fisted actions as the leader of the Thirty made his name the emblem of their infamy. Many of the democratic leaders and their families were forced into exile during the period of the coup, but Socrates remained in Athens; to the suspicious he might appear a private accomplice and mentor of the tyranny.

Still other associations might have helped to lend further support to suspicions about Socrates. In the *Phaedo* (59c1–2) Plato represents him as having among his closest comrades and admirers a number of foreigners with Pythagorean commitments. The Pythagoreans were no democrats; their political views might well have been seen as disturbingly akin to the oligarchic values of the likes of Critias and Charmides, and hence quite hostile to the now shaky democracy of Athens.[64] Yet another potentially damaging association may have been the one with Alcibiades, who appears frequently in the works of Plato and Xenophon, and who was perhaps seen as having a most intimate connection with Socrates; his infamous career, amply chronicled in a variety of ancient sources, does not need repetition

[62] Indeed, these are among the principal charges in Polycrates' pamphlet (see note 14, above).

[63] The story is repeated by D. L. (2.29). See also Xen., *Symp.* 4.32, where Charmides' association with Socrates is said to have damaged *Charmides'* reputation!

[64] The extent of this has, we think, been greatly overstated by A. E. Taylor ((1), 26), who gives Socrates, at least early in life, 'a perfectly definite position as the leader of a group of largely Pythagorean adherents' (see also Taylor (7), 59–68). Winspear and Silverberg (79–80) go even further, and claim that Socrates was rightly seen, even late in life, as perpetrating 'this semi-mystical, half-fanatical Pythagorean creed upon the excitable minds of patrician young men' (80). Winspear and Silverberg dismiss the obviously contrary evidence to be found in the early works of Plato as well as in those of Xenophon as obscuring 'historical objectivity' (80). Some early interest in Pythagorean teachings cannot be ruled out, however, nor, as we say, should a continuing casual acquaintance with the scientific and philosophical trends of the day. A very clear-headed reply to Taylor's views can be found in Robin (2).

For discussions of Pythagorean political activity and theory, see Kurt von Fritz, *Pythagorean Politics in Southern Italy* (New York, 1940); E. L. Minar, Jr., *Early Pythagorean Politics in Practice and Theory* (Baltimore, 1942).

here. His damaging association with Socrates, though not a fresh memory (Alcibiades had left Athens years ago, and had died a handful of years before Socrates' trial), may have lingered in the jurors' minds.[65]

Reports of certain of Socrates' philosophical views may have exacerbated any ill will generated by these associations. Some Athenians, no doubt, thought that democratic ideals were deserving of unquestioning loyalty. To the extent that Socrates' own views were seen as conflicting with the democratic ideology of the time, he may well have been regarded as a subversive. There are a number of passages in Plato's early dialogues in which Socrates sharply criticizes the arrogance and ignorance of many of the most beloved political figures of the period. One such example is found in the *Apology*: at 21b9-22a8 Socrates says that he is convinced that the politicians so often revered by the people are ignorant, and yet think they are not. Now it is not clear that Socrates was likely to criticize democrats more strenuously than oligarchs,[66] but in 399 the democratic faction was in power, and hence his criticisms of democrats would be the ones that would cause the most concern. But he had been in trouble with the oligarchs when they were in power, as *Apology* 32c4-e1 shows; that is even more forcefully evident in their reported passing of various laws against inquiry (see, for example, Xen., *Mem.* 1.2.31-8).[67]

Moreover, certain aspects of Socrates' thought might have been

---

[65] See esp. Polycrates (note 14, above). Isocrates (*Bus.* 5) tries to relieve Socrates of responsibility for Alcibiades by making the careful stipulation that the latter was never the disciple of the former, but allows that there may have been a friendly relationship between the two, and thus some influence. Xenophon (*Mem.* 1.2.24-48) defends Socrates in view of these associations, and appears to refer to Polycrates when referring to Socrates' 'accuser' (e.g. at 1.2.26, 49, 51, 56, 58, 64).

[66] We must not confuse the apolitical Socrates of the *Ap.* (31c4-32a3, 32e2-5) with the anti-democratic Socrates of Plato's later dialogues. We shall have more to say about Socrates and partisan politics in Chapter 2.

[67] Winspear and Silverberg (75-6) dispute this story, noting that Socrates is also reported by Xenophon to have continued to teach the question-and-answer method (at 4.4.3). They go on to say, 'We cannot believe that the uncompromising terrorists, who were responsible for something like fifteen hundred political murders . . . would have hesitated to put the dissident philosopher out of the way' (76). There can be no doubt that the Thirty were quite prepared to eliminate dissidents, but Socrates' earlier friendships with Critias and Charmides would almost certainly have slowed their normally swift retaliation, and it must be remembered that they stayed in power less than a year. Perhaps the order to arrest Leon was designed to give Socrates one last chance to show his allegiance to their authority; he certainly did not construe it as a token of friendly feeling. For what might be further evidence of tension between Socrates and the Thirty, see Diod. 14.5.1-3, and Section 4.3.4.2, below.

taken as particularly anti-democratic: for example, his commitment to expertise (especially in politics), which we see even as he makes his defense to the jury in the *Apology* (24c9–25c1; see also 31e1–32a3). Although we shall subsequently show that these remarks do not reflect a partisan political point of view, they do show that Socrates believes that only a few people, at best, can make other persons better.[68]

Even his appearance could (and no doubt by many would) be considered provocative. All sources agree that Socrates eschewed any but the most minimally serviceable clothing. His appearance is employed by the comic poets as a sure-fire way to arouse laughter, but even in comedy it was associated with emulating Spartan ways.[69] A different but equally hostile interpretation of the way Socrates appeared is recalled by Alcibiades in Plato's *Symposium*:

There was one time when the frost was harder than ever, and all the rest of us stayed inside, or if we did go out we wrapped ourselves up to the eyes and tied bits of felt and sheepskins over our shoes, but Socrates went out in the same old coat he'd always worn, and made less fuss about walking on the ice in his bare feet than we did in our shoes. *So much so, that the men began to look at him with some suspicion and actually took his toughness as a personal insult to themselves.* (*Symp.* 220b1–c1, trans. M. Joyce)[70]

Appearances can make a difference, and that Socrates' ascetic taste in clothing was seen as an important statement is evident in its becoming *de rigeur* among the later Cynics. The Athenian populace would doubtless not take kindly to such a rejection of their taste for greater personal comfort and decoration.

On similar grounds, Socrates' (apparently self-imposed) poverty and disinterest in pursuing a political life may well have counted against him. We need only recall a few lines from Pericles' Funeral Oration (Thucydides 2.40.1–2) to see the likelihood of this. Reporting Athenian values, Pericles says:

wealth we employ rather as an opportunity for action than as a subject for boasting. Poverty is nothing shameful for a man to admit; *the real shame comes in not seeking to escape it by action.* Here the same man can attend to

[68] Contrast the paean to democracy Plato puts in the mouth of Protagoras at *Prt.* 320c8–328d2.
[69] See Eupolis, *PCG* V, fr. 386; Ameipsias, fr. 9; D. L. 2.27; Ar., *Nub.* 103, 175, 362; *Av.* 1282.
[70] Compare D. L. 2.21, and Ar. *Nub.* 412–417, quoted at D. L. 2.27.

private affairs without neglecting those of the *polis;* even those mostly engaged in their own occupations have no lack of insight into affairs of the *polis.* *For we alone do not regard a man who takes no part in political life as one who minds his own business; we regard him as having no business here at all.* (Thuc. 2.40.1–2, trans. C. M. Reed)

On these standards, Socrates would plainly be counted shameful and useless. Worse, these crucial differences in personal style may have aroused the conviction that he was a threat to Athens.

Such suspicions and biases had been building long before Socrates faced the jury. Once in court, he said a number of things that may have further antagonized the jurors. As we shall argue, this was never intentional, though he was well aware that he could have this effect upon them. No doubt many things to which he refers in his speech could have contributed to the biases against him: his combative philosophic methods, to which he refers throughout his defense; his claim concerning the Delphic oracle to Chairephon, as well as that concerning his 'divine sign'; the anti-materialistic, apolitical, and élitist sense of his life and thinking; indeed even his fearless and unemotional mode of defense. Since these play such a vital role in his presentation, we shall discuss them in more detail later.

One might well wonder why Socrates had not been brought to trial much sooner. About this we can only speculate.[71] No doubt the fact that he had friends from among the powerful of both factions, especially the oligarchs, preserved him through 404/3. After the reinstatement of the democracy in 404/3, however, his powerful friends among the oligarchs could offer him no further safety, and his best democratic friend, Chairephon, was dead. Still, not until four or five years later (399) did Anytus, Meletus, and Lycon make their charges. We might suppose that in the first year or so people had more basic problems with which to concern themselves. The general instability was no doubt so pervasive that irritants like Socrates would not have been seen as requiring immediate attention; he could become a target for action only after things became more settled. Similarly, we might suppose that Socrates' accusers would wait for what they saw as a propitious moment before they took action, when the magistrates and jurors likely to be involved would provide a favorable climate for their allegations. We might suppose at least that the King-Archon was taken seriously in their plans, as he had to forward their

[71] See, e.g., Chroust (3), 181–2.

case to trial—a fact apparently noted as evidence for their case by Anytus (*Ap.* 26b9–c3).[72] Possibly an antagonistic conversation between Socrates and one of the three accusers such as the one we find in Plato's *Meno* (89e9–95a6) could have been the final straw, though this is mere guesswork.

In any case, we should suppose that Socrates' accusers were sufficiently confident of their case to bring it to court, despite the threat of substantial penalty for harassment if they got less than a fifth of the votes.[73] Widespread prejudice against Socrates would surely have bolstered their confidence. In fact, though the ultimate outcome shows their confidence to have been well founded, we have good reason to imagine that the close margin by which the case was ultimately decided surprised Meletus as much as it did Socrates, as Socrates suggests at 36a3–4. Perhaps Meletus' very confidence accounts for his apparent ignorance of Socratic views and commitments (see *Ap.* 23d2–e4; 26a8–28a1).

1.4   The Trial

1.4.1   PROCEDURE

The indictment against Socrates was made by Meletus.[74] The procedure appears to have followed the requirements of Athenian legal due process, according to which the indictment was brought to the King-Archon,[75] who convened a preliminary hearing (ἀνάκρισις) to

---

[72] See note 75 below.   [73] See *Ap.* 36a8–b2; MacDowell (2), 64, 252.

[74] It is clear from what is said in the *Ap.* (19b1–2, c7, 24c4–8, 26b2–4, d6, e7–9, 27a4–5, 27e3–5, 28a3, 31d2, 35d1–2, 36a7–b2, 37b6) and in the *Euthphr.* (2b8–9, 12e2–3) that Meletus is the one who made the official indictment. (See also Xen., *Mem.* 4.4.4, 4.8.4; D. L. 2.38, 40; Plut., *Mor. de gen.* 580B–C. Xenophon's plural at *Mem.* 1.1.1 is insignificant.) There has been a great deal of speculation about who was the actual instigator of the trial (an issue to which we shall return), but C. Phillipson's flat claim (211) that the charges were registered by Anytus is plainly wrong.

[75] It is not clear the degree to which the King-Archon's decision to forward the case to trial reflected a judgment as to quality of the evidence against the defendant, for though accusers who prosecuted poorly conceived charges had to pay penalties (see *Ap.* 36a7–b2 and MacDowell (2), 64), we know of none that had to be paid by the King-Archon who forwarded such poorly conceived charges to trial. *Ap.* 29b9–c3 may count against this, however. One who supposes that the King-Archon's decision to forward the case to trial reflects his judgment that there is at least some substantial indication of the truth of the charges is Allen, who views the King-Archon's judgment at the end of the preliminary hearing a 'preliminary

decide if the case was sufficiently serious to merit a trial,[76] and having decided it was, forwarded it to the 'Hλιαία,[77] the appropriate court for cases of impiety.

On the day of the trial,[78] the indictment would be read before the assembled jury (and observing public[79]), followed by a period of time allotted to the prosecution for presenting their case. An equal period of time followed for the presentation of the defense.[80] Athenian law during this period permitted a variety of different trial procedures for criminal cases. The relevant one in this case was called an ἀγών τιμητός, a trial for which there was no penalty set by the law. In a trial of this type the accuser (in this case, Meletus) would propose a penalty (τίμησις) which was stated at the end of the indictment. If the jury voted to convict, a new stage of the trial began. The prosecution was allowed, after the verdict was in, to present an argument in favor of the penalty proposed in the indictment, and the newly convicted man was given an equal time to propose an alternative penalty (ἀντιτίμησις).[81] The jurors would then in a second vote choose between the two proposals. They could not invent a third alternative if neither the prosecution's nor the defendant's proposal suited them.[82] This trial structure accounts for Socrates' first two speeches in the *Apology*: in the first speech he presents his defense against the charges; in the second, having been convicted, he proposes a counter-penalty. (We shall

finding' in the case, and likens the trial itself to an appeal of that finding ((5), 6–7). We believe Allen has somewhat over-estimated the King-Archon's authority. On the King-Archon's role in Athenian legal procedure, see MacDowell (2), 32–3.

[76] See MacDowell (2), 240–2; C. Phillipson, 248–9

[77] This court is frequently referred to as the *Heliaia*, but as MacDowell points out ((2), 30), inscriptions show that the proper form began without the 'H' (or 'rough breathing'). On the nature of this court, see MacDowell (2), 35: C. Phillipson, 229–39.

[78] The type of case is called a γραφή (writing), on which see MacDowell (2), 57, 197–202. The most extensive discussion of impiety trials may be found in Derenne (see esp. chs. 4 and 5 on Socrates, 70–184, and ch. 8 on the procedure, 217–45). An ancient definition of ἀσέβεια may be found in Ps.-Arist., *De virt. et vit.* 7. See also Lipsius, 359–60.

[79] That the public was present is apparent from *Ap.* 24e10, and perhaps 33d8–9. See also the sources cited by MacDowell ((2) 248, n. 566); C. Phillipson (251, n. r).

[80] For details concerning the methods by which these time-periods were allotted and measured, see MacDowell ((2), 249) and C. Phillipson (252).

[81] MacDowell simply says that both sides presented brief cases for their proposed penalties ((2), 254) and cites *Ath. Pol.* 69.2. C. Phillipson says that the prosecution's second speech came after the convict's, but cites no reference for this (260).

[82] See MacDowell (2), 253; Harrison, vol. 2, 80–2; Lipsius, 248–62.

discuss the status and meaning of his third speech in Chapter 5.) The entire procedure would be completed in a day (*Ap.* 37a7-b1).

1.4.2 THE JURY

We do not know the exact number of jurors at the trial, though there has been much conjecture in the literature.[83] Juries during this period could number anywhere from a few hundred to some thousands, depending upon the seriousness of the case.[84] Five hundred was typical for cases of this sort;[85] it is not uncommon for scholars to report the number of jurors at Socrates' trial as 501,[86] the odd number designed to prevent ties. This, however, presumes a system of jury selection devised later in the fourth century.[87] All we know from Plato's *Apology* is that Socrates addressed a sizeable number of jurors (24e9-10), and that if only thirty of those who found him guilty had instead gone his way, he would have been acquitted (36a5-6). Other sources give us other information, but attempts to render all such information consistent seem doomed to fail.[88]

The jurors themselves volunteered for jury duty. From the pool of volunteers, 6,000 were chosen by lot to be jurors for the year, and different groups of these were randomly assigned to one or another of Athens' bewildering variety of courts by a system that became increasingly complex as time went on.[89] Jurors earned three ὀβολοί (*oboloi*) per day for their work. As Douglas MacDowell says, this was

not a high rate. An able bodied man would normally be able to earn more by work of other kinds. Probably it was never intended that judging cases should be regarded as work, or the office of juror a full-time occupation; perhaps it was expected that many men would be glad to perform this service for the community, provided only that they did not have to starve while doing it. But

---

[83] See Riddell (xii–xiv) for a summary.　　[84] See MacDowell (2), 36–8.

[85] MacDowell (2), 36; Burnet (2), note on 36a5; Riddell, xiii; this is the count given by Allen as well ((5), 6).

[86] See, e.g., C. Phillipson (241), who is quoted on this by Guthrie (2), 64; Riddell, xii–xiv; Gomperz (2), 98; Grube, 21.

[87] MacDowell (2), 37–9; Burnet (2), note on 36a5.

[88] The numbers reported by D. L. (2.41) are senseless in themselves, and certainly cannot be made sense of consistently with Plato's account at *Ap.* 36a5-6. Riddell's attempt to do so requires him implausibly to suppose that Socrates' reference to 30 votes *really* means 31 (xiv). Bury ((2), 393) also counts the first vote in a way we find wholly unjustified. See Burnet ((2), note on 36a5) and Zeller ((2), 200 n. 1) for sensible analyses.

[89] The various systems of jury selection are described by MacDowell (2), 35–40.

what happened in practice was that relatively few able-bodied men volunteered; many of the volunteers were old men who were no longer fit for ordinary work and could not earn money by other means. Thus the juror's pay could serve the purpose of an old-age pension; and although the device of paying jurors succeeded in producing a fair (perhaps more than fair) representation of poor citizens, it did not produce a fair representation of different age groups.[90]

1.4.3 THE PROSECUTORS

At 23e3–4 and at 36a7–9, Socrates names his three accusers as Meletus, Anytus, and Lycon. As we have said, Meletus is the one who made the official indictment.[91] Anytus and Lycon supported Meletus in making the charges, which, among other things, meant that they would have to share in any of the consequences of bringing the case to trial (such as preparing and presenting the case and, if fewer than one-fifth of the jurors happened to judge Socrates guilty, contributing to the fine for harassment[92]). Such actions, in which the nominal prosecutor was supported by others, were not unusual. It would be extremely interesting to know what role each of these three persons played in the prosecution, but the evidence is insufficient for anything but speculation on this issue.[93]

Our understanding of the trial would be much improved if we could determine the motives of each of the prosecutors, and whether or not their charges reflected sincere concerns. Socrates suggests that the three had somewhat different motives for making their accusations (23e4–24a1), and we see no reason to doubt at least the effect of his suggestion. Unfortunately we know next to nothing about two of the prosecutors (Meletus and Lycon), and though we have rather more information about the third (Anytus), the reliability of much of that is highly suspect.

Some insight into at least Meletus' degree of sincerity might be gained if we could accept the view, offered by a number of scholars,[94]

---

[90] MacDowell (2), 34–5; see also C. Phillipson, 241.

[91] See note 74, above.   [92] See note 73, above.

[93] See esp. Grote (1), vol. 7, 147; C. Phillipson, 267–8.

[94] See Beckman, 60; Burnet (2), notes on *Euthphr.* 2b9 and *Ap.* 32d6; Bury (2), 391, n. 1; Calder (2), 83; Chroust (3), 171; Hackforth (2), 78; Keaney; A. E. Taylor (3), 95. Blumenthal finds the evidence inadequate to make the identification with confidence (see his bibliography on 169–70), whereas others deny the identity; see, e.g., Zeller (2), 193–4, n. 6; A. N. W. Saunders, 65, n. 5; MacDowell (1), 208–10; Mazon, 187; W. D. Ross in the *Oxford Classical Dictionary*, 2nd ed. (Oxford,

that the Meletus who indicted Socrates was also the man who prosecuted Andocides in the same year. If we also suppose that this
Meletus' speech against Andocides is preserved even in spirit in the
version attributed to Lysias, we have some grounds to think that
Socrates' accuser was a bona fide religious fanatic, unlikely to employ
religion casually as a mere pretext for more serious concerns. But, as
Burnet points out, the Meletus who prosecuted Andocides was one of
the men sent by the Thirty to arrest Leon (Andoc., *Myst.* 94),[95] a
grossly unjust episode in which Socrates himself would take no part
(32d4-7). Now Burnet may be right in arguing that Plato's Socrates
would not stoop to the *ad hominem* appeal of reminding the jury of
Meletus' past misdeeds,[96] but it is implausible to suppose that the same
lofty restraint would also have silenced Xenophon, who recalls the arrest of Leon in his *Memorabilia* (4.4.3), but fails to connect Socrates'
accuser to the incident.[97] It is also hard to imagine that the Meletus who
had been involved in such a notorious scandal could reasonably have
been described as an 'unknown', as he is in Plato's *Euthyphro* (2b8).
Nor for that matter could the prosecutor of Andocides be so described,
assuming that the trial of Andocides preceded that of Socrates.[98] Finally, whatever the order of the two trials, they could not have been so far
apart as to render it likely that the prosecutor of Andocides would join
forces with Anytus, whom Andocides calls to testify on his behalf (see
150). The best, indeed the only, evidence that can be claimed in support
of the identity of the two prosecutors is that they bear the same name[99]
and make a charge of impiety (ἀσέβεια) against two very different
men, in two very different cases. And though we might well imagine
that Andocides' accuser would have wished to have Socrates condemn-

1970), 667, s.v. Meletus, see F. Stoessl in supplemental volume 12 of the *RE*, cols.
852-4, s.v. Meletus.

[95] See Chapter 2, note 61, below.

[96] Burnet (2), note on *Ap.* 32d6. Keaney suggests that the provisions of the
amnesty (see note 113, below) would have prohibited Socrates making this
connection at the trial. That no such restriction would apply, however, seems certain
(see Chapter 2, note 43, below).

[97] In fact, such a connection is made by none of the ancient sources (see, e.g.,
Diogenes Laertius' silence at 2.24).

[98] See MacDowell (1), 204-5; A. Saunders, 270-1.

[99] Burnet ((2), note on *Euthphr.* 2b9) claims it is an unusual one, but himself
cites too many instances of it to be convincing. Guthrie flatly claims that 'the name is not
common' ((2), 61, n. 2). A. Saunders, on the contrary, says 'There were several persons
called Meletus' (65, n. 5). On this issue, Saunders seems to us to be right. See also
MacDowell (1), 208-10, who counts at least four, and 'quite possibly as many as six or
seven' (210).

ed, the evidence, in our opinion, weighs against his being the same man who prosecuted Socrates.

Many commentators have supposed that the main instigator of the charges was not their nominal author, Meletus, but rather Anytus,[100] a man of great political influence at the time[101] and a man (Plato tells us) with a mindless and fanatical hatred of the sophists.[102] Such hatred could easily enough be directed at Socrates, given Socrates' popular representation as a sophist, or for that matter it could be the result of an unpleasant conversation, such as the one Plato portrays in the *Meno* (89e9–95a6) or the one Xenophon has Socrates recall in the *Apology* (29). If there was a political motive for the trial (an issue we shall address in Chapters 2 and 3), it would most strongly impel Anytus, as Socrates may be suggesting at 23e5–24a1.[103]

Least of all do we know Lycon. Socrates says that he acts on behalf of the orators (24a1, repeated in D. L. 2.38), and this has led some to identify him with the Lycon whose wife Aristophanes slanders at *Wasps* 1301.[104] He has also been supposed the same man as the proud father of Autolycos in Xenophon's *Symposium*; but the friendly attitude the *Symposium*'s Lycon shows towards Socrates at 8.43 would seem to cast some doubt on this identification—Socrates' accuser was plainly not a friend.[105] Unfortunately, we do not know enough about the Lycon who accused Socrates even to begin to speculate about his

---

[100] This view is lent some support by Diogenes Laertius' endorsement of it at 2.38, and by Plato's first reference to his accusers in the *Ap.* (18b3) as 'those men around Anytus' (see also 29c1, 30b8, 31a5). Many commentators endorse this view of the matter without hesitation; see, e.g., Guthrie, who calls Meletus 'a puppet whose strings were pulled by the powerful Anytus' ((2), 61); Blakeney, who calls Meletus 'one of the creatures of Anytus' (22); and Burnet (2), who says that Anytus 'stooped to make use of the fanaticism of Meletus' (101). (See also Chroust (3), 170.) This account of the matter is not, however, universally accepted; see, e.g., Hackforth ((2), 77–8).

[101] See Plato's description of him at *Meno* 89e9–90b3. For other ancient references to Anytus, see Zeller (2), 194, n. 1; P. J. Rhodes, *A Commentary on the Aristotelian Athenaion Politeia (Oxford, 1981)*, 343–4, 431–3; J. Davis (1), 40–1; and *RE* s.v. Anytus, col. 2656.

[102] See note 61 above.

[103] Schanz and Cobet bracket the 'καὶ τῶν πολιτικῶν' at 23e5–24a1 that would confirm this, however.

[104] See Chroust (3), 36, J. Kirchner, *Prosopographia Attica* II (Berlin, 1891), 9271, q.v. *Lukon Thorikios*; W. J. M. Starkie, *The Wasps of Aristophanes* (London, 1897), note on *Vesp.* 1301, 355.

[105] See *RE* s.v. Lycon (8), col. 2302, for references to both sides of this issue. Mazon (177) and Tovar ((2), 370) identify the two Lycons.

motives in serving with Anytus as supporter (συνήγορος) for Meletus' indictment.

1.4.4 THE FORMAL CHARGES AGAINST SOCRATES

At 24b8-c1, Socrates recalls the formal charges against him as follows:

Socrates is unjust both because he corrupts youth and because he does not recognize the gods the state recognizes, but rather other new divinities.

According to Diogenes Laertius, the precise wording of the indictment (reported by Favorinus to be preserved in the Metroon—the temple of Cybele, where the Athenians kept their state archives) was as follows:

This indictment and affidavit is sworn by Meletus, the son of Meletus of Pitthos, against Socrates, the son of Sophroniscus of Alopece: Socrates is guilty of refusing to recognize the gods the state recognizes, and of introducing other new divinities. He is also guilty of corrupting the youth. The penalty demanded is death. (2.40; trans. after R. D. Hicks)

Diogenes' report is supported by the fact that Xenophon offers the same version with only one word changed.[106]

Despite the differences in wording in the three accounts, the nature of the charges is the same in each. There are thus three distinct charges:[107]

1. Socrates does not recognize the gods that the state recognizes.
2. Socrates introduced new divinities.
3. Socrates corrupts the youth.

Let us consider these in order.

1.4.4.1 Οὓς μὲν ἡ πόλις νομίζει θεοὺς οὐ νομίζων *(The gods the state recognizes [Socrates] does not recognize)*

Noting the connection between 'νομίζειν' (to recognize) and 'νόμος'

---

[106] Xenophon's version has εἰσφέρων instead of εἰσηγούμενος, which does not change the sense of the indictment (*Mem.* 1.1.1).

[107] Some commentators refer to only two accusations, the corruption charge and the impiety charge, and thus take 'not believing in the gods the state believes in, and introducing other new divinities' to be one accusation. As will be made clear in our argument to follow, Socrates and Meletus in Plato's *Apology* understand the expilicitly religious part of the indictment as making two distinct charges. A similar understanding of this issue can be found in Tate (3).

(custom, common practice), John Burnet, A. E. Taylor, and Reginald Allen[108] argue that this charge must be construed as saying that Socrates did not conform in religious practice to the religion sanctioned by the law of Athens, not that Socrates was some form of atheist. He was accused, that is, not of unorthodox belief but of non-conforming practice. The arguments for this view have been effectively refuted, in our opinion, by R. Hackforth, W. K. C. Guthrie, James Beckman, and especially J. Tate[109]; so we need not repeat their refutations at length. Rather, a few simple observations will suffice for our discussion.

First, Burnet *et al.* attempt to secure a distinction between οὐ νομί-ζειν θεούς (not to recognize the gods) and οὐ νομίζειν εἶναι θεούς (not to recognize that there *are* gods[110]), only the latter of which would imply atheism on their view. But the alleged distinction is neglected by the very people to whom it would mean the most: by Socrates himself, who uses the two expressions interchangeably in his interrogation of Meletus on this point (at 26b2–28a1; see also 29a3), and by Meletus, whose 'παράπαν (completely) οὐ νομίζεις θεούς' without the allegedly necessary 'εἶναι' (to be) at 26c7 none the less leaves his meaning clear. Meletus' charge is not that Socrates completely neglects proper religious practice; it is that Socrates is a complete atheist.

Secondly, and despite Burnet's explicit claim to the contrary,[111] it is clear that Xenophon also understood the charges against Socrates to involve atheism.[112] Burnet's point that Xenophon so carefully stresses Socrates' orthopraxy in his *Apology* is quite correct but irrelevant; after all, such activities would naturally be taken as good behavioral evidence that Socrates was no atheist. Nor is the emphasis in Greek law on proper practice good evidence that orthodox belief was not a major concern; practice and belief are inextricably tied together. The

---

[108] Burnet (2) notes on *Euthphr.* 3b3, and *Ap.* 18c3 and 24c1; A. E. Taylor (7), 98, Allen (4), 62. Another who is convinced of this view is Chroust (see (3), 236, n. 119).

[109] Hackforth (2), 58–79; Guthrie (1) vol. 3, 237, n. 2; Beckman, 55–6; Tate (1), 3–5, and (2), 3–6. See also MacDowell (2), 202; Wilamowitz, vol. 1, 158. Tate argues (in (3)) that the sense of the first charges is supported by Socrates' agnostic attitude towards the myths, but on this see Section 3.1.5, below.

[110] See, e.g., Burnet (2), note on *Ap.* 26c2.

[111] Burnet (2), note on *Ap.* 24c1.

[112] See Xenophon's rendering of the issue at *Mem.* 1.1.2–5 and esp. at *Mem.* 1.1.5. Plutarch also appears to have interpreted the charge as involving atheism (see *Mor. de gen.* 580B).

argument in Pseudo-Lysias' 'Against Andocides' (32) is illuminating
on this point: people will become more atheistic if the law allows its
citizens to ignore or violate established practices.

Finally, there is the matter of the decree (ψήφισμα) of Diopeithes,
the relevance of which Burnet greatly overestimates. This decree,
reportedly passed in order to prosecute Anaxagoras, would have
outlawed as atheism any attempt to give naturalistic explanations of
meteorological and astronomical phenomena. Even if we uncritically
accept the existence of the decree, as does Burnet, its nullification by
the general amnesty under the archonship of Eucleides provides no
reason to suppose that a charge of atheism could no longer be legally
valid.[113]

Now, however, Dover has questioned the existence of the disputed
psephism,[114] and of the action against Anaxagoras.[115] But whether or
not there ever was such a psephism, even Dover admits that 'we do
not have to suppose that the legislation of 403 [the amnesty] redefined
piety in such a way as explicitly to include types of behavior proscribed by Diopeithes; to be the victim of a γραφή at Athens it was not
necessary to have committed an act which was forbidden by the law in
so many words.'[116]

Yet despite Dover's objections we do not believe that sufficient
sense can be made of what Socrates says at *Ap.* 26d6 (about which
Dover is surprisingly silent) unless there had been an action against
Anaxagoras or, at the very least, unless such an action was conceivable on the very sorts of grounds specified in the disputed

---

[113] The amnesty created during the archonship on Eucleides called for the
complete revision and codification of the laws of Athens. It further required that all
prosecutions be for alleged violations of the newly codified laws and that there could
be no prosecutions for alleged violations of decrees passed by the Assembly, one of
which may have been the psephism of Diopeithes. (Ancient sources on the
reconciliation agreement of 403/2 and the amnesty that was one part of it include
Andoc., *Myst.*, 85–97; Arist., *Ath. Pol.* 39.1–6, 40.1–3; Diod. 14.33.5–6; Lys.,
Against Hippotherses 11.38–48; Nep., *Life of Thrasyboulas* (III); Xen., *Hell*
2.4.38–9. The most reliable commentary on the subject may be found in Loening.
Other discussions include: Burnet (2), 100–1; Paul Cloché, *La restauration
democratique à Athenes en 403 avant J.-C.* (Paris, 1915); A. Dorjahn, *Political
Forgiveness in Old Athens: The Amnesty of 403 BC (Evanston, 1946);* R. Grosser, 'Die
Amnestie des Jahres 403 v. Chr.' (dissertation, Minden, 1868); Harrison, vol. 1, 47–8;
J.-H. Kuhn, 'Die Amnestie von 403 v. Chr. im Reflex der 18 Isokrates-Rede', *WS* 80
(1967), 31–73; J. Luebbert, 'De amnestia anno 403 a.c. ab Atheniensibus decreta',
(dissertation, Kiel, 1881); and MacDowell (2), 46–8, and for its influence on impiety trials,
199–200.)

[114] Dover. (2), 39–41.   [115] Ibid., 27–32.   [116] Ibid., 41.

psephism. Hence, although Dover is right when he points out that the evidence for these incidents in inconclusive, we remain convinced that there is some justification of our view to be found in the stories about the prosecution of Anaxagoras, whether or not there really was such a prosecution, and whether or not it was performed under the psephism of Diopeithes. Again, our point is only that there is no reason to suppose that the charge of impiety, on the grounds of atheism, would be viewed by the Athenians as either illegal or even perverse.

In any case, Socrates was not charged with violating the decree of Diopeithes but of violating the law against impiety.[117] Since the latter law was vague,[118] its extension would almost certainly be determined in each instance *ad hoc*, first and provisionally at the preliminary hearing before the trial[119] by the King-Archon, and then decisively by the jury at the trial. Greek religious sentiments would have been remarkable indeed if the Greeks saw atheism as not impious in itself, so long as proper rituals were performed (in utter hypocrisy, *ex hypothesi*) by the atheist. The very existence of the decree of Diopeithes, and of the action against Anaxagoras (whether or not it was done under the decree), would by themselves provide sufficient evidence against the claim that intellectual orthodoxy was of no particular concern to the Athenians; the decree explicitly concerned ideology and the case against Anaxagoras was based upon his teachings and not upon any specific violation of ritual. Of course, the decree was annulled, along with all of the others that had been passed in prior years, by the general amnesty of 403/2. But it was hardly singled out for annulment and there is no reason to suppose that its effects could not be obtained under a constitutional law, in this case the one proscribing impiety. This, on our view, explains why Socrates does not undertake to dispute the legality of the charges against him,[120] despite Meletus' interpretation of them at 26c7 and despite

[117] This is made obvious by the fact that Socrates is being tried in the 'Ηλιαία, which would not have been used to try the case had the accusation concerned an alleged violation of the psephism of Diopeithes (see MacDowell (2), 35, for a discussion of the workings of the 'Ηλιαία). For further evidence of the nature of the law under which Socrates was indicted, see also *Euthphr.* 12e2–3. Osborn nevertheless manages to get this wrong (187), as does Navia ((2), 14).

[118] See MacDowell (2), 199–200.

[119] On the importance of the preliminary hearing in clarifying the issues to be set forth in the indictment, see MacDowell (2), 240–2.

[120] Plato could quite naturally have reminded us of such an illegality in any number of dialogues, and the same goes for Xenophon, yet there is complete silence among the ancients on this issue.

Socrates' willingness to challenge the Athenians' conceptions of the laws when he thinks those conceptions incorrect, even when doing so involves great risk to himself (see 32b4–c3).[121]

1.4.4.2   ἕτερα δὲ καινὰ δαιμόνια εἰσηγούμενος *(introducing other, new divinities)*

In order to introduce new divinities one need not give up the traditional ones, and giving up the traditional gods does not entail replacing them with new divinities. So the two explicitly religious charges against Socrates are logically independent of one another; each requires independent support and interpretation.

The first thing to notice about this second charge is that it does not say that Socrates introduces new gods (θεοί); it makes instead the less specific accusation that he introduces new divinities (δαιμόνια).[122] The second charge is vague: does Socrates introduce new gods, or does he introduce new divinities of other sorts, or does he perhaps introduce some of each?

Equally important to this charge is the sense of illegitimacy inherent in the divinities so described. The divinities Socrates introduces cannot be real divinities that the Athenians simply had not heard of before, for then Socrates' introducing them would be a boon to the city. If the charge is to make any sense as a charge of impiety, it must be that Socrates introduces as divinities new entities that are not real divinities at all. So, even if Socrates called these new divinities 'gods' (sincerely believing in them as such or not), they would not merit that label from Meletus; the only *real* gods, on Meletus' view, are the gods identified in the first part of the indictment, the gods the state

---

121 See also *Grg.* 473e6–474a1 (but see Chapter 4, note 29, below, on this). For other ancient references to the Arginousai affair, see Chapter 4, note 24, below.

122 At *Euthphr.* 3b1–4, however, Socrates says that Meletus is charging him with making new gods ('φησὶ γάρ με ποιητὴν εἶναι θεῶν, καὶ ὡς καινοὺς ποιοῦντα θεοὺς τοὺς δ' ἀρχαίους οὐ νομίζοντα ἐγράψατο τούτων αὐτῶν ἕνεκα, ὥς φησιν'). This discrepancy, we believe, is sufficiently accounted for by our following analysis of the specific charge, by the fact that Socrates at *Euthphr.* 3b1–4 is not reporting the actual words of the charge, but is rather speaking loosely, and by the fact that Euthyphro, immediately after Socrates' remark, unhesitatingly infers that the 'new gods' are no other than Socrates' private *diamonion* (about which, more below). Apparently this was not the last time such a charge was made against an individual. Some fifty years after Socrates' trial, the courtesan Phryne was indicted on a similar charge (Euthias, fr. 1 (Mueller); see A. Raubitschek *RE* 20 (1941), cols. 893–907); and Josephus (*Ap.* 2.267) reports the case of the priestess Ninus. We do not know if there were any examples of this charge earlier than 399 BC.

recognizes.[123] What sorts of new divinities then, is Socrates being charged with introducing?

At 31c7-d5 in Plato's *Apology* Socrates tells the jury about the 'something divine and spiritual' (δαιμόνιον/*daimonion*)[124] that he has had since his childhood, which warns him away from doing what he should not do. Both Plato and Xenophon explicitly tie the second charge to this *daimonion* (Pl., *Ap.* 31c8-d2, *Euthphr.* 3b5-7; Xen., *Ap.* 12),[125] to which Socrates refers frequently in the accounts of both men.[126] Given that our two principal sources of information about Socrates interpret the charge in this way and are contradicted in this by no other ancient sources, we see no reason to doubt them.

But as a number of scholars have noted,[127] the charge of 'introducing new divinities' almost certainly also reflects a strategic decision on the part of the prosecution, for it well accords both with the portrayal of Socrates in Aristophanes' *Clouds* and with the widespread prejudice that Socrates was a nature philosopher (*Ap.* 18a7-c2; 19a8-c5; 23d2-e3). Such men, the jury might be convinced, replace the old gods with new sorts of (often explicitly called 'divine'[128]) powers. This

[123] As Gregory Vlastos has pointed out to us, this would fit nicely with the picture of Socrates Aristophanes offers in the *Nub.*, for there Socrates says that 'the gods have no currency here' (247) and flatly denies the existence of Zeus (366); instead, he calls the Clouds 'our divinities' (252). This would also explain the otherwise peculiar qualifications in pseudo-Lysias' speech 'Against Andocides', 51: 'the gods in whom we believe and whom we worship and to whom we sacrifice in purity and pray'; that is, the *real* gods, not just anything that might be called by that name.

[124] ϑεῖόν τι καὶ δαιμόνιον'; on the vagueness of Socrates' terminology, see Burnet (2), note on *Euthphr.* 3b5. M. Nussbaum denies that Socrates thinks of his *daimonion* as a religious phenomenon at all (in her (2), 234-5). If she is right, Socrates' characterization of it is extremely misleading, especially at a trial for a religious offense. Given that the ancient sources unanimously characterize Socrates' belief in his *daimonion* as a religious belief, we take Socrates at his word.

[125] Burnet doubts this connection (see Burnet (2), note on *Euthphr.* 3b5, *Ap.* 24c1, 31c7, and d1). A. Ferguson provides an excellent argument for rejecting Taylor's suggestion (in (6), ch. I) that it was Pythagorean/Orphic gods that Socrates allegedy introduced, and gives a variety of compelling reasons for accepting Plato's and Xenophon's association of this charge to Socrates' *daimonion* (see esp. 158-9, 169-75). See also Ciholas's article.

[126] Plato, *Ap.* 31c8-d1, 40a4-6, c2-3, 41d6; *Euthphr.* 3b5-7; *Euthyd.* 272e4; *Rep.* VI 496c4; *Phdr.* 242b8-9; and the spurious *Theages* 128d2-131a7; see also *Alc.* I, 105d5-106a1; Xen., *Mem.* 1.1.2-4, 4.8.1; *Ap.* 4-5, 8, 12-13; *Symp.* 8.5. See also Plut., *Mor. de gen.* 580C-582C, 588C-E, 589F, 590A.

[127] See, e.g., Burnet (2), note on *Euthphr.* 3b2; Beckman, 57; A. E. Taylor (3), 101-2.

[128] For one of many examples of this, see the references to Anaximenes in Hippol., *Haer.* 1.7.1; Aet. 1.7.13; Cic., *Nat. D.* 1.10.26; August., *De civ. d.* 8.2. See also Aristotle's more general remark at *Ph.* 3.203b7-14.

is no doubt why the second charge is in the plural, so as to be purposefully vague. Socrates' *daimonion* can be cited directly in court;
the other 'new divinities' need never be cited by the prosecution
directly. Insinuation is all that is needed to call the jury's attention to
their own long-standing prejudices. In this, however, his prosecutors
erred; as we shall argue in Chapter 3, his desire to preserve these insinuations leads Meletus into obvious inconsistency.

1.4.4.3 ἀδικεῖ δὲ καὶ τοὺς νέους διαφθείρων *([Socrates] also
wrongs the youth by corrupting them)*

Youth can be corrupted in any of a great number of ways; precisely
how is Socrates supposed to have corrupted them? At 26b2 we find
Socrates requesting clarification of this very point from Meletus:

> In what way is it that you say I corrupt the youth, Meletus? Or is it clear, ac-
> cording to the indictment you wrote, that it is by teaching them not to
> recognize the gods the state recognizes, but rather other new divinities. Is this
> not what you say, that by teaching I corrupt them? (26b2–6)

Meletus unhesitatingly replies, 'That is exactly what I say' (26b7). So
the third charge of the indictment, as Meletus himself interprets it, is
intrinsically related to the first two parts, as least in Plato's account
(the sense of which is repeated at *Euthyphro* 3b1–4).

It might be thought that the connection Meletus makes between this
part of the indictment and the part explicitly concerning religious
matters is a tactical mistake; after all, it might be easier to obtain a
conviction if *any* evidence of corruption will count as relevant. But
the purpose of the preliminary hearing was to decide whether the
evidence warranted a trial, and, if it did, to delimit the issues to be
decided by the court.[129] It is extremely unlikely that the King-Archon
would have forwarded only the vague accusation that Socrates corrupted the youth unless Meletus specified in the indictment the actual
manner in which Socrates actually did so. For one thing, there is no
record of any law proscribing corruption of the youth.[130] Yet, as we
have already noted,[131] one of the conditions of the amnesty required
that a defendant be charged with violating some particular, written
statute. In order, therefore, to bring the charge of corruption within
the jurisdiction of the court, Meletus may have been obliged during

---

[129] See note 76, above.
[130] See Burnet (2), note on 24b9, and our next paragraph, however.
[131] See note 113, above.

the preliminary hearing to link formally the two parts of the indictment by charging that Socrates corrupted the youth by teaching them
his own impious beliefs.

There is no reason to believe, however, that corrupting youth could
not in a general way be subsumed under the law proscribing impiety,
especially given the powerful religious sanctions supporting proper
respect for one's parents and elders. If Socrates could be shown to encourage children, as the character of that name plainly does in
Aristophanes' *Clouds*, to turn against their parents, especially on
religious issues, he might well be viewed as guilty of impiety.[132]

Regardless of its legal status, Socrates' bad reputation in Athens
was most assuredly on the minds of both accusers and jurors. The
prejudices that had grown over the years against Socrates, which he
attributes to nameless slanderers he calls the 'first accusers' (*Ap.*
18a7–b2; d7–e4; 24b3–4), have a great deal to say about such things.
Accordingly, Socrates' two initial responses to this charge in the
Apology (about which we will say more in Chapter 3) interpret its
scope more broadly than Meletus specifies it. And that such broader
concerns were serious issues, even if they lacked legal status, is supported by all of the ancient sources. So whether or not Socrates' accusers wished, by innuendo or otherwise, to make more of the charge
that he corrupted the youth than Meletus did explicitly, it is certain
that there was a good deal more to it in the air at the trial.

1.5 The Style and Motives of Socrates' Three Speeches

1.5.1 THE PROBLEM

Although other commentaries often provide widely differing interpretations of individual passages in Plato's *Apology*, they are strik-

---

[132] This is also the interpretation of this charge Meletus offers during Socrates'
cross examination of him in Xen., *Ap.* 20. Heidel takes Plato's *Euthphr.* as
providing a defense against this more general conception of the charge, in 'the
emphatic utterance Socrates gives to his surprise at Euthyphro's conduct towards his
father. Socrates was often charged with inciting sons to disrespect and even do
violence to their parents. What more effective means of meeting this calumny than
this could be devised by his friend?' ((1), ((1), 166). Heidel's view is perhaps somewhat
supported by the fact that Diogenes Laertius claims that Euthyphro abandoned his
suit against his father as a result of his conversation with Socrates (2.29).

Yet another sense of this charge might be derived from *Cri.* 53c1–3, where
Socrates seems to assume that inducing disrespect for the laws in the youth would

ingly similar in their defense of the general theses that Socrates'
speech was not intended to be a serious response to his accusers. Instead, we are told, Socrates was primarily interested in proclaiming
the paramount importance of the philosophical way of life and cared
little or nothing about securing his own acquittal. The great Hellenist
George Grote, for example, writing in the nineteenth century, tells us,
'No one who ever reads the *"Platonic Apology"* of Socrates will ever
wish that he had made any other defence. But it is the speech of one
who deliberately foregoes the immediate purpose of a defence—persuasion of the judges'.[133] Similarly, John Burnet, whose edition of the
Apology set the standard for future generations of Socratic scholars,
writes: 'the *Apology* is not really a defence at all, but that makes it all
the more characteristic of the man'.[134] Much the same view is echoed
by A. E. Taylor, who argues that, by giving the kind of speech he
does, Socrates 'chooses to martyr himself' with words sounding more
like 'an avowal of guilt' than a serious defense against the charges.[135]
The most recent commentaries express this same view. In his 1979
book on the *Apology* Thomas West maintains that 'when Socrates
says that he will tell the whole truth, and yet refuses to give the whole
truth an outward order and attractiveness, he guarantees that the jury
will not believe it'.[136] And we find the following in R. E. Allen's recent book: 'An *apologia* is a defense. But the *Apology* is something
other than a defense'.[137] 'Socrates' aim was to gain neither conviction
nor acquittal, but to tell the whole truth in accordance with justice'.[138]

In this book we shall affirm what so many other scholars have one
way or another denied; for we shall try to show how the Platonic
Socrates' own moral and religious commitments, announced in the
Apology but also to be found in other early dialogues, require him to
undertake a sincere and effective defense to his jury. We shall naturally have to provide an explanation of the many aspects of the speech
that appear at least odd or even incomprehensible to contemporary
readers. Most scholars are inclined to view such puzzling passages at
instances of Socrates' notorious irony.[139] Other scholars claim that

---

count as corrupting them, and that if Socrates were to be guilty of this he would
thereby prove that the verdict of his trial had been the right one. (We owe this point
to Gregory Vlastos.)

[133] Grote (1), vol. 7, 157.   [134] Burnet (1), 146.
[135] A. E. Taylor (2), 156-67.   [136] T. West, 79.   [137] Allen (3), 4.
[138] Ibid., 13-14. See also Allen (5), 16. A similar view is expressed by Cornford
(1), 303-4; Guardini, 31; Seeskin (1), 60-4; and Shero, 111.
[139] There are a variety of such views, offering different rationales for Socrates'
use of irony in this particular context. Allen ((1), *passim*, and (3), 3-16), Calogero,

Socrates shows no real interest in defending himself against the charges and instead uses his time in the court to mock the ignorance of his prosecutors and jurors.[140]

1.5.2 SOCRATIC IRONY VERSUS SOCRATIC CONCERN FOR THE TRUTH

Socrates' irony is well attested. He is often enough explicitly accused of it in Plato's dialogues (*Grg.* 489e1, *Rep.* I 337a4, *Symp.* 216e4; cp. *Ap.* 38a1), and Aristotle reports it as well (*Eth. Nic.* 1127b22-6). His self-deprecating remarks about his own abilities[141] and his unabashed flattery of interlocutors,[142] so familiar in the other early dialogues, are transparently disingenuous. And though his dissembling is typically calculated to lure another into discussion in order to bring about the beneficial effects of his questioning method of philosophizing (the ἔλεγχος/*elenchos*), his teasing insincerity can sometimes appear entirely gratuitous.[143] Nor are these episodes restricted to playful rhetorical traps and other non-philosophical banter; even when the conversation concerns quite serious issues, he sometimes appears willing to propose or endorse the opposite of what he believes, to test the coherence or sincerity of his interlocutor's beliefs.[144]

Feaver and Hare (205-16), and Seeskin ((1), 56-61, and (2)), for examples, see the entire speech as an ironic parody of fifth-century rhetoric. A. E. Taylor ((2), 160) maintains that all Socrates says about the 'old accusers', roughly one-third of the entire speech, 'has abundant traces' of irony. See also Bassett, 58; Sauvage and Sauvage, 102.

[140] Burnet ((1), 181-2), for example, says 'Socrates treats the accusation with contempt, and even goes out of his way to import things into the case that were hardly of a nature to conciliate the judges.' Seeskin ((1), 63), says that 'given the closeness of the vote [to convict] (36a), there is reason to think that a speech containing fewer taunts and insults might have produced a different result'. Other proponents of the view that Socrates' arrogance influenced the outcome of the trial include Friedländer (vol. 2., 157), Jowett (106), Sesonske (229), Skemp ((1), 20), A. E. Taylor ((3), 109), and Zeller ((2), 195). An ancient version of this view may be found expressed in Ath. 611A.

The view that Socrates alienated the jurors with arrogance is plainly compatible with the ironic interpretation of many parts of the speech, and thus many interpreters can be found endorsing both views. See, e.g., Allen ((1), 35), Guardini (31), Grote ((1), vol. 7, 154), and T. West (76); also compare A. E. Taylor (3) with A. E. Taylor (2).

[141] See, e.g., *Euthyd.* 295e1-3, *Meno* 71c8, *Grg.* 461c5-8, *Rep.* I 336e2-337a2.

[142] See, e.g., *Euthphr.* 5a3-8, *Ion* 530b5-c5, *Prt.* 328d8-329b5, *Euthyd.* 295e1-3.

[143] For a discussion of this point, see Vlastos (1), xxiv-xxv.

[144] The argument Socrates has with Critias in the *Charm.*, for example, leads to the conclusion that temperance cannot be the craft of good and evil (see esp. 174d3-6). But Socrates almost certainly believes that temperance is just such a craft.

Moreover, numerous passages in the *Apology* itself might be taken as evidence that the defense was, at least in some places, not intended to be taken seriously and literally. For example, rather than directly answer his accusers' charges, Socrates spends most of his time talking about what he calls the 'first accusations' (18a8), which have no legal status. He then portrays his practice of philosophy in Athens as 'a service to the god' (23c1), a mission assigned him when the Delphic oracle answered 'no' to his friend Chairephon's question, 'Is anyone wiser than Socrates?' Many scholars disbelieve the whole story, and those that are willing to accept it at all find the connection between the oracle's simple negative and Socrates' developed conception of its jussive function anything but obvious. In other passages, Socrates claims to be ignorant of what he says is the most important thing in life—virtue (for example at 21b4–5); yet elsewhere he claims with great conviction that his actions are so paradigmatically virtuous as to make him the state's greatest benefactor (36c3–4). These apparently incompatible claims have prompted considerable dispute among interpreters of the *Apology*.

When Socrates considers the possibility that the jurors might let him go unharmed if only he would stop philosophizing, he flatly pronounces that he would disobey them (29c5–d6), despite his professed commitments to the law and legal authorities in the *Crito* and without apparent regard for the anger such a pronouncement might arouse among the jurors. When convicted and asked to propose a counter-penalty, he first considers the appropriateness of maintenance at the Prutaneion (36d1–37a1); and then, after considering and rejecting a number of counter-penalties that might satisfy the jury, he finally offers a fine that is, according to most scholars, so small as to be a mockery (38b4–9). Moreover, Socrates' predicament is itself a bitter irony: he stands trial for impiety as a result of activities stemming from the pious pursuit of what he takes to be the god's will (23b7, 28e4–5, 30e5–31b5). It therefore might be seen as only fitting for the tone of his response to the accusation to be equally ironic. These and other features of Plato's *Apology* are cited as evidence of Socrates' playfulness, arrogant defiance, or mocking artistry—anything, that is, but sincere and relevant trial behavior.

Despite such apparently abundant textual evidence for viewing the *Apology* as a portrait of Socratic irony and defiance, many passages indicate that, because of his various commitments, Socrates must offer a sincere and effective defense, intended to convince his jurors of his innocence. For one thing, Socrates' speech is punctuated with at least an apparent concern for the truth. He continually reminds the jurors that they will hear only the truth from him (18a5-6, 20d5-6, 22b5-6, 28a6, d6, 32a8, 33c1-2), and he is careful to contrast the truth of his statements with the many falsehoods of his accusers (17a5-b8, 31b7-c3, 34b5). He also frequently reminds the jurors that it is their sworn duty to put aside their prejudices against him and to listen only to the truth (18a3-6, 18e5-19a4, 35b9-c5). Of course, his insistence that what he says is truthful might itself be ironic, and is in any case consistent with other parts of the speech being mordantly sarcastic or slyly disingenuous. But we will try to show that the emphasis he places on the need for truth merits more attention and explanation than it is given in most scholars' accounts.

It might be argued that irony can be used as an instrument of truth, for only a mistakenly literal interpretation of an ironic remark would render it a falsehood. Irony and dishonesty, then, are hardly identical. But the *Apology* is unique among the dialogues in (among other things) presenting Socrates in a setting where he cannot practice his *elenchos* upon his principal audience. Though he does so engage Meletus (24c9-28a1), he cannot question the jury and respond in stages as their answers are given. So if he is to employ irony in this setting, it cannot be as bait for an elenctic trap; and if the jury should take literally an ironic remark, their mistake could not emerge in subsequent conversation for Socrates to correct. So if Socrates speaks ironically on a matter of substance at his trial, he risks causing some jurors to believe what is false, the degree of risk corresponding inversely with the jurors' present ability to interpret calmly and intelligently such wry playfulness or subtle sarcasm. Their ability to do so would never be a matter of complete confidence and in any case is especially impaired in the present circumstance, given the grave and slanderous allegations they have heard against Socrates.[145]

1.5.3 SOCRATES' RELEVANT MORAL COMMITMENTS

Though he alludes to it only briefly in the *Apology*, Socrates also believes that one must always uphold just laws and institutions; this commitment provides the basis of his arguments in the *Crito*, for ex-

---

[145] It is unfortunate that Vlastos never addresses the special problems concerning irony in the *Apology* in his most recent paper on Socratic irony (Vlastos (11)), though he is well aware that '[w]hen irony riddles it risks being misunderstood' (79).

ample.[146] Moreover, Socrates never once challenges the legitimacy of either the impiety law he has been charged with violating or the juridical process by which he is being tried.[147] He simply believes that he is innocent of the charges against him. Had he chosen to flee Athens, we may safely assume that he would have been convicted and sentenced to death *in absentia*. But the authorities would probably not have ordered that he be pursued,[148] so that such a conviction would have been nothing more than a *de facto* exile, one in which Socrates would be well cared for by his foreign friends. But in the light of his commitment to law and legal authority, it is not surprising that he elects instead to remain in Athens and defend himself, telling the jurors at the outset: 'I must obey the law and present a defense' (19a6–7).

No law directly required the defendant, or for that matter the prosecutor, to tell only the truth at a trial, though to be caught in a lie would no doubt be very prejudicial to one's case. Both defendant and prosecutor were required to take oaths at the preliminary hearing,[149] but each was only required to swear to the truth of his case—in this instance, Meletus to the truth of the charges he brought and Socrates to his innocence of those charges. Neither prosecutor nor defendant was sworn to tell only the truth to support his claim in court, nor was either required to take an oath prior to their presentation to the jury. Finally, the law against perjury pertained only to false testimony

[146] There has been considerable controversy recently over whether the principles Socrates announces in the *Cri.* commit him to obeying all or only some laws and legal institutions. The issue turns on whether he believes that all laws, or only some, are just. On either interpretation, however, Socrates believes that all just laws and institutions must be obeyed. We shall have a great deal more to say about Socrates' commitment to obey the laws in Chapters 3 and 4.

[147] The nature of Socrates' defense is consistently to deny that he is guilty of any wrongdoing as specified by both the 'first' and the 'later' accusers. Nowhere, however, does he challenge the law or the procedure under which he is prosecuted, although he does suggest after his conviction that the procedure would be improved by taking more than one day for trials of capital cases (37a7–b2). See also *Cri.* 52a6–d5 and 53a3–4.

[148] This is suggested by the concern that the danger Socrates presents to Athens is only in the continuation of his mission (see 29c3–d1). Moreover, Crito strongly implies that Socrates' life is endangered only because he chose not to flee Athens prior to his trial (*Cri.* 45e3–4). This remark makes sense, however, only if Crito at least believes that Socrates would not have been pursued had he simply fled. See also Guthrie (1), vol. 3, 383–4.

[149] Socrates refers to the oath called the ἀντωμοσία, at 35c2–d5. For more on the role the oath played at the preliminary hearing, see Harrison, vol. 2, 99–100; MacDowell (2), 240.

given by witnesses, not to what the litigants themselves might say.[150] Were Socrates, therefore, to mislead the jury, either through irony or simple mendacity, he would not *ipso facto* have violated his principle of legal obedience.

But in the *Apology* Socrates is careful to point out that each of the jurors has sworn an oath 'to judge according to the laws' (35c2–5),[151] an oath that binds each juror as a matter of both piety and law. He thereby reminds them that they must set aside whatever prejudices they may have against him and restrict themselves to judging whether or not he is guilty of the charges brought against him. As we said above, Socrates believed the function the jurors have sworn to perform to be a just one, though when the trial is over he will be convinced that a majority of the jurors have not performed it correctly. Socrates' principles require that he honor and obey just legal institutions; so as he presents his defense he must do everything within his power compatible with law and morality to make the truth known to the jurors about the real nature of the activities for which he has been brought before them. Were Socrates intentionally to risk misleading the jurors in any way, he would be guilty of the very disregard for law, justice, and the truth of which he accuses Meletus (24c4–8, d7–9; 25c1–4; 26a8–b2, 34b5). And if he should in any way encourage the jurors to fail to perform properly their sworn duty, he would thereby become guilty of impiety, the very crime he has been wrongly accused of committing (35c5–d5). If irony is to be found in Socrates' presentation, therefore, it must in no way interfere with the jurors' capacity to judge the case correctly.

Socrates, we believe, is convinced of his innocence. For him to act in such a way as to risk carelessly the condemnation of the jury would show a disregard for the law requiring juries to discern the relevant facts of the case; it would also demonstrate an impious disregard for the oath each juror swears to uphold that law. Socrates' sense of obligation to the state and its laws, therefore, requires him not only to undertake a defense, but to make this defense as effective as possible within the limits of the laws, time, and his other principles. Because of the limitations the law places on jurors, Socrates may not seek special favors from them or appeal to irrelevancies that might predispose them in his favor (34b6–35d8). Even if doing so might encourage

---

[150] See Plescia, 33–57.
[151] The actual oath seems to have been 'I will hold no grudges and not be influenced, but will judge according to the current laws' (see Andoc., *Myst.* 91).

them to arrive at the correct verdict, they would not judge the case in the right way. Socrates must do all in his power to enable the jurors to carry out their sworn duty: he must avoid willful dishonesty, misdirection, or even irrelevant playfulness if he is not to undermine the jury's performance of its pious and legal duty. Indeed, even the most transparent irony still carries a risk as long as one or more jurors would not understand it or would respond prejudicially to it.

Neither can Socrates be arrogantly defiant towards the jurors. Although he may well disapprove of their shameful ignorance as individual citizens, he must not lose sight of their legal function as judges: 'to judge according to the laws'. He knows that it will be exceedingly difficult for many of them to carry out their function, due to their prejudice against him (19a2–5). Were he to be pridefully defiant, he would risk deepening the prejudice of those already biased and creating it in at least some of the others. Just as he cannot appeal to their sense of compassion by bringing in his family and relatives, as other defendants often do, since that would interfere with the jurors' objectivity and hence their performance of their proper function (34b7–35d5), so he cannot intentionally or carelessly inflame them with irrelevant and defiant rhetoric.

There is yet another reason why Socrates must avoid saying anything that would risk prompting the jury to reach an incorrect verdict in his case. Socrates is convinced that one must never do an injustice to or harm another, or return injustice for injustice or harm for harm;[152] he also believes that the possession of a false belief about virtue and about virtuous activity brings about the greatest harm that can befall a person (*Grg.* 458a8–b1).[153] In the *Apology* Socrates claims not only that his life in general has been blameless (37b2–3); he also argues that the philosophical activities for which he stands accused of impiety are paradigmatically virtuous. Were Socrates to mislead or annoy the jury about these matters, whether by irony or arrogance, he would not only risk creating or sustaining false belief about virtue, the most important of all things; he would also risk bringing about or contributing to the worst possible harm to his judges. But that is

---

[152] See, e.g., Socrates' discussion with Polus at *Grg.* 469b12 ff., esp. 479c8–e9, and his concluding remarks at the end of the dialogue, at 527a5–b7; *Cri.* 49a4–c11; *Rep.* I 335b2–e5; *Ap.* 25c5–26a7, 29b7–9, 37a5–6, b2–5.

[153] This view also follows from Socrates' beliefs that vice is the greatest harm that can befall a man (see, e.g., *Ap.* 30c6–d5, *Cri.* 47e6–48a7, and *Grg.* 477c2–e6), and that wrongdoing is always the result of false belief about what we ought to pursue (see, e.g., *Meno* 77c5–78a8 and *Prt.* 358c4–d4).

what he must never do. Since the very issue the jury must decide is the moral quality of Socrates' activities, it follows that he must in no way contribute willingly to their reaching the wrong verdict. He must therefore not mislead the jury about any matter substantive to the judgment of the case. Those who wish to argue that Socrates was ironic in any particular claim must be prepared to show that he believed such irony was at least as likely as the literal truth to get the jury to see the facts of the case clearly and without prejudice.

But perhaps even more important than the above implications of Socrates' moral commitments is the nature of the mission for which Socrates has been haled before the jury. The heart of his defense is that, far from being impious, he has spent his life in pursuing the expressed will of the god, seeking virtue, and encouraging others to do the same. He gives no reason to suppose that he is permitted to abandon this pursuit in the face of difficulty. On the contrary, Socrates has followed the god's will *despite* numerous disadvantages: lacking the time for other personal or civic pursuits (23b7–9), he has earned only suspicion and enmity from his countrymen (21e1–2; 22e6–23a3, c7–d2) as well as great personal poverty (23b9–c1). As he stands before the jury he is in danger of further loss; but though he risks even death, he is not released from his mission. As he presents his defense, he must therefore continue encouraging people to give up their pretense of wisdom (23b4–7); he must exhort them to care for wisdom, truth, and the perfection of the soul more than wealth, reputation, and honor (29d2–30b4).

Suppose we set against these considerations even the most cautious version of the view that portrays Socrates as at least sometimes consciously and purposefully engaging in displays that might reasonably be expected to be less effective than the simple truth in calming prejudices and convincing the jurors to whom he spoke that his mission was indeed a pious one. The comparison makes clear the inconsistency between even the most moderate of such views and the demands of Socrates' mission. For him to behave as these interpretations say he does would be for Socrates to abandon his mission without permission and thus become guilty of impiety, the very crime for which he is inappropriately on trial. Neither may he risk encouraging the jury, through his own arrogant defiance, to follow the wrong path, nor may he show a lack of concern for the path they might select by themselves in their ignorance and hostility. The former would be to act in a way exactly contrary to the god's will, and the latter would be to give up the mission assigned by the god. Either way is one of disgrace, a fate worse than death (28d6–29a4).

Socrates' concerns to honor the law, avoid injustice, and follow the god's instructions are each amply attested in Plato's and others' portrayals. The constraints they place on Socrates convince us that another interpretation of the *Apology* is required, for it seems to us that his life and moral convictions require an explanation of his defense quite different from that provided to us by the interpretations we have challenged. We are not suggesting that Socrates' speeches aim *solely* at winning the case and being released; as he speaks to the jurors he cannot act in such a way as to violate his principles, even if acting in that way would be likely to arouse the sympathy of the jurors. As he speaks to the jury, he must continue as scrupulously as he can to follow the dictates of his mission, even if to some degree doing so jeopardizes what he would count as a favorable outcome to the trial. We are also not insisting that Socrates' principles require him *never* to engage in irony, but only never to do so in such a way as might needlessly interfere with the jury's capacity to judge the case correctly. In fact, we believe that characteristic Socratic irony can be found in his speech, though never on any issue of direct substance to his defense. It is certain, for example, that Socrates thinks that Euenos' actual service is worth nothing (see 20a2–c1); so in saying that Euenos' cheap sophistry is a bargain, Socrates is being heavily ironical.[154] Euenos is neither a blessing nor a bargain, though surely he would be both if he really could make people into better citizens, as he claims to do. But we believe that Socrates' own most cherished commitments rule out any interpretation of the *Apology* that portrays Socrates as intentionally and gratuitously putting the correct outcome and procedures in jeopardy. We find such interpretations inherently suspect and thus shall devote the remainder of this book to finding meaning in Socrates' remarks in a way that is informed by and consistent with the other aspects of his life and philosophic mission.

Of course, some of these aspects—for example, Socrates' account of his religious mission—are themselves disputed as instances of irony or playfulness, and must themselves be defended as providing motives

---

[154] A certain Euenos mentioned in the *Phd.* (60d3–61c9) is described as both a poet (60d8–10) and a philosopher (61c6–7), which are compatible with his being the same man as the sophist from Paros Socrates discusses in the *Ap.* But the Euenos of the *Phd.* is described in such a way as to suggest that he was among Socrates' friends, and Socrates appears not to know the sophist mentioned in the *Ap.*

for sincerity in the form and content of his defense. Furthermore, a number of Socrates' individual statements and strategies, such as those we mentioned in 1.5.2, have been cited in defense of the line of interpretation we oppose; in order for our analysis to be complete, we must provide an alternative interpretation of each of them that is compatible with our general view. In the remaining chapters of this book we shall consider each case as it occurs in the context of Socrates' other remarks to the jury.

2

SOCRATES' DEFENSE, PART I
(17a1–24b2)

2.1 The Prooimion

2.1.1 THE PROBLEM

There was little that was ordinary about the trial of Socrates. One of its most extraordinary aspects was the way in which Socrates behaved in the courtroom: whereas other litigants might employ highly emotional stratagems to win a favorable verdict, all the ancient accounts show Socrates proudly disdaining any posture of supplication or fearful humility that might have helped to earn him the jurors' mercy. In this respect, Plato's *Apology* is no exception. But as we have said, commentators have typically inferred from Socrates' refusal to appeal to the jurors' emotions that he betrayed insolence towards the jurors and was indifferent to the legal outcome of the case.

By contrast, students of ancient rehetoric find that one aspect of Socrates' defense conforms entirely to standard practice. Forensic speeches of the fifth and fourth centuries generally began with a brief introduction called the προοίμιον *(prooimion)*.[1] As the term itself suggests,[2] its purpose was to 'pave the way' for the main body of the speech.[3] In this respect Socrates' first speech to the jury has appeared to a number of readers to fit the standard rhetorical practice of the period. Not only does it contain such a *prooimion*; in many respects the style and substance of the *prooimion* appear very conventional. Those who believe this see such a stark contrast between the *prooimion* and the remainder of his speech as to conclude that Socrates himself would never have seriously offered such a conventional opening.

Although we are wholly unconvinced by such accounts, they are

---

[1] See, e.g., Pl., *Phdr.* 266d7–8; Arist., *Rh.* 1354b17 and 1414a1–1416a2; Dem., *Exordia* 1.1–56.3. See also Kennedy, 53–8.

[2] The root, οἶμος, means 'course' or 'path'.

[3] The expression is Aristotle's: ὁδοποίησις τῷ ἐπιόντι (*Rh.* 1414b20). We follow the translations of J. H. Friese and W. Rhys Roberts in rendering ὁδοποίησις as 'paving the way'.

nevertheless worth careful consideration. If we are correct, they are classic instances of the kind of reasoning that has led so many serious and intelligent scholars to invent subtle and elaborate interpretations of Socrates' words, despite his explicit announcement in the *prooimion* and throughout his defense that he will be blunt and honest. In fact, we believe that the *prooimion* is entirely consistent with what we know of Socrates' principles, and that it provides a natural and sensible introduction to the defense he subsequently offers; we therefore find nothing in the *prooimion* so extraordinary as to require ingenious explication. But let us begin by reviewing the evidence usually cited by those interpreters with whom we disagree, in order to show why we believe that such evidence does not warrant their conclusions.

2.1.2 SOCRATES AND RHETORIC

An anecdote recorded by Diogenes Laertius perhaps illustrates best the interpretative problem posed by the *Apology*'s *prooimion*. According to Diogenes (2.40), the great Attic orator Lysias actually wrote a defense for Socrates, which the latter refused to accept on the ground that it was 'more forensic than philosophical'. We have no way of knowing if there is any factual basis for Diogenes' report. But the spirit of the anecdote fits perfectly the criticism launched by Plato's Socrates against the oratory employed by his contemporaries. Nowhere is his hostility to contemporary rhetorical practices put more bluntly than in the *Gorgias*, where he argues that rhetoric is typically a form of persuasion that promises real benefit but in fact aims only at gratifying an audience and thus is actually harmful (*Grg.* 462b3–465e1; 502d5–503b5). Nevertheless, as Riddell noted in his 1877 edition of the *Apology*, various elements of the *prooimion* in Plato's version of the speech 'may be completely paralleled, piece by piece, from the Orators'.[4] As instances of these parallels, Riddell cites Socrates' denial that he is a clever speaker and his counter-accusation that his prosecutors are lying. From this observation Riddell infers that Plato's version bore little resemblance to the speech Socrates actually gave at his trial, since 'the subtle rhetoric of this defense would ill accord with the historical Socrates, even had the defense of Socrates been as we certainly know it not to have been the offspring of study and premeditation'.[5] Burnet accepts Riddell's observation regarding the similarities between the various topics of the *Apology*'s

---

[4] Riddell, xxi.   [5] Riddell, xx.

prooimion and those of other legal speeches, but he rightly denies that these similarities support the conclusion that Plato's account is largely a fiction. Instead, Burnet argues that the historical Socrates, was 'perfectly familiar with contemporary rhetoric, and . . . thought very little of it.[6] Burnet thus perceives an incongruence between the portrayals of Socrates elsewhere in the Platonic corpus as the avowed enemy of the rhetoricians and his depiction in the *Apology* as being willing to conform to standard rhetorical procedure. This perception leads Burnet to conclude that the *prooimion* of Socrates' speech to the jury must be seen as a parody of the very forensic rhetoric Socrates held in contempt.[7] Using their own devices to mock them, Burnet maintains, fully accords with what we know of the way Socrates treats his opponents.

Burnet's reading of the *prooimion* has attracted the endorsements of a number of the more recent commentators on the *Apology*.[8] Yet, exactly what justifies Burnet's view remains unclear. Such a reading, obviously, does not follow immediately from the mere existence of similarities between Socrates' *prooimion* and other forensic speeches. A parody, after all, is an imitation of something else for the purpose of achieving a satirical or humorous effect. Burnet claims that further evidence for his view may be found in Socrates' lack of respect for the likes of Gorgias and Hippias. But Socrates' genuine contempt for sophistry and for the Sophists' ignorance of moral virtue clearly does

---

[6] Burnet (2), 67.

[7] Ibid. A number of scholars have found what they saw as tell-tale similarities between Plato's *Apology* and Gorgias' *Apology of Palamedes,* but none can agree on what the tale is that these similarities are supposed to tell: Calogero (1) says that it shows Socrates' debt to Gorgias as a teacher; Coulter supposes it shows Socrates' explicit rejection of Gorgianic rhetoric; Seeskin ((1), 56–9, and (2)) is convinced that Plato's Socrates is parodying Gorgias' speech. Our own view on this is simple: there is no reason to suppose that a later work is a copy, criticism, or parody of an earlier work (if, indeed, Plato's *Apology* is later than Gorgias' *Palamedes*) unless there is no natural reason for the later work to be the way it is. Since we argue that each aspect of Socrates' speech in the *Apology* makes very good sense by itself, we find no reason to suppose its *real* motivation is anything but what it appears to be—Socrates' sincere attempt to defend himself before the jury. To understand whatever similarities we find between the words of (Plato's) Socrates and Gorgias' Palamedes, we may need to understand only that the *Palamedes* is, as Seeskin says, 'a collection of . . . tried and true devices for winning acquittal' (59), and that Socrates is a highly intelligent and educated man, on our view seriously seeking acquittal.

[8] Examples include Allen (1), 33 and (2), 5–6; A. E. Taylor (2), 160–1; T. West, 72, 74–5. Hackforth ((2), 55–7) resists Burnet's view, but does little to explain the various aspects of the *prooimion* that led Burnet to suspect Socrates' sincerity.

not require that he be only mock-serious whenever he calls attention to their practices. Nor does Plato's masterful ability to imitate other prose stylists,[9] evidenced in the 'middle period' dialogues, justify the conclusion that the *prooimion* of the *Apology* is a parody. Even if Plato elsewhere imitates others for ironic comic effect, it does not follow that he is doing so here. Before we accept the view that the *prooimion* is a parody, then, we must be shown better evidence that Socrates says what he does in the introduction to his defense in a satirical or mock-serious way. But therein lies the problem. If the evidence adduced by Riddell actually shows that the language of Socrates' *prooimion* closely resembles other standard forensic phrases, it is all the more difficult to see how the former is an attempt to ridicule or mock the latter. Parodies cannot be so close as to be indistinguishable from what they parody. And we may be quite confident that others' use of the standard rhetorical maneuvres Socrates is alleged to employ in his *prooimion* was intended to be no laughing matter.

Of course it might be thought that the *prooimion* must be seen as a parody simply because what is said comes from the mouth of *Socrates*, a known and outspoken critic of the rhetoricians. For *him*, of all people, to be heard uttering stock rhetorical phrases would of itself be amusing, and the mere fact that Socrates adopts such rhetorical techniques has been taken as evidence that he does not intend what he says to be taken seriously. This interpretation, however, assumes that those for whom the speech is intended, either the jurors or the readers of Plato's version of the speech, could be relied upon to notice the similarity between what Socrates says and what Riddell maintains are typical oratorical attempts to manipulate the jury. But this is a highly questionable assumption, since there is no evidence that ancient theorists of rhetoric prescribed any specific set elements for the *prooimion* of a legal speech,[10] nor do any of the speeches cited

---

[9] The six encomia on *eros* in the *Symp.* display Plato's ability to affect different prose styles. For a detailed account of the stylistic differences among these speeches, see R. G. Bury, *The Symposium of Plato* (Cambridge, 1933), vii–lxxi. In fact, scholars still remain divided over whether Plato actually composed the first speech of the *Phdr.* in an attempt to imitate Lysias or whether he used one of Lysias' actual speeches. For more on this point, see Guthrie (1), vol. 4, 443.

[10] Aristotle's treatment of rhetorical theory is by far the most extensive that has come down to us from Ancient Greece. In his discussion of *prooimia* (*Rh.* 1414a1–1416a2), however, he sets down only the most general guidelines to be followed.

by Riddell have more than two of the many 'standard' features Riddell finds in Socrates' *prooimion*.[11] Naturally, the less obvious or common the similarities are supposed to be, the more tenuous Burnet's inference becomes.

There are yet other reasons to be puzzled about the inference Burnet draws from Riddell's observation. At least parts of the Socratic *prooimion* are plainly true. It is clear, for example, that Socrates believes his prosecutors have lied about him in their speeches (17a3–4). And there is no reason to doubt his claim that this is the first time that he has appeared before a court of law (17d2–3). No doubt he does consider it inappropriate for a man of his advanced age to go into court 'fabricating a speech' like a young boy (17c4–5). Of course, the fact that parts of the *prooimion* are true does not show that they are intended by Socrates to be taken in earnest, since he might still be intending to amuse the audience by showing them that even he, the notorious enemy of rhetoricians, can truthfully say the same things they have so often heard from other litigants. But at least one part of the *prooimion* cannot be dismissed as a Socratic (or Platonic) attempt at parody, namely, its concluding remark, in which Socrates reminds the jury that it is his duty to tell the truth and their duty to decide what is just. Given his commitments to promote truth, justice, and the proper administration of just legal institutions, it would be exceedingly odd for him to remind the jury of his and their respective duties only in an attempt to ridicule other speakers. But if Socrates' final remark must be seen as sincere, Burnet's characterization of the *prooimion* is faced with at least *prima facie* implausibility, for it would be odd for Socrates to have engaged in an attempt to satirize contemporary rhetorical practice in the preceding parts of the *prooimion*, only abruptly to end his introduction on such an important and serious note.

Finally, there is no reason to think the Socrates' objections to the rhetoricians derive from the *form* their speeches take or from their

---

[11] Riddell, xxi. In fact, there are a number of extant forensic speeches that appear to contain *none* of the common elements Riddell claims to find in Socrates' *prooimion* (see, e.g., Antiphon, *Chor.* 141, 1–6; Andoc., *Myst.* 1–10; Lys. 1.92.1–5, 3.96.1–4, 13.130.1–4). Hence, it seems to us that Riddell and Burnet have both greatly exaggerated the degree to which Socrates' first remarks to the jury may be said to be in conformity with recognizable conventions. And if Bonner is right (see 176), Socrates' use of legal terms throughout his speech betrays a lack of close knowledge of forensics. But this point is not essential to our argument here, which seeks to prove only that even if we accept Riddell's and Burnet's premiss, we are in no way compelled to accept either of their conclusions.

willingness to use certain stock phrases and topics for their speeches. Rather, his complaint is with the *content* of their speeches. As we have said, the essence of Socrates' complaint is that, despite their professions to the contrary, those who engage in non-philosophical rhetoric fail to promote moral virtue because they gratify their listeners with what is the most pleasing rather than what is true (see, for example, *Grg. 462b3*–465e1). Other defendants may therefore even be telling the truth when they point out, say, that they have never been in court before or that in the past they have given distinguished service to the state. But Socrates would nevertheless condemn the mention of such facts if they are not pertinent to the charges but instead are merely being used to curry favor with the jury. (It is precisely for this reason that he later refuses to engage in the common practice of parading his children, other members of his family, and his friends before the jury (34b6–c7),[12] although it is of course true that he has young children and that his family and friends will be anguished if he is condemned.)

But in so far as the conventions of rhetoric *per se* are compatible with a scrupulous regard for using the truth to serve justice, we find no reason to suppose that Socrates would condemn such conventions. Perhaps more important, if the use of such conventions assisted a speaker in communicating the truth to his audience—if, for example, a certain style of opening remarks was expected by the jury—then we might well suppose that Socrates would prescribe it as preferable to a less conventional and more obscure approach. So if what Socrates says in his own *prooimion* is true and relevant to the defense he subsequently presents, the fact that the things he says are similar to at least some of the things said by various other litigants gives us no reason, *pace* Burnet, to question his sincerity or to think that in his opening remarks to the jury he strays from his commitment to the goal of philosophical rhetoric. On the contrary (and as we shall subsequently argue), the specific use he makes of his *prooimion* may only indicate just how seriously he regards his legal plight, and how eager he is to make plain to the jurors the truths he is obliged to make known to them.

2.1.3 SOME INDIVIDUAL PASSAGES

At this point adherents to Burnet's view might well respond that, even if there are parts of the *prooimion* that are true, there are also parts

---

[12] On such appeals to jurors' mercy, see Ar., *Vesp.* 568–74, 976–8; Lys. 20.34; Dem. 21.99, 21.186–8; Xen., *Mem.* 4.4.4.

that Socrates himself knows are plainly false: his flat denial that he is
a clever speaker (17a5–b1) and his assertion that he is 'an utter
stranger to the manner of speaking in court' (17d3). He immediately
goes on to tell the jurors that through his speech he will show that he is
a 'clever speaker *in no way whatever*' (17b2–3). But the extreme
cleverness of Socrates, which takes a variety of guises thoughout the
early dialogues, is patent to everyone except his most dim-witted opponents. And we need look no further than the *Apology* itself to find
out that Socrates could not seriously disclaim familiarity with the
manner in which litigants speak before the court. At 34b7–35a7 he
acknowledges that he knows that other defendants often parade their
families before the court in an attempt to arouse the sympathy of the
jury. He goes on to say explicitly that he has often witnessed trials
(35a4). On Burnet's view, 'It would be just like Socrates to say that he
knows nothing about forensic diction at the very moment he is showing his mastery of it'.[13] From such evidence, one might conclude that
Burnet's thesis is correct because at least parts of the *prooimion* cannot be construed as sincere.

But before we accept even this more restricted version of Burnet's
view we would do well to re-examine each of the statements at issue.
First, when Socrates disclaims cleverness to the jury, it is clear in context that he is employing the sense of 'clever' introduced by his accusers, which contrasts clever speakers with truthful ones (17b4–5).
Any truths he tells the jury, no matter how logically subtle or
rhetorically appropriate, would not qualify as clever in this sense. One
must convict Socrates of deliberately misleading the jury in some particular claim (other than the one in question, which would entail cir-
cularity) in order to establish that he is indeed a 'clever speaker' in the
relevant sense. And although Socrates' disclaimer relies heavily upon
a distinction between cleverness and honesty whose legitimacy is questionable, there is nothing sneaky or sophistical in his employment of
this distinction, for it had already been established by the prosecution. When he tells the jury that he is not clever, therefore, they know
precisely what he means by 'clever'.

Secondly, the scope of Socrates' disclaimer is unclear. In order for
what Socrates says here to be false, as Burnet insists, we must suppose
that Socrates is not merely denying that he will display cleverness in
the defense to follow, but also denying that he has ever been clever.[14]

---

[13] Burnet (2), note on 17d3. See also Seeskin (1), 59.   [14] Burnet, ibid.

But the way Socrates states the denial suggests a much narrower scope, for what he denies is the charge the prosecutors make in admonishing the jury to be 'on their guard lest they be deceived because he is a clever speaker' (17a5–b1). Socrates' denial is quite compatible with the claim that he can be a clever speaker when he wishes to be; it merely requires that the jury is in no danger of being deceived by such cleverness in this case. Our view that Socrates here affirms only the narrower claim, that he will not deceive the jury, is further supported by the conclusion he draws from his disclaimer: 'Therefore, as I say, they have said little or nothing true, but you will hear only the truth from me' (17b6–8). Because the inference drawn from his disclaimer refers to what the jurors *will hear*, it is plain that Socrates denies only that he will be clever in his subsequent attempts to convince them of his innocence. So if in the rest of his defense speech he displays in court what he calls 'the virtue of a speaker'—in other words, the virtue of telling only the truth—then, the evidence for Burnet's view in Socrates' disclaimer of cleverness vanishes, for what Socrates says here is the unvarnished truth. The jury need not be on their guard against Socratic deceit, whether or not he is capable of such 'cleverness' in other circumstances.

Socrates has good reason to single out the issue of clever speaking for special emphasis in his *prooimion*. It is not just Socrates' life that is in jeopardy; also at stake are the future of his philosophic mission and the jury's evaluation of it. If they err in their decision, they commit a grave wrong, for they condemn and extinguish what they should preserve. Socrates' various moral commitments therefore require him to attempt to disabuse the jury of whatever false or unjust claims his prosecutors have made. But the prosecutors have told the jurors not to believe what Socrates says; so the first thing he must do is to establish, or at least to profess as strongly as possible, his own credibility.

The second passage cited in defense of Burnet's interpretation, Socrates' claim to be 'an utter stranger to the manner of speaking in court', also invites an alternative reading. On Burnet's reading of this line, Socrates is saying that he lacks any experience whatever with the particular kind of diction used in law courts. If Burnet is right, Socrates is lying, since as we have seen Socrates later admits to have witnessed legal proceedings in the past. But we think Socrates' claim should be taken to mean only that he has never before presented a speech in court. On this reading there is no reason to doubt the truth of what he says. In deciding which of the two readings is the more plausible, we would do well to notice that Socrates' claim to be 'an utter stranger to the manner of speaking in court' is introduced with 'oὖν', which suggests that it is an inference, presumably drawn from the preceding remark. But the preceding line merely states that now it the first time that Socrates has appeared before the court, although he is seventy years old (17d1–2). Taken as a premiss that assertion clearly does not warrant Burnet's reading of the following line, since one could obviously have extensive familiarity with forensic diction without ever before having appeared in a court as a litigant. If fact, Socrates' familiarity with various rhetoricians[15] and his having witnessed other trials were presumably well known, which only heightens the illogicality of Socrates' claim if we take it Burnet's way. But the inference makes perfect sense if we adopt the more specific reading of Socrates' claim to be a 'stranger', namely that he has never before presented a legal speech. The conclusion, read in this way, plainly follows from his preceding remark.[16]

Socrates has good reason to remind the jury of his inexperience. For one thing, he has a reputation as a sophist and a deceitful speaker, a reputation on which the prosecutors certainly relied in bringing the charges against him. But two considerations weigh against the prosecutors' insinuations: in seventy years he has never sought to exercise his alleged artistry in one of its most natural fora; and secondly, he will keep his vow to employ no such oratorical artistry in his subsequent speeches. Socrates' credibility as an honest and decent man is further underscored by the fact that never before in all those years have any of his fellow citizens in a notoriously litigious society been moved to undertake legal proceedings against him.

As we have said, Socrates' moral commitments require that he en-

---

[15] At *Ap.* 34a4–7 Socrates states that he has often observed people on trial. That Socrates is quite familiar with the practices of people on trial is also apparent at 34b7–c7 and 35a4–7. See also *Menex.* 235c6, where Menexenus indicates that he is aware of Socrates' familiarity with the rhetoricians, and claims that Socrates is always making fun of them. Also, *Grg.* 462b3–466a3 suggests that Socrates' view, that rhetoric as it is practised by the likes of Gorgias is not a craft, has been developed as a result of some familiarity with rhetorical practice.

[16] Further evidence for our reading can be derived from the actual word Socrates uses in saying that this is the first time he has appeared before the court. Socrates says 'νῦν ἐγὼ πρῶτον ἐπὶ δικαστήριον ἀναβέβηκα' (17d2). 'ἀναβαίνω' is a verb that clearly indicates participation in an activity, and hence it would be inappropriate for someone to use the verb or its cognates to refer to cases in which he was a mere spectator. See LSJ, 9th ed., 98, s.v. ἀναβαίνω II.6.

courage the jury to discharge their duty in the right way, and this means that he must tell them the truth. He realizes that the truths he must tell will require him to undertake a very unusual style of defense, for, as we have noted, he must defend not just himself but the philosophic practices that led to his being charged with impiety. But he does not want his jurors to view his departures from the standard rhetorical embellishments as a sign of disrespect for them or for the law (see, for example, 20d4–6, 30c2–6, 34b7–d1, 38a1, 38d3–e5). So he warns them that he cannot deliver the kind of speech they expect to hear. This will be partly due to inexperience in presenting speeches before panels of jurors. Partly, too, Socrates thinks that undertaking to offer a carefully prepared speech after all these years of inexperience at such things would ill-befit a man of his age (17c4–5). But after all, it is Socrates' own philosophic practices that are on trial; so the style of his defense must in no way mislead the jurors about the unique manner in which he has conducted his mission. Hence he tells them that he must speak 'in the manner to which [he is] accustomed to speaking at the bankers' table and elsewhere' (17c7–10, see 32a8), and pleads with them not to be offended by the style of that defense.

2.1.4. FINAL REMARKS ON THE *PROOIMION*

As we have interpreted them, the various remarks that constitute the *prooimion* of Plato's *Apology* should be seen as an apt introduction to a serious defense, one intended to persuade the jury and to assist them in arriving at a just decision by informing them of what is true. Socrates accordingly begins by contrasting the prosecutors' many lies with the truths his speech will contain, taking special care to counter his accusers' warning that the jury should not listen to him because he is so clever. Knowing that he cannot but speak in his accustomed manner and that he thereby risks angering some of the jurors, he warns them in advance of the style his speech will take and explains to them why he must speak as he does. He concludes his introduction, not by protesting his innocence or pleading for mercy, but by reminding the jury of what is most fundamental to the proper outcome of the process in which they are engaged: that he tell the truth and that they decide what is right.

If this interpretation is correct, nothing in the *prooimion* of Plato's *Apology* need be seen as untrue or as an attempt to parody fifth- and fourth-century forensic rhetoric; thus the similarities between Socrates' first remarks and the introductions to a number of other legal speeches provide no grounds for doubting Socrates' sincerity. Nowhere does Socrates say that he is unfamiliar with the way in which rhetorical techniques have been practiced in Athens, nor is it likely that the jury would have assumed him to be saying so. Even if it could be shown that the *prooimion* Socrates offers is self-consciously conventional and thus atypical of Socrates, it does not follow that he has been insincere or inappropriately manipulative, for the *prooimion* serves to introduce the style of defense Socrates will offer, in a fashion that will best be understood by the jury. It is not, strictly speaking, a part of the actual defense itself, which Socrates promises will be in his customary style of speech. Because each of the claims Socrates makes in his *prooimion* is true, there is nothing untoward about his drawing upon knowledge of forensic techniques to convey persuasively those truths in the *prooimion* to the jury, though (as we have said) he must revert to a more natural style in the actual presentation of his defense. Indeed, employing a recognizable manner of presentation at first would best serve his cause, for it offers him the opportunity to explain the unconventional remainder of his speech to a jury otherwise likely to respond with uncomprehending hostility.

But though we accept, with Riddell, that there are some similarities between the *prooimion* in Plato's *Apology* and those of at least some other legal speeches, we are not committed to the view that these similarities betray Socrates' attempt to offer a self-consciously conventional introduction to the defense that follows. As we have pointed out, the conventions of forensic rhetoric were only loosely defined, and even if there were recognizable conventions they were after all designed for the purpose of winning cases. Any intelligent litigant might thus employ some of the prescribed strategies without self-consciously following the conventions *as conventions*. So, to establish that any of Socrates' introductory remarks were intentionally conventional, one would have to show that there would be no natural reason for him to proceed as he did. We do not believe that this can be shown. But even if it could, it constitutes no threat to the position we have urged, so long as it involved no willful attempt at deception on Socrates' part.

Let us conclude by noting two important limitations on our thesis. First, though our account of the *prooimion* construes it as the introduction to a serious defense, we have not yet proved that the subsequent defense is in fact a serious one. If the defense Socrates subsequently offers should prove to be unceasingly ironical or humorously irrelevant, our view of the *prooimion* is thereby undermined. Our purpose here was therefore quite modest: having noted in Section 1.5.3 that his moral principles require him to undertake a serious defense, we have now removed the evidence that some commentators have found in the *prooimion* for supposing that Socrates violates them. Secondly, we have not shown that Plato's version of Socrates' speech is essentially historical or even remotely accurate, though we believe that nothing in the *prooimion* of Plato's *Apology* counts as evidence against its essential historical accuracy. Plato may have invented the entire *prooimion*; if he did, we have shown that it at least fits with what little we know of Socrates and provides the man with a consistent and effective introduction to his defense. If what we have argued here is correct, Socrates achieves this end without once compromising his commitment to persuading the jury through philosophical rhetoric, as opposed to gratifying the jury by means of mere conventionality.

2.2   Socrates' Pessimism

2.2.1 WHY DID SOCRATES STAY IN ATHENS?

The final words of Socrates' *prooimion* show that he is not at all sanguine about his prospects for winning the case (19a4–5; see 28a4–b2); in fact, it later becomes clear that he believed that he would be convicted by a wide margin (36a2–5). If Socrates so doubted that he could succeed in defending himself against such serious charges, why did he remain in Athens after being indicted? We know that it was common enough for accused persons to flee before their trials (see Thuc. 6.60; Ps.-Lys., *Against Andocides* 18). And though the predictable result would be a trial and condemnation *in absentia*, with subsequent confiscation of all of his property, by the time of his trial Socrates was a poor man;[17] so such economic concerns would apply neither to him nor to his family. In fact, there is reason to suppose that Socrates and his family would have been well cared for in exile by concerned and wealthy friends (see *Cri.* 45a6–c4, 53e5–6).

As we argued in Section 1.3.3, the doubts Socrates expresses at 19a4–5, 28a4–b2, and 36a2–5 are not likely to be exaggerated; every

---

[17] See Section 1.3.1.

scrap of evidence we have supports the view that Socrates had ample reason to suppose that he was the victim of profound and widespread prejudice. Might he have recognized before the trial that his intended style of defense would antagonize the jury so thoroughly as to ensure his conviction and condemnation? In Section 1.5.3 we suggested a number of reasons for being cautious about such a suggestion. But the question must be asked: why undertake a defense when doing so will almost certainly be fatal, especially when one has other non-fatal (and, indeed, apparently comfortable) options?

2.2.2 TWO INTERPRETATIONS OF SOCRATES' MOTIVES

It seems to us that two general classes of views on this question are possible, both of which have impressive ancient authorities to cite among their proponents. According to Xenophon, Socrates decided that he had lived long enough and that death had become preferable to life (*Ap.* 1, 5–8, 27, 32; *Mem.* 4.8.1). His appearance in and defense before the court was therefore part of a premeditated suicide. This view has appealed to a number of modern interpreters,[18] who find in it an excellent explanation of so many of Socrates' actions and words they would otherwise find, as Xenophon puts it, 'quite foolish' (ἀφρονέστερος—*Ap.* 1). But Plato's Socrates, though conceding that it is better for him to die and be freed from troubles, claims to recognize this only *after* his condemnation, as (at least part of) the explanation for his *daimonion's* non-intervention (41d5–6; see 40a3–c3). What Xenophon thus portrays as Socrates' prior motives, Plato offers only as grounds for a retrospective acceptance of his fate after condemnation. Though Plato never addresses Socrates' prior motives as explicitly as does Xenophon, a clear enough account of them may none the less be found in Socrates' words before the jury, the most telling of which he utters just before beginning his actual defense:

I should like it to come out that I succeed in my defense, if doing so would be better for you and for me; but I think it is difficult and I am not at all unaware of the problems I face. None the less, let this be in such a way as is pleasing to the god; the law must be obeyed and a defense must be made. (19a2–7)

[18] See, e.g., Peterman; Shero (2), 109; Walton. Kostman argues that Plato's *Crito* provides grounds for thinking that Socrates committed a kind of suicide (as per Xenophon's account), but we are more inclined to the interpretations of Socrates' actions in that dialogue proposed by A. Barker and by Kraut (3), who recognize the sincerely moral concerns behind them.

Unlike Xenophon's Socrates, Plato's is not confident of the outcome he desires; he does not say, as Xenophon would have it, 'I know this will turn out for the best. Indeed, I shall ensure that it does by the style of defense I shall undertake.' He says instead, 'I should like it to come out that I succeed in my defense . . . but I think it is difficult .' And he does not imply, as Xenophon would have it, that he thinks it will be better for him to be condemned. He says instead that he hopes that he might succeed in his defense. Finally, he at least hints that his motives are not merely self-interested, as Xenophon made them, but rather derive from an independent obligation: 'the law must be obeyed.'

2.2.3 THE EFFECTS OF SOCRATES' MORAL CONVICTIONS

It is altogether appropriate that much of the evidence cited by modern followers of Xenophon concerns the style and tone of Socrates' speeches at the trial, even as they are reported by Plato. But since we have not yet looked at these speeches we must defer our final assessment of Socrates' motives until Chapter 5, when we will have reviewed all the pertinent evidence. Before we go any further, however, it is worth pointing out just how serious is the conflict between Xenophon and Plato on this point, for if we are right, Socrates' most profound moral commitments, at least as Plato describes them, should disqualify the motives Xenophon attributes to Socrates. We argued in Section 1.5.3 that Socrates' commitments to uphold just laws, to promote truth and virtue, to attack falsehood and vice, and to carry out the god's bidding despite the many dangers and hardships it caused him would all prevent him from encouraging the jury to hand down the verdict it did. At least in these senses, then, Socrates' defense must be assessed a failure; for a majority of the jurors misjudged Socrates' case, remained or became convinced of one or more false moral beliefs, contributed to an injustice, and brought to an end a philosophical mission ordained by god. But Xenophon's Socrates purposefully forfeited his case, not in the pursuit of any such lofty considerations, but rather to avoid the hardships of his impending old age and to ensure the deepest feeling of loss among his loved ones (*Ap.* 7).

Plato's and Xenophon's accounts diverge similarly in regard to Socrates' appearing in the court rather than fleeing to the comfortable safety of exile. Xenophon's Socrates presumably chose not to flee because so little would be gained by it. His body and mind would soon

begin to fail him, and he would become 'troublesome' to his loved
ones (*Ap.* 7), leaving them 'shameful' memories after his death (*Ap.* 7);
better by far to die the beloved martyr now. But Plato's Socrates says
he has a mission in Athens commanded him by god, and

> wherever a man stations himself, deeming it best, or is put there by a com-
> mander, he must stay there, on my view, and run risks, thinking neither of
> death nor of anything else more than what is shameful. (28d6–10)

Socrates, that is, believes that he should not abandon his mission in
Athens merely because he has been indicted on capital charges, nor
should he acquiesce in suicide because his body and mind will soon
deteriorate; he must remain steadfast in his post. And since the law
does not say that those indicted should flee from prosecution but says
rather that they should defend themselves against the charges, Plato's
Socrates respectfully obeys the law and makes his defense, despite his
bleak prospects. Finally, because Plato's Socrates is committed to
pursuing what is just, even when it appears that he will not succeed,
he tells the jury that he wishes that his defense will succeed, 'if it is better
for you and for me. . . . Let this be as is pleasing to the god' (19a2–7).
These words of Plato's Socrates are not those of a haughty suicide, but
rather those of a resolutely dedicated man who recognizes that a deadly
destiny is close at hand. If there is evidence to be found in Plato's
Apology to support Xenophon's view of Socrates' motives, therefore,
it must also be evidence for supposing that his wish at 19a2–7 and his
proud words at 28d6–10 were a sham: we would have to assume that on
the day of his trial Socrates did not see clearly enough, or did not see fit
to live up to, the consequences of the philosophic mission that had
governed his life. Despite his pessimism, then, Socrates' commitments
oblige him to try to refute the various accusations made against him.
We find it most unlikely that Socrates, of all people, would be unaware
of this obligation.

2.3 The 'First' Accusations against Socrates

2.3.1 THE TWO SETS OF ACCUSATIONS

Before Socrates actually begins his defense, he explains why it is
necessary for him to refute two sets of accusations, the 'first' accusations and the 'later' ones. The 'later' accusations are the formal
charges contained in the indictment by Meletus, on the basis of which

Socrates has been ordered to appear before the court. But he is convinced that his jurors are already deeply biased against him because over the years they have come to be convinced of the truth of other accusations against him (18c4–7). Indeed, Socrates says that it was Meletus' acceptance of such slanders that led him to bring the formal charges (19a8–b2). Because the 'first' accusations have been allowed to stand unchallenged for so long, Socrates regards them as even more dangerous to him than the formal indictment (18b1–6).

The *Apology's* account of the nature of the 'first' accusations is reasonably straightforward. Socrates reports them at 18b6–c1 and 'reads their sworn statement, as if they were prosecuting accusers' at 19b4–c1:

there is a certain Socrates, a clever man (σοφός), a thinker about the things in the heavens, and who has inquired into the things under the earth, and who makes the weaker argument the stronger. (18b6–c1)

Socrates does wrong and is too curious, inquiring into the things under the earth and in the heavens, and making the weaker argument the stronger, and teaching others these same things. (19b4–c1)

Though Socrates adds, in the second version, that he teaches others, and though the actual wording in the Greek is (only very) slightly different in the two accounts, the sense of these 'first' accusations is clear: Socrates undertakes naturalistic inquiries, argues sophistically, and teaches others to do the same.

As we have said, Socrates believes that his 'first' accusers are his most dangerous enemies. They are many and have made their accusations for a long time: they influenced the jury from the time the jury was young and most impressionable (18c5–6). Worse, their accusations gained credibility because no one ever defended Socrates against them; their 'case' was won by default (18c6–8). But worst of all is that one cannot even know who they are and provide their names, unless one of them happens to be a comic poet (18c8–d2). The rumors and suspicions having spread unhindered and anonymously for so many years, Socrates must defend himself 'as if against shadows' (18d6–7), leaving him with only a little time (19a2; see 37b2) to disabuse the jury of their acquired prejudices.

Socrates faced the enormous disadvantage of being unable to name (with one exception) or cross-examine any of his 'first' accusers. As we try to understand just how his shadowy 'first' accusers had slandered him, we are lucky to have the very paradigm of the 'first' accusations Socrates can and does mention, Aristophanes' *Clouds*. Socrates says the character identified by his name in that play claims to walk on air and proclaims all kinds of nonsense (19c3–4). But apart from all the silliness, the 'accusations' in the *Clouds* are precisely as Socrates in the *Apology* identifies them: the head of the 'think-shop' undertakes naturalistic inquiries, argues sophistically, and teaches others to do the same.[19] Let us, then, take a closer look at these accusations.

2.3.2 NATURALISTIC EXPLANATION

Precisely why would the enterprise of natural science comprise grounds for a grave accusation? For the answer we must look at natural sciences as it was practiced in the fifth century and (at least as importantly) at what popular prejudice held it to be. Though much has been lost, we know that one of the common aspects of Greek science, even from its Ionian beginnings, was an interest in explaining phenomena in such a way as to demythologize or demystify them. In the 'new' Greek science, the roots of the natural world, the 'first principles' (αἰτίαι), as Aristotle called them, were no longer gods or other divinities engaged in anthropomorphic struggles and strivings. Rather, early Greek science sought to explain the workings of the cosmos by some one or more of the 'elements'—earth, air, water, and fire.[20] The sun was not the shining chariot of Apollo moving in its stately way across the sky; it was burning clouds, a bowl of fire, or a red-hot stone.[21]

Such modes of explanation sought to discard those provided by Greek religion; earth, air, fire, water, clouds, and burning stones

---

[19] Lord says that 'it is impossible to escape the conclusion that this play [*Nub.*] was one of the chief causes for his [Socrates'] conviction and execution' (41). This view of Aristophanes' influence strikes us as perhaps a bit overstated. Plato's Socrates merely lists it as an example of a widespread phenomenon. Thus, when Lord later claims that 'Plato in the *Apology* represents Socrates blaming Aristophanes more than anyone else for the misconception of his teaching prevalent among the Athenians' (80), we cannot agree. Aristophanes is in fact the only 'first' accuser named, but nothing in the *Apology* warrants the claim that Aristophanes is any more responsible for Socrates' fate than any of the many other 'first' accusers.

[20] For examples and references, see Kirk, Raven, and Schofield, 88–98 (on Thales' water), 144–62 (on Anaximenes' air), 172–8 (on Xenophanes' fire, water, and earth), 197–202 (on Heracleitus' fire), 286–312 (on Empedocles' four elements plus Love and Strife), 441–5 (on Diogenes' air).

[21] See Kirk, Raven, and Schofield, 172–4 (on Xenophanes), 200–2 (on Heracleitus), and 380–2 (on Anaxagoras).

replaced the gods of tradition. It also became common for philosophers to attack traditional notions of the gods themselves, not just by replacing religious with naturalistic explanations, but also by showing the traditional accounts to involve indecency, incoherency, or some other implausibility. Xenophanes complains that 'Homer and Hesiod have attributed to the gods everything that is a shame and reproach among men, stealing and committing adultery and deceiving each other'.[22] Socrates himself may have been implicated in such scepticism (see *Euthphr.* 6a6-8; *Phdr.* 229c6-e4),[23] and after him Plato (see, for example, *Rep.* 377d4-383c7). In lampooning science, Aristophanes makes the principal scientist at the 'think-shop' inquire into the orifice 'from which gnats buzz' (156-64) and run experiments that fitted 'little Persian booties' on fleas (148-52). More ominously, the same scientist scoffs at the gods and denies the existence of Zeus (366) in favor of Vortex (379); he also proclaims that the other gods are obsolete (247) and must be replaced by Chaos, Clouds, and Tongue (424). So when Socrates worries about being slandered by the charge that he 'inquires into the things under the earth and in the heavens', it is because 'those who hear this think that those who investigate these things also do not believe in the gods' (18c2-3).

2.3.3 MAKING THE WEAKER ARGUMENT THE STRONGER

The word we have translated as 'argument' in this charge is λόγος, one of the most difficult words to translate precisely into English. However we translate it, this charge holds Socrates guilty of specious reasoning and deceptive speaking: he makes poor reasons or explanations appear to be excellent ones, presumably by a variety of devious tricks and verbal traps.[24] This facility enables him to tell lies and justify evils with impunity. In other words Socrates wins arguments he should not win, and convinces people of what should not be believed. This charge is not only identical to the one implicit in his 'later' accusers' warning to the jury that Socrates is a 'clever speaker' (17a5-b1); it is also tantamount to the charge of corruption, inasmuch as Socrates dazzles the youth into accepting improper beliefs.

In the context of the trial, the ability to 'make the weaker argument

---

22 Fr. 11, Sextus *Math.* 9.193 (trans. Kirk, Raven, and Schofield (168)).

23 But see Section 3.1.5, esp. Chapter 3, note 23.

24 This charge is echoed in Hyperides, fr. 55: καὶ Σωκράτην οἱ πρόγονοι ἡμῶν λόγοις ἐκόλαζον.

the stronger' would be the ability of a guilty defendant to convince the
jury to find him innocent, or, in the case of a malicious prosecutor, to
convince the jury to find an innocent defendant guilty. But skill in
forensic rehetoric is not all that is at stake in this charge; *any* instance
of persuading an audience of what they should not find persuasive
would be a case of 'making the weaker argument the stronger'. The
demagogues who convinced the Athenians to invade Sicily 'made the
weaker argument the stronger', as did those who convinced the mob
to try the generals *en bloc* after the battle of Arginousai (about which
see 32b1–7, and Section 4.3.4.1, below). In brief, then, one who
'makes the weaker argument the stronger' is one who is skilled at being persuasive even when in the wrong.

2.3.4 TEACHING OTHERS

The indictment of the 'first' accusers first identifies the areas in which
Socrates is supposed to be involved in suspicious intellectual activities; the charge of corruption is added at 19c1. It is bad enough
that Socrates himself studies nature-philosophy and practises verbal
treacheries, according to the 'first' accusations; worse still, he also
teaches others these same evils. Socrates thus spreads his own evil by
training Athens' youth to become atheistic nature-philosophers and
dangerous word-twisters who scoff at tradition and subvert Athens'
assembly and courtrooms with sly and seductive treacheries.

The head of Aristophanes' 'think-shop' recruits students and offers a variety of courses of study, including in particular natural
science and sophistic argumentation. The results are alarming:
Pheidippides becomes a star student who demonstrates his new expertise at the end of the play by assaulting his father and threatening to
do the same to his mother, all of which he is eager to defend by the
most shamelessly tortured reasoning.

2.3.5 SOCRATES' PRELIMINARY RESPONSES TO THE 'FIRST' ACCUSATIONS

Socrates has little to say in direct response to the 'first' accusations.
At 18c2–3 he says he fears the accusation that he is a nature-
philosopher because those who hear this accusation think such people
are atheists. He does not tell us what *he* thinks about this—he does
not say, that is, whether or not he believes that such men *are* atheists,
for this is not at issue. He says only that he has no wish to dishonor

the scientific understanding such men may have, if anyone really is wise in such matters (19c5–7); but he categorically denies having any understanding of such things himself (19c4–5), claiming that he has never had anything to do with such things (19c8) or even talked 'much or little' (19d4) about them. He invites any of the jurors who have earlier heard him to act as witness on his behalf against these claims (19d1–5).

Socrates does not selectively respond to the second charge—that he makes the weaker argument the stronger. Some have found this a weakness in Socrates' defense, apparently because they take what Socrates says in response to the 'first' accusations as applying only to the charges that he is a nature-philosopher and a teacher of nature-philosophy.[25] But he has already said in the *prooimion* that the very nature of his defense will give the lie to his accusers' charge that he is a clever speaker, for he will speak only the truth, without rhetorical garnish or frill (17b1–d1). He promised to demonstrate only the real virtue of an orator: truthfulness (17b4–8; 18a5–6). And since he knows well that the 'first' accusers made him the victim of the very stereotype presented in the *Clouds*, in which scientific and rhetorical interests are lumped together indiscriminately, Socrates does not separate the accusation that he is a nature-philosopher from the accusation that he makes the weaker argument the stronger and then respond only to the former, ominously calling attention to the charge he never answers. He simply tells the jurors that he has nothing to do with any of the things with which he is charged (19c8), and calls the jurors themselves as witnesses to the fact that they have never heard him discussing such things (19d1–5). In case 'such things' are taken to refer only to natural philosophical inquiries, he adds that the same lack of evidence is suffered by the accusations included in 'the other things the many say about me' (19d5–7), including, that is, the charge that he makes the weaker argument the stronger.

---

[25] Sesonske has argued that Plato's Socrates does not offer a direct refutation of the 'first accusation' that he makes the weaker argument appear the stronger, for ' "someone makes the weaker argument defeat the stronger" asserts that the accused speaks in terms and forms quite different from those familiar within the tradition, *and yet somehow compels* assent. All of Plato's dialogues proclaim that this was true of Socrates!' (224—Sesonske's emphasis). Thus, on Sesonske's view, 'to see the *Apology* clearly is to see that the whole of Socrates' defense is vitally concerned with this charge. In its entirety his first speech to the jury constitutes, paradoxically, both a refutation and a confirmation of the charge, allowing the jury to decide which to heed' (222). (See also 226.)

Socrates says other things that would surely count against the charge that he makes the weaker argument stronger. At 17d2–3, he reminds the jury that, though he is seventy years old, this is the first time he has ever appeared before the court. Surely if Socrates were an expert at persuasion he would not have avoided forensic actively for so long. Aristophanes tells us that one of the main reasons to learn how to make the weaker argument the stronger is so that one can swindle others in lawsuits and defend oneself effectively when one's swindles are grounds for indictment (776–78). Later on, Socrates shows that he has also eschewed the Assembly and other political activities (31d5–7). There still other natural fora in which the orators practiced the sort of rhetoric Socrates is accused of practicing; he clearly hopes that his inexperience in them will weigh heavily against the accusation.

Socrates repeatedly contends that he has never been anyone's teacher (19d8–el; 20c1–3; 33a5–6; 33b5–8), and that he has never taken money for what he does (19d9–el; 31b5–c3; 33a8–b2; see also 23b9–cl). So Socrates seeks neither political or material gain by 'making the weaker argument the stronger'. It would appear, therefore, that he has no motive for such a practice.

What more could Socrates say in his own defense against such a charge? He says that, unlike the stereotypical practitioner of sophistic rhetoric, he tells only the truth as he sees it, he does so not for material or political gain (indeed he suffers great personal loss in doing so), and he does not engage in formal pedagogy. These considerations all demonstrate the implausibility of the charge that he 'makes the weaker argument the stronger' and distance Socrates from the charge that he is a practicing professional sophist. Beyond this, there is only the now wholly unsubstantiated suspicion that he somehow persuades people of what is wrong or false, a suspicion that obviously counts against any defense he might attempt to offer. If he managed to begin to persuade the juror who had deep suspicions of this sort, the minute that Socrates began to sound persuasive would be the signal for something like the following response: 'He *is* a clever devil. . . . Why, look, he even began to get *me* going there, for a moment!' So Socrates does not belabor the point; what he says is nevertheless a sufficient defense against the effects of this particular slander.

2.4 Were There Other 'First' Accusations?

2.4.1 POLITICAL CONCERNS

The character named 'Socrates' in Aristophanes' *Clouds* is generally seen by scholars to be to some extent a composite of stereotypes of 'nature-philosophers' and sophists through which Aristophanes sought to make a broad attack on the 'new intellectualism' that had swept through Athens during the Periclean age.[26] It is equally clear, however, that by introducing a character named 'Chairephon' as one of the principals at the 'think-shop' and by naming its master charlatan 'Socrates' and protraying him in a variety of quite specific and personal ways, Aristophanes also sought to satirize the actual Socrates.[27] Because the caricature of Socrates is so unmistakable, Aristophanes must have thought that he had found in him a credible representative of the new intellectualism.

Aristophanes' caricature is instructive because it shows what the stereotype of the 'new intellectual' amounted to. It also shows that as early as 423 Socrates' philosophical activities were sufficiently close to that stereotype in the minds of the mass of Athenians to serve effectively as an exemplar of the whole movement. Striking by its absence

---

[26] Reference can be found in the *Nub.* to the doctrines of Anaxagoras, Diagoras, Gorgias, and Prodicus (see William Arrowsmith, introduction to *The Clouds* (Ann Arbor, 1962), 3). Though one might wonder how Aristophanes could have succeeded in using a single figure to caricature both 'nature philosophers' and sophists, the disparity between the two groups in the popular mind may be easily exaggerated. The most successful of the sophists, and those best known for the teaching of rhetorical skills, Protagoras, Gorgias, Prodicus, and Hippias, all wrote treatises that were presumably taught to their students, in which they attempted to explain such things as the nature of the heavenly bodies and the causes of natural events (See Kerford, 43, 45, 47., Guthrie (4), 276–7). Even Socrates himself groups the best-known living sophists together as if they all practised the same thing (*Ap.* 19e1–20a2).

[27] The various ways in which the historical Socrates is specifically picked out for attack by Aristophanes' play are explored in admirable detail by M. Nussbaum in her (1)—see esp. 51–3, 66–7, 69–76, 79–88. Edmunds agrees with Nussbaum that the real Socrates is singled out for attack, but on quite different grounds—grounds which Nussbaum herself rejects (in her (2)). Nussbaum explicitly contrasts her view of Aristophanes' Socrates to that argued by Dover (in his (4)), whose argument is also disputed by Kleve. Karavites suggests that the only serious similarities between Aristophanes' character and the historical Socrates were their physical characteristics.

from the *Clouds*, however, is any suggestion that the danger of this movement in general, or Socrates' activity in particular, lay in the promotion of dangerous partisan political propaganda, or indeed of any political theory at all. The 'Socrates' of the *Clouds*, whatever his other flaws, is wholly apolitical, and none of his students are prominent politicians. Rather, the dangerous features of the intellectual movement Aristophanes lampoons are its concern with naturalistic explanation, its unscrupulous teaching of rhetoric, and its undermining of traditional values.[28] The indictments of the *Clouds* are clearly just the same as those Socrates identifies as the 'first' accusations in the *Apology*: naturalistic explanation is tantamount to atheism, and teaching the art of persuasion breeds contempt for what is right.

In spite of the fact that, according to the *Apology*, the 'first' accusations consisted only of quite general charges of atheism and immorality, many commentators maintain that at least part of the prejudice against Socrates was far more specific and decidedly political in nature.[29] The principal evidence cited in support of this claim is adduced from the 'Socratic literature' produced after Socrates' execution,[30] some of which we mentioned in Section 1.1.2. As early as 414, Aristophanes himself had begun to add a political taint to his jokes about Socrates; in the *Birds,* produced during the agonies of the Peloponnesian War, we are told that those who talk with Socrates end up being 'laconized' (1281–4). Even Xenophon contributes to this taint. Reviewing one of the accusations made

[28] According to M. Nussbaum, 'The *Clouds* . . . attacks Socrates on three counts: (1) his lack of attention to the necessary role, in moral education, of character and the habituation-training of irrational elements; (2) his lack of a positive program to replace what he has criticised; (3) his openness to misunderstanding—his failure to make clear to his students the difference (if there is one) between his aloofness and the immoralism of Anti-Right' ((1), 81). We, none the less, prefer our own analysis of the nature of Aristophanes' attacks, though we believe Nussbaum's item (2) and (3) are assimilable to the second of our two charges. We would accept her item (1), however, as one specification of a charge of intellectualism, which undercuts convention in favor of unrestrained (and thus dangerous) critical inquiry, with its commitment to reason as providing the only source justification (as opposed to custom or tradition). (See M. Nussbaum (1), 66–7, on this issue.)

[29] See, e.g., E. Barker, 93–4; Bonfante and Raditsa; Burnet (2), note on 18b3; Bury (3); Chroust (3), 26, 164–97; Hansen; Lofberg, 602; MacDowell (2), 202; Montuori (5), 167–8, 177–86; Roberts, 243–6; Seeskin (1), 75–6; Stone; Vlastos (3); Winspear and Silverberg, esp. 64–85. Zeller ((1), 217), holds that the prejudice against Socrates was only partly political. Zeller's view is supported by Guthrie ((2), 62–3). Indeed, as far as we know, only Hackforth holds that the trial was not politically motivated ((2), 73–9).

[30] See Section 1.1.2, esp. Note 13.

against Socrates by 'the accuser' (almost certainly Polycrates[31]), Xenophon tells us that Socrates was said to have

taught his companions to despise the established laws by insisting on the folly of appointing public officials by lot, when none would choose a pilot or a builder or a flautist by lot, nor any other craftsman for work in which mistakes are far less dangerous than mistakes made in statecraft. Such sayings, [his accuser] argued, led the young to despise the established constitution and made them violent. (*Mem.* 1.2.9)

Gregory Vlastos finds ominous significance in the fact that although Xenophon defends Socrates against every other accusation mentioned, he says nothing whatever to rebut the charge that Socrates was an anti-democrat who encouraged others to recognize the irrationality of democracy.[32] And despite differences between Xenophon and Plato on a number of other aspects of their portrayals of Socrates, on this issue they agree utterly: Plato's Socrates also disputes the rationality of allowing non-experts to make political decisions (*Prt.* 319b3–d7). In fact, explicit and implicit criticisms of Athenian democratic leaders, sentiments, and policies abound in Plato's early dialogues.[33]

2.4.2 SOCRATES' EVIL ASSOCIATES

Other ancient authors suggest yet another source of prejudice against Socrates. Some time after 394, the sophist Polycrates wrote his *Accusation of Socrates*.[34] The speech itself has been lost, but it seems to have taken the form of a rhetorical display (ἐπίδειξις), in which Polycrates sought to demonstrate various rhetorical techniques. Speeches in this genre are designed only to demonstrate their authors' rhetorical mastery; no commitment to the truth of their

---

[31] The first to argue that Xenophon's 'accuser' in this section of the *Mem.* is Polycrates was C. G. V. Cobet, *Novae lectiones* (Lugduni Batavorum, 1858), 668–82. This is now the generally accepted view (see, e.g., Chroust (3), 45, 71–2, *et passim*). Hansen has questioned this identification, however (59–64).

[32] Vlastos (3), 497. See also Chroust ((3), 192) and Lofberg (602). Seeskin appears to share this view, saying that Plato was 'strangely silent' about the political motivations for Socrates' indictment ((1), 76).

[33] See, e.g., *Ap.* 24e4–25c1, and esp. 31e1–32a3; *Cri.* 47a2–48c6; *Prt.* 319c8–320b3; *Meno* 93e3–94e2. The extent to which these sentiments are the results of Platonic exaggeration is, however, a matter of concern.

[34] For a reconstruction of Polycrates' speech, see Chroust (3), esp. 69–100. Raubitschek holds that Polycrates' speech was published partly as a response to Plato's *Apology*, though composed before it ((1), 78–9).

specific claims would have been supposed. Indeed, the most effective advertisement of a rhetorician's talents would perhaps be made in a convincing speech whose thesis the speaker could be presumed *not* to believe. But whether or not Polycrates' accusations were sincere, the reactions to them on the part of various Socratic apologists indicate that they were taken seriously enough to be refuted, even in the first few decades after the actual trial. One charge in particular concerns us: Isocrates in the *Busiris*, in direct response to Polycrates, states, 'And when your purpose was to accuse Socrates, as if you wished to praise him, you gave Alcibiades to him as a pupil'.[35] Xenophon repeats a similar charge in the *Memorabilia* (1.2.12): 'his accuser [again, almost certainly Polycrates] argued thus: Having become the associates of Socrates, Critias and Alcibiades did great evil to the city'. The charge that Socrates had corrupted Critias was still in the air some fifty years after the trial: Aischines Rhetor, in a remark directed at an Athenian jury, says, 'You put Socrates, the sophist, to death because he was shown to have educated Critias' (Aisch., *In Tim.* 173).

Elsewhere, Plato confirms these and other potentially damaging associations. Alcibiades and Critias are present in Plato's *Protagoras* (316a3–5, 336b7–e4), in which Socrates' attraction to the former is also mentioned (309a1–b2) as it is in the *Gorgias* (481d1–4) and the *Symposium* (213c6–d6, 214c8–d4, 216e7–219e5, 222c1–d3).[36] In the *Charmides*, we learn that Critias is a long-time acquaintance of Socrates (156a7–8).[37] The *Charmides* (see esp. 155c7–e2) and *Symposium* (222a8–b4) also portray Socrates' attraction to Charmides, who would later disgrace himself as one of the Thirty.[38] Although Plato's portrayals show that Socrates was concerned only to improve those with whom he talked, the prominence assigned to these men and

[35] The quotation is from *Bus.* 5. That the speech is in response to Polycrates is made explicit fom the very first line of the speech.

[36] Although the *Symp.* is a 'middle dialogue' and hence cannot be counted as presenting anything of the philosophy of the historical Socrates, Alcibiades' speech in praise of Socrates (214e9–222b7) can safely be considered to refer to features of the actual relationship between the two. Some close relationship is implied as well in both *Alc.* I and *Alc.* II, but these are considered spurious by most scholars.

[37] Critias also appears in the later dialogues, *Ti.* and *Criti.* Vatai has suggested that Critias and Socrates had been lovers (65), but we see no evidence for this, and Vatai cites no texts in support of this claim.

[38] Charmides is also present in the *Prt.* (315a1). The most extensive prosopographical study of those associated with Socrates in Plato's dialogues is in Hansen (73–6 and nn. 81–91). It will become obvious that we do not agree with the conclusions Hansen draws from his study, however.

the friendly relations obtaining between them and Socrates in the dialogues lends support to the view that they were regarded as members of a Socratic circle. Why then does Socrates not explicitly recognize and respond to the sinister effects of these associations in minds of his jurors at the trial?

2.4.3 THE OPTIONS

Now it might be supposed that Socrates did not need to consider the issue because of certain legal protections he enjoyed. According to the terms of the amnesty that had been passed under the archonship of Eucleides in 403/2, [39] in the advocacy and passage of which Anytus had been centrally involved, Socrates could not legally be charged with crimes committed before and during the period of the Thirty Tyrants' reign. But Critias and Charmides had died during the attack on Mounichia in the Piraeus, [40] during the civil war that eventually ended the Tyrants' authority, and Alcibiades seems also to have died at about this time. [41] So any corruption of youth involving those persons had to have occured by or before the establishment of the Thirty (in fact, before—none of the men in question would have qualified as youths by that late date), and hence would be exempted as grounds for prosecution by the amnesty. So the 'later' accusers would have been prohibited by the law so closely associated with one of them (Anytus) from charging Socrates with having corrupted any of the men in question. It might be supposed that this legal restriction would have been enough to prevent the prosecutors from making the corruption of Critias or Alcibiades issues before the court, and thus that Socrates would not have any need to mention this prejudice as he addressed the jury. [42]

But even if this were the case, the amnesty would not prohibit *Socrates* from mentioning the bias such relationships might have aroused against him, and if the bias was significant enough in the eyes of the jury, as we have argued, he would have had to bring it up in court even if the prosecution had not called the jury's attention to it. In fact, however, the provisions of the amnesty only ensured that the

---

[39] See Chapter 1, note 113.   [40] See Krentz, 90–2.   [41] Ibid., 79.
[42] Allen ((5), 12), Burnet ((2), 101), Bury ((2), 393), Davies ((2), 187), Navia ((2), 14 and 39, n. 20), and Roberts (245) have suggested that the amnesty of 403/2 would have prevented the prosecution from any open references to Socrates' relations with Alcibiades and Critias.

corruption of Alcibiades or Critias (and maybe Charmides) could not
have been a legal specification of the accusations made against
Socrates by the 'later accusers' in 399. The amnesty provided for a
complete revision and recodification of the laws. All prior decrees
were annulled, and no offenses under the old law could be prosecuted
subsequent to its passage. Thus, Socrates could not be formally
charged with breaking any of the annulled laws, or with complicity in
any of the more notorious acts of the two villains. But there was no
provision in the amnesty that would prevent Meletus *et al.* from making unmistakable references to Socrates' associations with Alcibiades
or Critias, through obvious insinuation, or even quite explicitly, by
way of character assassination.[43] In fact, references to crime
antedating the amnesty, aimed at poisoning juries about the actual
legal allegations before them, were not uncommon in trials that came
after the amnesty. Thus, for example, the amnesty plainly did not prevent Lysias from associating the younger Alcibiades with the evils of
his father (Lys. 14.30–42).[44] The amnesty declared which legal actions could and could not be taken. It did not in any way inhibit
litigants from making ample and unmistakable references to events
that antedated the restoration of the democracy. In Socrates' case,
this means that 'recent' corruptions need only have been the feature
of the charges that gave the proceedings legal warrant as evidence of
continuing misbehavior; the more notorious and less recent associations could remain the most actually damning in the minds of the
jurors. Nothing in the amnesty, therefore, helps to provide the reason
why Socrates never mentioned his alleged corruption of Critias or
Alcibiades.

Yet another explanation might be proffered. Might it not be that
Socrates' silence derives from his concern that the mere mention of
some of his personal associations would further inflame the jury's
prejudice against him? On this view, it is his wish to win the case that
makes Socrates avoid this most sensitive point, perhaps because he is
convinced that he could never explain away such associations to the

---

[43] As Loening puts it, 'It was permissible to cite the conduct of an individual
under the oligarchy at scrutinies and other processes in the way of character
evidence' (vii; repeated verbatim on 203), and if one's activities during the oligarchy
could be cited in this way, so could one's activities prior to 403. See also Hansen
(60–2).

[44] For a list of the Lysianic corpus's other hostilities to Alcibiades, see K. J.
Dover, *Lysias and the Corpus Lysiacum* (Berkeley and Los Angeles, 1968), 53–4.

jury's satisfaction. There are a number of reasons why we do not in-
cline to this view, however. For one thing, Socrates' principles, as we
have said, require him to offer a defense that is both effective and exhaustive. Hence, he must be sure to speak to what he thinks are the
likely sources of the bias and hostility he perceives in his jurors. If he
were unprepared to address some accusations of such gravity as to
be substantially prejudicial to his case, then, he would to that degree
fall short of what his principles required. Nothing in the *Apology* suggests that there are topics too sensitive for Socrates to mention; on the
contrary, Socrates says that he will have to review openly the very
things that have led to such widespread prejudice against him. So if
other ancient commentators' attention to Socrates' associations is
taken as a sure sign that these associations would have concerned the
Athenian jury in 399, and if Socrates' defense failed adequately and
explicitly to address this concern, this failure would almost certainly
be seen by the members of the jury as a concession of the implications
drawn later by Polycrates. Socrates could not allow his defense to
appear to make such a concession.

It need not follow from this, however, that Socrates would have to
reply to all the specific sources of prejudice in his own speech. According to Xenophon, there were others who made formal speeches on
Socrates' behalf at the trial (*Ap.* 22).[45] Xenophon's testimony is unique, neither explicitly supported nor contradicted by any of the other
ancient sources. But the use of supporters who would speak on one's
behalf (συνήγοροι/*sunēgoroi*) was common, and we see nothing in
Socrates' principles that would have led him to forbid others to speak
on his behalf.[46] One thing we find in Plato's *Apology* at least slightly
supports Xenophon's claim that Socrates had *sunēgoroi*. Socrates'
defense speech itself is not an especially lengthy one, yet twice he
mentions how little time he had to speak to the jurors (19a1–2,
37a6–7). Since equal amounts of time were allotted to the prosecution
and the defense,[47] and since we know that at least three speakers
spoke for the prosecution, Socrates' entire defense could take up at
least as much time as the three prosecutors' speeches. But Socrates'

---

[45] Xenophon's report is perhaps slightly supported by Justus of Tiberias' claim
(*ap.* D. L. 2.41) that Plato himself had attempted to speak as a *sunēgoros* at
Socrates' trial.

[46] Socrates seems quite ready to have others speak on his behalf in Plato's version
(33c8–34b5, esp. 34a4–7), and accepts at least one other form of assistance from his
friends (38b6–9).   [47] See Chapter 1, note 80, above.

own defense speech is not likely to have taken more than an hour to
deliver,[48] so there seems no way to account for what Socrates perceived as a shortness of time unless some of the time he had been allotted had to be set aside for others to speak on his behalf.

If others did make formal speeches on Socrates' behalf, we have no
way of knowing what they said. It was customary for the defendant's
supporters to speak after the defendant himself.[49] Socrates might not
know exactly how long their speeches would be, and so he might well
be especially aware of the passage of time in his own speech. But surely
Socrates would know in advance that his *sunēgoroi* would support
him, and assuming that in his opinion they would do a reasonably
good job of covering one or more aspects of his defense, he would no
longer need to cover that ground in detail in his own speech. The
presence of *sunēgoroi* then, might be sufficient to explain Socrates'
silence on political issues as well as whatever concerns may have been
raised about Socrates' personal associations with evil men. If our
argument is correct, Socrates would feel required to ensure that any
serious suspicions his jurors might have toward him would be adequately refuted. But since he would not feel required in his own
speech to cover ground adequately covered by his *sunēgoroi*, nothing
follows from Socrates' silence on any specific topic. It could be that
he was confident that his supporters' speeches would provide sufficient replies. Thus if we trust Xenophon on this point and suppose
that others made speeches on Socrates' behalf, even if a close scrutiny
of his own speech shows that Socrates did not mention something
important, it does not necessarily follow that he had decided to avoid
the issue altogether. [50]

But two other options remain open. Firstly, we might show, contrary to the apparent sense of other ancient reports, either that there

---

[48] Figuring roughly two minutes of speaking time for each page of the Greek, we
calculate that Socrates' first speech would take about 53 minutes to deliver.
MacDowell ((2), 249) suggests that the defendant would be given 44 χόες of water in
the water-clock (κλεψύδρα) in which to present his defense. Given 3 minutes per
χοῦς of water (MacDowell figures 6 minutes per two χόες in (2), 250), Socrates
would have 2 hours and 12 minutes to present his defense. If these calculations are
even close to being correct, Socrates' own defense-speech would have taken up less
than half of his allotted time.

[49] The few examples we have seem to follow this pattern, but it is unclear whether
this order of speeches was legally prescribed or just standard practice. See Bonner
and Smith, 8; Kennedy, n. 4, 126; MacDowell (2), 251.

[50] We are indebted to Mogens Herman Hansen for suggesting this line of
explanation to us. His paper also considers this point (see esp. 63).

was no reason to suppose that Socrates' associations with Alcibiades and/or Critias were especially serious concerns of the jury, or at least that there is no reason to suppose that Socrates would see them as such. Alternatively, we might show that the way Socrates construes the 'first' accusations, and the way he replies to these, might reasonably be supposed by him to be sufficient to allay any concern the jury might feel about his associations with such notorious men (especially if, as per our hypothesis above, others had already addressed or would be addressing these concerns in Socrates' defense). These alternatives are not mutually exclusive: Socrates may have seen no special reason (as per the first suggestion) to focus on his associations with Alcibiades or Critias (or anyone else in particular), especially if the negative sense of any such association would be sufficiently removed (as per the second) by the defense he offers. Let us review the evidence for these two options.

2.4.4 DISTINGUISHING THE TWO CHARGES

Scholars have tended to treat the two accusations, (*a*) that Socrates was somehow to blame for the treachery of Alcibiades and the tyranny and violence of Critias and (*b*) that Socrates was an antidemocratic ideologue, as if they were the same accusation, one of a political nature. But this makes little sense. To be sure, an association with Critias, taken by itself, might suggest an affinity for oligarchic politics. Yet it was plain to all that Alcibiades' rise to power derived from his relationship with Pericles and the democratic faction in Athens. And though he proved to be a traitor, Alcibiades was never thought to be an oligarch.[51] Moreover, Socrates' friendship with Chairephon,[52] whose loyalty to the democracy was beyond reproach, was at least as well known as his associations with Alcibiades and Critias.

---

[51] Though he has been accused of tyrannical aims (see Ps.-Andoc., *Against Alcibiades* 21-2, 25-32; Thuc. 6.16, 6.53). It might be supposed that Thuc. 6.28 is evidence to the contrary, but it seems clear that Thucydides takes the charge of antidemocracy to be purely opportunism on the part of Alcibiades' detractors. In fact, we have good evidence for Alcibiades' popularity among the people, and none for supposing that he was involved in any partisan political activity favoring oligarchy.

[52] In addition to what is said about Chairephon in the *Ap.* in connection with the Delphic oracle (21a3; see also Xen., *Ap.* 14), Plato also portrays him as a companion of Socrates in his appearances as one of the *dramatis personae* in the *Charm.* and the *Grg.* Confirmation of this association in Plato's accounts is to be found in Ar., *Nub.* and *Av.* (see esp. 1554–64), and Xen., *Mem.* 1.2.48 and 2.3.

In the *Apology*, Socrates reminds his jurors that Chairephon was a member of the democratic faction (21a1) who had gone into exile with many of the other democrats, and returned with them during the restoration of the democracy (21a2). We cannot accept Burnet's point (see his note on 21a2) that Socrates would have been better off not reminding the jury that he himself had not been one of those who went into exile. First, the jury would not have needed to be reminded of the fact; and secondly, although his mention of Chairephon is needed to explain Socrates' reputation for wisdom by the oracle story, it also serves to remind the jury that among Socrates' lifelong friends could be counted a man who had scrupulously served the democracy. It is astonishing to us how many of the scholars who favor the view that the trial of Socrates was essentially political neglect to consider Socrates' close friendship with Chairephon.[53] None of this is to say, of course, that Socrates could be counted as a partisan democrat, for his refusal to join sides in the highly partisan atmosphere in Athens at the time could itself be seen as suspect.[54] So even if some of the jurors thought that Socrates had been to some degree responsible for Alcibiades' and Critias' crimes against Athens, they could not seriously have believed that his responsibility lay in promoting some particular anti-democratic political theory. Rather, it would have been that he loosened the hold of traditional restraints on his students by questioning even (or especially!) the most cherished of their society's values. And despite his criticisms of Athens and her ways, Socrates' exemplary military record,[55] especially at Potidaia and Delion (28e2–3), surely established his willingness to lay down his life for the city he criticized. Thus at least his patriotism could not have seriously been in question.

[53] See, e.g., Chroust, who wholly overlooks this fact in the 34 otherwise densely argued and meticulously documented pages he devotes to 'the political aspects of the Socratic problem' ((3), 164–97). One who does not overlook the importance of Chairephon's political sympathies is Bonner (176).

[54] See Bonfante and Raditsa.

[55] Laches praises Socrates' stand at Delion in the *La.* (181b1–4), as does Alcibiades in the *Symp.* (220c1–221c1). Socrates' fighting at Potidaia is also mentioned in the *Charm.* 153b4–c4. Socrates himself refers to his willingness to obey his commanders even in the face of death at *Ap.* 28d6–e4. For other ancient sources that partially confirm Plato's account of Socrates' heroism in battle, see Guthrie (2), 59.

A. W. Gomme (*A Historical Commentary on Thucydides*, vol. 3 (Oxford, 1956), 638) and Burnet ((2), note on 28e2) have questioned Socrates' claim at 28e2 to have participated in the fighting at Amphipolis. Calder (2), however, has in our opinion shown their scepticism to be unwarranted. See also Libanius, *Ap.* 131.

Furthermore, the evidence for Socrates' anti-democratic sentiments we find in Xenophon and Plato is not as decisive as commentators have made it out to be.[56] Socrates disputes the use of the lot,[57] it is true, but implies at the same time that the selection procedure by which it should be replaced is that by which one selects experts in the crafts. Those associating such remarks with an oligarchic ideology are guilty of *non sequitur*, for their inference would be warranted only if it followed from Socrates' suggestion that statecraft would automatically become the sole province of members of the oligarchic faction in Athens. We are also owed an account of why we should suppose that the selection procedure Socrates thus endorses would be incompatible with the procedure currently in use by the Athenians for selecting civic craftsmen, for example, the city architect, the master sculptor for civic monuments, or the ten generals; that is, by election. The fact that Socrates dislikes the lot may show only that he prefers more frequent use of the vote; and even if he disputes the good sense of any number of political decisions that were made by the vote, it does not follow that he must be construed thereby as calling for the elimination of a democratic constitution. Most of us now living in democratic states frequently dislike the officials who get elected, and we may have numerous suggestions as to how to attain better results. But despite all our dissatisfaction, we might still advocate constitutional democracy in practice. Nothing in Xenophon or the early Plato rules this out for Socrates either. In fact, despite the plainly oligarchic sympathies of both authors, nowhere in either's work (until Plato's later dialogues) do we find Socrates calling for a constitutional alternative to democracy. Of course, any criticism of the cur-

[56] An excellent review of the evidence for and against Socrates' anti-democratic sentiments may be found in Kraut (3), ch. 7, 194–244.

[57] In addition to Xen., *Mem.* 1.2.9 (quoted above), evidence for Socrates' criticism of sortition may be found in Arist., *Rh.* 1393b3–8. On the way in which such criticisms might have been seen, see ibid. 1365b30–31. If fact, however, there is at least some reason to suppose that a criticism of selecting officials by lot would not suggest anything of particular consequence for partisan politics. According to Anaximenes Rhetor (*Ars rhet.* 2.14 (Ps.-Arist., *Rhet. Alex.*) 1424a17–20)) the only appointments made by lot even in democracies were to minor posts; the important ones were elected. Moreover, the same author contends that appointment by sortition was possible in oligarchies as well (2.18, 1424a40–b3). If so, Socrates' criticism would apply to oligarchies no less than to democracies, and might only reflect the view that any public post would be important enough to elect. See G. E. M. de Ste. Croix, *The Class Struggle in the Ancient Greek World* (Ithaca, NY, 1981), 285, and L. Whibley, *Greek Oligarchies: Their Character and Organization* (London, 1896), reprinted Chicago, 1975), 145–6, for discussions.

rent laws might be interpreted by those hostile to Socrates as partisan bias, and, according to the ancient conception, one of the principal foundations of democracy is the selection of civic officials by lot. Accordingly, Socrates' criticism of sortition might have been interpreted by his enemies as evidence of broadly anti-democratic sentiment. So prejudice, which does not require good reason for its support, could easily have made Socrates out as an enemy to democracy. But if Socrates' remarks about the fundamental importance of respect for the law in Plato's *Crito* are taken seriously, remarks called to mind by his frequent professions of respect and concern for the law in the *Apology* (see 19a6, 25d2–3, 28d6–8, 29b6–7, 31e3–4, 32b1–c4, 35b9–c5), we must conclude that though there might be much he would advocate changing, the changes would be within the constitution of the Athens in which he was raised and nurtured, and according to due process under the democratic laws that constitution establishes. Such can hardly be accounted the political theory of a dangerous oligarchic revolutionary.

But as we have said, prejudice does not require its tenets to be grounded in reason, so even if Socrates' actual views show him to have posed no partisan threat to Athens' democracy, it remains possible that he was seen as an anti-democrat. Socrates' various anti-democratic beliefs, despite their lack of supplementation with oligarchic sympathies, may have been enough to arouse the partisan hostilities of the democratic faction in Athens, especially in the uneasy times around the turn of the century. Is there reason to suppose, then, that Socrates would recognize this prejudice as sufficiently widespread to be a concern? And if so, does he respond to it in the *Apology?*

In fact, apart from later writers, we have no real evidence from the time before Polycrates wrote his pamphlet to assure us that the specific prejudices against Socrates were in part political. Aristophanes' *Clouds*, as we have said, involves no partisan political aspect, and his jab in the *Birds,* for example, may require no more than an observation of Socrates' ascetic appearance and reputation (see *Av.* 1282), aspects of style associated with the Spartans. But if we suppose that there was at least some suspicion about Socrates' political sympathies, we also find aspects of his defense speech that make clear how little connection he has with partisan political activities. As we have said, he reminds the jury, for example, that one of his dearest and best-known friends (Chairephon) was a democrat.

Later, he shows them that his style of life and commitments to justice have got him in trouble with both factions equally (32a9–33a1). His point in this passage is clear: he is no partisan enemy of democracy; his mission is not political in the ordinary way at all. Socrates believes that a truly good man cannot function for long in the political arena and live. Finally, Socrates reiterates throughout his speech that he has no dogmas to teach (see esp. 33a5–b8). If there is partisan political prejudice against Socrates, then, these are his answers: (1) at least one of his best friends was a democrat; (2) his moral mission in Athens has all along put him outside the political arena; and (3) since he teaches no dogmas, it follows that he teaches no partisan political dogmas. We concede that (1) is not an especially convincing reply, and that (3) would be unlikely to convince those already prejudiced against him. But for (2), Socrates offers what he calls 'great proofs' for what he says (for a more detailed discussion of these, see Section 4.3), and his position is made very clear as one that does not lend itself to partisan political maneuvering. His jurors may not find his reasons or the sentiments behind them very pleasing, to be sure. But Socrates cannot be convicted of not offering, in his first speech, reasons for the jurors to abandon whatever political prejudices they may have had against him.

What then is the effect Socrates is supposed by Polycrates and perhaps others[58] to have had on Alcibiades or on Critias? We believe that the only hypothesis that would make sense of this charge, given the factional diversity of Socrates' known associates and the conflicting evidence about his own political commitments, is that the slander against Socrates is no other than what he says it is in the *Apology*: he is a sophist who teaches his students to hold all morality in contempt and instead to act in whatever way happens to suit their own purposes. As a result, Critias is ready to use mayhem and terror during the reign of the Thirty, and Alcibiades flatters the democratic faction and seduces them into electing him general. Political ideology is not what is common to such men; flagrant disregard for the common good in favor of the advancement of their own interests is. And both

---

[58] If fact, as we shall subsequently argue, we think that it is entirely possible that Polycrates alone invented this charge, perhaps out of whole cloth. Its subsequent repetitions, we believe, may be in direct response only to his speech. Chroust also notes that much of the 'Socratic literature' may have been in response to Polycrates' accusations ((3), 176), and acknowledges the possibility that Polycrates may have invented the charge concerning Alcibiades (181), though the political taint he supposes to have an 'Antisthenian origin' (184; see 135–63). (See also Ehrenberg (1), 372.)

may have been seen, one way or another, as guilty of irreligion.[59] So Socrates' influence is exactly what the 'first' accusations make it out to be: he is an atheist and an immoralist, and he teaches others these same things.

2.4.5 SOCRATES' SILENCE

Our argument thus far has been that good sense requires construing the charge that Socrates was in some way to blame for the activities of Alcibiades or Critias as identical to the charge made by the 'first' accusations, against which he defends himself in the *Apology*. Now we believe that the defense against the 'first' accusations Socrates offers in the *Apology* is fully adequate in general to remove whatever stain these or any other associations may have put on Socrates' reputation. A final review of the elements of that defense, however, will not be complete until the end of Chapter 4. Let it suffice for now to recognize that Socrates offers a defense against these accusations, and that, as we have argued, the sense in which the associations with Critias or Alcibiades may have been thought by the jury to be damaging to Socrates is the sense that would be given them by making them paradigms of the sort of corruption with which Socrates is charged in the 'first' accusations.

But might it not still be the case that Socrates would need to single out his associations with Alcibiades or Critias for direct discussion? If any such specific associations were especially emphasized by the prosecutors or particularly important in some other way to the jury, it would still seem necessary for Socrates to speak explicitly and directly to these associations, if only to subsume them under the more general defense he offers. Let us suppose, for the sake of the argument, either that Socrates did not employ *sunēgoroi* in his defense or that his *sunēgoroi* did not emphasize defending him against suspicions involving his associations with various and specified evil men. Xenophon offers elaborate defenses against the charge that Socrates was in any

[59] Alcibiades was prosecuted *in absentia* for profaning the Mysteries, and some attribute a fragment from the satyr play *Sisyphus* to Critias (see Diels and Kranz, 88B25), which offers an atheistic account of the origins of religion. (See also Plut., *De superst.* 171b.) The evidence that Critias was an atheist has been disputed, however. (See, for the various views on this, Festugière (114); A. Dihle, 'Das Satyrspiel "Sisyphus" ', *Hermes* 105 (1977), 28–42; Harald Patzer 'Der Tyrann Kritias und die Sophistik,' in *Studia Platonica* (Festschrift for Hermann Gundert), Amsterdam, 1974, 3–20; Dana F. Sutton, 'Critias and Atheism', *CQ* NS31 (1981), 33–8.)

way responsible for Critias' and Alcibiades' notorious evils (*Mem.* 1.2.12–47).[60] Why does the subject get no explicit attention in Plato's account, especially if there is so much to say on Socrates' behalf in this regard? Given his general defense against the 'first accusations', all that would remain for Socrates to do would be to make explicit that the defense he offers is especially mindful of the cases of Critias and Alcibiades. Was there reason for Socrates to take this one extra step, all that would be needed, on our view, to complete an adequate defense against the charge with which so many ancient authors concerned themselves?

We think not. First, the evidence that Socrates had at least some falling out with Critias is both ample and various, and such evidence may well have been widely known at the time of the trial. Later in his speech Socrates reminds his jurors of the grave danger he faced in defying the authority of the Thirty in his failure to participate in the arrest of Leon of Salamis (32c4–e1).[61] His behavior in this instance, for which he offers 'many witnesses' at his trial (32e1), might of itself be sufficient to disengage Socrates from too close an association with Critias. Thus there is at least some reason to wonder just how close Socrates' relationship with Critias would have appeared to his jury to have been. A number of such unfriendly incidents between Socrates and Critias may be found reported or at least implied in other ancient sources.[62] If his influence on Critias had been so great, why would there have been such subsequent (and, to Socrates, dangerous) enmity between the two? And though there is no specific evidence of a falling out between Socrates and Alcibiades, there is also no evidence for a continuing relationship between them after Alcibiades' departure for Sicily some fifteen years before Socrates' trial. Nor was Socrates in

[60] See also the account of Socrates' salutary influence on Alcibiades in Ps.-Dem., *Eroticus* 45.

[61] The name 'Leon' appears only in Plato's account, and that of D. L. (2.24), apparently following Plato. But other references to the Thirty ordering Socrates to arrest someone appear in Plato, *Letter VII* 324d8–325a3, 325c1–5, and Xen., *Mem.* 4.4.3. Yet other references to this event do not name Socrates as one of those ordered to make the arrest, but are compatible with what we find in the above passages in Plato and Xenophon. See Andoc., *Myst.* 94; Lys. 12.52 and 13.44; and Xen., *Hell.* 2.3.39. On the identity of Leon, see MacDowell (1), 133, note on *Myst.* 94; W. James McCoy, 'The Identity of Leon', *AJP* 96 (1975), 187–99.

[62] Other reports of conflict between Socrates and Critias or the Thirty in general, not concerning the arrest of Leon, may be found in Xen., *Mem.* 1.2.29–38, and Diod. 14.5.1–3. Krentz, however, disputes the report in Diod., favoring that in Plut., *Mor.* 836 f., in which it is Isocrates and not Socrates whose actions are reported (77, n. 21).

any way implicated in the profanation of Mysteries in which many Athenians supposed Alcibiades had been involved.

Secondly, we are inclined to find the apparently widespread concern for so narrow a conception of the primary causes of Socrates' prosecution potentially misleading. All the instances in which Socrates' responsibility for the acts of Critias or Alcibiades is reported or refuted by ancient authors are compatible with its invention as an issue by Polycrates. As we have said, both Isocrates and Xenophon are generally agreed to have been writing in direct response to Polycrates,[63] and Aischines' remarks, fifty years later, may be nothing more than a continuation of this same debate.

If fact, Isocrates' complaint may actually *suggest* that Polycrates invented the issue. Most commentators who rely on Isocrates' claims as evidence for the effects of Socrates' relationship to Alcibiades neglect to cite the relevant passage (in *Busiris* 5) in full. Isocrates says

and when you undertook to accuse Socrates, as if you sought to praise him, you gave Alcibiades to him as a student, who, as far as anyone perceived, never was taught [by Socrates].

When Isocrates says that no one had perceived that Alcibiades was a student of Socrates, he may only mean that, contrary to the common belief at the time of the trial, no one really had any direct evidence that Alcibiades had been Socrates' student; this is presumably how most scholars have read the passage. But Isocrates' remark may also be understood as saying that no one until Polycrates had ever perceived Alcibiades as having been a student of Socrates.[64] Thus despite the

---

[63] The same can plainly be said for the much later, explicit responses of Libanius in his *Apology of Socrates,* and the similar charges against Socrates to be found in plut., Cat. Mai. 23. It is not irrelevant to our speculation in this regard that no association between Alcibiades and Socrates is made in the otherwise vehement slanders to be found in Ps.-Andocides, *Against Alcibiades* (probably an earlier work), though see Chroust ((3), 180) on this.

[64] This is how Dupreél reads it, for example (227–8), and though he rejects Isocrates' account he does so precisely because he sees that it would entail that Polycrates invented the issue, which he cannot accept on (quite dubious) historical grounds (namely, that Plato's *Prt.* could not, in his opinion, have been written after Polycrates' pamphlet). Instead, he concludes that Plato and Aischines invented the relationship between Socrates and Alcibiades, and that Polycrates was merely responding to their fictions (279)! On the other hand, we accept Dupreél's dating of the *Apology* before Polycrates' pamphlet, and thus reject Ehrenberg's view ((1), 372) that the former was one of the many things written in response to the latter. It is plainly not irrelevant to this that nothing in Plato's *Apology* provides a direct response to Polycrates' most notorious charges.

number of authors involved in reporting the effects of Socrates' associations, no reflection of common sentiments at the time of the trial is necessarily implied. We know that Polycrates' pamphlet was quite provocative, and this may be enough to explain later authors' concern for the specific charge that Socrates was held responsible for Critias and Alcibiades.

Finally, there is good reason to suppose, from Socrates' own rhetoric, that the identities of Socrates' allegedly corrupted students were never clear during the trial. At 34a2–b5, Socrates challenges Meletus to produce even a single one, or else a relative of such a 'student', who will testify to his corrupting influence.[65] It may be true that Meletus would have been reluctant to take up Socrates' offer to call witnesses who could testify about any role Socrates may have had in the 'corruption' of Alcibiades or Critias, since perhaps that could be construed as testimony to substantiate the formal charges and, hence, as a direct violation of the amnesty.[66] But immediately prior to his offer to allow Meletus to call any additional witnesses, Socrates *himself* invites anyone who claims to have been corrupted, or a relative of such a one, to come forward to testify against him. Testimony offered by a witness called by Socrates himself would clearly not violate the provisions of the amnesty. This is significant because, in Plato's version of the speech, Socrates wants the outcome of the trial to be determined by the full truth, not by the bias of the jury nor any fortuitous legal protection he may happen to enjoy as the result of the amnesty. Thus, Socrates' offer at 34a2–b5 to have anyone who wishes speak against him is not an empty gesture secured only by a legal nicety that protects him from damaging testimony about his relationship with either Alcibiades or Critias, for he enjoys

[65] For the evidence that it would not have been unusual for Socrates to invite Meletus to speak again, see Burnet (2), note on 34a5. In the same note, however, Burnet is sceptical of the possibility that Meletus could have used the opportunity to introduce new evidence on the ground that any legally permissible evidence at the trial would already have had to be introduced at the preliminary hearing before the trial. Against such a restrictive view of what was legally permissible evidence, see Harrison, vol. 2, 97–8; Bonner, 173–4; and Lofberg, 605.

[66] Since the charges themselves could legally specify only allegedly criminal activities that took place after the amnesty, the testimony of witnesses would have to pertain to Socrates' conduct after 403/2 BC. But, in fact, nothing legally prevented the prosecution from employing testimony concerning the prior corruption or Alcibiades and Critias as paradigms of the results of corrupting activities in which Socrates had continued to engage after the amnesty. The prosecutors would thus be reluctant to call witnesses to the corruption of Alcibiades and Critias *only if* doing so might be construed as providing the *only* evidence against Socrates.

no such legal protection once he himself invites the damaging testimony.

In any case, if the names of allegedly corrupted youths had already been named by his prosecutors, even if only by insinuation or through slanderous asides—indeed, even if their identities were so obvious to those present at the trial that they did not need attention called to them—Socrates and his jurors would have been well aware of what particular 'students' his prosecutors had in mind. On any such hypothesis, Socrates' challenge to Meletus at 34a2–b5 becomes so transparent a pose that even the most sluggish member of the jury could see past it, whatever Socrates' actual legal protection may have been.

As we have pointed out above, the prosecutors could have sought to impugn Socrates' character through mention of his association with Alcibiades or Critias without fear of being perceived to violate the conditions of the amnesty. And we can be quite confident that had they thought that making legally permissible references to those associations would have damaged Socrates in the eyes of the jury, one or more of the prosecutors would have made them. Given this fact, if Socrates' challenge to Meletus at 34a2–b5 makes sense it follows that neither Alcibiades nor Critias (nor for that matter any other specified individual) was seen as a recognizable paradigm of Socratic corruption, even in the minds of the very men who were most hostile to Socrates. Of course, Socrates' challenge to Meletus may be supposed only to be a case of Platonic embellishment. But in supposing that it is, we condemn Plato of making Socrates look foolish, for a damning reply to the challenge Plato puts in Socrates' mouth would be obvious to all Plato's readers. Even if Socrates had anticipated speeches by *sunēgoroi* who would argue compellingly against the response we can imagine Meletus making, Socrates' challenge—whether or not it was invented by Plato—would be nonsense if a damaging reply to it were obvious, especially if that reply were already a matter of record as an explicit controversy at the trial.

For these reasons one may reasonably doubt that Socrates' associations with Alcibiades and Critias were a specific and profound concern to a significant number of the jurors. If we are right, Socrates' defense against the 'first' accusations is suited well enough to any slander that may have made him responsible for anyone's misdeeds, and to focus on individual instances would be a needless waste of the precious time allotted to him. There is no compelling evidence, later testimonia notwithstanding, to believe, and, as we have seen, at least some reason to deny, that Socrates' associations with Critias and/or Alcibiades represented matters of special and specific concern to the jurors, apart from what Socrates identifies as the 'first' accusations. Hence, we find no jurisprudential fault in Socrates' failure to apply his defense explicitly to a summary review of these or any other specific associations.

2.5 Socrates' Mission

2.5.1 THE ORIGIN OF SOCRATES' REPUTATION

At 20c6 we find yet another aspect of Socrates' response to the 'first' accusations that has been widely seen as strong evidence of his lack of interest in convincing the jurors of his innocence. Having said he has had nothing to do with natural philosophy, rhetoric, and teaching, despite the many and vehement slanders against him, Socrates imagines the jurors asking the obvious question: 'Clearly all this talk has not arisen while you were doing nothing unusual', he says on behalf of the jury, 'unless you were doing something out of the ordinary; so tell us what it is, so we may not act unadvisedly with regard to you' (20c6–d1). So begins Socrates' notorious tale of the oracle to Chairephon, upon which so much of the rest of his defense depends.

The very activities that have aroused the anger of his accusers amount to nothing less than a 'divine mission', he tells his jurors, and Socrates repeatedly reminds them that he has pursued this mission as a fundamental obligation, honoring it above all else, even though it has brought him only poverty and the enmity of his fellow citizens. But why does Socrates believe that he has such a mission?

According to the *Apology*, a Delphic oracle set him on the path of divine service. He tells the jurors that his friend, Chairephon, once had the audacity to ask the oracle if there was any man wiser than Socrates. The oracle responded that no one was wiser (20e8–21a7). Commentators are divided over how the references to the oracle are to be understood in connection with the origin of Socrates' mission. Since Socrates' account of his mission is so vital to his defense, we must explain how Socrates came to believe that his life must be spent in the service of the god. To do this, we shall show how the oracle can be

construed as having been the seminal element in the genesis of
Socrates' understanding of his specific mission.

2.5.2 SOCRATES' MISSION

Many scholars have been puzzled by what is said in the *Apology*
about the oracle and the origin of Socrates' mission.[67] By the time he
concludes his speech, it is clear that his mission is a complex one. He
must free men from their pretense of wisdom (23b7, 37e5–38a6), and
exhort them to care rather for its actual attainment, for truth, and for
the perfection of their souls (29d7–e3). Moreover, he must also attempt to free them from the bondage of their concern for material
things (29e3–30b4) and urge them to strive for the possession of that
most precious of all goods, virtue (30a1–2, 31b4–5). How could
Socrates possibly derive such a complex injunction from the oracle's
simple declaration that no man is wiser than he?

It is tempting to think that Socrates simply interpreted the oracle as
a veiled directive from the god to pursue a life of philosophy,[68] but
though Socrates does think that the oracle is in need of interpretation
(21b3–7; 23a7–b4), the interpretation he arrives at shows that he does
not believe that the oracle was directed specifically to him—rather, he
sees it as addressed to mankind in general. Moreover, as a number of
commentators have pointed out, there is nothing jussive in either the
oracle itself or in Socrates' later interpretation of it,[69] nor is there
anything in either to suggest that he must encourage men to pursue
wisdom, truth, the perfection of their souls, and virtue. Yet later in
the speech he insists that he is obliged by the god to encourage men to
care for these things.

These puzzles prompt many commentators to argue that a plausible
account of Socrates' reasons for understanding his mission simply
cannot be generated from Plato's account, despite the more than
three Stephanus pages devoted to the allegedly life-changing impact
the oracle had on Socrates. These commentators tend to adopt one of

---

[67] See, e.g., Bury (1), 580; Chroust (3), 31–2; Doering, 57; Dupreél, 45; Gigon
(2), 99; Parke and Wormell, vol. 1, 402–3; Renouvier, vol. 1, 299; Thirlwall, vol. 4,
288. See also notes 80 and 81, below. Guthrie suggests that perhaps the Pythia only
told Chairephon what he wished to hear ((3), 7). Montuori ((5), 57–143, esp.
133 ff.) doubts the entire oracle story. A distinctly original interpretation of the
meaning of the oracle is offered in Ps.-Lucian, *Erotes* 48.

[68] See, e.g., Grote (2), vol. 1, 284–7; C. Phillipson, 293–6; Friedländer, vol. 2,
162.   [69] E.g., Chroust (3), 31–2; Hackforth (2), 89–91.

two positions. Some maintain that Plato never intended what is said about the oracle to be taken seriously; rather, it is but an example of Socrates' notorious irony.[70] Others, however, maintain that the references to the oracle are intended to explain Socrates' mission, but that the explanation simply fails. On this view, though Plato sought to portray Socrates in the best light possible by underscoring the pious nature of his activities, he attempted in vain to tie Socrates' philosopical life to the well-known oracle regarding his wisdom.[71]

Both of these positions, however, raise questions at least as troublesome as those they are intended to answer. The first position, that what is said about the oracle is intended as irony, raises difficulties with other Socratic doctrines, as we have shown in Section 1.5.3. And even if it were true that there are many places in the *Apology* where Socrates' remarks ought not to be taken literally, it is most unlikely that he would resort to mere irony on a matter of such substance to his defense. On these matters, Socrates repeatedly reminds the jurors that he tells only the truth (for example, at 17b4–8, 20d5–6, 22b5–6, 24a4–5). Were he then to risk being intentionally misleading about such a substantive point, he would be guilty of the very sort of dishonest rhetoric for which he condemns the prosecution (for example, at 17a1–b5), as any attentive juror, or Plato, would see. Indeed, at 37e5–38a8, Socrates explicitly anticipates such a suspicion from the jurors and denies its basis utterly, while recognizing that it is not easy to allay such a suspicion.

Socrates' emphatic claims that his actions have been ordained by the god is the very heart of his defense against the charges, and he

---

[70] Kidd, e.g., claims that the entire oracle episode is but an example of 'characteristic Socratic irony' (482). Similarly, A. E. Taylor dismisses the mention of the oracle as Socrates' 'native humor' ((2), 160); see also Burnet (1), 107.

[71] Hackforth, e.g., dismisses this section as an utter Platonic fiction, arguing that Plato was himself perplexed about Socrates' reasons for undertaking the mission and invented what is said about the oracle in a vain attempt to explain it ((2), 101–4). Wolff maintains that the episode is not intended to explain the origin of Socrates' mission, but is rather a rhetorical device employed by Plato to underscore Socrates' sincerity in exhorting others to examine their lives (72–4). Montuori dismisses it as part of the Socratic 'myth' ((5), 140–3). Fontenrose allows that it is 'not impossible, though perhaps incredible' (34) that the oracle is a fiction of the Socratic circle (see also 245–6). (For other sceptics, see note 67 above). Against Montuori, however, it should at least be noted that D. L. (2.37–8) supports Plato's version, and that Xenophon's story would be a natural expansion on Plato's especially assuming, as we should, that Xenophon had Plato's *Ap.* in mind when he wrote his own *Ap.* (about which, see Chroust (3), 18–19, 39). (For a list of the other ancient sources on the oracle, see Fontenrose, 245.)

does at least say things about the oracle and the origin of his mission that might reasonably lead the jurors to believe that his sense of mission was sincerely derived from the oracle. The view that Socrates is not telling the plain truth on this point implies that he is willing to risk swaying the jurors by creating false belief about the nature of his actions. Unless we are to explain away Socrates' apparent concern that the full truth be told, together with his insistence that the jurors reach the right verdict, we cannot plausibly construe these remarks as irony.

Equally implausible is the second view, that in order to convey the pious nature of Socrates' motives Plato chose an explanation of Socrates' mission that does not cohere with the rest of the speech. Even the proponents of this view must concede that the rest of the *Apology* bears all the marks of careful composition. This view, however, requires that Plato's powers as a philosophical rhetorician failed him on a matter crucial to the coherence of the speech he imputes to Socrates. This seems unlikely. At the very least, such an attempt to dismiss the apparent importance the *Apology* assigns to the oracle should be adopted only as a last resort.

Both of these interpretations are unsatisfactory then, but they do have this merit: they call attention to the fact that neither the oracle itself nor Socrates' subsequent understanding of it plausibly generates a divine command that he spend the rest of his life philosophizing with his fellow Athenians. But from this it does not follow, contrary to what has frequently been assumed, that the oracle played no role in forming Socrates' conviction that he must spend the rest of his life in the service of the god. It is not the case, after all, that the only way Socrates could have come to recognize his duty regarding the god is through the god's issuing a direct command to him.

Plato's Socrates could easily have attempted to persuade the jury that his actions are benign and thus should not be considered unlawful, but instead he chooses to underscore the great irony of the charges he faces. Socrates is convinced of his innocence, not simply because he has scrupulously avoided harming anyone, but also because he has been laboring at the behest of the god. If his conviction that he is innocent is to make any sense, he must believe that his actions are in accordance with what piety demands of him. And although he believes that the god desires that he perform these acts, it is very unlikely that he believes these acts are pious simply because the god desires that they be performed (*Euthphr.* 10a2–11a6). An understanding of Socrates' conception of piety, then, might cast light on his reasons for undertaking his mission and the role the oracle apparently played in prompting it.

2.5.3 SOCRATES' CONCEPTION OF PIETY

The *Apology* does not contain an explanation of Socrates' conception of piety, and the one dialogue in which the concept is discussed in any detail, the *Euthyphro*, ends in irresolution (ἀπορία). This is not to say, however, that the *Euthyphro* reveals nothing positive regarding Socrates' own view. On the contrary, there are several reasons for believing that 11e1–14c3 presents Socrates as holding at least some unfeigned beliefs about the nature of piety. First, as if to indicate that a fresh start is to be made, that passage is set apart by means of an interlude from Euthyphro's previous failures to arrive at an acceptable definition. But more importantly, Socrates himself takes the lead in this argument, thus attempting to aid the confused 'expert'. His offer to help Euthyphro is perplexing if Socrates is himself confused in every way about the proper conception of piety. Finally, although Euthyphro eventually stumbles and is unable to complete the definition to Socrates' satisfaction, the passage is punctuated by Socrates' apparent endorsement of several of the claims made about the nature of piety.

The passage begins with Socrates asserting that piety is a part, but not the whole of justice.[72] When Euthyphro adds the differentium of attending to the gods, as opposed to the rest of justice, which requires attending to men, Socrates, without any apparent irony, readily agrees. But he is equally quick to point out that the definition is as yet incomplete, since Euthyphro has not made clear how the notion of 'attendance on' (θεραπεία) is to be understood.

To help Euthyphro better understand what is called for, Socrates suggests that piety be understood as a craft (τέχνη). Since each craft aims at producing some specific product (ἔργον), or beneficial product, Euthyphro will be able to clarify the notion of 'attention' by specifying the benefit produced by the craft of piety. Although Euthyphro agrees that piety is a craft, he is careful to deny that the gods stand to the craft of piety in the way that horses, for example, stand to the craft of horsemanship. The product of the horseman's craft is the improvement of his horses, but the improvement of the

---

[72] For a similar claim, see *Grg.* 507a5–b4, which provides further evidence that Socrates is expressing his own views at *Euthphr.* 11e1–14c3.

gods cannot be the benefit produced by the craft of piety (13a2–d3). No man, he points out, can improve a god. Once again, Socrates agrees.

A second model is then suggested. The pious man attends to the gods by performing a service (ὑπηρέτημα) on their behalf in much the same way a slave attends to his master by performing a service on his behalf. Just as the aim of the slave is not the improvement of his master but the carrying out of the master's wishes, so the aim of the pious man is not the improvement of the gods but the carrying out of the gods' wishes.

Socrates agrees with the aptness of the second model, but presses Euthyphro again to specify the 'all-glorious product' (πάγκαλον ἔργον) that the gods wish the pious man to accomplish with his craft of service (13e10–11). It is at this point that Euthyphro fails to provide what is called for and is berated by Socrates: 'You are not eager to teach me; that is clear. For just now when you were right there, you turned away. Had you answered it, I should already have gained an understanding of piety from you' (14b9–c3). Thus it appears that Socrates has at least some conception of piety and that Euthyphro has made real progress towards what he would consider the proper definition. If so, Socrates sees the pious man as a craftsman who justly serves the gods by producing some truly beneficial end that the gods desire.

In spite of the numerous indications to the contrary, some commentators are nevertheless disinclined to accept the view that the *Euthyphro* presents Socrates as having any conception of piety whatever.[73] Allen, for example, argues that Euthyphro's final attempt to find a satisfactory definition fails because Socrates does not believe that piety has a product. Thus Socrates is aware that the attempt will fail as soon as Euthyphro accepts the analogy between piety and a craft. To bolster this conclusion, Allen cites numerous examples in other early dialogues where attempted definitions

---

[73] Those who are sceptical about inferring that Socrates endorses the conception of piety sketched in *Euthyphro* 11e1–14c3 include Allen ((4), 56–8); Robin ((1), 254–5); and Shorey ((3), 78–9). Given our argument, and the fact that the view we derive from the *Euthyphro* accords so plainly with other uncontroversially Socratic doctrines, we believe such a degree of scepticism to be unwarranted. With us, others who would disagree with such sceptical arguments include J. Adam (*Platonis Euthyphro* (Cambridge, 1908), xii–xvii), Arnim (141–54); Haden (2); Rabinowitz (108–20); and Versenyi ((1), esp. 11–20, 95–134). By far the most plausible and exhaustive of such positive arguments, we believe, may be found in McPherran (2).

founder on the interlocutor's inability to specify the product of the particular virtue under discussion.

But the fact that Socrates takes issue with the product suggested by an interlocutor does not, by itself, justify the inference that the virtues do not produce beneficial products, not the least of which is the improvement of the virtuous man himself. Indeed, Socrates' frequently drawn analogies between virtues and crafts[74] make little sense if crafts produce products but virtues do not. That Euthyphro is unable to specify the product of piety does not, then, warrant the conclusion that Socrates does not believe piety to be the craft of just service to the gods that produces some all-glorious benefit. And it is surely significant that Plato had Socrates, and not Euthyphro, introduce this view. If Socrates does not believe it, he must be viewed as merely tricking Euthyphro, rather than as making a sincere effort to attain the truth. And since Euthyphro had already admitted that he is confused (11b6–8), the passage cannot reasonably be seen as an attempt to reduce Euthyphro to a state of confusion (ἀπορία), for such would be redundant.

A second objection to our view that the *Euthyphro* reveals at least something of the view of piety Plato imputes to Socrates may be developed as follows: if our reading of the *Euthyphro* is correct, then Socrates understands what piety is and merely tries to guide Euthyphro to the same understanding. But in the *Apology* and throughout the early dialogues Socrates claims to be ignorant of the nature of all the virtues, and his persistent profession of ignorance cannot be dismissed as wholly ironic.

The objection, however, implies that when Socrates claims to be ignorant of what moral virtue is, he is saying that he has no conception of it. But that he is not saying anything as strong as this is plain, for he frequently expresses a variety of moral convictions, such as that virtue is always a good thing for its possessor, or that virtue is the same thing in a man and a woman, or that virtue is to the soul what health is to the body. Had he no conception of what virtue is, these convictions would be baseless, and (what is worse) he would have no reason to be convinced, as he plainly is in the *Apology*, that his life had been blameless (*Ap.* 37b2–3). It seems decidedly more likely, therefore, that Socrates' profession of ignorance amounts to a denial that he

[74] See *Charm.* 164a5–166d6; *Grg.* 464b2–466a3; *Rep.* I, 341c4–342e11; *Euthyd.* 289b7–292e5.

possesses understanding of precisely what any specific virtue is, but not to a denial that he has some (no doubt incomplete) conception of it, a conception about which he may be quite confident. Thus, his avowed ignorance of the nature of moral virtue in no way undermines our view that this passage in the *Euthyphro* reveals at least part of Socrates' conception of piety.

Although the specific product of piety is never revealed and therefore, to that extent, the definition is left incomplete, what is agreed upon fits well with what Socrates says in the *Apology* regarding the 'Heraclean labors' he has undertaken at the behest of the god. He claims that his actions have been a 'service to the god' (23c1, 30a6–7),[75] a 'mission' on behalf of the god that aims at producing what is truly beneficial (30a7–b4, 38a1–3). As if to leave no doubt about the benefits of his work, he tells the jury that he is nothing less than a 'gift' given to Athens by the god and that if they, his judges, decide to destroy him they will not soon find another to replace him (30d5–31a3).

It is impossible to know the exact date of Chairephon's fateful journey to Delphi.[76] Although the *Apology* indicates that the divine mission began only after Socrates had discovered the real meaning of the oracle, its account requires that Socrates was already philosophically active by the time of Chairephon's departure. Had he not already gained a certain reputation in Athens as a result of such activities, Chairephon, who, as we have seen, is portrayed by a variety

[75] In the *Euthphr.* Socrates calls the pious man's service an ὑπηρετική. In the *Ap.* he refers to his service to the god as a λατρεία. Both terms connote work done by a subordinate on behalf of his superior. Thus, the different terms for service in the two works do not represent different conceptions of service.

[76] Parke and Wormell (vol. 1, 401–2) argue that it is unlikely that Chairephon could have made his journey to Delphi during the war years, 431–422 and 413–404. Thus, the oracle must have been given prior to 431 or between 422 and 413. They conclude that the earlier date is more likely. A. E. Taylor ((3), 78–9) concurs, arguing that in the *Charm.* Socrates is presented as returning from a battle at Potidaia and inquiring about the state of philosophy in Athens. The battle at Potidaia took place in 430. (See also Fontenrose, 34, 245.) Against the earlier dating, J. Ferguson (2) argues that the date must have been closer to 421. Ferguson points out that Socrates did not appear as the object of comic treatment at the hands of Aristophanes and Eupolis until the 420's, and that the Delphic oracle could only have been responding to his newly gained reputation for wisdom. We are unconvinced by Ferguson's argument, since the Pythia's answer may have been determined by the draw of a lot, and not necessarily in recognition of any special facts (see Fontenrose, 219–24). But because Plato and Xenophon provide us with no clues on the date of the oracle, any confident dating of the oracle remains impossible.

of ancient authors as a devoted companion of Socrates,[77] would never have been prompted to pose his question to the oracle. And even if the Pythia and priests for Delphi were generally inclined to give the supplicant the answer he wanted to hear, it is unlikely they would have given the answer they did in this case if Socrates had not already had a considerable reputation as a wise man.[78] Otherwise, they would have risked discrediting themselves.

Two of Socrates' responses subsequent to his receiving the news of the oracle strongly suggest that the conception of piety sketched incompletely in the *Euthyphro* was one of the views Socrates had developed prior to Chairephon's departure for Delphi. First, he undertook to investigate the meaning of the oracle, not out of any idle curiosity, but because he believed at the time that he must assign 'the god's business the highest importance' (21e4–5). Secondly, once he discovered the real meaning of the oracle, his immediate reaction was to 'give aid to the god', by 'undertaking a service on the god's behalf' (23b7–c1). If this is correct, it is clear why attempts to find a command to serve the god in the oracle's specific pronouncement, or in Socrates subsequent interpretation of the oracle, are otiose. Socrates' sense of obligation to the god derives from his already-held belief about the requirements of piety, not from a direct command issued through the Delphic oracle.[79] But we are still left with three questions: (1) Why did Socrates believe that he must serve the god in the particular way he does? (2) Why does he not begin his service until the

---

[77] See, e.g., his appearance at *Grg.* 447a7–8 and *passim,* and the relationship to Socrates they imply; *Charm.* 153b2–4 and *passim;* Ar., *Nub;* Xen., *Mem.* 1.2.48.

[78] On this point see Guthrie (2), 86, and A. E. Taylor (3), 78. The fact that Socrates must have already gained a reputation for wisdom as a result of his views does not imply that he had already begun his particular 'service to the god' prior to Chairephon's journey. Thus, we see no reason to agree with Wilamowitz-Möllendorff (54) or Daniel and Polansky, who say that the oracle could only have served to confirm Socrates' belief in the necessity of his mission, but contributed not at all to that mission's origin.

[79] Socrates repeatedly argues in a way that suggests that he views the god as having commanded him in a way analogous to being assigned a military post (see 28d6–e4, 33c4–7). Guthrie ((2), 88) is certainly correct, however, in pointing out that Socrates sees the oracle as a 'message' and not a 'command'. However, Guthrie fails to show what motivated Socrates to undertake his mission. But some account of his motivation is precisely what is needed to explain why Socrates took the oracle so seriously, and why he responded the way he did. Our argument is that Socrates sees the oracle as expressing the god's concern in a way that, when combined with Socrates' commitment following the god's wishes, yields his mission. In this way, the god has given Socrates his 'post', even though the oracle is not, of itself, a command.

oracle was presented to Chairephon? and (3) Why does Socrates not explain why the oracle so greatly affected his life?

2.5.4 THE MEANING OF THE ORACLE

Socrates says that he was initially perplexed by the oracle's claim that there was no man wiser than he, since he believed himself not to be wise at all. Knowing that oracles are often in the form of riddles whose real meaning is not easily discerned (21b3–7), he set out to refute its apparent meaning by finding at least one man wiser than he.

It might be thought that the fact that Socrates actually sets out to refute the oracle is evidence that he did not really take it seriously, and that he has only mock reverence for it. Burnet actually goes so far as to say that Socrates 'tries to prove the god a liar'.[80] Similarly, Alexander Nehamas construes Socrates' examination of the oracle as a test 'in order to determine whether or not it is true', and speaks of 'Socrates' effort to prove the oracle wrong'.[81] This view, however, rests upon a misunderstanding of Socrates' intent when he sets out to find at least one wiser than he. Because he believed himself not to be wise at all, and he knew that oracles' words often had the form of riddles (21b3–7), he sets out to refute the oracle's apparent meaning. This is not an impious attempt to prove the god wrong, but only an attempt to understand what the god sought to convey.[82] He refers to his investigation as 'labors' (22a7) that he performed 'on behalf of the god' (22a4). Far from showing any irreverence for either the god or the oracle, Socrates' attempt to refute the apparent meaning of the oracle only reinforces the view that he sees piety as requiring that he always make 'the god's business' take first priority. So Nehamas is surely wrong in saying that Socrates 'tests the oracle's wisdom as rigorously as he tests the wisdom of those by means of whom he tests the oracle itself'.[83] Though Socrates surely does test the oracle, he does so to determine the truth he is entirely confident it has expressed (however darkly). In testing his interlocutors he can have no confidence that the views he tests are true in any way. His interlocutors need testing not because what they mean is unclear—though sometimes it is—but because they frequently say something that is entirely clear *and entirely false*. Nothing in what Socrates says about the

---

[80] Burnet (2), note on 21b8. [81] Nehamas, 306.
[82] See Guthrie (2), 87–8. [83] Nehamas, 305.

oracle suggests that it might turn out to be simply and fundamentally false—if it were, the god would either be lying (which he surely is not (21b6–7)), or confused (which he surely cannot be).

When he began to examine those Athenians renowned for their wisdom, the focus of his questioning was not their reputed understanding of just anything, but their claims to understand what is good and noble (see 21d4–5, 22c2–6, 22c9–e5). He found the politicians and poets to be utterly lacking in this regard, but when he turned to the hand-craftsman, he found that they did indeed understand many noble things (22c9–d4). For example, they had the understanding requisite to practise their crafts well. But because they possessed this understanding, they mistakenly believed they were wise about the greatest things (22d4–e1). Socrates goes on to say that he then asked himself on behalf of the oracle whether it is better to be as he is, wise about his ignorance, or to be as they are, wise about their crafts but foolish about the greatest things. Not surprisingly, his answer is that it is better to be as he is (22e1–5).

Nowhere in this passage does Socrates say what the greatest things are. We do know that Socrates thinks the question, 'What is virtue?' is the most momentous a man can ask. Thus when he says that his examination of the craftsmen led him to the conclusion 'It is better to be as he [Socrates] is', he must have meant: 'It is better to recognize that one understands nothing than to possess some worthy understanding and yet also think one understands what virtue is when one does not.' He reaffirms this conviction when he tells the jury that 'the unexamined life is not worth living' (38a5–6). Viewing the passage in this light we can better understand how Socrates reaches his conclusion concerning the real meaning of the oracle, namely, that 'human wisdom is of little or no worth' and that a man would be 'wisest, who, like Socrates, recognizes that he is in truth worth nothing with respect to wisdom' (23a6–b4). Although he finds some men who do possess wisdom of a sort, it is only craft-wisdom with respect to material goods. Socrates realized that this sort of wisdom is of no value if those having it think they understand what virtue is when they do not.

There is good reason to suppose that Socrates is presented as believing, even before Chairephon's startling news, that piety requires one to serve the gods by promoting what is good. But his astonishment at the oracle and his subsequent understanding of its real meaning show that he had not realized the full extent to which his fellow Athenians had pursued and possessed only apparent goods. The god's message, therefore, is that the Athenians lack the supreme benefit, virtue, a deficiency of which they are arrogantly ignorant. As the god's servant, Socrates must free them from the pretense of real wisdom that is the cause of this deficiency and urge them to acquire virtue. This, he says, he has done, for he has tirelessly carried out his pious duty to convey the god's message to all who will listen.

This account explains why Socrates describes the oracle as the crucial turning-point in his life. Moreover, it explains how the oracle prompted the specific activities he says he is duty-bound to perform, activities from which he cannot shrink as long as he remains alive. Still, why does Socrates not explain to the court his belief that, because of the oracle, he is obliged to do as he does? All who read the speech would agree that he nowhere explains just how the oracle was responsible for his undertaking his mission.

An explanation of the importance Socrates attaches to the oracle, however, is not essential either to his defense against the 'first' or to that against the 'later' accusers. He initially refers to the oracle in connection with his response to the 'first' accusers, whose insidious attacks, he says, are far more dangerous to him than the charges formally brought against him by Meletus (18b2–4, 28a6–8). It was their slanders, after all, which aroused the prejudice against him and which prompted Meletus to bring the 'later' formal charges against him (19b1– 2). Although Socrates is well aware that he is not likely to disabuse his judges of their false beliefs about him in the few hours allotted to him to make a defense, he realizes that the success of his defense rests at least in part on his rebuttal of the 'first accusations'.

After Socrates explains that he is neither a nature-philosopher nor a sophist, as the 'first' accusers had claimed, he realizes that he must explain why he has nevertheless gained such notoriety for wisdom. To do so, he refers to Chairephon's question and the oracle's perplexing answer, his investigation of all reputed for their wisdom, his eventual understanding of what the god really meant, and his subsequent mission to make men aware of their lack of real wisdom. One product of these events was that he became known for a certain cleverness. But another was that his ill-deserved reputation for wisdom grew as a result of the many young men who began to follow him and imitate his elenctic method (23c2– d2). His mention of the oracle and its connection with his divine duty to philosophize is, then, a crucial part of his defense against the 'first' accusers. But his initial reason for mentioning the oracle, to explain this reputation for sophistry, does not require that he provide a detailed explanation of how the oracle actually prompted his mission.

Once the point is made that, because of the oracle, he believes he is under a moral compulsion to serve the god in the way he has, Socrates uses it as the focus of his defense against the 'new' charges of impiety brought by Meletus. As we have seen, he chooses to emphasize the irony of the formal charges by suggesting that his actions, far from being impious, are actually precisely what piety requires of him. Although Socrates sees the pious man as a kind of craftsman who aims at the productions of an 'all-glorious product' and thus, to the extent, his conception differs from the view commonly held,[84] there is at least one important feature that the two conceptions share: both hold that piety requires one to attempt to aid the gods by carrying out what the gods ordain. In order to convince the jury that he is indeed pious, Socrates is not obliged to explain his own conception and the way in which his investigation of the oracle led him to understand what product his craft of service to the god must promote. Rather, he needs only to persuade the jury that he has sincerely attempted to aid the god following his discovery of what the god wished him to do. And this is precisely how he tries to demonstrate the irony of the formal charges against him.

2.5.5 CONCLUSIONS

We have shown that Socrates takes the oracle with the utmost seriousness and that it represents to him the fundamental motive for his mission on behalf of the god. Moreover, we have argued that Socrates did not see the oracle as a divine command issued to him by the god. Instead, we have tried to show that, at the time of Chairephon's journey to Delphi, Socrates already believed that piety requires that a man engage in just service to the god. The oracle and his subsequent realization of its meaning provided Socrates with an understanding of what the god wanted most for men: the abandonment of their pretenses to wisdom and the comprehension that their material concerns profit them nothing until they have first achieved the most precious of all goods, human virtue.

Socrates realizes that many of the jurors will take what he says about the oracle as sheer arrogance. But it is evidence for the strength

[84] For more on the commonly held conception of piety, see Dover (3), 246-9.

of his convictions that he must serve the god and tell his jurors the full truth that he none the less proclaims his message once again at his trial. And that this conviction was seen by Plato to be fundamental to Socrates' way of life and thought is manifest from its repetition throughout the early dialogues.

2.6 Socrates' Ignorance

2.6.1 THE PARADOX OF SOCRATES' DEFENSE

The principal lesson of the oracle story, according to Socrates, is that he is the wisest of men because only he recognizes the extent of his own ignorance. As he puts it, at 21b4– 5, 'I am aware of being wise in nothing, great or small'. Such confessions of ignorance on Socrates' part are common enough in Plato's portrayals.[85] But how, one may fairly ask, can Socrates so persistently confess his ignorance, and yet be utterly convinced, as he plainly claims to be, that his philosophic mission is of supreme moral value, and thus that he is utterly innocent of any wrongdoing as a results of its pursuit? As Gregory Vlastos has put it, '[Socrates'] avowals of epistemic inadequacy, frequent in the dialogues, are never paralleled by admission of moral failure; the asymmetry is striking'.[86]

Throughout the early dialogues, Socrates searches for a correct conception of virtue (or excellence—ἀρετή). Without this, he says, true moral understanding is impossible.[87] But this should strike us as

---

[85] See, e.g., *Ap.* 20c1–3, 21d2–7, 23b2–4; *Charm.* 165b4–c2, 166c7–d6; *Euthphr.* 5a7–c5, 15c12, e5–16a4; *La.* 186b8–c5, d8–e3, 200e2–5; *Lysis* 212a4–7, 223b4–8; *Hip. Ma.* 286c8–e2, 304d4–e5; *Grg.* 509a4–6; *Meno* 71a1–7, 80d1–4; *Rep.* I, 337e4–5. See also Arist., *Soph. El.* 183b6–8; Aisch. Soc., *Alc.* 10C (Dittmar).

[86] Vlastos (7), 6, n. 14. This 'striking assymetry' is missed by Allen ((1), 39–40 and (5), 16), who argues that Socrates can offer no real defense against Meletus' charges because he does not know that he is innocent of them.

[87] We identify Socrates' epistemic concern as being for the pursuit of 'understanding' rather than 'knowledge', though we recognize that this is not the common practice. For reasons why one should select this terminology in the Socratic/Platonic context as the best translation of ἐπιστήμη, see Moline (esp. 3–31) and Moravcsik. But see Jean Robert's quite negative review of Moline in *OSAP* 2 (1984), 223–35, esp. 225–9. We shall continue to use 'knowledge' and 'know' when referring to other scholars' analyses, however, to be consistent with their practice. We also find it quite proper to refer to cases of particular cognitions Socrates claims to have as instances of knowledge (but not, as our argument will show, as instances of understanding), and so we will refer to such cognitive claims by Socrates as claims

puzzling, for we often correctly and confidently identify things and yet would be utterly at a loss to provide anything like a formally adequate conceptual analysis of the term we use to identify them. None of us feels the slightest uneasiness in our identifications of any number of ordinary things, but who would not feel at least a little uncertain if challenged to say what it *really is* to be a table, or a rock, or a man? But many commentators maintain that Socrates would deny that any identification of particulars is possible, since they claim that he believes that the ability to recognize a token of any general type presupposes the more formal knowledge of the type's proper analysis.[88] If this is correct, the confident stance Socrates takes at his trial is indeed paradoxical, since the moral urgency he attributes to his mission, and the moral knowledge he claims to possess, would require the very understanding he professes not to have.

2.6.2 SOCRATES ON KNOWLEDGE OF INSTANCES

The natural way to escape a paradox is to deny at least one of the assertions that generate it. So it is that legions of commentators have sought to deny the sincerity of either Socrates' profession of ignorance or his disavowal of guilt.[89] But such denials are unconvincing. Socrates claims throughout the early dialogues to be committed to discovering the truth, and in the *Apology* he places the pursuit of this goal at the heart of his philosophic mission in Athens (29d7–e2). Though ironic insincerity, for example, might be defended as part of the means by which the ends of his mission are pursued,[90] Socrates' commitment to philosophic inquiry does not allow him to advance an untruth willingly as an *end* of inquiry. Yet his claims of ignorance and innocence are plainly and emphatically stated and elaborated in various parts of his defense in the *Apology*, as plain truths for his

to knowledge. Thus, on our view, Socrates knows many things, but sincerely claims to understand nothing.

[88] See, e.g., Allen (1), 39; Beversluis; Crombie, 57; Geach; Guthrie (1), vol. 3, 352; Robinson, 51.

[89] For examples of those who deny the sincerity of Socrates' profession of ignorance see Gulley, 69; Shero (2), 109; Vlastos (4), 7–8 (though Vlastos explicitly reverses this opinion in his more recent work (7)). For examples of those who deny that Socrates seriously intended to defend himself, see Chapter 1, notes 133 through 140.

[90] See, e.g., Gulley (69), who calls Socrates' confession of ignorance 'an expedient to encourage his interlocutors to seek out the truth, to make him think that he is joining Socrates in a voyage of discovery'. Gulley does not see the consequences of this view for the *Apology*, in which there is no interlocutor to manipulate in the relevant way.

jurors to contemplate. (His innocence, in fact, he has already sworn to in an oath at the preliminary hearing.[91]) To dispute the sincerity of either of these claims, therefore, is to convict Socrates of outright mendacity, and thus of running afoul of his mission.[92]

But there is a good reason to question the third proposition from which the paradox is generated, that Socrates requires that one have a developed conceptual understanding of virtue before one can confidently identify an instance of it.[93] First, despite the number of commentators who attribute this view to Socrates, there is surprisingly little that can be found in the texts to support such a claim.[94] And the passages that are cited in its support are also compatible with the weaker (and certainly less controversial) view that an understanding of virtue is necessary only for knowing *why* something is an instance of virtue.[95] If Socrates is making only the weaker claim, then confident identification of instances is possible without the more general understanding he seeks in his philosophic pursuits, and his belief that he is innocent thus does not presuppose the understanding he claims to lack.

If Socratic epistemology is to make sense, moreover, there is good reason to resist the stronger interpretation of his view. If the very process by which one is to attain the conceptual understanding Socrates says he and his fellow Athenians lack is to take place at all, one must first

---

[91] See Chapter 1, note 149.

[92] In fact, we are convinced that other problems of equal magnitude could be shown to be generated by the sort of approach we have disputed here (see Section 1.5.3).

[93] For excellent criticisms of this alleged Socratic principle, see Irwin, ch. 3, esp. 37–41 and 294 n. 4, and Vlastos (7), 23–6. As will become apparent, our own view differs somewhat from Irwin's and Vlastos's, however.

[94] *Charm.* 176a6–8; *Euthphr.* 6e3–6. *Hip. Ma.* 286c3–e4, 304d5–e3; *La.* 189e3–190b1; 190b7–c2; *Lysis* 223b4–8; and *Meno* 71b1–8 are the passages usually cited to support this claim. Nehamas offers an interpretation of these passages that does not convict Socrates of committing what Geach calls 'the Socratic fallacy'.

[95] At *Hip. Ma.* 286c4–7, Socrates testifies to having strong beliefs about instances of beauty and ugliness without being able to give an account of either. And at *Grg.* 508d6–e3 Socrates says that although he is ignorant, he is convinced that it is better to be wrongfully struck or slashed or robbed than to do the striking or slashing or robbing. Such convictions are incomprehensible unless, in claiming to be ignorant, Socrates does not intend to rule out rationally maintained moral convictions. Irwin (loc. cit., see note 93 above) endorses the view that Socrates has beliefs about the natures of the virtues, beliefs for which he does not claim certainty, But as we have argued elsewhere (in Brickhouse and Smith (5)), and as Vlastos has more recently argued ((7), see esp. 7–11, 24–5), Irwin's view is unable to explain the strength of many of Socrates' claims.

have access to the cases that give sense to any search for a theory to explain them. If Socrates could never be confident that any case was or was not a case of piety, for example, he could never hope to determine that a given theory of piety was adequate or not, for we would be left with no undisputed instance to capture in theory.[96] We would not even be in a position to suppose with any confidence that there are, or even could be, instances of piety. Any view of his principles that requires an adequate theory before some fairly confident judgments can be made of individual cases, therefore, reduces Socrates' enterprise to methodological nonsense.

Happily, that he does not hold any such view is plain enough from his characteristic use of mundane and uncontroversial examples in his investigations; unless we are to suppose this employment to be senseless or purely rhetorical, we must allow that Socrates finds some degree of confident judgment possible without a prior attainment of theoretical understanding. It still remains, of course, to determine the grounds other than theoretical understanding on which Socrates thinks such judgments can be made, and the degree of confidence with which Socrates thinks that such judgments can rationally be made.

Though we shall be returning to these questions in Chapter 3 and 5, in our discussions of individual passages where Socrates makes startlingly confident claims, the specific case that concerns us here is Socrates' certainty that his mission is of supreme moral value. About this, Socrates' conviction appears to be absolute. Such certainty cannot be explained in terms of the strength of any conception of virtue Socrates might have, since he is convinced that he must continue to test his conceptions by means of the *elenchos*. His conception, therefore, if he has some specific one, must be either fallible or at least susceptible to revision.[97] But his conviction regarding the moral virtue of his mission (and thus of his utter innocence of any wrongdoing as a result of its pursuit) is complete and unyielding. 'As long as I am capable of doing so', he tells the jury, 'I will not stop philosophizing' (29d4–5). One part of the puzzle, therefore, remains: how can Socrates be so certain of the morality of his activities?

---

[96] Someone who convicts Socrates of being caught in the jaws of this dilemma is Geach. Our first statement of this objection to Geach's view was in Brickhouse and Smith (5), 126. Others who make this objection include Irwin (40–1), and Vlastos ((7), 23–4).

[97] See *Ap.* 28e5–6, where Socrates states that he must continue to examine himself.

2.6.3 TWO INTERPRETATIONS

One way of seeing Socrates' numerous confident claims has been proposed by T.H. Irwin,[98] who argues that although Socrates' profession of ignorance is quite sincere, it does not rule out the possibility of anyone's having any number of true beliefs, some of which might be extremely strongly justified and thus held with great conviction. On Irwin's interpretation, Socrates may begin with confidently held beliefs about particular instances, and seek to derive through philosophy the sort of conceptual understanding that will convert such beliefs into moral knowledge. Can this account for Socrates' confidence in his own innocence?

We believe not. Notice that the particular issue here (the value of philosophizing) is fundamental to the entire process of inquiry by which knowledge is, on Irwin's account, to be attained. If the epistemic status of this is only that of belief, then the best Socrates can claim for the method by which he supposes knowledge might be attained is that he *believes* it is valuable, he *believes* the results he gets from the process are not deceptive and worthless. If the very process by which one's results are obtained is not held as a matter of complete confidence, then whatever results one may obtain by the method are infected by at least that same degree of uncertainty. Should he hold the value of his own mission as less than certain, its products—the propositions Socrates has come to believe through its pursuit and the courses of action to which Socrates accordingly commits himself (as, for example, in making the sort of defense he does in the *Apology*, or deciding to remain in prison in the *Crito*), his effects on the young people that have witnessed his elenctic probings of Athens' prominent citizens, and all the rest—are at least equally matters of incomplete certainty. On Irwin's view, then, that philosophizing is of supreme moral value may be a matter of true belief for Socrates, but since he cannot *know* that it is true, it must be viewed as at least to some degree held in a qualified way. But Socrates does not speak in this way to his jurors; he demonstrates such confidence before them that centuries of commentators have seen his words as unbridled arrogance.

A rather different problem of explaining the degree of Socrates' commitment to his mission arises for the analysis offered recently by Gregory Vlastos. Vlastos argues that Socrates may consistently claim both that he is ignorant and that he knows a number of things,

---

[98] Irwin, 40–1. See also Burnyeat (1), 384; Santas (2), 120 and 311 n. 26; Woodruff, 140.

because he finds in Socrates' discussion of knowledge and ignorance a separation of the meaning of 'know' into two different senses: what Vlastos terms 'knowledge$_c$' or knowledge construed as entailing infallible *certainty*, and knowledge$_e$' or knowledge construed as whatever can be elenctically justifiable, which involves no claim of infallibility.[99] On Vlastos's view, Socrates' ignorance is the total lack of knowledge$_c$, and his convictions are instances of knowledge$_e$. But is Socrates' conviction that his mission in Athens is worthy an example of knowledge$_e$?

As we have argued, Socrates' elenctic probings became a *mission* partly as a result of their prior practice in Socrates' attempt to uncover the meaning of the oracle, about which we have already spoken. But Socrates' claim that his mission has value has not actually at some time or times been put to the test of the *elenchos*, nor does Socrates attempt to justify its worth, in the one instance where its worth is at question—at his trial—by providing an elenctic test. That is, Socrates has not undertaken to test elenctically whether testing elenctically is worthy, and found it to pass the test. Indeed, such a procedure would have to beg all its own questions so profoundly and transparently that the degree of philosophy's value cannot even have been construed by Socrates as 'elenctically *justifiable*'; surely it is not *elenctically* justifiable, even if it is in some way justifiable. Therefore, his confidence in the value of his mission cannot derive from elenctic justification. But we know that Socrates believes that its worth is justifiable, for we know that Socrates attempts to defend its worth in the *Apology*. We also know that whatever degree of conviction one evinces must be conditioned upon the confidence one invests in the mode of inquiry by which that conviction was reached. Since, therefore, there is no trace of epistemological qualification in Socrates' defense of his mission, we can conclude that whatever brought him to his evaluation of it must be at least as potent a method of discovery as Socrates' claims in his defense betray confidence in his innocence. How, then, did Socrates assess the value of his mission?

2.6.4 DIVINATION AS A SOURCE OF CONVICTION

Commentators often ignore, or at least play down, what is admittedly one of the oddest features of Socratic philosophy: Socrates'

---

[99] Vlastos (7), esp. 18.

trust in various forms of divination as sources of truth.[100] Nevertheless, the *Apology* leaves no doubt about his certainty that his *daimonion* is something divine in nature (31c8–d1, 40b1) and that it will always warn him away from what is wrong.[101] His trust in divination is, moreover, by no means limited to his *daimonion*. His faith in the oracle that began his mission, though sorely tested by its astounding content, is evident when Socrates says of the god, 'he doubtless is not lying, for that is not appropriate (ϑέμις) for him' (21b6–7). Socrates refers again to his trust in divination while recounting his examination of the poets, whose works, he says, 'were done, not by wisdom, but by a kind of nature and inspiration, like the seers and oracle-givers; for these too say many fine things, but do not know anything of what they say' (22b9–c3).[102]

Socrates realizes that at least some of the truths resulting from divination may not be readily apparent and, thus, the particular form in which they are revealed may stand in need of interpretation (see 21b3–7). But it is equally clear that he believes that the correctness of a particular interpretation can be corroborated by other divine revelations. Thus, because he wishes to leave no doubt in the minds of the jurors that he serves the god by philosophizing, he tells them: 'I have been commanded to do this by the god, both by oracles and by dreams and in every way in which divinity had ever commanded a man to do anything' (33c4–7).[103] And, as we have seen, so strong is his certainty that he knows what the god wishes him to do that nothing could make him voluntarily abandon his service (see 29d4–5).

Two important consequences regarding the paradox with which we are concerned follow from Socrates' trust in divination. First, it is clear that it is a mistake to assume that Socrates' concern for an understanding of virtue is a concern merely for certainty about what things are virtuous. It is true that he thinks understanding is stable and cannot be refuted (*Meno* 97d6–98a8; *Euthphr.* 11b6–e1; see

---

[100] Unconvincing attempts to explain away Socrates' trust in various forms of divination may be found in M. Nussbaum (2), 234–5 and Nehamas, 305–6.

[101] See also Xen., *Mem.* 1.1.3–4, where it appears that Socrates' trust in his *daimonion* is within accepted Athenian orthodoxy. The fact that the *daimonion* may have given grounds for the charge of introducing new divinities, however, undercuts Xenophon's claim. (See Sections 1.4.4.2, 4.3.2, and 5.5.)

[102] The establishment of this claim is also the main point of Plato's *Ion*.

[103] Other passages in which Socrates refers to taking dreams seriously occur at *Cri.* 44a6–b4 and *Phd.* 60e1–61b7.

also *Grg.* 508e6–509a4) but these are only necessary conditions for understanding, conditions it shares with his confidence, derived from divinations, that he must serve the god by practicing philosophy in Athens. The divinations Socrates cited, however, provide him with certainty only about one particular sort of action: his engaging in philosophy with his fellow Athenians. The understanding of virtue that he seeks, by contrast, would enable him to understand *why* each virtuous thing is virtuous.

Secondly, the certainty of Socrates' assessment of the moral significance of his mission is logically independent of whatever beliefs he may have about the nature of virtue. As we have seen, his certainty about the moral importance of his mission is derived from various forms of divination, and not from whatever conception of virtue he has developed and continues to test by means of the *elenchos*. Thus, no specific degree of confidence about his conception of virtue is implied.

We are now in a position to see why Socrates' profession of ignorance is actually consistent with his absolute confidence that he is innocent of any wrongdoing. As we have seen, when Socrates proclaims his ignorance it is likely that he means that he lacks the understanding of what virtue is and hence cannot provide a correct general account of why something is virtuous. But since he is certain that divinations, properly construed, provide truth, and because he is certain that the god's will has been revealed to him, Socrates has what he at least considers decisive grounds to be convinced that the activities for which he has been brought to court are morally good. Thus, even though Socrates is certain that his philosophical activities are morally good, he cannot provide the account (λόγος) by which their goodness could be explained. And this he cannot do because, as he tells the court, he does not have the understanding of goodness he would need to do so.

2.6.5 A FEW FINAL REMARKS

We have argued that Socrates' philosophic method presupposes some access to pre-theoretic confidence in judging individual cases, and we have explained what is perhaps the most important instance of such confidence by showing its connection to Socrates' belief in divination. We need not suppose, however, that Socrates believes that this is the only way to gain convictions. Plainly, another would derive from the understanding of virtue he seeks; indeed, this would be the best and most comprehensive way of all. But since he believes that the method of inquiry he employs has been sanctioned by the god, to the extent that it is successful in deriving some part of a proper understanding, to that same extent Socrates can be confident in judging accordingly. The god would not sanction a deceitful instrument. This process might well explain a number of moral convictions Socrates repeats throughout Plato's early dialogues, as, for example, the virtue is like a craft,[104] or that one should never harm another or do an evil, even in retaliation for harms or evils done to oneself,[105] or even his knowledge that he is 'in truth worth nothing with respect to wisdom' (23b3–4). When Socrates has witnessed his method lead to the same conclusion in many different arguments with many different people, he begins to see that conclusion as being 'held down and bound . . . with reasons of iron and adamant' (*Grg.* 508e7–509a2), yet, because he does not yet have the comprehensive account he requires for true understanding, even when he has 'reasons of iron and adamant' he nevertheless protests in the next breath that 'as for me the story is always the same: I do not know how these things are' (ἐπεὶ ἔμοιγε ὁ αὐτὸς λόγος ἐστιν ἀεί, ὅτι ἐγὼ ταῦτα οὐκ οἶδα ὅπως ἔχει—509a4-5). Socrates can derive compelling reasons with his god-sanctioned philosophic methods; but he cannot derive the exhaustive understanding that constitutes 'divine wisdom'—in comparison with which Socrates' lacunose, incomplete, and fragmentary 'human wisdom' is 'worth little or nothing' (see *Ap.* 23a5–7; also, *Symp.* 175e2-3, *Meno* 98b3-5, *Euthyd.* 293b7-8).

---

[104] For an excellent discussion of this analogy, and many references to relevant Platonic texts, see Irwin, 24–5, 71–7, 96–7, 100–1.

[105] See *Cri.* 49b2–e4; *Grg.* 469a9 ff., esp. b8–c2 and 479c8–e9; *Rep.* I, 335b2–e5.

3

SOCRATES' DEFENSE, PART II
(24b3–30c1)

3.1 Socrates' Defense against the Formal Charges

3.1.1 THE 'LATER' ACCUSATIONS

From 24b3 to 28a4 Socrates elects to reply to the 'later' accusers by interrogating one of them, Meletus, the official[1] author of the indictment against him. This interrogation has been the source of a good deal of puzzlement, for during the interrogation Meletus seems to be ill-prepared to defend his own charges coherently. To some, this is a decisive sign that the entire interlude is largely, if not wholly, invented by Plato to discredit Socrates' prosecutors as inept and unprincipled.[2] Other readers see the interrogation as showing that neither Socrates nor Meletus takes the formal charges as the real motive for the prosecution. To Meletus and his collaborators, the formal charges, we are told, are a legal pretext for other complaints that could not themselves be brought forward legally; but these other complaints were so prejudicial that the prosecutors could rely on them to ensure a conviction on the charges they could bring. And on this view, the legal fiction involved was so evident that Socrates would not honor the formal charges with a serious refutation. Instead, he undertook in his interrogation of their nominal author merely to demonstrate to the jury that his prosecutors had shown a careless disregard for morality and

---

[1] Meletus is at least nominally the principal prosecutor of the case, but this of course does not rule out his acting on someone else's behalf. Many believe that Anytus was the real force behind the prosecution (about which see Section 1.4.3).

[2] The clearest statement of this position can be found in Hackforth (2), 104–10. Seeskin ((1), 55) dismisses the interrogation as 'not terribly important' (55). An absurd extreme of this view is argued by T. West (134–50), who assesses Socrates' arguments in this section as 'among the most ridiculous used by him anywhere in Plato' and sees this as proof that the entire interrogation is Plato's attempt at comedy writing (135).

We propose, on the contrary, to show that Socrates' arguments in the section of the *Apology* do indeed provide him with an excellent defense against Meletus' charges, even if the defense in question is only one of Plato's invention.

the law by employing such patently senseless and unsupportable charges against him.[3]

We believe, on the contrary, that both Socrates and his prosecutors viewed the formal charges as reflecting important issues to be decided by the court, even if (as we also believe) other concerns also influenced the prosecution and outcome of the case.[4] We shall argue that the three prosecutors can reasonably be assumed to have intended the official indictment to be taken as specifying serious crimes actually committed by Socrates. We shall then show why Socrates must be supposed to have taken the formal charges seriously, and why and how the arguments Socrates develops during his interrogation of Meletus are designed not merely, as other commentators have claimed, to confuse Meletus, and thus discredit him before the jury, but rather to refute the legal charges themselves by showing that they are based upon incoherent and thus indefensible prejudices.

3.1.2 THE PROSECUTION'S COMMITMENT TO THE CHARGES

Against the view that the formal charges were not taken seriously, it is worth recalling what we discussed in Section 2.3, namely, Socrates' conviction that the jury is predisposed to find him guilty because the 'first' accusers have insinuated that he is a sophist and nature-philosopher. If these 'first' accusations are believed, the formal charges against Socrates would appear at least superficially to be quite appropriate in the eyes of a contemporary Athenian. That sophists currupt young people by teaching them to disregard their elders and the laws is exactly the point of Aristophanes' *Clouds*, the one instance of a 'first' accusation Socrates explicitly cites. That sophists and nature-philosophers convince the young that the gods are dubious inventions of old-fashioned fogeys is also explicitly a part of that comedy. Since the essence of the 'first' accusations is the charge that Socrates is in some way or other a dangerous innovator against established religious beliefs and a corrupter of youth—that is, the

---

[3] See, e.g., Beckman, 60-3; Blakeney, 118; Burnet (1), 146-7, (2), 100-1, and note on 24c9; Chroust (3), 39, see also 43; A. Ferguson, 169; Guardini, 43; Shero, 110; A. E. Taylor (2), 162-3, (3), 100 and (5) 15.

[4] See Section 1.3.3. For other discussions, see also Dover (2), esp. 51-4; C. Phillipson, 157-67, 200-12. We agree that ulterior motives may have encouraged Socrates' accusers to make their charges, but we disagree with the inference often made from this view that the formal charges were not themselves seriously at issue before the court.

sense of these charges is the same as that of those lodged by the 'later' accusers[5]—these 'later' accusers have every reason to believe that their accusations will be seen as important and serious ones. And since so many jurors may be supposed to be convinced by Socrates' 'first' accusers, there is at least equal reason to suppose that some such blind prejudices may also have infected his 'later' accusers. Socrates says as much at 19b1–2 and at 23e3–24a1, where he states that the formal indictment itself derives from prejudices spawned by the 'first' accusations. Hence, there is at least this much reason to allow that the 'later' accusers may have believed their own accusations to be true.

Whatever one believes about this issue, however, it remains true that Meletus, Anytus, and Lycon managed not only to persuade a King-Archon to forward the case to a paid jury, but also to persuade a majority of the jurors to convict Socrates and sentence him to death. Of course, all these people may have ignored the formal charges. But such flagrant and widespread disregard for the letter of the law, however compatible with Plato's and Xenophon's uncharitable assessment of the honor of their fellow citizens, needs some imagination to endorse without at least some uneasiness.

Such considerations do not imply that the motives of Socrates' prosecutors were all the same, or that they would all have endorsed the formal charges, with equal vigor. In fact, as we argued in Section 1.4.3, we know so little about the prosecutors themselves that it is impossible to determine the degree to which any of them privately believed in their accusations. Their choice of accusations may have been somewhat tactical. Our argument is only that the prosecutors had good reason to select the charges they did, for they had excellent reason to suppose that such charges would be taken seriously by the jurors they had to convince. The degree to which the private motives of the prosecutors are expressed in the formal charges, however, is both impossible to determine and irrelevant. At least this much can be said, however: we have good reason to suppose that the King-Archon and the jury took the formal charges seriously as issues to be argued

[5] On the relationship between the 'first' accusations and the formal charges made by Meletus, see our paper on the formal changes (Brickhouse and Smith (3)). Another who claims there to be a close correspondence between the 'first' and the 'later' accusations against Socrates is Montuori ((5), 233–6). A. Ferguson also suggests this when he says that Meletus' interpretation of his own charges in Plato's *Ap.* betrays a commitment to the truth of the 'first' accusations (170–1).

before the court, and we have no reason to suppose that the prosecutors themselves saw things any differently, whatever other
reasons each may have had for acting as they did.

One aspect of this is often forgotten by commentators. The passage
of the amnesty of 403/2 required that individuals be charged only for
crimes (other than homicide) committed since its passage, crimes as
defined by the recently codified laws. But a puzzle arises if Anytus is
supposed not to take seriously the formal charges he supported
Meletus in bringing against Socrates: how could the man well known
for his sponsorship of the amnesty so plainly violate its spirit (if not its
actual terms), by prosecuting Socrates on grounds that could not be
legitimate according to the amnesty? Of course, people are frequently
inconsistent in their values, and in their applications of their own
most cherished beliefs. But surely some argument is needed before we
convict Anytus of this here. And it is not enough to point out that
Anytus may have had other motives in prosecuting Socrates. That
may be. Our contention is that whatever other motives Anytus may
have had, there is good reason to suppose that he also believed the
charges he supported against Socrates, and no reason to think he did
not.

3.1.3 SOCRATES' RESPONSE TO THE CHARGES

Despite the differences between scholars' opinions about the sincerity
and gravity of the charges, there is virtual unanimity in their
assessments of Socrates' interrogation of Meletus: Socrates, they say,
makes no attempt to refute the specific charges, but rather
demonstrates his own dialectical ability to 'entrap'[6] Meletus into confusion and contradiction

The initial appeal of this interpretation is evident enough. For one
thing, the discrediting of Meletus seems to be all that Socrates intends
to achieve through the interrogation: before he begins his questioning, he tells the jury only that he will show that Meletus is 'joking by
lightly involving men in a lawsuit' (24c4–6); he does not explicitly say
that he will actually refute the charges. Moreover, the interrogation
itself is unmistakably similar to the elenctic refutations Socrates has

---

[6] It is interesting to see how often this word or one of its derivatives is used in
describing the interrogation. See, e.g., Allen (1), 34, and (5), 11; Beckman, 61;
Burnet (2), notes on 24c9, 26a4, and 26d4; A. Ferguson, 170; Hackforth (2), 104;
Lofberg, 603; A. E. Taylor (3), 100.

always employed with such devastating efficiency against others who claim to be wise when they are not. Such a process is, after all, an essential part of his mission in Athens. And if the *elenchos* is taken to demonstrate only a contradiction in his opponent's assertions, and not the truth or falsity of individual propositions,[7] it is difficult to see how the interrogation could possibly result in a proof of Socrates' innocence of the formal charges.[8] Finally, if, contrary to our arguments of Section 2.4, there were other important considerations against Socrates that could not be made explicit given the amnesty of 403/2, it would not be surprising for Socrates pre-emptively to dismiss the formal charges as a purely superficial legal maneuver by showing that even their author had given them only little thought. The irony of Meletus' position would therefore be evident to all. The charges he actually prosecutes are ones for which he cares little;[9] and the charges he considers to be serious are ones he cannot prosecute.

But despite its initial plausibility, this view is not unproblematical. Socrates begins his speech by telling the jury that he is hopeful that his defense will succeed (19a2-4). Nevertheless, he is keenly aware that acquittal is possible only if he can remove the long-standing prejudice against him that has been engendered by the 'first' accusations. And the same reasoning as we applied above to the prosecutors and jurors also applies to Socrates' own response to each set of accusers. In so far as there is good reason to suppose that the prosecutors, accusers, and jury would take the charges seriously, there is equal reason to

[7] For the view that the *elenchos* demonstrates only the inconsistency of a set of propositions, see, e.g., Vlastos (1), xxvi-xxxi; Robinson, 17-8. Recently, however, Irwin (ch.3) and even Vlastos (9) have argued that individual propositions may be established. Though in our reply to Vlastos's article (Brickhouse and Smith (11)) we criticized his general account of the *elenchos*, it will at least be plain from our interpretation of this instance of a Socratic argument that we believe it intended to provide a positive proof of Socrates' innocence. Hence, we agree with Irwin and Vlastos at least this far: elenctic arguments may be used to establish the falsehood of a given proposition.

[8] It might be thought that by reducing Meletus to a state of confusion Socrates would have proven his innocence, since the prosecution would not have carried its burden of proof. But Athenian law recognized no such burden and it is unlikely that an Athenian jury would have acquitted a defendant simply on the grounds that the prosecutor had failed to provide a strong case against him, especially (as in this instance) if the jury felt it had independent grounds for finding the defendant guilty of the prosecutor's charges.

[9] It is likely that Socrates is punning on Meletus' name throughout the interrogation. The name 'Meletus' is derived from μέλειν ('to care for' or 'to be an object of care'), yet Socrates shows how little Meletus cares about a series of vital issues.

suppose that Socrates recognizes that fact. And even if he believes, as he says he does, that the 'first' accusers are the more dangerous, since the charges of each set of accusers are in essence the same, Socrates cannot sensibly take those of one set seriously and reject the others as patently absurd. Of course, Socrates may take the 'first' accusers more seriously as adversaries, despite the fact that they charge him with the same crimes as do the 'later' accusers, and this seems to be the sense of what he says in assessing the relative dangers of each. He says that he fears the 'first' more than the 'later' accusers because the former have been at it for such a long time, insinuating their calumnies to Socrates' jurors from childhood (18b5, c5-7); they are many (18c4); the case they may have made has gone without rebuttal by a defense (presumably until now) (18c7-8); they are for the most part anonymous, except for the comedy writers (18c8-d2); and, most importantly, they cannot be cross-examined (ἐλέγξαι—18d5).

But, unlike the 'first' accusers, Meletus can be cross-examined. In the cross-examination he accordingly undertakes, shall Socrates neglect this opportunity to demonstrate his innocence through cross-examination, or engage in a flashy demonstration of his ability to 'entrap' Meletus with verbal tricks? The latter strategy would be certain only to confirm in his jurors' minds the connection made by his most dangerous enemies (18b2-4) between Socrates' methods and the slick dialectical skills of the sophists. Such behavior would not only be imprudent in the extreme, it would constitute an unnecessary incitement to the jury to follow prejudice instead of law, and thus to come to a verdict that was both inappropriate and immoral. It would make little sense, then, were Socrates to dismiss the formal accusations and to use his opportunity to question Meletus only to make an ironical or rhetorical point, having already expressed his recognition of the danger posed to him by the formal accusations and his desire for his defense to be successful. Yet such verbal trickery is precisely what the established view portrays Socrates as employing in his interrogation of Meletus.

Although Socrates' initial remarks suggest that he will defend himself against both sets of accusations, his principles do not allow him to defend himself in whatever way may prove most expedient, no matter how great the danger. Unlike both the 'first' and the 'later' accusers, who have engaged in slanders and deceptions, he must tell only the truth (18a5-6, 20d5-6, 22b5-6, 28a6, 31e1, 32a8, 33c1-2).

Therefore, he would convict himself of impiety for having disobeyed the command of the god were he not to use the occasion of the trial to attempt once again to convince his fellow Athenians—especially those jurors who confuse philosophy with sophistry—that he has done no wrong in pursuing his mission.

As we said in Section 1.5.3, Socrates' principles do not allow him to say whatever happens to be true in order to promote a just decision. He cannot, for instance, employ a strategy whose sole purpose is to arouse the compassion of the jury even if what he says is true and would have the effect of preventing the jury from condemning an innocent man (see 34b7–d1). In telling the truth he must enable the jury to perform its assigned legal function. Thus, he concludes his first speech not by issuing a final emotional plea for acquittal—as was the usual practice of defendants—but rather by lecturing the jurors once again about his and their respective duties. A speaker, he says, ought to 'inform and persuade' (35c2) and 'the juror does not take his place in court to grant favors', but 'to judge these matters' (c2–3). And in order to leave no doubt about the domain of the specific judgment the jury is to make, he reminds them that the oath they have taken obliges them 'to judge with respect to the laws' (c5).[10] Socrates is thus committed to promoting the jury's performance of its proper legal function by telling the truth relevant to the question of his guilt or innocence of the charges. Given his conception of these restraints, therefore, he must attempt to 'inform and persuade them' that he had not violated the laws.

The law the jury is sworn to consider in this case is the statute proscribing impiety. In order to clarify the issues for consideration by the jury, Meletus has been required to state in the indictment the specific ways in which he is accusing Socrates of impiety.[11] And it is clear that, in Socrates' view, neither he nor the jury may carelessly disregard the formal accusations, given the importance he places on the jury's duty 'to judge with respect to the laws' and hence to judge with respect to the truth about the way in which those laws apply in this case. On the contrary, if justice is to be done, Socrates must do everything in his

---

[10] According to Demosthenes (24.149–51) the exact wording of the juror's oath is as follows: 'I will judge according to the laws and decrees of Athens, and matters about which there are no laws I will judge by the justest opinion'. We cannot, of course, be certain that precisely the same oath was administered to jurors in 399. However, Socrates' references to the oath suggest that they are very similar. For more on the oath taken by jurors, see MacDowell (2), 43–4.

[11] At the preliminary hearing before the trial; see Chapter 1, note 76.

power in the short time allotted to him to convince the jury that Meletus' accusations are false. Were he, then, simply to ignore these formal accusations in favor of an attempt only to discredit Meletus in the eyes of the jurors, he would be guilty of diverting the jurors' attention from the real issue they must determine: whether or not he has violated the laws of Athens.[12]

Of course, it might be argued that exposing Meletus' thoughtlessness and confusion goes a long way towards discrediting his accusation, and thus an *ad hominem* attack on Meletus need not be seen as requiring Socrates to abandon his own defense. But though we do not deny that the discrediting of Meletus would contribute to Socrates' defense at least in some sense, we believe that doing so cannot of itself be a goal for Socrates. For one thing, the fact that he is able to confuse Meletus in court is entirely consistent with Socrates being guilty of the charges. So long as Socrates' interrogation of Meletus involves no actual argument against the truth of the charges, therefore, it is no more than a diversion from the issue before the court. The issue is not whether Meletus can survive a clever cross-examination without becoming flustered and foolish-looking; the issue is whether or not his charges are true. If Socrates can show that Meletus is a stupid, impulsive man, that would most assuredly assist Socrates in securing acquittal. But it would do so irrelevantly, for it would have this consequence whether or not Meletus' charges were in fact true. In other words, such an *ad hominem* display would encourage the correct verdict for the wrong reasons, for it would function only by the creation of a bias against Meletus himself, and not by securing a judgment against the truth of the charges. Hence, even though the established view need not convict Socrates of abandoning his defense, it does convict him of failing to adhere to the principles he repeats throughout his speech. If Socrates seeks to demonstrate an incoherency or confusion in this part of the speech, therefore, that incoherency or confusion cannot merely be one he induces *ad hoc* in

---

[12] In addition to the above reasons, Socrates' rhetoric suggests that he intends his interrogation of Meletus to be seen as a defense against the formal charges. The expression Socrates uses to complete his interrogation of Meletus (ἱκανὰ καὶ ταῦτα —28a3) is a standard sign employed by forensic orators to mark the completion of a refutation. A similar and equally standard forensic marking expression (ἱκανὴ ἀπολογία) is used at 24b4 to mark the end of his defense against the 'first' accusers. (On the use of these expressions in forensic rhetoric, see Burnet (2), note on 28a4.)

Meletus himself. Rather, it must have its source in the actual charges to be considered by the jury.

3.1.4 SOCRATES' INTERROGATION OF MELETUS

According to Plato, before Socrates calls Meletus forward to be questioned he recalls the indictment with the charges in reverse order of the way they appear in both Diogenes Laertius' and Xenophon's accounts (see Section 1.4.4). Hence, when he takes the charges up in order, Socrates considers the corruption charge first.

Surprisingly, Socrates' two initial arguments regarding the corruption charge treat the phrase 'corrupts the youth' as if its meaning were unproblematical. The first argument (24c9–25c4) is formulated on the basis of Meletus' agreement with the proposition that 'all Athenians make the youth excellent and Socrates alone corrupts them'. Socrates immediately points out that such a claim violates the rules suggested by analogous cases, since it is plain in the case of horses and all other animals that only the one person with the appropriate understanding, namely the trainer, actually improves the animals under his care, whereas all other men injure them (25a13–b6). Moreover, if Meletus' assertion were true, it is unlikely that the youth have been harmed at all, since it is unlikely that one man could succeed in corrupting them when everyone else is acting to make them better (25b7–c1).

It is not uncommon for scholars to suggest that this argument is in some way unfair to Meletus.[13] But Socrates in no way forces Meletus to assert that he alone corrupts the young, and, in any case, the view that the great majority of Athenian citizens are good men who work to improve those around them was widely held.[14] And far from being disingenuous, Socrates' use of the analogy between the improvement of animals and the improvement of persons is a familiar one in the works of Plato (*Euthphr.* 13b9–c1; *Rep.* I 342c4) and Xenophon (*Mem.* 4.1.3-4), as is the point he seeks to make with it here, namely, that the majority of his fellow citizens are thoroughly incapable of improving anyone (see *Cri.* 47a2–48a11). Finally although this argument does not show that Socrates is innocent of the accusation, it does suc-

---

[13] See, e.g., A. E. Taylor (2), 164; T. West, 137, 144.

[14] See, e.g., Pl., *Prt.* 322d5–328d2, where Protagoras endorses the view that every citizen is capable of improving the youth by teaching them what virtue is. Of course, he also believes that some sophists provide better training, and he the best of all. The former view, but most strenuously not the latter, is averred by Anytus in the *Meno* (92e3–6).

ceed in showing that his guilt, if there is such, is at least to some degree shared by all his fellow Athenians, since the analogy indicates that they too injure the young because their attempts to improve the young are made without the understanding of how to do so. Thus, if the jury is to convict Socrates on this ground, they must convict virtually all of Athens as well.

The second argument (25c5-26a7), like the first, develops a familiar Socratic doctrine. Meletus agrees that bad men do something evil to those who are with them (25c7-8), and that no one wishes to be harmed rather than benefited (25d1-2). When Meletus subsequently claims that Socrates has corrupted the youth voluntarily, Socrates is quick to point out that this is completely unbelievable given Meletus' former admissions (25e4-6): no one would voluntarily make those around him worse, for from bad people one can only expect to receive harm and evil. Thus, either he has not corrupted the youth at all, or if he has, he has done so involuntarily. Either way, Meletus' accusation is a sham, since the law has no interest in prosecuting the innocent or those who act involuntarily (26a1-7).

The obvious ease with which Socrates derives this conclusion might well have the effect of making Meletus look foolish in the eyes of the jury. But even if some of the jurors take this argument to be no more than a bit of sophistical trickery, it does not follow that Socrates is dissembling or insincere when he asserts it. In fact, since the argument is a version of one we see elsewhere in Plato's Socratic writings,[15] there is every reason to take it here as being presented with the utmost seriousness, despite what the jurors or, for that matter, we might think of it. And although this argument, like the first, does not show that he has not actually corrupted the youth, it does show something of considerable importance regarding the accusation: corrupting his youthful followers is something Socrates would never willingly do.

Socrates says that he is convinced that he has never corrupted anyone. Because he must tell the jurors the full truth about his mission, he does not want them to think that his philosophical pursuits have ever harmed anyone, even unintentionally. For Socrates, believing philosophy to be harmful is itself impious, for it involves supposing that the god had commanded something evil (see 33c4-7 and our discussion in Section 4.3.3). In order, then, to show that the accusation of corruption is actually false, Socrates asks Meletus about the man-

[15] Related arguments are to be found in *Meno* (77b6-78b2), and *Prt.* (351b3-358d4). See also Arist., *Eth. Nic.* 1145b23-8; and Xen., *Mem.* 3.9.4-5.

ner in which he allegedly corrupts the youth and Meletus replies in such a way as to make clear that he predicates the charge of corruption upon the religious charges (26b3-7). On Meletus' own interpretation of the charges, therefore, Socrates can prove the corruption charge false by showing that the religious charges are false.[16]

In turning to these parts of the indictment, Socrates' first move is to have Meletus clarify the phrase, 'does not recognize the gods the state recognizes'. In doing so, Socrates might be supposed only to be baiting a rhetorical trap. But we must not forget that in the Athenian legal system individuals charged and prosecuted other individuals; Athens had no legal equivalent of our public prosecutor, who is duly authorized by the state to prosecute charges in the state's name. Hence, the prosecutors' interpretation of the charges is *the only* interpretation that is legally at issue before the court, and on this point Meletus must be supposed to speak officially for his fellow prosecutors no less than himself. It could not be that each of the three prosecutors had a different but equally official interpretation of the charges, each of which had to be disproved by Socrates in order for him to defend himself successfully. Of course, other interpretations of the charges might be open to the jurors as a matter of *psychological* fact, and to the extent that Socrates can anticipate this, it would be prudent for him to defend himself in such a way as to cover these as well. But it is not sensible, and certainly not legally necessary, for Socrates to have to anticipate and defend himself against any possible interpretation of the charges.

Under the circumstances, moreover, Socrates might well be puzzled by the locution 'the gods the state recognizes'; neither Athenian law nor custom prescribed the recognition of a clearly specified set of deities, even if, as we argued in Section 1.4.4.1, atheism was impermissible. But, of course, atheism was just what Meletus was charging Socrates with, and thus to make sure that both he and the jury understand the charge, Socrates asks Meletus:

Do you say that I teach that I recognize some gods to exist, and therefore I myself recognize gods to exist, and that I am not a complete atheist nor unjust in that way, but that these gods are not the ones the state recognizes, but dif-

---

[16] Strictly, to show that the corruption charge is false Socrates must show that it is false that he teaches the young not to recognize the gods the state recognizes *and* that this is the *only* way in which he corrupts the youth according to the indictment. It is clear from what follows, however, that both Meletus and Socrates are assuming the proper conjunction.

ferent ones? Is this what you accuse me of, that I recognize the different ones? Or do you say that I do not myself recognize any gods at all, and that I teach this to others? (26c1–6)

Meletus' unequivocal answer is that Socrates does not recognize any gods at all (26c7). Now the standard view of this is that Meletus has been 'entrapped' into answering as he does. But the first thing we should notice about the way this argument proceeds is that Socrates has hardly tricked Meletus into his answer. Instead, Socrates plainly lays out all the options Meletus might take, clearly offering as one of them that Socrates is not a complete atheist, only a theistic innovator. Meletus' answer, then, is in no way forced; rather, Meletus freely and eagerly contributes it.

Of course, Meletus' answer does in fact allow Socrates subsequently to derive a contradiction in the charges so conceived, and thus it might be thought that Meletus has made an unbelievable blunder that he would eagerly wish to retract if given the slightest opportunity; surely a more careful and evasive answer could have been given. But as we argued in Section 3.1.2, there is every reason to suppose that Meletus and his collaborators actually believed they could convince the jury that Socrates was an atheist. Many Athenians would have thought any number of the sophists and nature-philosophers were atheists, and in so far as they were inclined to see no important distinction between these fellows and Socrates, a charge of complete atheism would come naturally to mind. Playing upon such a presumption would not be tactically unreasonable either, even if the prosecutors themselves did not believe it. Given the long-standing suspicion that Socrates is one of these 'atheistic' nature-philosophers, a prejudice upon which the prosecution has relied so heavily in bringing Socrates to trial in the first place, Meletus and the others would lose a major advantage if they were to attempt to revise that prejudice. One could hardly expect the jury to abandon what they had believed all along and suddenly believe instead that the danger Socrates presented was actually quite unlike that posed by the stereotypical sophist or nature-philosopher, namely, complete irreligion. Had Meletus attempted to select Socrates' other option, therefore, he would be committed to showing Socrates in a very new light. The old prejudices would thus have to be abandoned, for now it would turn out that Socrates was in fact religious in some recognizable sense, even though his religious beliefs were not the customary ones. Of course, it is still possible that Meletus would be able to convince the jurors that Socrates was guilty of impiety even on these grounds, but now he would have to do so without the aid of the 'first' accusers. Understandably, Meletus seeks to avoid incurring such a loss by maintaining the stereotypical portrayal of Socrates as an atheist. We must recall, as well, that Meletus and the other prosecutors have already made their speeches, and may well have relied to some degree in them upon the very stereotype Meletus is now forced to maintain. An abrupt abandonment of it at this point would damage his credibility.

But once it is clear that the charge of 'not recognizing the gods the state recognizes' is really an accusation of atheism, Socrates can point out its implausibility. For one thing, even if this conception of the accusation were true, the youth of Athens would hardly have needed to come to Socrates to learn such a doctrine, since the books of Anaxagoras, which are filled with the very sort of views Meletus has in mind, are so easily accessible (26d6-e2). But Socrates also advances an additional argument that, he says, will show that the indictment is 'hubristic, unrestrained, and rashly conceived' (26e8-9). The first point is that anyone who believes in (again, νομίζειν—recognizes) divine matters (δαιμόνια πράγματα) of whatever sort must also believe in the existence of divinities (δαίμονες/*daimones*) in the same way: for example, anyone who believes in matters pertaining to horses must believe in the existence of horses (27b3-c10). The second point is that recognition of the existence of *daimones* requires recognition of the existence of gods (θεοί/*theoi*), since *daimones* are themselves either gods or the children of gods. The two points taken together form the premises of a hypothetical syllogism, the conclusion of which is that anyone who recognizes any sort of divinities must also believe in gods. Since the additional premiss, that Socrates recognizes some divinities, is provided by the indictment itself, the senselessness of Meletus' charge is apparent: on the one hand, Meletus accuses Socrates of not believing in any gods; but the last part of the indictment can be true only if Socrates does believe in gods.

Some have found treachery in one of the vital premises of this argument, arguing that Socrates could not really believe in *daimones* as they are conceived in the argument.[17] But though Socrates was

---

[17] Guardini, for example, proclaims that 'it is hardly to be assumed that Socrates believed seriously in "illegitimate children of the gods, either by the nymphs or other mothers . . ." ' (43). Seeskin dismisses Socrates' argument on this point as 'feeble' (84).

critical of some aspects of the religious orthodoxy of his day (see *Euthphr.* 6a6–8), in not one of the ancient sources do we find any reason to suppose that he did not hold orthodox beliefs as regards the nature of *daimones*. And even if he did not, his argument is not thereby reduced to an *ad hominem* one, as many have held,[18] for it still shows that Meletus' own indictment is internally inconsistent. In other words, nothing in the passage requires that Meletus has been tricked into admitting what he did not really mean. Rather, in relying on the prejudicial stereotypes against Socrates, Meletus trapped himself into incoherency: atheistic sophists and nature-philosophers do not believe in *new* divinities; they do not believe in divinities *at all*.

Could Meletus not have avoided such an embarrassing conclusion? Let us reconsider his options. As we said above, he could have selected the alternative Socrates offered him by saying that Socrates does recognize some gods, but not the gods of the state. That, however, would actually support Socrates' defense against the 'first accusers', for now Socrates could say, 'you see, even Meletus and his supporters do not believe I am really like the character of my name in the *Clouds*; even Meletus and his supporters realize that I am no Anaxagoras.' If Socrates is right about the relative dangers posed by the two sets of accusers, then it would be a great advantage to his defense to be able to call his current accusers as witnesses, as it were, against the more dangerous 'first accusers'. As we have noted, Meletus could have selected Socrates' other proffered interpretation of the charges, then, only by undermining the very thing most dangerous to Socrates: the well-established prejudice that he is an atheistic nature-philosopher like Anaxagoras.

What if Meletus denied the connection between *daimones* and *theoi*? If anything, this would be an even worse strategy, for now he would have to deny one of the standard religious beliefs of his day, an odd position for the prosecutor of an impiety charge to have to endorse in open court. But could Meletus not simply deny that *Socrates* accepted the traditional connection between *daimones* and *theoi*? No, for not only could Meletus not provide evidence for such a claim, but any such denial would appear implausible to the average Athenian; such distinctions were simply not made. We know of no case in which someone held sincere beliefs in *daimones* but denied the existence of

---

[18] See, e.g., Guardini, 43. A view more like ours is expressed by Burnet (2) in his notes on 26a4 and esp. 26d4.

any gods. Finally, Meletus could also not deny that Socrates' belief in *daimones* was sincere. After all, Socrates' belief in his *daimonion* was apparently well known,[19] and provided Meletus one natural ground for the charge that Socrates invented new divinities. Any attempt to say that Socrates did not really believe in the existence of his *daimonion* would be instantly rejected by anyone with sense on the jury.

But now it might appear that Socrates' arguments are so easily won that Meletus and his fellow accusers could not have failed to see them coming when they undertook to write the charges. Certainly, Meletus shows great reluctance to answer Socrates' questions in the courtroom, but this might only represent uneasiness about being interrogated by one so renowned for dialectical wizardry. It is more likely, however, that Meletus and the other accusers were simply blinded by the same prejudices upon which they relied, as Socrates says, in bringing the case before the court, prejudices deriving from the 'first accusers' (19b1-2; 23e3-4). Prejudice, as we know, does not work according to rational processes; so if the prosecutors were guilty of prejudice, then their critical faculties as regards Socrates' real character and beliefs were at their worst, and the charges they sought to bring may well have reflected that fact.

Nor can it be that the King-Archon would of necessity prevent incoherent charges from being brought to trial. If Socrates' reputation was as bad as we might suppose, there is no reason to believe that the King-Archon would not be infected with the same prejudice. It is possible that the prosecutors charged Socrates when they did (and not earlier or later) because they felt confident that the King-Archon would forward their charges without resistance or interference of any kind.[20] Anytus, after all, was a man with many powerful connections in Athens at the time.

And if this was the case, it would not even matter if one or more of the prosecutors recognized that Socrates could not both be a complete atheist and hold a sincere belief in his *daimonion*, for example. A prosecutor who realized the charges were flawed in this way might still be willing to go to court: he might make the tactical assumption that even

---

[19] Socrates tells the jury that they have heard him talk about his *daimonion* 'at many times in many places' (31c7-d2). See also *Euthphr.* 3b5-6. For other ancient references to Socrates' *daimonion* see Chapter 1, note 126.

[20] According to MacDowell ((2), 32), by 399 BC King-Archons would almost automatically forward cases to trial; the time for more active participation and judgment from this magistrate had long passed.

logically flawed charges could inflame the jury's prejudice against
Socrates, regardless of whatever incoherence Socrates might (and it
turns out does) expose in them. Whatever the prosecutors believed,
their tactics worked; for the jury, despite Socrates' refutation of
Meletus' charges, convicted Socrates anyway.

3.1.5 SOCRATES ON RELIGION AND ORTHODOXY

One final worry about Socrates' defense against the 'later' accusations must be addressed. Many readers have been struck by the
unconventional nature of Socrates' defense. They observe, rightly, that
it is open to Socrates to declare his religious beliefs and practices simply and straightforwardly, and that he nowhere does so.[21] Might this
not be because his beliefs and practices would not bear scrutiny? So it
might be argued that the reason for conviction was at least in part that
Socrates interrogation of Meletus had the effect of leaving intact in
the jurors' minds the one interpretation of the charges that does
render them consistent not only with one another, but also with
Socrates' sincere belief in his *daimonion*: Socrates does not recognize
the gods of the state, but introduces new divinities in which he sincerely believes, but that are nevertheless false and offensive to orthodox
religion. Socrates plainly does not ever explicitly refute any such interpretation of the charges; for example, not once in the *Apology* does
he ever directly assert his belief in the gods of the state *under that
description*. Moreover, though his claim to have a personal divine
guide may well have troubled many jurors, he never tries to defend its
compatibility with conventional religious belief.[22] Taking these two

---

[21] See, e.g., Seeskin (1), 90. Allen ((1), 34), Bury (3), Chroust ((3), 28), Lofberg
(602), Lord (30), and Shero ((2), 110) also convict Socrates of a dangerous degree of
religious innovation. Despite their differences on other issues, both Lofberg and
Bury (in (3)) agree that Socrates could not honestly have claimed to have orthodox
religious beliefs, though Lofberg plainly allows that Socrates is quite religious in his
own way. H. Neumann ((4), 202) and Shero ((2), 110) also claim that Socrates is tellingly
silent in regard to the charge of religious innovation, and (astonishingly) Allen ((5),
11-13) and Gontar both go so far as to say that Socrates' defense includes no real
denial or rebuttal of any of the formal charges.

[22] Xenophon argues that Socrates' belief is no novelty in *Mem.* 1.1.3-4. But the
very fact that Xenophon feels he must undertake this defense in the first place leaves
one with the sense that there might have been something in Socrates' belief that
troubled the jury after all. It is also true that when Euthyphro is told that Socrates is
being charged with impiety he immediately supposes that the charge is based on
Socrates' belief in the *daimonion* (see *Euthphr.* 3b5-6). Euthyphro's readiness to
make such an inference indicates that Socrates' belief was potentially troublesome to
those of traditional convictions. None the less, it remains true that Socrates himself

facts together with Socrates' suggestion at *Euthyphro* 6a6–8 that the motive for his prosecution is his scepticism concerning many of the generally accepted myths and characterizations of the gods, we might even suppose that he could not defend himself convincingly before the jury against this interpretation of the charges.

A number of considerations count against this supposition, however, although we do not believe thay any decisive resolution of this issue is possible. For one thing, we must recall that the interpretation of the charges in question is not the one in fact before the court, since Meletus is the authority who defines how the charges are to be interpreted, and he has defined them differently. Hence Socrates is under no legal obligation to 'inform and persuade' (35c2) the court about an allegation that he is unorthodox in his beliefs, though sincerely religious within his unorthodoxy; no such allegation has been made. Let us also remember Socrates' remarks about the influence of the 'first accusers' on his actual prosecutors. Since the interpretation of the formal charges we are considering diverges so far from the 'first' slanders, which plainly influenced Meletus, whatever scepticism Socrates may have had is for all practical purposes moot. Socrates does not consider it, on this line of reasoning, since no one else in the courtroom is likely to be concerned by it either. Moreover, what Socrates says in the *Euthyphro* is for at least a few reasons not strong evidence for the view at issue. For one thing, Socrates in the *Euthyphro* has not yet been through the preliminary hearing, and so does not yet know what the specific interpretation of the charges to be argued before the court is going to be. His speculation about the motive and meaning of the charges at 6a6–8, therefore, is not an informed one, and turns out, as what actually happens in the *Apology* would appear to show, to be incorrect. Again, since Meletus in fact put another interpretation on the charges, we have no reason to suppose that the issues Socrates raises in the *Euthyphro* were ever considered (at least explicitly) by anyone at the actual trial. Secondly, the nature of the scepticism Socrates confesses to feeling in the *Euthyphro* does not in any way entail that he disbelieves in the gods of the state. Rather, all he says is that he finds it difficult to believe

---

sees nothing wrongful or impious in his belief in his *daimonion* and gives no indication that he perceived it as being a significant concern to the jury. One who entirely accepts that Socrates' belief in his *daimonion* shows sincere religious feeling is Norvin (93). A view contrary to Norvin's is (unconvincingly) suggested by M. Nussbaum in her (2)—see esp. 234–5.

stories that would seem to degrade and diminish them. (In fact, it appears elsewhere that Socrates' views and practices are well within the range of what was normal for Athenians—see *Euthphr.* 14e11–15a2; *Euthyd.* 302b4–d6.) Finally, it is not at all obvious that the kind of doubts Socrates had about the myths would qualify as criminally impious even to the most orthodox Athenians.[23] For example, though the devout Euthyphro does believe the stories Socrates doubts, he shows no pious outrage at Socrates' scepticism, and we must suppose that what would qualify as acceptably orthodox allowed some degree of latitude.

Of course, Socrates never explicitly expresses his views about the gods in court; he never says 'I recognize Athena, my fellow Athenians, and Zeus and Apollo and all the rest of the gods you recognize.' But two things must be said about this. First, how very like Socrates it is not to affirm beliefs dogmatically for which he feels he does not have 'reasons of iron and adamant' (see *Grg.* 508e7–509a2). In a passage in the *Phaedrus* (230a1–3), in which Plato gives us no reason to believe that he is fictionalizing, Socrates says that despite whatever doubts he may have about the traditional conceptions of the gods, he accepts the customary views. The alternative to doing so, he says, would be undertaken with what he calls 'a bumpkinish sort of wisdom' (ἄγροίκῳ τινὶ σοφίᾳ—229e3), for which he has no leisure (229e4). So he does not disbelieve in the gods, as the indictment would have it, but neither does he affirm a dogmatic belief in them, for both would involve 'the most disgraceful form of ignorance' (*Ap.* 29b1–2), which Socrates defines as behaving as if one knows what one does not know. Socrates is thus not hiding anything in his lack of aggressive affirmation; he is showing the very sort of epistemological modesty he wishes to induce in others. Acceptance of the customary views about the gods of the state is all that is required for Socrates to be innocent of the charges against him. Sheer

---

[23] Tate has argued that Socrates' scepticism about the myths was the sense of the first of the three formal charges ((3), 144–5). This may be true, but his claim elsewhere (in Tate (5))—that even though it was not the actual specification of any of the formal charges, his disbelief might reasonably be supposed to have got him into trouble in Athens—seems less certain. Except for Socrates' casual speculation at *Euthphr.* 6a6–8, there is not the slightest sign that his doubts about the old myths ever actually caused concern. When he expresses a kindred scepticism at *Phdr.* 229c6–e4, it is in response to Phaedrus' own questioning, and is prefaced by the observation that such scepticism is not uncommon (229c6–7). Other arguments follow. A view similar to ours is expressed by Burnet (2), note on *Euthphr.* 6a8.

dogmatism is not. We should accordingly not expect the latter of him, especially since such would involve a violation of the very sort he exhorts his fellows to avoid.

Secondly, his acceptance of customary religious belief is in fact strongly suggested by various things Socrates does say. For example, he is likely to have left the strongest possible impression on the jury when he says to Meletus, 'O astonishing Meletus, why do you say this? Do I believe that neither the sun nor the moon are gods, as other men do?' When Meletus says that he does not, affirming instead that Socrates believes the sun is a stone and the moon, earth, Socrates asks him if he thinks he is prosecuting Anaxagoras, whose relevant views, Socrates adds, are quite absurd (26d1–e2). Now it is true that Socrates nowhere says that he *does* believe that the sun and moon are gods, but the impression that he does is such a strong rhetorical consequence of his attack on Meletus that supposing he does not accept the divinity of the sun and moon is to convict him of deliberately misleading the jury.[24] Similarly, at the end of his defense speech, he says that if he were to move the jury to make the right decision in the wrong ways he would convict himself of the charge of disbelief in the gods (35d2–5). He concludes

but this is far from how it is; for I do recognize them, men of Athens, as none of my accusers do ... (35d5–7).

Socrates does not merely say, 'I do recognize them,' and leave it at that; he says that he recognizes them as none of his accusers do. But again, the rhetorical effect of what he says on the jury will be that of an affirmation. Were this effect misleading, his concern to tell only the truth would to that degree be vitiated.

In this way, then, we believe that Socrates is indeed innocent of the charges against him, even if we construe them in a way Meletus did not. As we have argued, though there may be aspects of customary religious belief that appear to him to be problematical, nothing in what Socrates says is reason to doubt his general acceptance of it, and a number of things he says strongly suggest a general acceptance. If he did not accept customary religion, his leaving the impression that he did would cause him to run afoul of his mission; and there is no compelling reason to suppose that he did not accept it. Thus, although

---

[24] Notopoulos and B. Jackson (17) are convinced that Socrates sincerely believes in the divinity of the sun and moon. Adkins, however, is convinced that Socrates could not be serious in suggesting that he believes any such thing ((2), 231).

some find Socrates' failure to make a more direct affirmation telling, we see only that, from Socrates' point of view, he has given the jury ample evidence that the charge against him is false.

3.1.6 SUMMARY AND CONCLUSION

Our arguments should not be taken as saying that the interrogation provides Socrates' only defense—or even the principal part of it—for that is far from true. As Socrates himself says, the 'first' accusations have always been the most dangerous, and whatever the jury may think of it, it is plain that Socrates believes that his philosophical activity in Athens is an expression of the highest sort of piety, as an 'assistance' (23b7), 'obedience' (29d3), and 'service' (30a7) to the god. His interrogation of Meletus is not merely a defensive diversion from Socrates' refutation of the charges against him, but rather advances substantive grounds for his innocence.

We have argued that the charges against Socrates are intended to be taken seriously, and that Socrates' interrogation of Meletus addresses the formal charges directly in an attempt to convince the jury that these charges have no merit. Such an approach, we believe, is required by the principles Socrates refers to in his speech. But these principles also require that he make clear Meletus' ignorance and lack of concern for matters of the greatest importance. It is testimony to Socrates' consummate philosophical skill that he accomplished both goals with such precision and economy of argument, for by questioning Meletus directly he demonstrates that not even his most fanatical enemy can coherently believe that Socrates is guilty of the charges in the indictment.

3.2 What Socrates Does Know

3.2.1 'THIS I DO KNOW'

At the conclusion of his interrogation of Meletus, Socrates repeats his conviction that it will not be the indictment of Meletus, but rather the prejudice caused by the 'first' accusations that will lead to his condemnation (28a4–b2). He then imagines the jury asking him why, if he realizes so clearly the troubles his mission has led him into, he continues to pursue it. 'Are you not ashamed, Socrates,' he imagines his jurors asking, 'at having committed yourself to such pursuits that have now put you in danger of being executed?' (28b3–5). Socrates' reply shows how deeply committed he is to his mission:

You do not speak well, sir, if you suppose that a man who is of even a little worth should take into consideration the risk of life or death, and not instead consider when he acts only whether he does just or unjust things, and the acts of a good or bad man. (28b5–9)

He goes on to say how the same sentiment could be found in Achilles' disregard for his life when avenging the death of Patroclus (28b9–d5), and he reminds the jury that in his own military career he followed orders, as was proper, despite the risks of doing so (28d10–e4). But how much more important, he asks, is it for him to remain at the 'post' the god assigned him, and not abandon it for fear of death (28e4–29a1)? Such behavior would make him guilty of the charge he now faces, for by abandoning the mission they had assigned to him and by disbelieving their message (that 'human wisdom is worth little or nothing'—23a6–7) and thinking instead that he is wise when he is not, Socrates would show disbelief in the gods.

For all anyone knows death might even be the greatest of goods to man, but people fear it as if they knew it was the greatest of evils. But is not this the most disgraceful ignorance, supposing one knows what one does not know? I, gentlemen, perhaps differ in this matter, too, from other men, and if I were to say that I am wiser than they, it would be in this, that not knowing very much about what is in Hades, I do not think I know. *But I do know that to do what is unjust and to disobey one's superior, either god or man, is evil and shameful. I will never fear or flee from things that for all I know might be good, in favor of things that are evil, that I know are evil.* (29a6–b9)

The heart of Socrates' defense against the 'first' accusations is that he knows only the extent of his own ignorance, and thus has no 'wisdom' to profess about natural phenomena, rhetoric, or religion. In the passages just quoted, he allows once again that he is wiser than others in these things only because he does not think he knows about the afterlife. But something new seems to have crept in: whereas before he said that he was aware of having no wisdom, great or small (21b4–5), he now tells us that he does in fact know one thing, namely, that one ought never to disobey one's superior, and he suggests strongly that he knows a number of other things to be evil, as well. How does Socrates know these things?

3.2.2 MODES OF KNOWLEDGE

We argued in Section 2.6 that Socrates' belief in divination allowed him to make some claims of knowledge without violating his confession of ignorance. In fact, we believe that it was by divination that Socrates acquired his utter confidence in the value of his mission in Athens. No such warrant, however, is offered for his claims of knowledge at 29a6–b9; indeed, no warrant is offered for them at all. Three preliminary points are worth making on this. First, nothing rules out the possibility that these knowledge-claims were also derived from some divination or other. Although it seems unlikely that Socrates could have derived such substantive and general convictions from his *daimonion*,[25] nothing in this passage rules out the possibility that Socrates learned these things 'by oracles and by dreams and in every way in which divinity has ever commanded a man to do anything' (*Ap.* 33c5–7). Socrates' silence on the foundation of his claims to knowledge counts no more against their being grounded in divination than for it. Secondly, these convictions are not at issue in the *Apology*; the one explicitly stated (that one ought not to disobey one's superiors) would in fact almost certainly be accepted as uncontroversial by Socrates' jurors. Hence, Socrates might quite rightly feel no need to show the warrants for such convictions to those he addresses, however interested we might be on other grounds to discover them. His confidence in the moral value of his philosophic mission, however, which we argued was derived from divination, is precisely what is at stake in his trial. Thus, his specific demonstration of its grounding (in divination) is an essential ingredient of his defense. Finally, there is special reason for Socrates to stress his reliance on divine guidance, since he is defending himself against a charge of irreligion, and it is an especially effective rebuttal to this to argue, as he does, that the very activities in which people saw disrespect for religion were actually undertaken in obedience to a divine command. Although he may not obfuscate and conceal material information from the jury, there is reason to see the special emphasis Socrates puts on divination in the *Apology* as warranted by the trial setting. Other grounds for his convictions, especially if they are not of direct relevance to his defense, may without blame be de-emphasized or even omitted

---

[25] According to Plato, the *daimonion* only warned Socrates to refrain from actions; it never told him to perform them (31d2–4). (See Section 5.5, below.)

altogether (provided, or course, that there is no risk of misleading the jury by doing so).

But despite these reservations, it is natural for a philosophical reader to want to consider how Socrates might have come to the things he claims to know at 29a6-b9, and whether, given his confession of ignorance, he can even do so coherently, and since there is no particular reason to see divination as directly involved in this case it would be worth our while to consider other options. Of course, one option is simply to dismiss the claim as actually a claim to *knowledge*, on the grounds that it would appear to conflict with Socrates' claims of ignorance.[26] But Socrates says he knows, and as we have said, his confidence in this case is not utterly unique.[27]

Another option is offered by Gregory Vlastos, who interprets Socrates' claim only as a claim to having elenctic justification for what he says.[28] Something like this, it seems to us, is probably what is at work here, though there are a few restrictions we should like to put on the account. First, any knowledge-claim Socrates is prepared to make which is based upon his 'refutations' of his interlocutors will require a complex justification indeed. After all, Socrates' *elenchos* constructs arguments merely from his interlocutors' responses to Socrates' questions. Although in each case the conclusion reached always expresses the negation of some claim the interlocutor had made which Socrates had put under examination, and although his interlocutors invariably abandon the contested claims at the end of the examination, it is nevertheless unclear how Socrates could think that anything more than the *inconsistency* of his interlocutors' beliefs has been demonstrated. Nothing in the *elenchos*, taken by itself, would ever justify a knowledge-claim that the conclusion of a specific *elenchos* is true and its negation, the interlocutor's intial claim contested in the *elenchos*, is false.

Vlastos realizes this, and proposes two principles by which Socrates may be assured of deriving true conclusions:

[26] This would have to be the response of Irwin, who says that Socrates may only make claims of true belief, but never knowledge (see 39–42).

[27] Compare Irwin's remarks on this passage (58). Even Vlastos ((7), 7) claims that this passage is the only instance in which Socrates claims moral knowledge, but in fact there is at least one other in the *Ap.* itself: at 37b5-9, Socrates claims to know that a variety of punishments he might suggest to the jury are evil. It is also clear that Socrates claims to know that he is 'in truth worth nothing with respect to wisdom' (23b3-4).

[28] Vlastos (7), esp. 7, 18–20. A view somewhat similar to Vlastos's is expressed by Burge.

(A) Anyone who ever has a false moral belief will always have at the same time true beliefs entailing its negation.

(B) The set of moral beliefs held by Socrates at any given time is consistent.[29]

Given these two assumptions, Vlastos concludes that Socrates may be assured of the truth of his own moral beliefs. We have argued against this view elsewhere, however,[30] and see no particular value in reproducing those arguments again here. Suffice it to say that we find both assumptions far too strong for the Socrates of Plato's early dialogues, whose philosophic modesty leads him to proclaim his own ignorance more often than any other single belief he holds true.

Vlastos's error, we believe, it not merely in the strength of the principles (A) and (B) but also in assuming that Socrates regards the conclusion of *each* elenctic argument to have been proven true and hence that the interlocutor's initial moral claim has been proven false. We believe that Socrates finds moral significance in the demonstration of the *inconsistency* of his interlocutors' beliefs, together with *their* willingness to abandon the position under scrutiny, once the inconsistency has been pointed out, rather than any of their other beliefs making up the inconsistent set. When an *elenchos* is completed and an interlocutor abandons his initial moral claim, the interlocutor shows that, upon reflection, he, the interlocutor, finds the claim unworthy of belief. Through further examinations, Socrates finds that others, too, who make that same claim invariably end up in inconsistency, and subsequently abandon the controversial claim rather than their other beliefs. From these examinations, he comes to be in a position to infer inductively that no one can maintain that claim consistently with their other beliefs, beliefs which, as we have said, his interlocutors would invariably preserve over the contested claim, once they were forced to choose between them. For Socrates, a fully good life requires that one's conceptions of how to live be coherent, since one follows one's conceptions in living one's life. If one's conceptions are inconsistent, one will not consistently pursue the good in one's life. So, after sufficiently numerous examinations of various people, Socrates would come to have good reason to believe that anyone who sincerely makes the now-suspect claim will not be on the path to a fully good life. If we

[29] Vlastos (9), esp. 52, 55.
[30] See Brickhouse and Smith (11). On the basis of our criticisms, Vlastos now argues for a 'scaled down' version of these principles (see Vlastos (7), 18–19 n. 44).

are right, when Socrates claims 'to know' that one must obey one's superiors at *Apology* 29b6-7, he is only professing confidence in what, as the result of numerous elenctic tests he has found to be justified—elenctic testing has shown that those who reject such a belief have incoherent conceptions of how to live. Thus, if one is to have a coherent view of the good life one must believe that one must never disobey one's superiors.

Moreover, Socrates has what he takes to be additional, independent reason to think that his method of elenctic examination will lead to morally important results. His mission to have people examine their lives has been ordained by the god himself. Since the god is truly wise (23a5-6), and, most of all, is concerned for men (31a6-7; see also 41d2), he would not send Socrates on a fruitless mission. The results of this mission, if only people will attend to them, are crucial if men are ever to learn how best to live; they must examine themselves and others, root out the inconsistencies among their beliefs, and abandon those beliefs that, upon reflection, they themselves find implausible. Because it has been divinely ordained, Socrates believes that this method will never lead him, or his fellow Athenians, astray.

But lest we be taken to make Socrates run afoul of his professions of ignorance, let us draw out all the restrictions on this method of obtaining knowledge, and show why achieving a number of instances of such knowledge will still leave Socrates in a state he would unflinchingly and quite sincerely describe as ignorance.

3.2.3 WHAT SOCRATES DOES NOT KNOW

The first thing to notice about the elenctic warrants for knowledge-claims, even if, as we believe, Socrates supposed that he had divine assurance about the value of such warrants, is that by their very nature such warrants do not achieve certainty. Elenctic warrants are inductive, built up over many elenctic conversations. The god's wish for Socrates only certifies the moral uprightness of his mission, a lifetime of examining himself and others. It does not certify the truth of the conclusions of each elenctic argument Socrates attempts. Although Socrates is confident that employing the *elenchos* on all who will submit to his questions is a good thing, he cannot be certain that each of the beliefs he inductively generates are truly necessary for living the good life. On our view, Socrates had reason to think that anyone who believes that one may disobey his superior will never lead the good life; but he cannot be certain that he will never meet someone who believes the opposite and for whom—as far as Socrates will be able to ascertain—there is no inconsistency between the belief that superiors may be disobeyed and that individual's other beliefs. Although Socrates has never found such a person, even the divine sanction on his mission affords no guarantee that such a person does not exist.

Another problem with elenctic warrants is that they would never provide the exhaustive degree of applicability Socrates requires for the sort of wisdom he claims to lack. If the proposition that is to be warranted by elenctic trials is general in scope, as, for example, his claim at 29b6-7 that it is always wrong to disobey a superior appears to be, it may eventually be employed as a premiss in deliberations about how to act in particular instances. But Socrates plainly shows that he has confidence in only a few of the many general propositions he would need to know to become truly wise. In the case in question at *Apology* 29b6-7, Socrates can apply his knowledge of good and evil only if he knows who his superiors are and has clear orders from them, so he can recognize confidently what disobeying them would amount to. This is easy enough to do in war, where one's superiors are the officers invested with the legal authority to issue orders. It is not nearly so clear in one's private life, and it is even less so in politics, where there exist laws of due process, but where the law-makers themselves have to determine what laws to pass by due process. For the most important question of all, 'How should I live?' this instance of Socratic knowledge, then, is truly 'worth little or nothing'. Similar problems beset any other general rules or principles of morality Socrates can support with 'reasons of iron and adamant': though they are not without value, they are too few to generate a system of principles by which the most important questions could be answered with any confidence.[31]

If the proposition in question were particular (say 'Socrates should not escape from prison'), its survival through elenctic tests at most assures the morality of the particular act in question and no more. If Socrates managed to test some particular proposition with the necessary repetition and diligence, he could gain increasing confidence that the act in question, precisely as it is described in the tested proposition, had the value attached to it in the tested proposition.

---

[31] For a discussion of this, see Vlastos (7), esp. 19-21, and Kraut (3), 270-4.

Thus, Socrates could gain increasing confidence, for example, that his escaping from prison would be wrong, *given* all of the considerations brought to bear in the elenctic tests by which he considered the value of escape. If the tests he performs in the *Crito* are typical, the considerations that must be assumed in elenctic tests will be quite numerous and complex (such as: being born and raised in the city in question; demonstrating his satisfaction with the city in so many ways; having a legal structure according to which an argument from just agreements even makes sense, perhaps including, for example, the test for citizenship (δοκιμασία), and so forth[32]). Socrates' elenctic product is thus heavily qualified by conditions, the removal of any one of which creates the need for a new battery of elenctic tests.

In fact, in all of Plato's early dialogues, we find not one instance of any such particular and specific proposition to have enough elenctic warrant to permit Socrates to claim what Vlastos calls 'elenctic knowledge' concerning it. Certainly the example cited above, that he should not escape from prison, does not qualify: Socrates has but one conversation with Crito on the topic, and though much of Socrates' argument in this conversation is the product of frequent and elaborate tests in other contexts, some of the considerations that are brought to bear are unique to that dialogue. Of course, Socrates dies peacefully, untroubled by second thoughts, but he has other reasons for this beyond the conversation with Crito, at least one of which involves, again, a form of divination: in a passage about which we shall have much to say in Chapter 5 (*Ap.* 40a2–c3), Socrates says that the silence of his *daimonion* provides him with a 'great proof' that the death he has been condemned to is no evil thing. In any case, one does not need the full certainty of divine wisdom to follow a certain path of action with (at least qualified) confidence; belief buttressed by strong warrants and no contrary indications is quite enough.

There are, of course, particular claims that we believe Socrates would make with utter conviction: his claim to have a mission in Athens is one example; his claim at 40a2–c3 that his death will be no evil for him might be another. But we find no particular claim for the truth of which Socrates appears prepared to argue (to the degree required for conviction) that cannot be traced back to some source in divination. Numerous particular claims are made in the early

---

[32] For the complexity and detail of all these considerations, see Kraut (3), esp. ch. 4–6, 91–193. On the specific relevance of δοκιμασία, see 154–7.

dialogues that Socrates assumes with no sign of hesitation, namely, all
the examples he and his interlocutors employ in their searches for
definitions and their contests over general rules of conduct. Socrates'
very method requires there to be some particular examples that are
held as unobjectionable by his interlocutor, or the process of working
the *elenchos* could never begin. But this does not mean that such examples themselves are held as elenctically warranted. Nor is it likely
that all of them are held to be certain because of some revelation or
other in divination. Perhaps all that can be said in their defense is that
they are preconditions of the method Socrates believes he has divine
sanction in employing; so Socrates believes that a sufficient *stock* of
uncontroversial (*and veridical*) examples can be found to fuel the
method that requires their use. If a specific example is not accepted
immediately for the sake of argument, it may be replaced by another.
But though the general sense provided by the *stock* of examples may
be assured (otherwise, how could the god sanction the method?), the
same assurance need not extend to each individual member of that
stock of examples. To discern in this more specific way the value of
the individual example, one would have either to find support in
divination for the example in question, or else to engage in a series or
arguments like that of the *Crito*, to test the example in question elenctically. But those arguments would involve the employment of general
principles much like those Socrates and his interlocutors sought to test
by using examples such as the one now under scrutiny. This is why
Socrates is convinced that we need the principles and definitions that
will give us the *logos*, the account in virtue of which one achieves true
understanding. Without this *logos*, we will not have recourse to the
premises necessary to deliberate confidently and correctly about the
individual actions and decisions that constitute our lives. So it is that
with the sole exception of the *Crito* we never see Socrates arguing for
or against a particular course of action in the early dialogues. In fact,
in circumstances where such a particular proposition begs to be
scrutinized (such as whether or not Euthyphro should prosecute his
father), Socrates deflects the conversation into a discussion of general
principles.

   This, we believe, tells us something quite important about Socrates'
confession of ignorance: for all he may claim to know, we almost never
find Socrates directly defending or criticizing specific moral actions
other than those that can be settled by an appeal to divination. As we
have said, the only instances of particular actions he under-

takes to defend as moral in the early dialogues are in one way or another assured by divination (whether or not his actual defenses appeal to divination in their premisses[33]). It is in the very nature of morality, however, to guide our lives and daily actions. Socrates' relentless search for the principles of morality, together with his utter reluctance to proselytize and his paucity of dogmas, demonstrates more eloquently than the most elaborate defense he could offer in words the degree to which his confession of ignorance is sincere.

When Socrates confidently claims knowledge at 29b6-7, therefore, there is too much missing from his claim to create conflict with the ignorance he professes throughout the dialogues. Perhaps the knowledge he claims in this passage derives from divination; but perhaps it derives instead from diligent elenctic testing, a process divinely guaranteed to provide dependable results. None the less, what Socrates has come to know in either way provides an inadequate basis for deliberation and judgment in the most important decisions one must make in life, leaving him without the relevant moral skills. And since his epistemic position is nevertheless unexcelled, according to the god, it follows that 'human wisdom is worth little or nothing' and no man is wiser than he who has come to the realization that he is 'like Socrates, truly worthless in regards to wisdom' (23b1-4).

3.3 Socrates and Civil Disobedience

3.3.1 THE 'CONTRADICTION' BETWEEN THE *APOLOGY* AND THE *CRITO*

To emphasize the strength of his commitment always to obey his superior, the god, Socrates tells the jury:

Men of Athens, I hold you in high regard and I love you, but I will obey the god more than you, and just as long as I breathe and am able, I will never cease from philosophizing or from exhorting you and from declaring my views to any of you I should ever happen upon. . . (29d3-6).

Commentators have often pointed to this passage as a star example of Socrates' arrogant defiance of the jury's power to convict him and put him to death. But as we have already argued, Socrates' principles

---

[33] As we said, the arguments of the *Crito* may not be the sole ground for Socrates' peaceful resolve to remain in prison, given *Ap.* 40a2-c3.

do not allow him to seek acquittal by any means at all. Rather, he must urge the jury to decide the case according to the truth and, thus, he must tell them the full truth about why he has undertaken his 'mission on behalf of the god', and hence why he cannot abandon his commitment to philosophizing.

Socrates' assertion at 29d3–6 has troubled commentators for still another reason; for it seems to affirm at least a willingness to defy a legally constituted authority, the jury. Yet in the *Crito* Socrates seems to argue that one ought never to disobey the law, or any legal power or body. The strongest such obligation not to engage in such disobedience is suggested at *Crito* 51b5–c1 where Socrates says of the state:

> if it commands you to be flogged or imprisoned, or if it sends you to war to be wounded or killed, you must do it, and this is just, and you must not give in or retreat or desert this post, but in war and in court and everywhere you must do whatever your state and father land commands, or persuade it as to what is naturally just.

Critics have been led, by comparing such passages as these, to argue that there is a contradiction in Socrates' view of the moral acceptability of civil disobedience.[34] Others have urged that this shows Socrates' arguments with Crito to be intended less as philosophically decisive than as rhetorically adequate to persuade Crito himself.[35] Still others have sought to defend the consistency and sincerity of Socrates' arguments by providing a variety of interpretations of the problematic arguments that either weaken their apparent conclusions or recast their focus.[36] Though we are sympathetic with the motives of this last group, we believe the issue itself is a creature of modern scholarship. That is, we believe that a sizeable number of quite substantive but historically inaccurate assumptions are needed to motivate the issue. Thus, though we believe that a number of the solutions offered to this 'problem' are philosophically worthy,[37] we do not

[34] See e.g., James; R. Martin.; Momeyer; Stephens; Zinn.

[35] See, e.g., Congleton; Rosen; Young. Grote ((2), ch.8) holds that the positions regarding obedience to the law found in *Ap.* and *Cri.* are inconsistent, but attempts to explain the inconsistency by arguing that the *Ap.* is a faithful account of the speech Socrates actually gave at his trial, whereas the *Cri.* represents Plato's attempt to portray his master in a far more favorable light by writing an imaginary discussion between Socrates and Crito in which Socrates defends the prerogatives of the state. A position similar to that of Grote is found in Dybikowski (2).

[36] See, e.g., Allen (2) and (3); Kraut (2) and (3); Santas (2), 54–6; Vlastos (8); Wade; Woozley (1), esp. 44–6, and (2).

[37] See, especially, Richard Kraut's ingenious and compelling interpretation of the

find the problem itself to be an authentic one. In our discussion of these passages, then, we shall not attempt specifically to evaluate any of the many interpretations that have been offered on this issue, but rather to focus attention upon the actual context of Socrates' remarks in the *Apology* and the effect of this context on the issue of consistency in Socrates' outlook. If we are right, the effect is that even the strongest possible reading of Socrates' professed commitment to the law, that is, the reading most likely to generate conflict with Socrates' vow in the *Apology*, does not in fact generate such conflict, once the context of that vow is understood.

3.3.2 THE *APOLOGY* ON LEGALITY AND AUTHORITY

The question we must ask is whether or not in the *Apology* Socrates expresses a preparedness to defy legal authority, and thus his own proscriptions in the *Crito*. But his moral commitment to legal obedience is not unique to the *Crito*, for the *Apology* as well offers ample testimony to Socrates' belief that obedience to the law is a matter of moral obligation. It is important to recognize that the same Socrates who hypothetically vows to disobey his jury at 29d3–4 also said only moments before that a man must never leave the post he is assigned by his commander (28d6–10), and who says that he *knows* it is wrong to disobey one's superior, god *or man* (29b6–7).[38] He is also the same man who offers his defense (at least partly) because 'the law must be obeyed' (19a6), who exhorts his adversary in the name of the law (25d2–3), who makes at least some suggestion of a claim to being 'one who obstructs many unjust and illegal things from coming to be in the state' (31e3–4), who reminds his jurors of the grave risks he has taken to uphold the law (32b1–c4), and who even lectures the jury itself on

'persuade or obey' doctrine Socrates announces in the *Crito* (in Kraut's (3), 5–190, esp. ch. 3, 54–90). But though we appreciate Kraut's ultimate interpretation as philosophically worthy, we remain unconvinced that it accurately represents Socrates' view. At *Crito* 50e4–51b3 Socrates likens his own relationship to the laws to those of a child to his father or a slave to his master. If Kraut is right about the 'persuade or obey' doctrine, it follows that Socrates also thought that children or slaves who made sincere (however childish or slavish) attempts to persuade their fathers or masters, respectively, could then properly disobey them if their attempts failed. We find this implausible, precisely because it requires that what Socrates offers as models for the citizen's duty to the law be conceived by Socrates in ways that neither Crito nor any of Plato's original readers would accept without argument. For another discussion of these comparisons, with similar conclusions, see Panagiotou (1), 44–5.

[38] See Kraut (3), 23, n. 38; Santas (2), 33–40; Woozley (1), 49.

what their legal responsibilities are (35b9–c5). To generate the alleged contradiction, then, we need to employ the *Crito* only as a guide to interpreting the commitments to the law and legal authority Socrates affirms repeatedly in the *Apology* itself. It should be clear from the frequency and coherence of such affirmations that those who believe that a contradiction in Socrates' attitude towards the law is generated by his vow at 29d3–4 require an interpretation of that vow that puts it at odds with Socrates' many professions of his respect for the law in the *Apology* itself.

The many references to the law and one's responsibility to it in the *Apology* deserve comment. Those that appear after Socrates' vow at 29d3–4 we shall discuss in Chapter 4. But it would be worthwhile, in our attempt to understand the context of Socrates' vow, to look more carefully at what he says at 28d6–10 and 29b6–7, where Socrates says that one ought always to obey one's superiors. One thing to notice about each of these passages is what they do *not* contain, a lack shared by each of Socrates' remarks about the obligation of obedience to the law in the *Apology*: only in the *Crito* does Socrates add that the appropriate responses to the demands of law include persuasion (see 51b3; c1; e4; e6–7; 52a2); in the *Apology* we hear only about obedience. Arguments that attempt to reconcile the two dialogues by relying upon some conception of how persuading the laws permits just disobedience[39] thus begin with a problem: if the option of persuasion is so vital to Socrates' philosophy on this issue, why does it only appear in the *Crito*, and even there have each of its appearances occur within the brief space of 33 lines of text? Though we are disinclined to dismiss the claims Socrates makes in these lines as insincere, we are led to believe that the philosophy expressed in them alone could not have comprised anything like Socrates' most basic view of the relationship between morality and law. Instead, we are inclined to see Socrates there as considering for that one time the question as to whether anything other than obedience to the law might be moral. If this is true, it follows that nothing like the alternative of persuasion was on Socrates' mind as he made his infamous vow of disobedience before the jury at *Apology* 29d3–4, and thus anything involving the moral permissibility of persuasion cannot be cited as an element in the explanation of Socrates' vow.

When Socrates tells us of his commitments at 28d6–10 and 29b6–7,

---

[39] E.g. those of Kraut (3) and Woozley (1).

then, we are simply told that he believes one must obey legal authority. But, as Kraut rightly points out,[40] neither passage raises the issue
of what the citizen's moral obligation would be if the orders he had
received were unjust. This is what would be needed to generate the
contradiction, for unless the law asks him to do something wrong,
there is no reason to suppose that Socrates would believe anything but
simple obedience was appropriate. But Socrates' silence about the
justice of one's orders at 28d6-10 and 29b6-7 plainly cannot be taken
as evidence for the view that he merely assumes in these passages that
what the authority in question orders is just. The first of these two
passages does suggest that the issue of wrong is foremost in Socrates'
mind, for he says that in one's actions one should take into account
nothing more than avoiding doing what is disgraceful. Presumably,
then, the legal status of the order is not so much to be taken into account as whether or not disobeying it would be disgraceful. But
'nothing more' does not mean 'nothing *at all*'; that is, it does not imply
that there are *no* other considerations that apply, only that no other
considerations could outweigh the moral ones. Thus, one might suppose that there are various levels of priority within Socrates' moral
beliefs, according to which conflicts between the dictates of his
various principles might be adjudicated.[41]

But the second of our two passages strongly suggests an exceptionless requirement of obedience: Socrates flatly states that he knows
that disobeying his superior is wrong. So the issue here is what
Socrates would count as a superior, 'whether god or man', and plainly only the latter of the two candidates for superiority raises questions. The superiority of the gods over man is, we may suppose, both
universal and absolute. But what makes one man another's superior
in the relevant sense?

The only examples we are given are military: Socrates compares the
commands given him by the god with those made by his officers at
Potidaia, Amphipolis, and Delion (28d10-29a1). Now Kraut and
Woozley[42] seek to establish a broadly moral conception of the relevant superiority. Socrates, on their view, is saying that it is wrong to
disobey anyone morally superior to oneself. This strikes us, however,

---

[40] Kraut (3), 23, n. 38.

[41] See, e.g., Santas (2), esp. at 38-40. A similar view is expressed by Mulgan.

[42] Kraut (3), 23, n. 38; Woozley (1), 49. See also Nehamas, who denies that the
issue is whether or not one must *obey* one's superiors, but who also construes the
conception of 'superior' in this passage as restricted to one having *moral* superiority.

as a most bizarre and unlikely way to read what Socrates says at
29b6-7. If that were what Socrates meant, his actions at Potidaia,
Amphipolis, and Delion would very likely not be cases in point, for
though the men he obeyed were superior in military rank to Socrates,
there is every reason to suppose that Socrates would have found them
wanting in virtue, relative to himself. After all, he is the god's own gift
to Athens (30d7-e1), deserving of the greatest civic rewards Athens
has to offer (36b5-37a1). Instead, it seems plain to us that what
Socrates means to say is simply that one ought not to disobey one's
duly constituted superiors. This does, of course, strongly suggest the
utterly authoritarian political philosophy Kraut and others hope to
escape. But, again, it is only a suggestion; for Socrates does not consider instances in which one's military superiors' orders are unjust, or
even whether or not such orders could be unjust. That the question
occurs almost instinctively to us does not require Socrates to have it in
mind as he utters these words.

3.3.3 CONDITIONS FOR CONTRADICTION

Socrates' vow at *Apology* 29d3-4 is not the only instance in the
Apology in which he appears defiant of authority. At 32a9-c4
Socrates reminds the jury of the time when he alone opposed the plan
to try *en bloc* the delinquent generals after the battle of Arginousai.
We shall review this case in Chapter 4, but it may suffice for now to
note that Socrates' defiance in this case causes no problem of contradiction because it was at least his view of the matter that in resisting
the trial of the generals he was *upholding* Athenian law against the
Athenians themselves. At 32c4-e1, Socrates recalls the time when the
government of the so-called 'Thirty Tyrants' directed him to arrest
Leon of Salamis and bring him in for execution. Socrates disobeyed.
Though we shall have a great deal more to say about this in Chapter 4,
few have seen Socrates' disobedience to the Thirty as grounds for conflict[43] presumably because the allegiance Socrates argues is owed to
the state is never suggested by any of his arguments to extend beyond
the democratic regime.[44]

　　These cases provide at least some tentative grounds for deciding

---

[43] See, e.g., Mulgan, 209. We shall note the exceptions and reply to them in
Section 4.3.5.
[44] See Santas (2), 38. See also Dreisbach, who argues that the question of
agreement with an unjust state is never raised, even implicitly, by the *Crito*.

whether or not there is inconsistency in Socrates' philosophy concerning legal authority. For example, if it can be shown either that the directive Socrates imagines the jurors to issue could never be a legal one under the current constitution of Athens, or that they were invested with no constitutional authority for issuing such an order, Socrates' vow to disobey would be no more inconsistent with the doctrine that one ought always to obey the law than his resistance to the mass trial of the Arginousai generals had been. Though we concede that there might be other ways to resolve the paradox, which might be extremely edifying in themselves, we shall argue both that the imagined court order would have been illegal and that the jury lacked any relevant authority to make it. If we are right, it follows that the problem that has given rise to so many interpretations is in fact not a feature of the texts cited to generate it, and that the questions answered by such interpretations are not ones that could have occurred to Socrates as he made his vow before the jury. Hence, though such answers may be based upon legitimately Socratic principles, they cannot accurately be represented as Socrates' own answers.

3.3.4 THE LEGAL SETTING

It is important to recognize the circumstances under which Socrates makes his controversial vow: he is on trial for impiety and for corrupting the youth of Athens. Socrates imagines that the jury is not entirely persuaded by the prosecution's arguments, but is also not convinced that he is blameless and harmless, and thus offers to let him go on the condition that he give up philosophy. Socrates responds by saying that he would never obey.

There are two possible ways in which such a situation could occur: either (*a*) the jury offers to acquit Socrates of all charges, with this provision, or (*b*) the jury finds him guilty of the charges, but elects to sentence him to a cessation of his philosophic activities rather than the death penalty proposed by the prosecution. Let us consider these in order.

If the situation Socrates has in mind is (*a*), what is supposed to occur is that Socrates is found innocent of any charges, but is nevertheless required to eschew philosophy, on pain of death (29c8–d1).[45]

---

[45] Indeed, option (*a*) appears to be the option Socrates had in mind, given the way he presents the case. He says 'if you let me go *now*' (εἴ με νῦν ὑμεῖς ἀφίετε (29b9–c1)). Panagiotou (2) seems confident that something more like (*b*) is what Socrates has in

But there is not the slightest historical evidence that Athenian juries were empowered to enact any such conditional acquittals; nor is there any sense in supposing that there should have been provisions for this. After all, if the man is legally guilty of no crimes, then he surely deserves no penalties. If, on the other hand, he would deserve death for repeating his actions, then surely those actions are blameworthy and should thus merit conviction and not acquittal. Of course, it might be that one who was charged, as Socrates was, and put forward for trial, should, whatever the outcome, feel warned that whatever he had done had the potential of getting him in serious trouble. But again, there is excellent reason to believe that Athenian juries in trials of this type did not have the authority to find a man innocent, on the one hand, and yet issue a directive stipulating a penalty should the directive be disobeyed, on the other. Had they somehow made such a directive anyway, Socrates' vow to disobey it would involve no disobedience of the law.

In fact, it requires considerable imagination to picture an Athenian jury making Socrates the sort of offer he hypothesizes. Athenian juries did not debate and deliberate at the conclusions of trials. As soon as the prosecution and defense finished making their cases, the voting process would begin; no formal discussion would intervene.[46] The directive Socrates imagines the jury making would thus not only have no legal status, it would require a phase in the legal process itself that did not exist.

But what if the jury were to acquit Socrates without a provision of any kind, but subsequently pass a law saying either that philosophy was a crime punishable by death, or that Socrates' practicing philosophy was a crime punishable by death? The effect of this would be that though they found Socrates guilty of no crime (for what he had done was not against the law), they had become convinced that it *ought* to be against the law, and had thus resolved to make it so. Accordingly, they say to Socrates, 'We will let you go now, for you have

mind, except that the sentence of death is assigned and then Socrates is pardoned. Despite his different way of construing the conditions Socrates has in mind, Panagioutou (independently) comes to remarkably similar conclusions as those we argue for here and in our earlier article on the topic (Brickhouse and Smith (6)).

[46] See MacDowell (2), 251–2: 'When the speeches were finished, the jury proceeded to vote immediately. One of the most important differences between an Athenian trial and most modern trials is that in Athens no judge or other neutral person gave any directions or advice or summing up to the jury, nor did the jury hold any formal discussion'.

broken no law, but we shall act so as to ensure that if you go out and repeat the actions that have brought you before us, you *will* be breaking the law, a law the breaking of which earns you the death-penalty.' This would provide a reasonable reading of the jury's directive, one that does not generate some of the problems considered above. It would still require them to deliberate, however, and in any case would also require them to take on prerogatives they did not possess. Juries were not empowered to pass laws; rather, they acquitted or convicted those brought before them on formal charges, and, under certain circumstances (and with certain restrictions, about both of which we shall have more to say below), selected the penalty to be paid by those they convicted. If the jury acquitted Socrates, then, they would have no further power over him as a group, nor could they contrive as a group to retain any such power over him. Of course, as citizens, some, or for that matter all, of the members of the jury could propose legislation of the relevant sort to the council. But, as jurors, they could not guarantee its passage through the popular assembly. So not only could they not *in practice* issue the directive Socrates imagines, since that would involve a period of deliberation not available at Athenian trials, they also could not with any legal authority, actual or potential, enforce such a directive. Hence, were the jury to find Socrates innocent (as per (*a*)), his continued practice of philosophy would violate no law or legally constituted authority, no matter what the jury had otherwise proposed to him. His vow to continue, therefore, would in no way violate his avowed commitment always to obey the law.

But let us suppose (contrary to the sense of the way he presents it[47]) that Socrates had situation (*b*) in mind, in which the jury convicts him but then sentences him to give up philosophy, threatening him with death if he disobeys. This not only makes better conceptual sense than situation (*a*)—for now they would be assigning such a penalty as a sentence for a convicted criminal—but coincides well with Socrates' later discussion at 37e3–38a1, where having been convicted, he reconsiders the proposal that he quit philosophizing as the appropriate sentence.

It is clear that juries were empowered to sentence convicted criminals to a variety of penalties, at least in cases of this sort. And a sentence, once assigned, had to be carried out if the convict were not

---

[47] See note 45, above.

to be in violation of the law, or at least disobedient of a legally constituted authority empowered to make such assignments. Were
Socrates legally sentenced to eschew philosophy, disobedience would
then at least prima facie violate his purported view that one ought
always to do as one's country commands, and we would have a problem of interpretation on our hands.

Socrates' trial, as we have pointed out[48] was an ἀγών τιμητός, a trial
procedure for which there is no penalty set by law. In cases of this
type, the prosecution would propose a penalty at the end of the indictment.[49] If the defendant was then found guilty, he was provided the
opportunity to offer a counter-penalty. One thing that seems secure in
our knowledge of this procedure[50] is that the jury was then required by
law to vote a second time in order to choose the penalty from those proposed by the prosecutor and the defendant. There was no provision
made for them to concoct yet another possible penalty and then assign
that one.[51]

But this shows that Socrates' vow to disobey the jury, were they to
proscribe further philosophical activity, would in no way commit him
to disobeying either law or legitimate authority, for the jury could in
no way legally make such a proscription, even, as in situation (*b*), in
the course of sentencing Socrates. On the one hand, the prosecution
had asked for death. Telling Socrates that his sentence is to cease
philosophizing is thus plainly not to select the penalty proposed by the
prosecution. But it is not the penalty proposed by Socrates either, for
when he is called upon to propose a counter-penalty he explicitly and
emphatically rejects the one at issue. Instead, he offers a fine. Were
the jury to sentence him to silence, therefore, they would be assigning
a penalty proposed by neither of the parties empowered to offer alternatives. Hence, were they to direct Socrates to quit philosophy in
the way imagined in situation (*b*), their directive would not be legal.
Socrates' commitment to obey the law would thus not be in even
prima facie conflict with his refusal to obey this directive.[52]

[48] See Section 1.4.1.   [49] See Burnet (2), note on 36b3.
[50] See, e.g., Burnet (2), 149; Harrison, vol. 1, 80–2; Otto Schulthess, in *PW*,
Cols. 1251–5; Harp. s.v. ἀτίμητος ἀγών καὶ τιμητός. The principal ancient source is
Dem. 52.18, 53.26, 56.43, 58.70, and 59.6.
[51] See Chapter 1, note 82. Neither was the jury empowered to suspend sentences
or grant pardons, contrary to the scenario Panagiotou claims Socrates to have had
in mind ((2), 51 *et passim*).
[52] Moreover, the jury could not sentence Socrates to death but then suspend the
sentence under the provision that it would be carried out if Socrates continued

Of course, if Socrates proposed such a penalty the jury could legally select it, and his subsequent failure to act accordingly would be a violation of the law to which Socrates appears to profess utter obedience. But Socrates does not do this when given the opportunity, and there is every reason to suppose that he never would do such a thing. Alternatively, if the prosecution had made the abandoment of philosophy the penalty they attached to the indictment, the jury would have had the opportunity to command Socrates legally to do what he says he would never do. But the prosecution manifestly did not do this, and their failure to do so was already established by the time Socrates made his vow to disobey. And it is most unlikely that the prosecution would ever consider proposing such a penalty. For one thing, the notion that any indictment for a crime as serious as impiety would allow for even a conditional release of the guilty is absurd. But the prosecution could not afford to make less serious charges either; they needed to make charges that fitted the prejudice against Socrates. All these problems aside, even if Socrates' abandonment of philosophy were the penalty proposed by the prosecution, it is not clear that Socrates could not have proposed an alternative that would have better suited the jury—even death[53]—and thus have avoided the conflict that way. In short, the number of suppositions, all contrary to fact, that need to be made even to get the problematic case off the ground renders the problem itself prohibitively speculative.[54]

3.3.5 AN OBJECTION CONSIDERED

One final point remains which might be used as an objection to our view that no serious paradox is to be found in Socrates' vow. Whatever truth there is in the above observations, the fact remains that Socrates does not say that he would disobey because any such directive to cease philosophy would not be legal; he says that he would

practicing philosophy. We have not the slightest evidence that Athenian law permitted juries to suspend a sentence on a condition. Even if we supposed the jury did have such authority, and opted to exercise it in Socrates' case, his failure to cease philosophizing would not then be a violation of law, but rather the choice of death over silence; a choice provided by the terms of the suspension.

[53] It is unlikely that Socrates would ever propose such a penalty, despite his professed lack of fear of death, but the supposition that he might, under these conditions, is surely no less likely than are the conditions we have imagined.

[54] A view in a number of ways similar to ours is argued by Prosch, who also notices that the directive Socrates imagines the jurors making would not be legally valid (see esp. 181).

disobey because such a directive would conflict with his duty to the god. If the fact that the jury could not legally require Socrates to quit philosophy had had anything to do with his vow, surely he would have said so.[55]

Such an objection is based upon a misunderstanding of our argument, however, and in any case ignores the specific purpose of Socrates' vow. First, we have not attempted to argue that there could be no moral (for religious) principle overriding that which obliges Socrates to obey the law, though we shall consider this point in the next section. Secondly, we have not claimed that the fact that the imagined directive from the jury would not be legal is what *motivated* Socrates to vow disobedience. We have only argued that in vowing to disobey any such directive he is not vowing disobedience to the law or legal authority, and thus his vow creates no conflict with the arguments in the *Crito* or elsewhere.

But, more importantly, Socrates does not raise this topic to explain either his feelings of obligation to the law or any inclination he might have to violate the law. Rather, he wishes to underscore two points of fundamental significance in his defense: he wishes to show how much more deeply he fears doing that which is evil and shameful than he fears death, and he wishes to highlight the seriousness with which he takes his mission on behalf of the god. In doing so, he employs what is to the jury (if not to many modern readers) the plainly imaginary situation that he is released provided he gives up his mission. His answer is that to do so would be shameful and impious. The irony of this is that it is on the grounds of piety that he will not promise to cease what has led to his being charged with impiety, and this irony was not likely to be lost on his audience, the jurors. The gist of his vow, then, is only this: even if it meant freedom for him were he to give up his mission, and death were he to continue, he would continue. So much does he fear disgrace more than death. And even if the citizens of Athens would never forgive him for his actions, the will of the god means more to him.

The reason that Socrates would make such claims is that it is vital to his defense that it be understood that the actions which have offended his accusers (and many others besides) proceeded from the will of the god, and thus cannot provide grounds for the charge of impiety. And

---

[55] This appears to be the way Kraut construed our first expression of the arguments on these pages (in Brickhouse and Smith (6)), to which he refers in his (3), 13–14 n. 24; see his summary of the position on 14–15.

were he seen to be saying all these things out of fear of death, the jurors could doubt the sincerity of his repeated claims that his work is serious and vital to the welfare of the state. Thus, Socrates urges both that he serves the god and that he has no fear of death, and he urges it so strongly as to override an openly expressed love and respect for his fellow citizens. His vow to disobey the imagined directive does not reflect an arrogant disregard for the jury or their wishes. Rather, it stresses the extent to which he is deeply pious, contrary to the claims of the prosecution. Indeed, it is a repeated feature of his defense that his actions are designed to better the state and those who compose it.

3.3.6 CAN THE PROBLEM BE RECONSTRUCTED IN A MORE GENERAL WAY?

We have not argued that there is no need to consider the commitments of Socratic philosophy on the issue of competing or conflicting duties to god and to law. Indeed, we believe that there is a great deal of understanding to be gained from carefully considering this issue, and we have learned a great deal from many of the analyses of the passages we have argued do not really require such analyses. The grounds of our arguments thus far, then, have been what Socrates actually says and the contexts in which he says it. These grounds do not entail that no conflict of the relevant sort could occur.[56] Though such speculation, according to our argument above, is not required by the *Apology* and the *Crito*, it is worth while asking whether a situation could arise in which Socrates would face a conflict of duty, and, if it did, what Socrates' response would be.

The options appear to be three: (1) Socrates' principles would require him to obey the law even if it entailed defying the god's command; (2) Socrates' principles would require him to obey the god's command even if it entailed defying the law; and (3) given the ways in which he construes his duties to the law and to the god, Socrates could not conceive of a situation in which they would come into conflict.[57]

Establishing which of these would be the Socratic position is made problematic by the fact that no Socratic text offers anything explicitly addressed to this issue; as we have said, the statements of the *Apology*

---

[56] Thus, mindful of our objections, Kraut argues ((3), 15–17) that the power of Socrates' commitment to philosophy is such that he would be undeterred by a legal ban on philosophy.

[57] Though he is not necessarily committed to the interpretation that follows, T. H. Irwin's helpful comments had a great effect on the way we have structured it.

and *Crito* that have caused this controversy are not, once they are properly seen in context, sufficient to raise the question directly. Rather, they leave only the mere suggestion that such a conflict could occur. But (1) on the surface appears to conflict with at least the sense of Socrates' defense in the *Apology*, a defense that is founded upon repeated assertions to the effect that he has given up all else in favor of pursuing his duty to the god. Moreover, even if our argument above is correct, Socrates passes over the legal impossibility of the jury's imagined directive, citing only his allegiance to the god's will, as if that were all that mattered. These features of the *Apology* suggest that Socrates would consider his duty to the god first and foremost. And just as such observations would seem to render (1) an unlikely candidate for Socratic commitment, they would also seem to lend support to (2), the option unanimously chosen by those scholars inclined to say that there is a solution to the alleged contradiction. But there is an homologous difficulty with (2). In the *Crito*, Socrates' arguments never explicitly allow exceptions; they say only that one must 'persuade or obey', and they never explain what it would be for one to persuade, nor do they say that one may persuade *instead* of obeying.[58] For all that is explicit in that dialogue, Socrates' duty to obey the law is absolute and exceptionless. Of course, it might be argued that permissible exceptions are not provided in the *Crito* only because the moral and religious issues required to generate them are not at issue in that dialogue.[59] The unqualified character of Socrates' conclusions in the *Crito*, however, strongly suggests that the arguments are not supposed to be applicable solely to the specific questions raised by Crito.

It is curious that so few interpreters have considered option (3), perhaps because in order for it to work grounds must be given for ruling out possible conflict between civic and religious duties, yet since at least the time of Sophocles' *Antigone* the possibility of such a conflict appears undeniable. But more than a little evidence can be found for supposing that Socrates might have seen the issue in way (3), and indeed the very fact that he never raised the issue of competing duties in anything like the way commentators have craved suggests that he did.

[58] Kraut argues for such a position against those who construe the phrase in question 'persuade or *failing that* obey' (see Kraut (3), esp. 54–90).

[59] This is the move made by Santas (in (2)) to explain why Socrates does not mention in the *Crito* what Santas takes to be the overriding nature of his obligation to the god. Though we do not wish to be taken here as refuting that view, it should be clear from our argument that we do not find it required by any problems in the text. See, in addition, Prosch, 181.

First, there is at least some evidence that Socrates believed that unjust laws would not really be laws at all.[60] If so, Socrates would see no possibility of conflict between god and law, for any law that conflicted with the god's will could be condemned as unjust and hence no law at all. Moreover, it was generally supposed that the foundations for the legal code were divine in origin.[61] Any law, then, that conflicted with divine will would be a law in conflict with its own foundation. More importantly, Athenian law directly proscribed impiety, without proscribing particular acts or beliefs.[62] A conflict between law and god in Socrates' thought would thus become conflicts within the laws themselves, since any law that required Socrates to disobey the god would direct him in a way exactly contradictory to the legal directive prohibiting impiety. Socrates' categorical duty to obey the law could not in principle conflict with his categorical duty to the god under these conditions, for the latter was built into the former.

Let us consider what the effect of this would be on Socrates' position were he to face a duly enacted law prohibiting the practice of philosophy. Initially, Socrates might not consider it a law at all. In cases where one believed that a law was passed that contradicted a prior law, one could endeavor to have it cancelled by proposing a γραφὴ παρανόμων, a legal procedure in which the initiator of the later law is charged with having created such a contradiction, and during which that later law is suspended.[63] At least at the outset, Socrates might well have initiated such a procedure, for a law banning philosophy would penalize him for adhering to the law against impiety. Of course, it is conceivable that even if he did this, the offending law would be upheld, leaving Socrates to face a duly enacted, and now upheld, law forbidding him to philosophize.

Now Kraut simply states that 'a legally valid ban on the practice of philosophy would not be an impossibility in democratic Athens.'[64] But this depends entirely upon what might occur through what Socrates, *ex hypothesi*, would see as a corruption of due process. The issue is not whether or not the rest of Athens would see the offending law as legally valid. The issue needed to generate conflict is whether or not *Socrates* can imagine a law that he would recognize as legitimate yet

---

[60] See *Hip. Ma.* 284d1–7, *Minos* 314b8–315a3, 317c1–7, and Woodruff, note on *Hip. Ma.* 284d6–7, 41. Kraut disputes the applicability of this to the issue of conflict in (3), 21–2, n. 36.

[61] See Dover (3), 255–6.   [62] See MacDowell (2), 199–200.

[63] See MacDowell (2), 50–2.   [64] Kraut (3), 15.

none the less not to be obeyed. The fact that his fellow citizens see no contradiction does not entail that there is no contradiction, and this is crucial to the situation Socrates would now face. In Socrates' eyes, what Kraut calls 'legally valid' would be legally contradictory, for the imagined law would require him to commit impiety, which is against the law. When two laws contradict one another, even the most steadfast adherent to civil authority cannot find a way to comply with both. That Socrates could not defy a law of logic is no evidence that he would defy a law of Athens, yet it seems that the former is what would be required in this case, given Socrates' beliefs, in order to achieve the latter in some non-trivial way. Thus, Socrates could argue that both duties, to the law and to the god, are such as to be exceptionless. Given that Socrates makes no exceptions to such duties, and that Athenian law guarantees their compatibility, at least as he (if not all of Athens) construes them, we have reason to believe that (3) is the most likely reconstruction of Socrates' philosophy of duty to law and god. Properly understood, they cannot conflict.

There is but one possible set of circumstances in which Socrates might encounter the conflict we have so far ruled out. We might be able to generate such a case if we imagine Athens first to repeal her proscription of impiety (though this itself might end up generating nonsense[65]), and then to outlaw philosophy.[66] We have shown that no conflict can be generated from a proper understanding of the vow Socrates makes at 29d3-4, even when conjoined with the strongest rendering of the arguments of the *Crito*. We have further argued that, given the Athenian legal system as Socrates would have understood it, no such conflict could be generated. Though we concede that interest might be found in speculations as to how Socrates might have had to

---

[65] Such an adventure would itself be impious and thus against the law it sought to repeal, which would have a presumption of precedence over any procedure designed to repeal it. In all likelihood, then, its repeal would be legally impossible by due process under the laws of Athens. Notice that the same conundrum would not be faced in considerations concerning the repeal of any other law in Athens: the law against adultery, for example, would plainly not be broken by the legal procedure required to repeal it. We are inclined to suppose on these grounds, therefore, that the problem of conflict could not actually even be generated this way, but seek only to show how absurdly distant from Socrates' actual context one would have to go to generate the problem that has caused all the fuss among commentators.

[66] Even on the most superficial reading of the *Crito*, however, some provision is made for this: Socrates could choose to leave Athens, though it is not clear that this would not compromise his religious mission in Athens (see *Cri.* 51d5-8; but cp. *Ap.* 30e1-31a1, 37c4-38a1).

qualify his views, were Athens to undergo one or more drastic changes (or, for these purposes equivalently, if the god were to direct him to attempt to destroy the laws), such speculations lie considerably beyond the scope of philosophical exegesis. We do not deny the value of this issue in prompting much valuable and illuminating discussion of the texts. Nor do we doubt the value that might be found in reinterpreting Socrates' claims in such a way as to change their superficial meaning. But we have shown that in context, Socrates' various claims and vows can be taken at face value, with no violence to sense or logic. Finally, we see nothing in Socrates' remarks at 29d3–6 that requires that he be seen as engaged in arrogant defiance of the jury's special status to be judges according to the laws.

4

SOCRATES' DEFENSE, PART III
(30c1–35d8)

4.1 The Danger Faced by the Jury

4.1.1 'NOT FOR MYSELF...BUT FOR YOU'

Thus far, Socrates has constructed his defense by means of two sorts of arguments. By responding directly to his 'first' accusers and then to his actual prosecutors, he seeks primarily to show that he is not guilty of any of the various forms of wrongdoing specified in their accusations. And by claiming, after the completion of his 'interrogation' of Meletus, that his philosophical activities have been undertaken as a service ordained by the god, Socrates attempts to show that the very activities which have for so long been the object of popular suspicion and hostility have actually provided an invaluable benefit to the city of Athens.[1] Both kinds of arguments, those concerning his innocence of the accusations against him and those concerning the good his mission bestows on Athens, show how complete would be the injustice he would suffer by the court's condemnation.

But at 30c2–31c3 Socrates offers the jury a new reason for releasing him. He pleads, he says, 'not for myself, as one might think, but for you, that you do not err utterly regarding this gift of the god by voting against me' (30d5–e1). This claim may have appeared to many of the jurors (as it has to so many commentators) to be outrageous arrogance. We believe, however, that there is good reason to suppose that Socrates was nothing but sincere in expressing it. Viewed from one perspective, Socrates' notion that the jury should vote to acquit

---

[1] It was by no means uncommon for defendants to cite the various ways in which they had benefited the city in the past, for example through acts of largess or military service. (See, e.g., Lys. 20.30, 25.13; Andoc. *Myst.* 147.) For more on this aspect of Athenian trials, see Dover ((3), 292-5), and MacDowell ((1), 16), who offers an interesting explanation for the appropriateness of such a procedure, given the Athenian system of justice.) Whether or not such pleas would be appropriate in other cases, Socrates' substantial discussion of the benefits he has bestowed upon Athens cannot be construed as diverting the jury's attention away from the charges before them, since such 'benefits' refer, in fact, to the very activities that have for so long been said to be injurious to the city.

him for their own sakes is reasonably straightforward. He has already
told them of the twofold nature of his mission: he is obliged both to
free his fellow citizens from the bonds of their misguided belief that
happiness will come from wealth, power, and reputation, and to urge
them to care first for the acquisition of moral virtue, whence all real
goods flow (29d7–30b4). Because his fellow Athenians have been so
reluctant to pursue what is best for themselves, he has devoted his
entire life to urging them on, neglecting his own affairs while he attempted to advance the true interests of his fellow citizens (31b1–5).
Thus, he tells the jury that they will not easily find another 'gadfly'
who is willing to spend his whole life 'stinging' the city in order to
rouse it from its laziness (30e1–31a1).

4.1.2 INJUSTICE AND HARM TO THE SOUL

But Socrates' plea on the jurors' behalf expresses a more general and
profound sense of their potential danger. He introduces his appeal by
telling the jury, 'Know well that if you kill me, being the sort of person
I say I am, you will not injure me more than you injure yourselves'
(30c6–8). He immediately goes on to connect the injury an adverse
juror will inflict on himself by condemning Socrates with the sort of
harm Anytus and Meletus will have done to themselves.

Neither Meletus nor Anytus is able to injure me; for I do not believe it is god's
will (θεμιτόν) for a better man to be injured by a worse. He might perhaps kill
me or banish me or disenfranchise me; and perhaps he and others think such
things are great evils, but I do not think so. It is a much greater evil doing what
he is now doing, trying to kill a man unjustly. (30c8–d5)

Unless Socrates' remarks about Anytus and Meletus are utterly
parenthetical, Socrates must be pleading with the jurors that they not
injure themselves in the same way as Anytus and Meletus—namely,
by 'committing a great error regarding the god's gift'.

For all Socrates knows at this point, virtually all of the jury will remain convinced that he is a dangerous subverter of the public good;
none the less, he maintains that those jurors, if any, who are persuaded by his defense and who vote to acquit him will not have injured
themselves in the way Meletus and Anytus have done. Yet all the
jurors, and indeed all of Athens, will have been deprived of the
benefits of the 'god's gift'. Thus, the point of Socrates' plea cannot be
merely to warn the jury of the damage they do themselves by destroy-

ing this precious gift the god has bestowed upon them. Rather, it must pertain to the damage they do themselves *because* they, like Meletus and Anytus, will have participated in Socrates' condemnation. Not only will they have committed an injustice by putting an innocent man to death, but they will have also acted impiously for having terminated the very activities the god has ordained.

Socrates does not explain at this point just how the jury's and prosecutors' injustice and impiety will prove a greater injury to those who participated in his condemnation than anything he will have suffered at their hands. But if we review a few of the basic doctrines of the philosophy of Plato's early dialogues, it is easy to see what his explanation would be. First, it is axiomatic in Socratic philosophy that the soul is the most precious of our possessions (*Ap*. 29d7–30a2; *Cri*. 47e6–48a4; *Prt*. 313a6–b1; *Grg*. 512a5–7). Socrates articulates this doctrine only moments before warning the jury of the harm they will do themselves by convicting him: at 30a8–b2, Socrates tells the jury that it has been fundamental to his mission to urge his fellow citizens not to care about their bodies and their possessions until they have ensured the well-being of their souls. Equally fundamental to Socratic philosophy is the doctrine that moral virtue constitutes the good condition of the soul, whereas vice corrupts the soul (*Cri*. 47d8–48b2; *Charm*. 161a2–10; *Grg*. 507a5–7). When Socrates pleads with his jurors not to injure themselves by killing him, he must believe that, were they to do so, they would thereby in some way damage their souls, since obviously none of their other possessions would have been affected.

Socrates does not suppose, however, that *doing* unjust and impious things causes harm to the hitherto undamaged soul of the agent. Vice, considered as the corrupted condition of the soul, is nothing more than ignorance of what virtue requires (*Prt*. 350a4–357e2; *Meno* 76b6–78b2), and vicious action obviously does not simply *cause* the agent to become ignorant. Rather, vicious action springs from prior ignorance.

But vicious action also conditions the soul to accept ignorance and vice more readily. Since those who are ignorant of virtue will mistakenly think that their evil actions harm their victims, they will count what they have done as evidence for their mistaken view of how to live. So Socrates is concerned about vicious action both because its performance is a certain symptom of a soul already corrupted by ignorance, and because he fears its perpetrators will become ever more inured to their own corruption. In this case, by refusing to be persuaded about the value of his philosophical activities the jurors who vote against Socrates blind themselves to the single way in which they can rid their souls of vice. Like Meletus and Anytus, who think that Socrates' mission must be suppressed, those jurors who vote to convict Socrates are not likely to submit to the elenctic testing that would rid them of their pretense of moral wisdom. His warning to the jurors not to convict him, then, is at least in part a concern about whether or not they will continue in their prejudice that he is a wrongdoer and hence continue to maintain the false belief about what justice requires in this particular case. The consequence of their doing so is that they will endure the worst possible evil—the unrelieved corruption of their souls (see, for example, *Grg.* 479d74-6).

4.1.3 THE SOCRATIC LACK OF WISDOM VERSUS VICIOUS IGNORANCE

Although Socrates' plea on behalf of the jurors themselves makes little sense unless he is trying to save them from the devastating consequences of their disregard for the value of his mission, his remarks might nevertheless appear puzzling. He obviously believes that any jurors who are persuaded by his defense are substantially better off than those convinced of his guilt. Yet he also believes that all the jurors, like everyone else in Athens who has been subjected to elenctic examination and found wanting, lack an understanding of virtue. It can hardly be said that those jurors who are persuaded of his innocence have suddenly attained the wisdom for which Socrates has all these years been searching. Since Socrates regards vice to be nothing more than moral ignorance, and since he also believes that even those jurors who are not persuaded of his guilt nevertheless fail to be wise about 'the most important things', it might appear impossible to conclude that they could be counted as any better off than those who were unmoved by his defense.

Moreover, Socrates' apparent conviction that a juror will profit by having been persuaded to find him innocent may be paralleled by his own conviction that he is immeasurably better off than the likes of Anytus and Meletus, as well as all of the jurors who voted for his condemnation. As we have argued above,[2] Socrates must be taken at his word when claims that he, too, lacks the understanding of virtue. To

[2] See Section 1.5.2.

be sure, he tells us earlier in the speech that he did indeed come to see himself as superior to other men once he came to the realization that, unlike those whom he examined, he at least realized that he did not have the understanding of virtue (21e2–22e5). But the fact that Socrates is alone in being aware of his own lack of understanding does nor of itself, at least, give him substantively more understanding than other men about the nature of virtue.

When placed against the background of yet other Socratic doctrines found throughout the early dialogues, we see just how perplexing is his conviction that, regardless of what his enemies could ever do to him, he will always remain better off than they. For Socrates, happiness (εὐδαιμονία/*eudaimonia*) and wretchedness (ἀθλιότης) constitute the two conditions by which to judge the value of one's life (*Euthyd.* 278e3–279a1, 280b5–6; *Meno* 78a1–b2), and his belief that *eudaimonia* requires nothing less than virtue[3] must block any assessment that he is completely happy. More vexing still is a conclusion that follows from the conjunction of the two cardinal doctrines of Socratic philosophy—namely, that injustice is sufficient for wretchedness (*Cri.* 47e6–48a11; *Grg.* 480a1–4, 512a2–b2) and that injustice is nothing more than ignorance of what moral virtue is. Committed as he is to such views, how can Socrates, who recognizes more clearly than anyone else that he does not understand what virtue is, escape the conclusion, not only that he is not completely happy, but that, no less than those who would execute him, he is in a wretchedly impoverished condition?

4.1.4 THE SOLUTION: 'KNOW THYSELF'

The solution to this problem, we believe, is to be found in the view Socrates derived from his attempt to understand the Delphic oracle regarding his wisdom—that he is better off than those who have failed his elenctic tests. At 22d5–e5 he told the jury,

the good craftsmen, just as the good poets, seemed to me to have the same failing (ἁμαρτία). Because he performs his craft well, each believed he is wisest about the other most important things. And this error (πλημμέλεια[4]) of

---

[3] This doctrine follows directly from Socrates agreement in *Euthyd.* that happiness requires the possession of many goods (279a2–3) and nothing other than wisdom is good unless it is guided and correctly used by wisdom (281d2–e1; see also *Grg.* 470e4–11). See Brickhouse and Smith (9) for further discussion.

[4] Burnet (2), note on 22d8, suggests rendering πλημμέλεια, as 'want of tact'. But the fact that it is meant to parallel ἁμαρτία indicates that Socrates wishes to connote

theirs obscured their wisdom, so that I asked myself on behalf of the oracle, whether I should prefer to be thus as I am, being neither wise with respect to their wisdom (σοφὸς ὢν τὴν ἐκείνων σοφίαν) nor ignorant with respect to their ignorance (ἀμαθὴς τὴν ἀμαθίαν), or to have both things that they have. I then answered myself and the oracle that it would be better for me to be as I am.

It is important to notice that Socrates' conception of what makes him better off also has a Delphic warrant found in the renowned inscription at the shrine (see *Charm.* 164d4–5; *Prt.* 343b3; *Phdr.* 229e5–6; *Phil.* 48c10; *Laws* 11.923a3–5). Socrates knows himself. That is, on this account, he is aware of his own lack and human limitations, unlike the politicians, the poets, and the craftsmen.

Although Socrates here and elsewhere[5] disclaims any understanding of virtue, it is clear from what he says at 22d5–e5 that whatever his epistemic limitations are, he is nevertheless not ignorant in the same sense as the craftsmen are.[6] But what exactly is the others' failing, the ἁμαρτία that makes them ignorant in a way Socrates is not? Surely it cannot be that the politicians, poets, and craftsmen lack the understanding of virtue that Socrates and perhaps some others have, for though he allows that 'the god is truly wise' (23a5–6) he never identifies any of his fellow humans as having the understanding that the politicians, poets, and craftsmen suppose they have. And since Socrates suffers from this same lack and is nevertheless better off than the ignorant ones, it cannot be merely the lack itself that is the problem. Instead, their flaw has to be just that they suppose they have this understanding when they do not.

The importance of this false supposition is that those who suffer from it are likely to harm themselves more and more by affirming

something far stronger. In thinking they understand the 'most important matters' when they do not, the handicraftsmen and the poets are guilty of a very serious failing.

[5] For the various passages in which Socrates disclaims moral understanding, and the reasons for thinking these disclaimers are sincere, see Sections 2.6.1–2 and 1.5.3.

[6] See Hathaway, who finds a distinction between ἀμαθία, which he defines as 'proud ignorance, a defect of character', and ἄγνοια, 'intellectual ignorance, the simple absence of knowledge either of fact or art' (134). The difference between Socrates and his fellow Athenians, on Hathaway's account, is that Socrates suffers only from the latter and not from the former sort of ignorance. It is at least some evidence against Hathaway's distinction that Socrates characterizes his own ignorance as ἀμαθία at *Grg.* 488a3. But even if a terminological distinction cannot be found to support it, there is nothing impossible in the idea that Socrates could have such a distinction in mind, for even if both he and Meletus, say, are ignorant in the same sense of ignorant, there remains nevertheless an enormous difference in their intellectual and epistemic status. An exploration of this difference follows.

false moral opinions one after the other, and perhaps with ever graver moral consequences, without the benefit of the caution and moderation that self-understanding would provide. But those who, like Socrates, are aware of their own lack of wisdom do not merely escape these dangers. They may even be able, as we have argued in Section 3.2.2, to ascertain a number of moral propositions whose truth can be a matter of confidence, through a patient pursuit of examination through philosophy.

Because complete happiness requires wisdom 'about the most important things', the very wisdom that Socrates knows that he lacks, he cannot count himself completely happy. But then perhaps only the god(s) can be happy in this sense, for only the god(s) is (are) fully wise. The more modest and less secure happiness that is given to man to achieve, however, is Socrates', for he does have what he calls 'human wisdom' (20d8-9). So it does not follow from the fact that Socrates is not wise that he is wretched. Since the beliefs by which he has lived his life have been exposed to extensive scrutiny and continuous re-examination by a method of inquiry that he believes has been divinely sanctioned, not only is he free from the blinding arrogance that afflicts so many of his fellow countrymen, he may also be confident that much of what he believes is true and hence that those actions that derive from his true beliefs are good ones. So it is that he can fairly call himself a 'good man' (see 36d1-3, 41d1-2), one who has brought great benefit to his fellow Athenians (see 31a7-8, 36c3-4), and even one who has never done an injustice (37b2-3). And because he has never been unjust, having never acted upon a carelessly accepted but demonstrably false conception of justice, he can be equally confident that he has escaped the wretchedness that comes through injustice. Thus, although neither he nor any of his fellow citizens have fully attained the goal at which all aim, *eudaimonia*, Socrates can be assured that he has at least a share of happiness, such as is possible for humans, and thus that he is immeasurably better off than the multitude of Athenians, who labor under a variety of mistaken notions about the nature of virtue.

The same reasoning, we believe, may be applied to explain Socrates' apparent conviction that, for their own sake, the jurors should vote to acquit him. We have already pointed out (in connection with our discussion of the origin of this mission[7]) that Socrates is

---

[7] See esp. Section 2.5.4.

convinced that for all who lack virtue their understanding of how best to live will be improved by submitting their moral conceptions to elenctic examination. Those jurors who retain their prejudice that elenctic examination is wrongful and deserving of condemnation will continue to possess one or more disastrously false beliefs about virtue, for they will no doubt refuse to submit their lives to elenctic examination. Consequently, they are doomed to the wretchedness that is assured them by their continual ignorance. This is not to say, however, and Socrates nowhere implies, that voting for acquittal will *guarantee* those who do so escape from injustice and the wretchedness it brings its possessor. Friendly jurors may still have a number of false views about justice. They may still believe, for instance, that it is just to harm one's enemies or that virtue is merely the power to attain one's goals. Nevertheless, Socrates had good reason to urge the jurors to vote for his acquittal for their own sake. First, he can be certain that they will have avoided the great damage done to their souls by the impious and unjust belief that it would be right to kill him. Moreover, their vote to acquit him would indicate their repudiation of the false and dangerous moral view that one should attempt to suppress Socrates' philosophical activity. And since Socrates is convinced that improvement of the soul, the most important kind of betterment, can come only through philosophical examination, those who have at least come to tolerate his examinations are, in his eyes, at least, obviously far more likely to reap their benefits than are those who would seek to extinguish them altogether.[8]

4.2 Virtue and Immunity to Harm

4.2.1 HARMING A GOOD MAN

We are now in a position to interpret another feature of Socrates' warning to the jurors about the harm they will suffer in condemning him. At 30c8–d1, Socrates makes an astonishing claim: he says that

---

[8] A requisite of successful elenctic examination is the interlocutor's willingness to offer his sincerely held beliefs (see *Cri.* 49c11–d1, *Prt.* 331c5–d1, *Rep.* I 346a4–6, *Grg.* 500b5–c1). Those jurors who are unpersuaded by Socrates' arguments about the supreme importance of submitting one's beliefs to testing are thus unlikely to undergo the sort of questioning for which Socrates has made himself notorious. And even if they are 'cornered' by other Socratics (see 39c6–d3), they are unlikely to answer with the sort of sincerity Socrates demands of his interlocutors.

neither Meletus not Anytus can harm him. The apparent lack of qualification in this claim is puzzling, for Socrates is well aware of what Meletus and Anytus (with the help of the jurors) *could* do to him: immediately after his claim that they could not harm him, he allows that they 'might perhaps kill me or banish me or disenfranchise me' (30d1-2). Later on in the *Apology*, Socrates rules out a variety of counter-penalties he might propose, *including banishment*, precisely on the grounds that they would be evils to him (37b5-e2), and the sole virtue he cites of the counter-penalty he does propose is that it is no evil and will do him no harm (38a8-b2).[9] So it might appear that there is an inconsistency in the *Apology*.

Though he never cites the later passage, and thus does not offer his reading as a way to extricate Socrates from the apparent contradiction, Gregory Vlastos has suggested a way to understand the earlier passage that would solve our problem. According to Vlastos, we should weaken the sense of 'no harm' in the earlier passage to mean something like 'no harm by comparison with the enormity of the harm they will do to themselves'.[10] We accept that this provides a natural reading of the passage, especially given that Socrates concludes his remarks about what Meletus and Anytus can and cannot do to him by making the proposed comparison explicit (30d4-5). But as Vlastos well knows, it remains true that banishment and disenfranchisement, for example, are 'calamities'.[11]

A look at the context of the remark shows that what must be qualified in the earlier passage is not merely the strength of Socrates' actual claim, but the sense in which Socrates means that Meletus and Anytus cannot harm him. The point of Socrates' petition, after all, is to warn his jury not to harm their souls through ignorance and vice

---

[9] As we have discussed in Section 1.4.1, the jury is constrained by a provision in the law governing trials of this type to choose between the prosecutor's proposal and that of the defendant, and of course Socrates will not propose what he knows to be an evil. Since Socrates says that he does not know that death will be an evil, and since the jury must select either the prosecution's proposed penalty or else the penalty Socrates decides to propose, Socrates can be assured in this case that he is in no danger of suffering what he tells us are certain evils. But the protection moral betterment affords on his view is not contingent upon being lucky enough, as Socrates has been in this case, to have one's enemies not seek to perpetrate certain evils. For confirmation that Socrates recognizes that he could suffer harm at the hands of unjust men, see *Grg.* 469b12-c1, where Socrates tells Polus that he would never want to suffer injustice, although of course he would rather suffer injustice than do it.

[10] Vlastos (2), 193-4.   [11] Ibid, 193.

and thereby suffer the greatest calamity that can befall one. Since this is the sense of harm presumed throughout the passage, the reason why Socrates believes that what Meletus and Anytus can make him suffer is nothing in comparison with the enormity of what they are doing to themselves is clear: the harm they can do to Socrates is not a harm to his soul. Compared to the harm to their own souls that Meletus and Anytus suffer by doing Socrates an injustice, the harm they might do to him is as nothing.

All of this requires, of course, that Socrates relies in the two relevant passages upon different conceptions of what is harmful. The most catastrophic kind of harm is the wretchedness that derives from ignorance and vice. This is the only sense of harm at work in the earlier passage, for it is in this sense that Socrates worries that jurors will harm themselves. In this sense, it is unqualifiedly true that Meletus and Anytus cannot harm him, for they cannot make him ignorant and vicious. But they and the jurors can do a number of nasty things to him, and when, in the later passage, Socrates considers what he should invite the jury to assign him as a punishment, his remarks show plainly that he recognizes how nasty some of these things can be. But the catastrophic harm to the soul he is discussing in the earlier passage is not relevant in the later passage—nothing the jury assigns to him by way of a punishment will make him ignorant and vicious. Since the context of each remark protects against the danger that someone might suppose one of these two senses of harm to be at work where the other one is, the only risk of confusion here is to a commentator who insists upon interpreting various of Socrates' claims out of the contexts in which they are made.

4.2.2 THE SUFFICIENCY OF VIRTUE THESIS

A number of scholars have seen in Socrates' claim to immunity from the catastrophic sort of harm support for their view that he subscribes to the thesis that virtue is sufficient for happiness.[12] If it turns out to be true that for Socrates all evil things are harmful just in so far as they produce wretchedness for their possessor, and if Socrates cannot be made to suffer this harm, it might be supposed that though he can be deprived of many things—even life itself—he cannot be deprived of the share of happiness that is possible for men.

But is it true that the good man cannot be made to suffer wretched-

---

[12] See, e.g., Irwin, 100; Vlastos (2), 192-6; Burnyeat (3), 210-11.

ness, or is it only true that he cannot be made to suffer the most calamitous *sort* of wretchedness? As we have already said, it is clear that Socrates recognizes the virtuous man's vulnerability to a distressing variety of catastrophes: he could be deprived of all his material possessions, tortured, banished, disenfranchised, and even put to death. Given what he says about various possible counter-penalties, Socrates plainly supposes that at least some of these would be harms in some sense.

The logic of Socrates' various remarks about evils and harms makes clear that the loss of a good would qualify as a harm. Only slightly before his warning to the jurors on their behalf, as part of his explanation of his mission, he chastises his fellow citizens for caring more about 'money, reputation, and honor' and ignoring 'wisdom, truth, and the perfection of the soul' (29d7–e2). They are deserving of censure, he says, because they have mistaken what is of lesser worth for what is of greater worth (30a1–2). But he then goes on to explain the nature of their mistake (30a7–b4).

For I go about doing nothing other than attempting to persuade you young and old not to care so much for your bodies and your money (χρήματα) nor so vehemently, as for your soul, saying that virtue does not come from money, but *from virtue comes money and every other good thing for men in public and private.*

The Athenians' mistake of wanting what is worth less instead of what is worth more, then, derives from their mistaken conception of virtue. Because virtue is 'wisdom, truth, and the perfection of the soul', they will never attain virtue by making material attainments their chief concern.

Nowhere in the *Apology* does Socrates explain just why anything other than virtue may be counted as a good or how other goods besides virtue might contribute to happiness.[13] The passage just cited is nevertheless of considerable importance to our present concern because, although Socrates asserts that all other goods depend for their goodness upon virtue, he makes it clear that once virtue is ac-

---

[13] It is beyond the scope of our present concern to show just why and in what sense Socrates thinks that things other than virtue can also be goods. (For a full discussion of our view on this matter, see Brickhouse and Smith (9).) It should be pointed out here, however, that Socrates' apparent recognition of goods other than virtue in the *Apology* is not anomalous. In the *Euthydemus* (281d2–e1) Socrates explicitly states that a variety of things may be good subject to their being guided by wisdom.

quired a number of things—inclu   money—may nevertheless count as goods. Hence depriving the virtuous man of such things would have to count as harms.

It may seem paradoxical for Socrates to allow that loss of money could be a harm, when later (in his counter-penalty speech) he explicitly says that paying a fine would be *no* harm. But (1) in the later passage Socrates contrasts the loss of money with the catastrophic harms that other counter-penalties would be to him. The counter-penalties he considers and rejects would harm him by causing his life to become wretched and not worth living (see our discussion of Socrates' review of his counter-penalty options in Section 5.2). Paying a fine would not make Socrates wretched; indeed, paying a fine will not in any way interfere with what Socrates views as the real value in his life—the practice of philosophy. Moreover, (2) it does not follow from Socrates' view that money *can* be a good to a good man that money would count as a good to *any* good man. Goods other than virtue are goods, on the view we attribute to Socrates, only in so far as they contribute to one's virtuous activities. In Socrates' case, money is of no value at all, for his virtuous activities—as defined by his mission—are neither expedited by money nor hindered by the lack of it. Hence, *for Socrates*, paying a fine would be *no* harm. Not everybody lives like Socrates, however. For some, as 30a7–b4 suggests, the loss of money would be a harm, though still nothing like the disaster that the acquisition of vice would be.

It must also follow that Socrates' friends, who offer to help him pay the fine, will not suffer a harm by the consequent loss of money; otherwise, in accepting their offer Socrates would contribute to their being harmed. We do not know enough about these other men—or the kind of life one would have to lead to make virtuous use of money—to speculate on why his friends, like Socrates himself, would not be harmed by helping him to pay a fine. But since in accepting their offer to help, Socrates seems to suppose they are acting well, and since Socrates also thinks that in doing well one always achieves beneficial results (see Section 5.5.3), it follows that in assisting Socrates his friends would be benefited. Certainly, one relevant benefit would be their continued access to 'god's gift' to Athens, Socrates himself. One case in which the loss of money can be a good, we may assume, is when it is well spent.

But what is it to harm someone, and to what extent can a good man be harmed? Surely not all harms involve causing their victims to become wretched; some may involve only a diminution of happiness. So might it not be that despite the most grievous losses and injuries a virtuous man could still be happy at least to some degree? If so, the sufficiency of virtue for happiness doctrine still stands, for the virtuous man would still be assured of at least a significant measure of happiness.[14]

There is, however, strong textual evidence that Socrates believes that various harms can come to a virtuous person that would leave no trace of happiness in their victim. In the *Crito*, for example, Socrates attempts to convince Crito that the greatest harm that can befall a person is harm to his soul. But in arguing for the point, he compares the value of the soul with the value of the body, and reminds Crito that 'life is not worth living with a diseased and corrupted body' (47e3-5). But this is precisely the same reason that Socrates gives for avoiding life with a soul that has been harmed through injustice (47e6-49a2). Of course, it also follows from the comparison Socrates makes between the two that the life of the unjust man is none the less vastly worse than the life of the hopelessly diseased man, though death is preferable for both. Still, one might suppose that having a diseased and corrupted body would not be sufficient to make one wretched, thinking that there is an important difference between a life that is not worth living and a life that is wretched. But in the *Gorgias* Socrates states explicitly that a man with a chronically diseased body, like a man with a chronically diseased soul, is wretched, since he is 'bound to live badly' (512b1-3). Although the degree of wretchedness that comes with an unjust soul is always worse than what attends ills of the body, the point is clear that moral virtue is not sufficient always to protect a person from the wretchedness that renders his life no longer worth living.

4.2.3 CONCLUSION AND A PROMISORY NOTE

We have argued that what qualifies Socrates' claim of immunity to being harmed by Meletus and Anytus at 30c8-d1 is its presumption, obvious in context, that the harms to which Socrates is claiming absolute immunity are those that might afflict one's soul —ignorance and vice. We have shown how this passage may be read consistently with the comparative claims that surround it, as well as Socrates' later remarks that certain penalties he might be made to

---

[14] This is the position defended by Vlastos in his (2) (see esp. 191-213).

suffer would be evils and harms to him. Despite his goodness, therefore, Socrates might be harmed in other, lesser ways. We have also shown how what Socrates has to say about the various other ways in which the virtuous man can be harmed requires us to reject the attribution to him of the sufficiency of virtue doctrine, for it seems that even a virtuous soul does not protect one against certain calamities that would render one wretched and better off dead.[15]

One passage in the *Apology* remains to be discussed, however, and until an account can be offered of it that is consistent with all we have argued thus far, our results must be considered merely tentative. At 41d1–2, in his final speech to the jury, Socrates makes the unqualified pronouncement that 'no harm comes to a good man in life or in death'. It should be obvious that the interpretation of this claim is critical to the controversies we have pursued in this section, for it clearly appears to conflict with our reading of other passages according to which good men can suffer *some*, and indeed considerable harm. Though we believe the proper interpretation of this later passage requires precisely the same assumptions we made concerning Socrates' similar claim at 30c8–d1, it is best to postpone this discussion until a scrutiny of its context is timely. Those who may wish to continue the present discussion should turn now to Section 5.6.2.

4.3   Socrates and Political Life

4.3.1   MORALITY AND PRIVACY

A primary element of Socrates' defense is that, since the oracle at least, he has lived a life of exemplary service to the state, and its 'gadfly' (30e5), a 'gift from the god' (31a8), exhorting his fellow Athenians 'like a father or elder brother' (31b4) to care for virtue. But for all his unceasing moral activity, Socrates has not pursued a life in the political arena. This very fact, in the minds of many jurors, must have undermined Socrates' credibility, for in the Athens of his day moral

---

[15] Although we dispute the way scholars have understood the connection between virtue and happiness in Socrates' thought, we do not believe that they are wrong to see such a connection or to emphasize the interdependency of virtue and happiness. Elsewhere, we have argued that Socrates views virtue as one of a number of necessary conditions for virtuous activity, and that only virtuous activity is sufficient to ensure happiness for its agent. (See Brickhouse and Smith (9).)

and political activism were generally considered inseparable. As Thucydides' Pericles, in his Funeral Oration, says of the Athenians, 'we alone do not regard a man who takes no part in political life as one who minds his own business; we regard him as having no business here at all' (*History* 2.40). Since, then, as everyone knew, Socrates was not a politician, his claim to have made virtue his primary concern would be taken by many at least to be an empty boast.

At 31c4, therefore, Socrates begins to answer this unvoiced doubt concerning his moral integrity. His answer has three main parts. (1) Each time he has resolved to undertake political activity, his *daimonion* has opposed him (31c7–d5). (2) Though the opposition of the *daimonion* does not come with a built-in explanation, Socrates believes that the opposition is a good thing because he is convinced that 'one who fights for what is just, if he is to preserve his life for even a little time, must live as a private man and not lead a public life' (31d5–32a3). (3) Finally, lest anyone think that his lack of political activity is a sign that he has simply acted out of fear for his life, Socrates offers the jury 'great proofs' (32a4) of his fearless pursuit of morality in the face of grave danger: his opposition to the mass trial of the generals after Arginousai, and his failure to take part in the arrest of Leon of Salamis despite an order from the Thirty. Let us consider each of these in order.

4.3.2 THE OPPOSITION OF SOCRATES' *DAIMONION*

As we said earlier (Section 1.4.4.2), Socrates' claim to have a personal *daimonion* appears to have played an important role in the formal accusations against him (see 31d1–2). The role of this *daimonion* is a peculiar one in Plato's account, for, as Socrates says at 31d3–4, it always acts in such a way as to oppose an action Socrates might otherwise undertake, but it never tells him what he should do. In that sense, then, Socrates' *daimonion* is more like an alarm than a guide, for though it sometimes warns him of danger, it does not lead him to safety. So even with his *daimonion*, Socrates must find his own way in life.

We shall have a great deal more to say about the role of the *daimonion* in Socrates' life in the final chapter of this book, but for the present a few things are worth noticing. First, nothing in the passage suggests that the *daimonion* provides Socrates with an explanation of its opposition; it merely opposes and leaves the reason for such opposition for Socrates to puzzle out for himself. So the amount of information Socrates gets from the *daimonion* is extremely meager. In this case, Socrates does indeed think he knows why the *daimonion* has opposed his prospective forays into politics, but this is Socrates' own interpretation and it is not in any way given by the *daimonion* itself. Secondly, even the general principle that Socrates ought not to engage in politics is not given by the *daimonion*. Rather, it is clear that even though Socrates says the *daimonion* opposes his going into politics, what has in fact happened is that it has opposed Socrates *each time* he has thought about becoming politically involved (and we do not know how many times this has happened) and Socrates has inferred from this pattern that the *daimonion* is generally opposed to any move Socrates might make in the direction of politics. So even the generalization we are offered is the product of a Socratic inference, and not a direct message from the *daimonion*. We must not, therefore, be seduced into thinking that the *daimonion* offers Socrates greater access to important moral information than it does, lest we impugn Socrates' repeated confession that he has no wisdom. A divine moral guide might provide Socrates with at least some of the wisdom he consistently denies having, but Socrates' *daimonion* fails to provide this service.

But if what we have said so far is right, why should we (or Socrates' jurors) have any confidence in the conclusion he draws from his *daimonion*'s consistent frustration of his political impulses? Socrates *says* that his *daimonion* opposes his entering politics, but all that has really happened is that it has opposed him each time he has tried. Even if his jurors accepted what Socrates says about his *daimonion* (which doubtless many would not have done), they might worry that Socrates has made a faulty induction. For one thing, surely a sensible juror would like to know how many times Socrates has been tempted to undertake political activity only to be opposed. If it has happened only a few times, one might sensibly blame Socrates' own renitence and not his religious awe. The fewer instances that support Socrates' generalization, the more uncertain his inference becomes. Moreover, Socrates does not labor to support his inference at all. He tells the jurors that the *daimonion* has opposed him, but he does not impress them with the point by saying how often it has done so, and how many times he has tried to apply his moral exhortations in what the jurors would consider the most appropriate forum, politics. Without further argument or support, then, Socrates' point in this case would

be decidedly weak. If the jurors are inclined to be suspicious of someone who claims to live an aggressively moral life but does not also
take an active role in politics, it would hardly remove their suspicions
to show that one had made a few failed attempts to become political
and then had given up the whole idea as a lost cause. So even if the
daimonion provided Socrates' private motive for eschewing the
political life, more is needed to convince Socrates' jury of the sound-
ness of his judgment in doing so. On our view, this is precisely why
Socrates offers the other arguments, to which we now turn.

4.3.3 SOCRATES AND POLITICAL PHILOSOPHY

Having been opposed by his *daimonion* each time he thought to
engage in politics, Socrates must at some point have begun to wonder
why he encountered such opposition. The conclusion he reached is
reported to us at 31d5-32a3; he thinks that he would have been put to
death long ago, and thus accomplished no good for himself or others,
for he is convinced that anyone who really fights for the right cannot
survive long against the Athenians or any other mass of people
(πλῆθος). The startling and provocative anti-democratic sentiment of
this claim is stronger than anything else that can be found uttered by
Socrates in any of the early dialogues of Plato. But how can he make
such a negative assessment of his fellow Athenians and the very idea
of rule by the masses? After all, the personified Laws claim in the
Crito (52e2-53a5) that Socrates, of all Athenians, has proved himself
to be especially satisfied with Athens' ways, and Socrates himself
never disputes their assessment (see also *Phdr.* 230c6-d5).

Commentators have often charged that Socrates was an enemy of
democracy.[16] Claims such as the one Socrates makes at *Apology*
31d5-32a3 provide the most powerful evidence of all that Socrates
was opposed to democracy, for it seems quite clear in all this passage
that he is convinced that *anyone* who opposes *any mass of people* in
such a way as to prevent the numerous injustices and illegalities
Socrates assumes the masses will commit would be likely to suffer
the direst consequences. The *Apology* leaves no room to quibble
about the scope of Socrates' commitment on this point: he does

---

[16] See, e.g., E. Barker, 97; Guthrie (2), 94-6; A. E. Taylor (3), 141. The strongest
assertions of this view can be found in Stone; Winspear and Silverberg, 84; and Wood
and Wood, 97. See also the sources cited in Chapter 2, note 32, above, and Kraut's
extensive review of the evidence for and against this thesis in his (3), ch. 7, 194-244.

not merely accuse the Athenians; he says 'neither you nor *any other mass of people*' (οὔτε ὑμῖν οὔτε ἄλλῳ πλήθει).

None the less, Socrates has had his democratic defenders, most of whom attend exclusively to the rather more friendly statements Socrates makes in the *Crito*.[17] But the most cautious and balanced of Socrates' defenders is certainly Richard Kraut, who attempts in his recent book, *Socrates and the State*, to resolve the apparent conflict between the resolutely élitist moral philosophy one finds in the *Apology* and elsewhere and Socrates' professed satisfaction with Athens and her laws in the *Crito*.[18] On Kraut's view, Socrates is extremely pessimistic about our ability to discern moral truth.[19] But since, according to Kraut's account, undertaking positive moral action involves a presumption of moral wisdom, we must suppose that Socrates' principal moral commitments are strictly negative, and thus passive ones; so, for example, it is acceptable to suffer but never to perform an injustice. On this view, one avoids doing evil; one does not aggressively pursue good. How can one aggressively pursue that of which one understands little or nothing (see *Apology* 23a7)? Kraut tells us that this is why Socrates sees himself as obliged to play no active role in politics, and why he advocates no such activity for his followers, since their moral wisdom, like his own, is 'worth little or nothing'. Thus, it is Socrates' moral scepticism that leads him to advocate political passivism. Activism involves a presumption of moral wisdom.

Moreover, according to Kraut, the same epistemological pessimism leads Socrates to be an advocate of Athenian democracy, for, until a moral expert appears, 'in the meantime Athenian democracy provided the best conditions for the discovery of the correct moral system'.[20] But Kraut realizes that his view of Socratic pessimism about the possibility of moral expertise entails that 'this *meantime* might be a very long time indeed'.[21] So Kraut concludes that 'Socrates thought that it would be hard—perhaps impossible—to improve on Athenian democracy'.[22]

Socrates is very clear (in the *Crito* at least) that the Athenian democracy is a system he has preferred over all others. But Kraut goes too far, in our opinion, in supposing that Socrates thinks it 'perhaps impossible—to improve on Athenian democracy'. On the contrary,

[17] See, e.g., Gulley, 168–79; Popper, 128–33.
[18] Kraut (3), esp. ch. 7–8, 194–309.
[19] Ibid., 267–8.
[20] Ibid., 268.
[21] Ibid., Kraut's italics.
[22] Ibid.

surely Socrates would suppose that an Athens governed in strict accordance with the principle that one should never harm another or return harm for harm would be immeasurably preferable to Athens under the democracy. And even greater good would be assured if we added other changes, such as a battery of legal and political modifications designed to promote and protect a widespread commitment to the view that 'the unexamined life is not worth living', that 'human wisdom is worth little or nothing', and that 'one must always do whatever the state commands, or persuade it as to what is naturally just'. In short, in Socrates' eyes, a Socratized Athens would be an immeasurably better Athens, even though it, too, would lack the true expert. If so, a government composed of Socrates and/or his likeminded friends would be plainly preferable to the democracy.

It should be noted that nothing we have just said would commit Socrates to a non-democratic form of government. Rather, all these considerations are entirely compatible with the view that Socrates would maintain the democracy but change the moral commitments according to which it enacts and enforces its laws and statutes and determines its domestic and foreign policies. The point we wish to make, however, is that for Socrates the principal issues would not be constitutional but *moral*; there is every reason to suppose that Socrates would prefer, for example, a non-democratic system administered by benign Socratic philosophers to a democratic system run by ignorant and bellicose demagogues. And we find no evidence at all for supposing that Socrates would have preferred a democratic to an oligarchic constitution, *ceteris paribus*; Socrates never considers the relative merits of various constitutions at all, at least in Plato's early dialogues. On these grounds, then, we believe that Kraut overstates the degree to which Socrates is committed to Athenian democracy in principle (if not in fact, as we shall subsequently show).

But Kraut has every right to demand an account of the preference Socrates plainly professes in the *Crito* for Athens and her laws. Let us return, then, for a closer look at the passage in the *Apology* in which Socrates explains his lack of political activity. Socrates reminds his jurors that if he had undertaken to go into politics,

I should have perished long ago and done no good for you or for myself. And do not be vexed with me for speaking the truth; for no man will preserve his life who lawfully opposes you or any other mass of people and prevents many unjust and illegal things from happening in the state. One who fights for what is just, if he is to preserve his life for even a little time, must live as a private man, and not lead a public life. (31d5-32a3)

These are not the words of a man pessimistic about the possibility of moral expertise—after all, it allows that there might be someone who 'lawfully ... prevents many unjust and illegal things from happening in the state'; these are the words of one who is profoundly pessimistic about the possibility of such persons surviving the attempt to engage in political activity. *This*, then, is the reason Socrates would not encourage the few who follow Socratic moral principles to attempt to take over the government, even though he might well suppose that if they could do so successfully they would create a vastly better state than democratic Athens. And notice that despite this very depressing view of the respect for morality to be found in democratic Athens, it may well be true none the less that democratic Athens is the best of all realistically possible states, for at least in Athens one can pursue the noble life in private.[23] Elsewhere, even this might be impossible. In any case, it appears that Socrates' endorsement of Athenian democracy in the *Crito* is not the result of an epistemological pessimism, as Kraut would have it, nor is it based upon a respect for the peculiar constitutional merits of democracy. It is rather the result of a profound pessimism about the practical possibility of creating or maintaining a government by the sort of men who would prevent 'many unjust and illegal things from happening in the state'.

4.3.4 SOCRATES' 'GREAT PROOFS': ACTIONS THAT SPEAK LOUDER THAN WORDS

A major ingredient of Socrates' defense is that, at great cost and grave risk to himself, he has never abandoned the post assigned him by the god (28b5-30cl), refuting those who pretend to be wise and exhorting all to care more for virtue and the care of their souls than for money, reputation, or honor (29d7-e3). But the present passage (31d5-32a3) makes clear that there are limits to the risks that Socrates may take in the pursuit of his mission, for he has not brought his moral exhortations into the political domain. Again, he says he did not because the *daimonion* opposed such activities, but the reason he offers as to why he thinks this opposition was appropriate is that he would thereby

[23] A similar account of Socrates' preference for Athens is given by Anastaplo ((1), 14).

have been put to death long before he could have done himself or others any good.

As we said above, there is an unmistakably élitist sentiment in this assessment, and we might well suppose that such words would get a decidedly unfriendly reception from the democratic jury to whom they are spoken. Lest they dismiss his point as mere political hostility, therefore, Socrates undertakes to demonstrate its truth by means of what he calls 'great proofs. . . not words, but what you honor—actions' (32a4-5). He then reminds the jurors of his actions in two situations in which he chose, at terrible risk to himself, not to conform to what was expected of him because he would rather die than do evil. The two cases are nicely paired at this point, for one demonstrates Socrates' moral courage against the will of the democracy, the other, against the will of the Thirty. Socrates' 'great proofs' show his claim to be steadfast and courageous in his pursuit of the good to be no empty boast; they also show that he believes that Athenian democracy is not unique in the danger it poses to those with deep commitments to justice and law, and thus that his anti-democratic sentiments are not to be confused with partisan oligarchic hostility to democracy. Rather, his 'great proofs' support Socrates' more general claim that 'a man who lawfully fights for what is just, if he is to preserve his life for even a little time, must live as a private man, and not lead a public life'. This unhappy situation, then, is not unique to those living in democratic states, for the noble opposition to evil under the Thirty was at least as dangerous an undertaking as any opposition to the Athenian 'masses'. In fact, from the unqualified condemnation Socrates expresses for the oligarchs' reign this much is clear: however dangerous the Athenian democracy might be to the good man, it had been a safe haven for Socrates far longer than the oligarchy had proved to be. For one thing, Socrates portrays the trial of the generals under the democracy as an aberration (32b4-5); but he says the order to arrest Leon was typical of the Thirty's reign (32c7-8).

4.3.4.1 The Trial of the Generals
In 406 BC, only one year before their final defeat at Aigospotamoi and two years before their complete capitulation to the Spartans in the Peloponnesian War, the Athenians won their last great naval victory near a small group of islands in the Aegean between Lesbos and the coast of Asia Minor, the Arginousai.[24] After the battle a storm blew

[24] For the other ancient sources on the Arginousai affair and Socrates' role in

in, and in the rough weather and confusion the victorious fleet departed for home without picking up the crews of the ships that had been lost or disabled. Many men were lost—as many as or more than had been killed in any battle of the war. Though there is some disagreement in the ancient sources as to how many generals (στρατηγοί) were involved,[25] their victory was all but forgotten by the Athenians. Instead, their failure to save the lost crews became the principal issue.[26]

In fact, the generals apparently learned of the agitation at home before they ever returned to Athens. Two of the generals (Protomachus and Aristogenes, no doubt because they judged the situation too dangerous) simply elected not to return to Athens. But six generals decided to come home, and by the time they arrived public feeling was strongly against them. They were immediately called upon to testify before the Council (βουλή), and the Council decided to imprison the generals and then refer them to the Assembly (ἐκκλησία) for prosecution.[27] Accordingly, the Assembly undertook to consider the case and a number of men spoke up against the generals, including some of their own ship-captains (τριήραρχοι).

Apparently, the dispute raged, both sides exchanging accusations,

opposing the action against the generals, see Xen., *Hell.* 1.7, *Mem.* 1.1.18 and 4.4.2; Arist., *Ath. Pol.* 34; Ps.-Plato, *Axiochus* 368d6-369a2; D. L. 2.24; Diod. 13.101.1-103.2; Philochorus, *FGrH* (F. Jacoby) 328 F 142. Perhaps Plato's *Grg.* 473e6-474a1 refers to the same incident (see note 29, below). Good historical analyses that sort through this evidence and piece together the details of the events in question include Andrewes; Paul Cloché, 'L'affaire des Arginouses', *Rev. Hist.* 130 (1919), 5-68; Grote (1), vol. 6, ch. 64, 397-430. On Socrates' role in the legal proceedings, see Hatzfeld.

[25] Plato, Aristotle, Diogenes Laertius, and the author of the *Axiochus* all refer to ten generals. Xenophon refers to only eight in the *Hell.*, and is supported in this by Diodorus Siculus, who does not, however, list the same eight names as those Xenophon offers. But in his *Mem.* Xenophon says there were nine generals involved. Ten generals were in office at the time, but two of the ten were apparently not actually prosecuted: Conon, as not having been at the battle, and Archestratos, who was already dead. On Plato's reference to ten, see Burnet's (2) and Riddell's notes on 32b3.

[26] Following Andrewes, we have chosen in the following account to represent Diodorus' version of the events, wherever there is conflict between his and Xenophon's.

[27] Though (curiously) none of the ancients refer to the Arginousai generals' trial as an example of such, the procedure by which a trial is held before the Assembly is called εἰσαγγελία. For discussion of this, see Hignett, 233-4; MacDowell (2), 183-9; *Oxford Classical Dictionary*, q. v. *eisangelia*, 375-6; Mogens Herman Hansen, *Eisangelia: The Sovereignty of the People's Court in Athens in the Fourth Century BC and the Impeachment of Generals and Politicians* (Odense, 1975).

for so long that before any resolution could be reached the meeting
was adjourned due to the lateness of the hour and the case continued
at the next meeting of the Assembly. But the next meeting of the
Assembly was nothing less than a mob scene, with mourners appearing and screaming their accusations, and demanding the execution of
the generals. Eventually, a certain Callixenus proposed on behalf of
the Council that the Assembly take one vote on the guilt or innocence
of the generals. But three valiant efforts intervened. First, a (third?)
cousin of Alcibiades, Euryptolemus, son of Peisianax,[28] and others
charged Callixenus with having made an illegal proposal, claiming
that the law did not permit actions against groups, but rather required
that each individual be tried separately. If they had held to this indictment, the trial of Callixenus would have had to be held before the
generals could be dealt with. But the mob at the Assembly howled for
action, and a speaker in the Assembly, Lyciscus, stopped Euryptolemus' action by moving that those who made the indictment
against Callixenus be tried by the same vote as that proposed against
the generals. Recognizing the danger they faced, Euryptolemus and
his supporters withdrew their indictment. It is at this point that
Socrates intervened.

   As a result of its reform under the archonship of Cleisthenes in
508/7, the Council was composed of five hundred men: fifty, chosen
by lot, from each of the ten tribes of Athens. Each tribal group served
at the Presiding Committee (πρυτάνεις) for one-tenth of the year. As
it happened, Socrates had been one of those selected by lot to serve on
the Council that year, and his tribe was serving as the Presiding Committee during the current Assembly.[29] After Euryptolemus had been
bullied into withdrawing his indictment of Callixenus, Socrates and

[28] See J. Davies (1), s.v. Megakles (9688.8), 377–8.
[29] This is the extent of Socrates' position in the account he offers in the *Ap.*,
where he simply says he was a member of the presiding committee (32b5). This view
is consistent with the information we get from Xenophon's *Hell.* But in both of the
accounts in the *Mem.*, and also in the *Axiochus*, we are told that Socrates was
standing as ἐπιστάτης, or presiding officer, and that it was in this capacity that he
refused to put the question before the Assembly. Riddell (82–3, n. 7) finds this
evidence compelling, and adds that Socrates' reference to standing as ἐπιστάτης in
the *Grg.* may be taken as referring to the time of the trial of the generals. Grote ((1),
vol. 6, 421, n. 1) is unconvinced by this evidence, as are Burnet ((2), note on 32b6),
Hatzfeld (167–70), and Tovar ((2), 340, n. 124). We are inclined to follow Grote,
Burnet, Hatzfeld, and Tovar here, since no mention is made of Socrates being
ἐπιστάτης in the *Ap.* Moreover, as Burnet argues, it would be rather surprising for
Plato in the *Ap.* to overlook or diminish the lofty role Socrates would have played in
opposing the mob had he actually served as ἐπιστάτης at the time.

some of his fellow Presiding Committee members refused to put Callixenus' question to the vote on the grounds that it was illegal. But Callixenus responded by charging them along with the generals, and his supporters cried out to indict the members of the Presiding Committee who had refused to bring the case to a vote. Like Euryptolemus, the Presiding Committee was thereby scared into doing the mob's will, and all of its members but Socrates then agreed to put the case of the generals to the vote. Socrates continued to object that the procedure was illegal, but his objection was swept aside. Euryptolemus then attempted one last legal maneuver, but the Assembly rejected it and the generals were condemned. Those present were executed, including the younger Pericles, son of the great Athenian leader.

Socrates recalls these wild events at 32b9–c4, and reminds his jurors of the unyielding and courageous position he maintained throughout. He repeats his view that the mass trial had been illegal and claims that subsequently everyone else had agreed with him. In fact, this assessment was never really put to the test, since Euryptolemus' indictment of Callixenus was never tried. But the story Xenophon tells about all the maneuvers and objections to the procedure that preceded the actual trial suggests that Socrates' interpretation of the law was not merely idiosyncratic. And whether or not it was actually contrary to law,[30] all the ancient sources agree that a clear majority of Athenians had later changed their minds about what had been done. Plato's Socrates simply says that the democracy subsequently agreed that the trial had been illegal. On Xenophon's account, the Athenians repented and passed a decree indicting those that had been responsible for the mass trial. Callixenus and four others were arrested, we are told, but managed to escape before they could be tried.

Of course, even if we accept that the Athenians had a change of heart and attempted to prosecute Callixenus and his supporters, it does not follow that the change of heart was precisely because they thought the mass trial had been *illegal*. It could have been only that in retrospect they thought it imprudent or in some other way misguided. But Socrates' claim in the *Apology* that everyone later agreed that the trial had been illegal is not portrayed as greeted with shouts and denials from his jurors; we can conclude therefore that whatever the

---

[30] MacDowell raises this question (in (2), 189), but does not draw any definite conclusions. Hatzfeld (see esp. 165, 169) considers the trial illegal.

Athenians' (perhaps various) reasons had been for the reversal of feeling about the trial, to grant its legality would have been at best to
make a moot claim in its favor. Thus even if the jurors would not be
convinced that Socrates had been right all along on the specific legal
point, as he claims, they might still reasonably have been impressed
with the general morality of his position, and with his personal for-
titude in the face of dangerous mob. Since he offers his 'great proofs'
precisely to impress the jury in these ways, even if his interpretation of the relevant law was never established with certainty,
Socrates' remarks here are plainly well designed to show that his lack
of political activity has not been the result of cowardice. It also lends
support to his contention that those who stand unyieldingly for the
good take grave risks in the political arena.[31]

It might be supposed that there is at least a hint of inconsistency in
Socrates' first 'great proof'. If his point is that it is proper to avoid
politics because of the manifest danger involved, then why was it not
heedless bravado that led him to maintain such a dangerous position
in the face of the bloodthirsty mob he faced during his term on the
Presiding Committee? On the other hand, if his jurors are supposed
to be impressed by his actions then, how can they fail to find his
subsequent lack of involvement anything but cowardice? If taking the
sorts of risks he took during the Arginousai affair is admirable, then
why should we be moved to accept his subsequent political inaction?
It might appear that the very bravery he cites in his defense in this instance actually condemns his subsequent inactivity by contrast.

But Socrates' argument protects him against this objection. He tells
the jury that he has not been active in politics because his *daimonion*
has opposed him. Hence, though he allows that this opposition has
been a good thing, it was not his fear of danger that kept him from
politics. Presumably, the *daimonion* did not oppose his actions during the Arginousai affair, and in fact, despite the risks he had taken,

---

[31] In fact, the extensive evidence (presented admirably by Andrewes on 121-2) of
Theramenes suffering no ill effect from the Athenians' subsequent reversal of feeling
suggests strongly to us that Socrates' reading of their motive was precisely accurate.
(Theramenes was one of the ship-captains that testified against the generals.) Since the
Athenians later acted only against Callixenus' group, and not against Theramenes and
the other ship-captains it appears that it was not the damage done to the generals (to
which Theramenes had manifestly contributed) but rather the *way* the damage had been
done that had been the focus of the reversal. Hence the issue was the manner of the trial,
and not a change of heart about the generals, or surely Theramenes would have suffered
the same consequences as Callixenus.

he emerged from his one venture into politics unscathed. So when Socrates says that his *daimonion*'s opposition was a good thing, it may be supposed that the good fortune Socrates had enjoyed during his time on the Council would not have been repreated had he made other forays into the world of politics. Instead, having experienced the *daimonion*'s alarms often enough to discern their purpose, Socrates undertakes the unceasing practice of maintaining the good in 'private' practice; that is, not behind closed doors, but not in constitutionally established public fora, such as the Assembly. Socrates spends each of his days in the pursuit of his mission in public, but not in politics.[32]

4.3.4.2   The Oligarchy of the Thirty

Two years after the Arginousai affair, Athens unconditionally surrendered to Sparta. Sparta might well have elected to destroy Athens utterly, or to occupy and exploit the region savagely. Instead, the penalties were relatively lenient:[33] Athens had to cut her fleet to a total of twelve ships (to be used for local defense and police work), and to restore those who had been exiled in the years following the first restoration of the democracy in 410. These men, however, now bitter enemies of the democracy that had forced them to withdraw, returned with oligarchic schemes that had the support of Sparta's military leader, Lysander.

As essential role in the early phases of these events was played by a

---

[32] On Riddell's reading (in his note on 32b7) of the brief reference to Socrates' holding the position of ἐπιστάτης at *Grg.* 473e6, Socrates served on the council only one time, during which the Arginousai generals' trial was held. On Burnet's reading of the passage, however, there was yet another time in which Socrates served on the Council (see his (2), notes on 32b1 and 32b6). But even Burnet allows that 'to be a βουλευτήσ in his turn was not to play a part in politics, but to perform a citizen's duty, just as military service was ((2), note on 32b1). Hence, even Burnet's reading shows no inconsistency between Socrates' speech in the *Ap.* and the facts of his life, properly understood.

[33] Useful summaries of the following events can be found in Hignett, ch. 11 (285-98), and Krentz. See also Gabriel Adeleye, 'Studies in the Oligarchy of the Thirty' (Dissertation, Princeton, 1971); Knud Hannestad, *Der 30 Tyranner* (Copenhagen, 1950); T. Lenschau, *RE* 6 A 2 (1937), 2355-77, s.v. *hoi triakonta*; R. Loeper, 'The Thirty Tyrants', *Zhurnal Ministerstva Narodnago Prosvescheniya* (May, 1896), 90-101; W. James McCoy, 'Aristotle's *Athenaion Politeia* and the Establishment of the Thirty Tyrants', *YCIS* 23 (1975), 131-45; Pierre Salmon, 'L'établissement des Trente à Athenes', *AC* 38 (1969), 497-500.

Despite Krentz's arguments in favor of Aristotle's chronology in the *Ath. Pol.*, we shall follow Xenophon's. See the reviews of Krentz's book by D. M. Lewis (*Phoenix* 38 (1984), 293-4) and Christopher Tuplin (*JHS* 104 (1984), 242).

man named Theramenes, who had been a ship-captain at Arginousai
and had later testified against the generals. No matter what we make of
his motives,[34] his negotiations with the Spartans may have helped spare
Athens from harsher treaty provisions. Sometime later, at a meeting of
Athens' Assembly, Lysander instructed the Athenians to select thirty
men 'to codify the ancestral laws'[35] under which Athens would
henceforth be governed. Theramenes objected that Lysander's interference was in violation of the terms of the peace treaty. But
Lysander had an excuse to press the point, for it seems that the Athenians had failed to demolish their defensive walls, as the treaty had
also stipulated, within the time-limit. So Lysander could thus be confident that the Athenians had lost any reasonable hope of appeal, and
threatened Theramenes and the other Athenians with execution if
they did not do his bidding. Theramenes backed down, and the
frightened Athenians voted in favor of Lysander's scheme. So came
the notorious 'Thirty Tyrants' to power, men whose factional oligarchic sentiments were no secret to anyone.

Initially, the Thirty appear to have taken seriously their role in codi-
fying the old laws. But soon enough their activities became partisan
extremism of the worst possible kind. When they began to encounter
resistance, they applied to Sparta for a garrison to use in maintaining
their power, and seven hundred men were sent. Since Athens'
finances were already exhausted, the Thirty began to use their power
to confiscate property to support their regime, and a policy of execution and confiscation was thus employed against anyone who might
be seen as resisting their rule. Since these policies were backed by
Spartan troops, the Thirty operated for a little time with complete impunity, and what ensued was a government by execution and organiz-

---

[34] Xenophon is sometimes hostile to Theramenes, as is Lysias. But other writers,
including Aristotle and Diodorus Siculus, are more sympathetic. For discussions of
Theramenes' role in these affairs, see esp. Gabriel Adeleye, 'Theramenes: The End
of a Controversial Career', *Museum Africum* 5 (1976), 9-19; Philip Harding, 'The
Theramenes Myth', *Phoenix* 28 (1974), 101-11; Hignett, 285-90; Krentz, 28-77; W.
James McCoy, 'Theramenes, Thrasybulus, and the Athenian Moderates' (dissertation,
Yale, 1970); J. A. R. Munro, 'Theramenes against Lysander', *CQ* 32 (1938), 18-26;
Bernadotte Perrin, 'The Rehabilitation of Theramenes', *Amer. Hist. Rev.* 9 (1903-4),
649-69; Leendert van der Ploeg, *Theramenes en zijn Tijd* (Utrecht, 1948); S. Usher,
'Xenophon, Critias and Theramenes', *JHS* 88 (1968), 128-35.

[35] A slogan whose meaning in this context was that an oligarchic regime would be
established. See esp. M. I. Finley, *The Ancestral Constitution* (Cambridge, 1971);
Alexander Fuks, *Ancestral Constitution* (London, 1953); K. R. Walters, ' "The
Ancestral Constitution" and Fourth Century Historiography in Athens', *American
Journal of Ancient History* 1 (1976), 129-44.

ed robbery. As the oligarchs had done earlier, now democrats fled or were driven into exile, including Socrates' accuser, Anytus, as well as Socrates' close friend and associate Chairephon.[36] Socrates stayed in Athens.

Theramenes continued to play a vital role in these matters. Having initially been empowered to select ten of the Thirty, he was himself installed as one of their number. But the notorious Critias and his supporters appear to have outnumbered Theramenes' more moderate group and continued to cement their own authority with an escalating policy of terror, murder, and confiscation. Finally, a number of metics were selected by the oligarchs for destruction, and each of the Thirty was to be involved in the confiscation of these metrics' property. When Theramenes refused, Critias accused Theramenes in the newly formed Council of plotting against the oligarchy, and though Theramenes seems to have defended himself fairly impressively, Critias threatened to employ armed force and the Council was cowed into submission. Critias thus pronounced the sentence of death on Theramenes, who was accordingly executed soon after.

Socrates mentions nothing of the demise of Theramenes in the *Apology*; nor do we find any mention of it in any of the works of Plato or Xenophon. Diodorus Siculus, however, tells us that Socrates attempted to intervene at the last minute on Theramenes' behalf, but was forced to desist when it became clear that he would be killed in the attempt, which could not possibly succeed.[37] We are inclined to doubt that Socrates was ever involved in this way, but the story deserves further comment none the less.

First, we might wonder whether the story could be true yet not be reported by the more proximate sources, Plato and Xenophon. It seems unlikely (though admittedly not impossible) that Diodorus would know anything Plato and Xenophon did not know, so if we wish to allow the story any truth we must suppose that for some reason or other it was either ignored or suppressed by the earlier writers. In the case of Xenophon, we can hypothesize a plausible reason for its omission. Through most of the *Memorabilia* Xenophon labors to dissociate Socrates from any friendly connection to the Thirty or other controversial public figures (most prominently,

---

[36] See Section 2.4.4 and notes 52 and 53.

[37] Diod. 14.5.1–3; see also Plut., *Mor.* 836 f., in which it is Isocrates who intervenes on Theramenes' behalf. Krentz takes Plutarch's version to be the accurate one on the ground that we hear nothing of it from Socrates' apologists (77, n. 21).

Alcibiades). But Xenophon is also openly hostile to Theramenes; only when the latter is portrayed as being the victim of the Thirty does Xenophon's account become at all sympathetic.[38] Theramenes is thus precisely the sort of man with whom Xenophon's idol should not be associated, and hence the bravery with which we could credit Socrates might be seen by Xenophon as offset by the implied contamination of Socrates by what Xenophon considers repugnant political associations. Since there is other evidence (mentioned below) for friction between Socrates and the Thirty, Xenophon might have suppressed this incident as having only redundant positive value, but unique negative value.

Some of the same might be said for Plato, though here the case is even weaker. We do not know what Plato thought of Theramenes' career and associations, though it is not entirely immaterial that Plato's own relatives were among the Thirty, or that his later political philosophy remained immoderately anti-democratic. Despite Plato's obvious condemnation of the Thirty's actual practices, therefore, it is not at all clear that Theramenes' political views or activities would have repelled Plato the way they did Xenophon. But the jury at Socrates' trial might well be supposed to have little sympathy for Theramenes, whose political views, though moderate when compared to Critias', were none the less oligarchic. The fact that Theramenes was later attacked by the vicious government he had helped to appoint might have been seen as only a form of poetic justice. Hence, even if Diodorus' tale is true, Plato's Socrates (and indeed Socrates himself) may have seen only dubious advantage in saying anything about the affair. He may have needed to remind his jurors that he was no friend of the Thirty, but the story of Leon is far better suited to this purpose, since no possible taint attaches to it. And since the arrest of Theramenes was not directly material to his present situation, (Plato's) Socrates was not obliged to remind the jury of this event or any role he may have played in it. Thus, though we are inclined to doubt the truth of Diodorus' story, we see nothing in Plato's or Xenophon's silence to refute it.

But, similarly, we see none of the above reasons as compelling us to suppose that Plato or Xenophon would have to suppress the story, either. Diodorus' tale no more commits Socrates to a friendly association with Theramenes than his actions at the trial of the Arginousai

[38] On this, see Hignett, 290.

generals demonstrate a sympathy for the generals themselves or for their actions. Had a procedure been adopted to try each of the generals separately, Socrates might well have voted to convict each and every one of them. So in the case of Theramenes, as in the case of the generals, Socrates' objections could have been strictly procedural. This point could have been made to Socrates' jury, or to Plato's or Xenophon's readers, if necessary. But it would have had to be made carefully, and it would serve at best to do what can be more easily done by recalling Socrates' actions in the case of Leon. So we are left with no strong reason to believe Diodorus' account, but nothing important as regards Socrates' personal or political affilations would follow if we accepted it either.

Similar considerations apply to Xenophon's stories in the *Memorabilia* about Socrates' criticism of Critias for the latter's intemperate pursuit of Euthydemus (1.2.29–31), or about Critias' law against 'teaching the art of words' (or of arguments (λόγοι)—1.2.31–38), with Socrates specifically in mind. Plato says nothing about either of these things, but his silence does not tell against the accuracy of Xenophon's account. (Plato's) Socrates may well have neglected the first event as too trivial to recall.

As for Critias' law, Plato might reasonably see no advantage in reminding his jurors that even the hated Thirty believed Socrates to be a dangerous word-twister. But this is no reason to suppose that by silence he would be covering up any relevant guilt. Socrates says he has spent every day of his life, at least since the oracle to Chairephon, examining anyone who cared to talk with him. It is entirely believable that the murderous Critias might see this as a threat, and there is every reason to suppose that at least some of those who listened to Socrates could learn to reason better by doing so. So the fact (if it is a fact) that Critias tried to outlaw Socrates' activities would not support the jury in an unfriendly assessment of those activities, even if Critias' reasons for doing so coincided precisely with certain corresponding suspicions of Socrates held by the democrats. In fact, Socrates' method of reasoning would threaten any blind dogmatism. Hence, though (Plato's) Socrates might have seen good reasons not to raise this issue before the jury, nothing in it would discredit what he does tell them, and nothing directly relevant to the trial is covered up by failing to mention it. So again, as with Diodorus' story, the silence of other proximate sources counts neither for nor against the accuracy of Xenophon's claims at *Memorabilia* 1.2.29 ff.

One story that shows conflict between Socrates and the Thirty is shared by a number of the ancient sources, and this is the only one Plato gives in this regard. At *Apology* 32c4-e1 Socrates reminds the jury of the time the Thirty had ordered him to go out and arrest Leon of Salamis and return him to Athens for execution.[39] Though the other four went out and made the arrest (Leon was apparently executed), Socrates went home. Of this incident, he says 'that government, with all its power, did not frighten me into doing anything unjust . . . and perhaps I should have been killed for it, if that government had not quickly been overthrown' (32d4-8). He then says that there are many witnesses to this. The author of the *Seventh Letter* (325b5-c5) notes with bitterness that while Socrates' accusers were in exile, Socrates himself courageously refused to arrest their friend. In fact, the Thirty lasted only eight months in power before they were deposed, and since the evidence favors a steady increase in corruption during their time in authority, Socrates may well have been saved by their overthrow.

As we said before, by counting this incident Socrates demonstrates that there was no great friendship between Critias and him, in case any juror should be inclined to hostility towards him on that ground. So even if the other incidents (reported by Xenophon and Diodorus) in which conflict arose between the two were true, Socrates does not need to recite them, any more than he would need to recite other times (if any) in which he and the democratic government were at odds. His pont, that he has always stood for the right and never given in to evil despite the gravest dangers, is made well enough by the cases he cites, both of which are strong evidence in his favor and neither of which would be controversial in any way at this point. There may have been other similar cases; there may not have been. But these are surely forceful enough to make the point. If the jurors took Socrates' 'great proofs' seriously, and there was no reason they should not, they would know that the fact of his present danger would not alter his commitment to his mission, or to those values by which he had lived all of his life.

---

[39] See Chapter 2, note 61. Plato's *Ap.* is the only source that specifies that there were precisely four others (or five actually ordered to make the arrest, counting Socrates), but we see no reason to suppose this is significant.

4.3.5 SOCRATES' DISOBEDIENCE AND THE *CRITO*

One final concern should be addressed, the possible conflict between Plato's *Apology* and his *Crito* that might be implied by Socrates' resistance to the Thirty. We said earlier that the most celebrated passage in the *Apology* supposed to generate this problem does not in fact do so. Nor does Socrates' resistance to the mass trial of the generals, which he, at least, was convinced was illegal. But he disobeyed the order of the Thirty. Since the Thirty were appointed by an act of the Assembly, even if only because of Lysander's threats, and since Athens had unconditionally surrendered to the Spartans, one might be inclined to think that the arguments of the *Crito* should extend to the laws in Athens under the Thirty.[40] If so, Socrates' disobedience to their order would seem to violate the position he espouses in the *Crito*.

The situation gives rise to a number of interesting historical and legal questions, the most obvious of which concerns the actual legitimacy of the rule of the Thirty. These, however, are not questions for us to try to answer here. Instead, we need to ask whether the government of the Thirty satisfies the conception of legal authority assumed by the arguments Socrates makes in the *Apology* and *Crito*. If either of two conditions apply, it would turn out that even if the Thirty's authority to command Socrates to arrest Leon was in fact legitimate, Socrates would be guilty of no inconsistency in sincerely endorsing the arguments of the *Crito* and yet disobeying the Thirty in this case. (*a*) The Thirty may have been viewed *by Socrates* (or his intended audience) as not having the legal authority they had in actual fact, or (*b*) the arguments of the *Crito* may be conditioned by a number of considerations that would not be satisfied by the government of the Thirty. If (*a*) is the case, the actual legal status of the oligarchy is immaterial to the alleged inconsistency in Socrates' position. Though we might convict Socrates of poor jurisprudential analysis, we cannot convict him of inconsistency, for the government and/or command he disobeyed, on his view of the matter, would not

---

[40] This issue is raised by Kraut ((3), 17–24), Gavin, and Woozley ((1), 52–5). All three, however, subsequently reject the view that Socrates' resistance creates conflict with the *Crito* (see Kraut (3), 187). In criticizing our interpretation (as we expressed it in Brickhouse and Smith (6)), Colson has argued the stronger view, that this incident creates an inconsistency between the two dialogues.

have been a legal one. If (*b*) is the case, we cannot apply the arguments of the *Crito* to the situation faced by Socrates under the Thirty, for those arguments would now turn out to be conditioned by certain criteria not satisfied by the Thirty. In either of these cases, then, Socrates would be guilty of no inconsistency.

In fact, we consider the actual legality of the Thirty's rule questionable and doubt that it would have been accepted by the members of the restored democracy before whom Socrates was tried. But, in addition, we also believe that both conditions (*a*) and (*b*) above are satisfied by the evidence.

First, let us address the actual legal state of affairs in Athens at the time in question. Though the government of the Thirty was installed by a vote of the Assembly, we must not too quickly assume that the government thus installed was legal, and thus would have to be recognized as such by Socrates. For one thing, though the sources agree that there was such a vote that it was taken by the Athenians as decisive, they do not agree as to whether the vote in question actually satisfied the conditions for being legally binding as such conditions were specified by Athenian law. At that time, for an issue to pass into law it had to be voted in 'by a majority vote of the citizens present at the meeting'.[41] According to at least one source, this condition was not met. Lysias says that when the issue came to a vote, only 'a few . . . raised their hands in favor of [the new government]' (Lys. 12.75). If Lysias' account is accurate, even if no one raised his hand in opposition, it may not have been the case that a majority of the citizens present at the meeting voted for the Thirty, but only that a majority of those voting did so. Moreover, Lysias says that a number of people departed before the fateful vote, in which case the number required for a quorum may have been lost even before the voting was initiated. The evidence is sketchy, however, and Lysias is a very hostile witness, so it would be improper to base an interpretation on his testimony. We mention it only to show one of many uncertainties surrounding this matter.

Secondly, as we have said, at the very meeting of the Assembly in which the Thirty were installed there were legal objections made to the role played by Lysander. His playing any role more aggressive than giving advice was in violation of the peace treaty,[42] but the objections raised on this question were silenced by murderous threats from the

---

[41] This is a quotation from MacDowell (2), 45.   [42] See Krentz, 48-9.

Spartan, the same man who at Iasos had 'executed 800 men, sold the women and children into slavery, and razed the city to the ground'.[43] We must not simply assume that Lysander's excuse for this interference, that Athenians themselves were already in violation of the peace treaty, provides him *legal* warrant for the pressure he brought to bear. Unless the treaty stated that if the Athenians failed to live up to one or more of its terms Lysander could do whatever he wished (or some such stipulation), that inference would be a *non sequitur*. The fact is that his interference appears to have been contrary to the terms of the treaty. It might be argued that by non-compliance the Athenians had nullified the legal force of the treaty, but even that would not make Lysander's actions legal; it just makes the entire situation one in which legal constraints no longer applied. The point is that Lysander no longer felt constrained by the treaty, and the Athenians had left themselves in no plausible position to plead their cause to the Spartan kings who were the only ones who might restrain the Spartan general. The only plea they could make, being otherwise powerless, was on the basis of the treaty, but they had broken it themselves. None of this makes Lysander's actions legal ones, however, unless we are to conflate unopposable power with law. So the legal situation at the time of the Thirty's being installed is far from clear, and might easily have been disputed even by the Athenians themselves. What was not unclear, at the time, however, was that the Thirty had absolute *de facto* authority, were openly supported by Spartan arms, and any Athenian would resist them at his own mortal peril. Hence, the Thirty were in fact relatively unopposed in action, if not in spirit, by those remaining in the city.

Burnet dismisses the problem by arguing that the Thirty were not legally empowered to arrest or execute citizens, having been appointed temporarily to revise the laws.[44] But Richard Kraut challenges Burnet's conclusion, with what he finds a significant contrast between what Socrates says about the trial of the Arginousai generals and what he says about the order to arrest Leon. Of the former, Socrates says twice that it was *illegal*; of the latter he says nothing of its legal status, he merely says that it was unjust. From this Kraut concludes that '[Socrates'] silence suggests that he either thinks their order legal, or he does not care to discuss the issue'.[45]

---

[43] Ibid., 33-4.   [44] Burnet (2), 173-4.
[45] Kraut (3), 19. In this Kraut explicitly follows Krentz, who argues for the

We believe that Socrates is simply unwilling to rehearse the obvious.

1. Though Socrates never calls the Thirty's order 'illegal' he does characterize it as being a part of their general strategy to implicate others in their unjust actions. The words Socrates uses to express this view are extremely strong ones: ἀναπλῆσαι αἰτιῶν, 'to defile (or infect) others with the discredit of their acts'. As Burnet notes, this is the sort of language the Greeks used to refer to catching the plague from someone or to 'the *miasma* of bloodguiltiness'.[46] Socrates employs these words to describe the actions of notoriously bloodthirsty men. It seems to us to be the most unlikely that the Socrates who undertakes the arguments of the *Apology* and *Crito* would employ such strongly evocative language and yet still tacitly accept that the defilement in question was none the less entirely legal, or at least arguably so. And it seems to us even more unlikely that he would have felt the need to be careful about this issue before the jury whose very existence derived from the restoration of the democracy the Thirty had sought systematically to dismantle.

2. It is not irrelevant that Socrates views the case of disobeying the Thirty as another instance of the same kind as the case of resisting the mass trial of the generals. On Kraut's view, Socrates' silence on the legality of the former is significant, for it shows that the real issue to Socrates is avoiding injustice. But surely Socrates' silence on the legality of the Thirty's order is no more significant than his repeated concern for legality in the rest of the argument of this part of the *Apology*, in which his actions in defying the Thirty are supposed to provide one of two 'great proofs'. Socrates begins by referring to himself as one who would seek to prevent 'many unjust and illegal things' (πολλὰ ἄδικα καὶ παράνομα) from happening in the state, and as Kraut notes he subsequently refers twice to the illegality of the mass trial of the generals. Of course, Socrates also sometimes refers only to what is just, and does not add legality as a second concern. But since he begins this passage with a concern for legality, and refers again to this issue during the passage, it seems more reasonable to us to suppose that unless he makes some clear stipulation that a given case is only one of injustice *but not illegality*, the latter would be a presumptive element of any case he offers in the passage. If, as Kraut insists,

Thirty's legitimacy. Against this view, however, see the review of Krentz by Christopher Tuplin (op. cit., note 33, above).

[46] Burnet (2), note on 32c8.

there are really two very different sorts of cases in Socrates' 'great proofs', why does Socrates not tell us so? And if the cases are the same only because both concern injustice, why does Socrates keep bringing up the legality issue?

3. The Assembly's decision was to appoint the Thirty to codify 'the ancestral laws of Athens by which they would rule' and presumably in the interim to govern the state. What, then, was the presumptive state of the law in Athens by which the Thirty were to rule in the interim period? It seems to us that a number of alternatives might be argued. Two do not support the legality of the Thirty's command to Socrates: either (*a*) the democratic laws of Athens were still in effect until such time as the 'ancestral' laws were codified, or (*b*) the 'ancestral' laws were already in effect in an uncodified state. Plainly, under (*a*) the Thirty's order would be illegal, though it might be counted as evidence against (*a*) that before any 'ancestral laws' were codified the Thirty erased the democratic laws that were inscribed on a wall next the Royal Stoa.[47]

But let us suppose for the sake of argument that (*b*) was the presupposition of the Assembly's vote to establish the Thirty. By the employment of the term 'ancestral laws', it was clear that an oligarchy was to be set up. But the rhetoric of calling for 'ancestral laws' implies that this oligarchy was to be constituted in a way at least consistent with Athens' own history (or legendary history) prior to the establishment of its democracy. We submit that *no* sensible conception of such 'ancestral laws' would permit the sort of summary arrest and execution, with the former to be carried out by private citizens, that we find in the case of the Thirty's order to Socrates and the others. So unless an argument can be found to show that the Athenians at the time would view such an order as naturally falling within the domain of the 'ancestral laws of Athens', and another argument can be made to show that they would view such a law as already in effect at the time, we see no reason to suppose that Socrates or anyone else would have to count the Thirty's order as anything but illegal, according to the conditions under which they were installed.

4. It might be argued that there is a third possibility, that (*c*) all the laws of Athens were in suspense until such time as the 'ancestral' laws were codified, and that in the meantime anything the Thirty said had the force of law. What we know is only that they acted as if this were

[47] Krentz, 61.

the case, and that no one within the city (successfully, at least) opposed their doing so. Of course, they first set up a series of puppets
through which they would administer their demands: they hand-
picked a new council and a number of magistrates, ten to manage the
Piraeus, ten treasurers, eleven prison wardens and executioners, a
whip-bearing police force of 300, and maybe an Assembly-surrogate
of 3,000 (though the actual participation of the group might have been
minimal[48]). They appeared to take pains to operate through these
channels, at least whenever possible, but the issue is not whether or
not they thereby achieved a semblance of law (or even a set of proclamations that had all the practical force of law) but rather whether
or not Socrates or for that matter any of the Athenians in the restored
democracy would recognize the proclamations thereby set up as being
duly constituted laws, enacted by due process. Given the great difference between the legal state of affairs at the time of the Thirty's
rule and the legal state of affairs surrounding the arguments of the
Crito, and given the restored democracy's subsequent disregard for
the laws enacted by the Thirty (more on this in a moment), there is
good reason to wonder whether Socrates or his jurors considered the
edicts of the Thirty to have the force of the law at all.

5. As Burnet notes,[49] though Plato's Socrates may be silent about
the legality of the Thirty's directive, Xenophon is quite explicit.
Xenophon flatly states that the Thirty's order was illegal (*Mem.*
4.4.3). Kraut finds Burnet's citation of Xenophon on this issue
'curious',[50] but why should one doubt that Xenophon's view of the
legality question reflected the thinking of Socrates and his jurors?
Moreover, Xenophon's assessment has at least some ancient support:
Diodorus tells us that after a period of time during which their execu-
tions had been acceptable to those whom Diodorus calls 'the most
able' of the citizens (presumably the moderate oligarchs) the Thirty
sought to do more 'violent *and illegal* things' (14.4). Of course,
Diodorus does not specify the command given to Socrates as one of
those illegal acts, but certainly the sense of the passage is entirely compatible with Xenophon's assessment of the situation.

Since Xenophon's explicit view is precisely the one that would allow
Plato's Socrates to treat the Thirty's order as a case identical to that of
the trial of the generals, we see no reason to question it. Naturally,

---

[48] Krentz (68) points out that we hear of only one meeting of the 3,000 during the
Thirty's reign.   [49] Burnet (2), 174.   [50] Kraut (3), 19, n. 31.

this also allows us to avoid problems of inconsistency between the *Apology* and *Crito* without further argument, which might be counted as an advantage.

6. The actual legal status of any provisional government installed by conquerors to run a defeated state is almost certainly going to be a matter of dispute for a significant period of time, if the historical record is any guide. Of course, some of these governments become accepted as legitimate, once they have stood the test of time. But the Thirty lasted all of eight months, and a substantial part of this time was spent fighting the civil war that eventually ousted them. It seems most unlikely to us that the democrats who returned to power so soon after having lost it would recognize any feature of the Thirty's reign of terror as legitimate.

Further evidence for our conception of Socrates' and the restored democracy's view of the Thirty may be found in what transpired at Athens during the next few years. Though there was a formal reconciliation between the democrats and oligarchs, the members of the Thirty and at least some of their appointees were explicitly excluded from the terms of this agreement.[51] Moreover, during the restoration there is not the slightest sign that any of the constitutional or legal modifications undertaken by the Thirty were viewed as still in effect; indeed, they appear to have been entirely invalidated by a single broad provision of the restoration (Dem., *Tim.* 24.56). It is true that the amnesty associated with the reconciliation forbade subsequent prosecution of individuals for crimes committed during this period (crimes, that is, defined by democratic constitutional and statutory standards), but this prohibition implies that the actions in question were in fact illegal. Amnesties are not enacted to protect those who had engaged in uncontroversially legal activities.

7. Why, then, does Socrates remind the jurors of the illegality of the mass trial of the generals, but not remind them of the illegality of the Thirty's order to arrest Leon? The latter, we contend, was never a matter of controversy. But the mass trial had been a most important source of controversy between his fellow Athenians and Socrates. Indeed, the entire issue in that case had been the legality of the procedure, and not the guilt or innocence of the accused. So Socrates reminds his jurors of what the issue had been, and that though nearly everyone had initially disagreed with him, all had eventually come

[51] See Chapter 1, note 113.

round to his point of view. Thus, it is reasonable for Socrates to mention legality in the case of the trial of the generals, but not in the case of the Thirty's order to arrest Leon. So Socrates' silence on the legality of the Thirty's order appears to us in all likelihood to show that what Kraut says would involve 'a thicket of historical and conceptual questions'[52] was in fact obvious to everyone concerned, and did not need explicit specification.

So much, then, for the view that Socrates or his jurors would have supposed the Thirty's order to arrest Leon was a legal one. On the other hand, Kraut is certainly right in saying, as he does later,[53] that, regardless of what Socrates might have thought of the legality of the Thirty's order, theirs would not have qualified as a form of government to which the arguments of the *Crito* would apply. As Kraut says, the arguments of the *Crito* are conditioned by the fact that Socrates has lived under the laws of Athens some seventy years (see *Crito* 52e3), and that by staying he has demonstrated his satisfaction with them. Surely the same cannot be said for the reign of the Thirty, whose new ('ancestral') laws were at best incompletely codified, and whose rule by terror hardly endured long enough for Socrates' brief endurance of it to qualify as tacit approval.

In fact, to Kraut's argument we can add a few others. The personified Laws of Athens to whom Socrates owes obedience in the *Crito* also identify themselves as those according to whom Socrates' parents married and by which Socrates was born and raised (50d1–e2; 51c8–d1; 54b2–3). It was under these Laws that he raised children himself (52c2–3). It was also to the Athens of the personified Laws that Socrates gained citizenship via δοκιμασία (51d3).[54] Not one of these conditions is satisfied by the Thirty, so nothing follows concerning Socrates' duty to obey their administration from what in the *Crito* he says he owes to the personified Laws of Athens.

Hence, we find nothing at all in the case of Socrates' disobedience of the Thirty either to shed light on or to conflict with the arguments of the *Crito*. In fact, though we have discussed the issue at length, we believe the entire issue of such conflict to be greatly overworked by modern commentators who have put questions of a high degree of complexity to Plato's texts that neither Socrates nor Plato seem to have anticipated. Socrates never asks what a citizen owes an unjust

---

[52] Kraut (3), 18.   [53] Ibid., 187.

[54] See ibid., 154–7, for a discussion and explanation of the importance of this issue.

state such as that under the Thirty, nor does he ask what he himself would owe Athens if it were to change in some material but unspecified way. So neither is there clear conflict in these texts, we conclude, nor were all the proposed versions of the alleged conflict clearly anticipated and answered there either. Scholars themselves, and not the texts, have created these issues.

4.3.6 CONCLUDING REMARKS

Socrates takes great care to answer a possible objection to his self-portrait as an unceasing promoter of virtue. If he has such concern for morality, why has he not attempted to pursue that concern in the sorts of fora wherein he might achieve the most good for the state, that is, in political activities? His answer is at once direct yet richly complex, in that it allows him not only to answer decisively the specific question, but also to highlight a number of other points of significance to his defense. In its simplest form, his answer is that his *daimonion* has opposed him whenever he thought to undertake a move into the political arena. He does not embellish this answer, nor does he expect his jury to accept it on faith. But strictly speaking, this is his answer—the rest is no more than an explanation and demonstration of why he thinks his *daimonion*'s opposition was appropriate.

The rest, however, has much to offer his jury. Were a man like Socrates to engage in political activity, he would almost certainly and swiftly find himself in mortal danger. In the end, such a man would be killed without having ever really been of much service to himself or to the state. Because these are such jarring words to his democratic audience, he offers them 'great proofs' in actions that speak louder than words, actions that he himself has undertaken to advance the good, which have put him in the gravest danger. The two cases he offers as proofs serve well in showing that an uncompromising commitment to the good can be terribly dangerous when it is pursued in opposition to political authority. But his two 'great proofs' also demonstrate a point to which political partisans are too often blind: where two bitterly opposed factions exist, it does not follow that the critic of one is the friend of the other. Socrates makes no secret of holding a number of views opposed to democratic ideology; but he also reminds his jurors, by recalling his actions at the trial of the Arginousai generals, that the majority is not always right, and that in retrospect even the majority can regret the decisions they make in the heat of emotion.

This is no small point for Socrates to make, for here he is again, facing a suspicious and hostile majority whose emotions have been played upon by the lies and insinuations of his prosecutors. 'I was here before', says Socrates in effect, 'and so were you. Last time you threatened and bullied and nearly killed me, but so soon after you regretted what you did. How will you act this time? Will you forget the lessons of the past, or will you calm yourselves and listen to me now, before you once again do something you will regret?'

And lest his jurors suppose that his criticisms and resistance have only been directed at the democracy, Socrates offers a second 'great proof' in which he recalls his refusal to obey an immoral order by enemies of the democratic regime. In reminding the jury of this action he shows not only that he is as devoted to his mission as he claims to be, despite the most terrible risks to himself, but also that he is what he says he is: a private, not a political man. Socrates' equal opposition to the injustices and tyrannies of the democratic and the oligarchic factions show that he is not a partisan of either. He is precisely what he claims to be: a gadfly, a social critic, and a man who is convinced that he serves as the conscience of Athens. His 'great proofs', therefore, do more than show why his *daimonion*'s opposition was a good thing. They also allow Socrates to warn the jury of the danger of acting in haste and emotion, and to remove the taint of partisan politics that might be misread into other remarks he makes during his defense.

4.4　Socrates' Final Defense against Corrupting the Youth

4.4.1 'THOSE MY SLANDERERS CLAIM TO BE MY STUDENTS'

At *Apology* 32e2–33a1, Socrates reiterates the point of his 'great proofs', asking his jurors if they really believe he could have lived as long as he has if he had chosen to lead a public life 'acting as a good man should, giving assistance to what is just, and considering this of the highest importance?' (32e3–4). He answers his own question by saying once again that no one could do this. So it is that he has undertaken his moral mission in the streets of Athens rather than in her Assembly and jury-courts. But lest they suppose that by avoiding public life Socrates has been inconsistent in 'giving assistance to what is just', he says to his jurors, 'all my life, whether in public activity, if I engaged in such, or in private, I have always been the same, and have never given in to anyone contrary to justice, neither to any other, nor to *any of those my slanderers claim to be my students'* (33a1-5).

In Section 2.4.5 we discussed Socrates' failure to mention his association with Critias and Alcibiades, despite the suggestion of many later writers that his unsavory social contacts contributed to his trial and condemnation. We concluded there that even if these two notorious men were associated with Socrates in the minds of the jurors, his failure to mention them explicitly in no way detracted from the completeness of his defense. But to whom is Socrates referring when he calls attention at 33a4-5 to 'those my slanderers claim to be my students'? One might argue that Socrates' 'slanderers' would select the most damning of Socrates' associates to include in this category, and that history shows that Alcibiades and Critias (and perhaps Charmides) would be at the top of this list. On this reading, Alcibiades and Critias (and maybe Charmides) must have been mentioned as Socrates' students by the 'slanderers', and thus at 33a4-5 Socrates does directly refer to his most notorious associates, so that what follows will constitute Socrates' effort to clear himself of the very guilt by association that we have said does not figure in the *Apology*.[55]

When Socrates says that his slanderers identify certain people as his students, it is not at all clear that by 'my slanderers' he is referring to Meletus, Anytus, and Lycon.[56] In fact, we believe that the expression is much more likely to refer to the 'first' accusers than to these, the 'later' accusers. Throughout the *Apology*, Socrates is quite careful to indicate which of the two sets of accusations he is addressing (see 18a7-e4, 19a8-b2, 24b3-c2, 28a2-b2). At 28a4, Socrates tells the jury that what he has already said is a sufficient defense against the 'later' accusers, and immediately after this he reintroduces the dangers he faces from the long-standing prejudices against him (that is, the 'first' accusations). He never again makes an explicit general shift of attention to the 'later' accusers. It would thus be odd indeed for him abruptly to focus his attention on the 'later' accusers at 33a4 without some specific indication that he is doing so.[57]

---

[55] See, e.g., Burnet ((2), note on 33a4), who takes this view, as does Chroust ((3), 179-80). Mark McPherran called our attention to this issue.

[56] Burnet himself points this out ((2), note on 33a4).

[57] In fact, in the other two cases in which Socrates refers to a set of accusers as 'slanderers' (διαβάλλοντες) it appears that it is the 'first' accusers to whom he refers

But if 'my slanderers' refers to the 'first' accusers, the sense of the passage does not require us to suppose that the actual names of any so-called students had been introduced in court for Socrates to concede or dispute (though it might be that the identities of a number of such persons would be clear enough not to need explicit mention). Instead, Socrates' remarks become quite general—he has never given in to anyone, even those whom popular prejudice may hold to have been his students (whoever these may be). In fact, Socrates' subsequent remarks appear to have just this character, designed to cover any case regarding the teaching of evil ways for which he may have been blamed by the various shadowy 'first' accusers (see 18d6-7).

On the other hand, if we suppose that 'my slanderers' refers to the 'later' accusers, the sense of the passage at least strongly suggests that such alleged students had actually been named in the courtroom, for now Socrates would be referring to persons who Meletus, Anytus, and (or) Lycon had said were Socrates' students. But as we have argued (in 2.4.5), there is excellent reason to suppose that no one had been named in court as Socrates' student.

Let us suppose for the sake of argument that, despite our reservations, Meletus and Anytus did make clear in their speeches that they considered Socrates to have been the 'corrupter' of the notorious Alcibiades and Critias. In what way would they have attempted to raise this issue before the jury? We can be entirely confident that no attempt would have been made by the prosecutors to detail Socrates' subversion of Alcibiades and Critias in an *exclusive* attempt to give content to the vague charge of 'corrupting the youth', for that would violate the conditions of the amnesty;[58] Alcibiades and Critias could, however, serve as paradigm cases of corruption by Socratic teachings that had continued after the passage of the amnesty.

Recall, however, that at 28a4-b2 Socrates declares that if he is condemned it will be only because of the strength of the prejudices and enmity brought about by the 'first accusations', and *not because of Meletus and Anytus*. Thus, even if the prosecutors did refer in specific ways to associations of Socrates' that antedated the amnesty, they could not have singled out particular instances that constituted special damage to Socrates' case, beyond what had been said for so many years by the shadowy 'first' accusers. It would be worth asking, then,

(see 19b3, 23e3). Whenever he plainly refers to the 'later' accusers, he uses some form of 'κατήγοροι'.

[58] See Section 2.4.3.

who might have been said to have been corrupted by Socrates, according to the comic poets, gossip-mongers, and popular prejudices of the day. Unfortunately, virtually all of the evidence on this (with the exception of the *Clouds*, in which Chairephon is the only historical person associated with Socrates) comes from sources later than the *Apology* itself. Of course, this does not show that Alcibiades *et al.* were not included prominently among the alleged 'students' in the minds of many jurors or that the prosecutors did not mention them explicitly in their speeches. The point is simply that we have no reason, other than that given us by later writers, to focus so narrowly on these men.

From these considerations, we conclude that *Apology* 33a4–5 does not of itself compel us to suppose that Socrates alludes specifically to his alleged corruption of Critias, Alcibiades, or Charmides, as opposed to the indefinite number of Athenian youth who, according to the 'first' accusers, were ruined by associating with him (see 23c2–d2). The most probable reading of 33a1–5 is that Socrates never gave in to anyone at all, including *anyone* whom prejudice might hold as having been one of Socrates' students. Hence our earlier presumption, that Alcibiades, Critias, and Charmides are in no way singled out specifically in Socrates' speech, remains justified.

4.4.2 CONVERSING VERSUS TEACHING; LISTENERS VERSUS STUDENTS

Socrates 'slanderers' have claimed that he is a teacher, whose students are corrupted by his teaching. In his initial reply to these accusations, Socrates makes it clear that those prejudiced against him accuse him of being one of the sophists, who corrupt young men for pay (19d8–20a2). Socrates flatly denies being a paid teacher (19d8–e1), for he has no wisdom to offer students (20c1–3). He also reminds his jurors more than once of his poverty, a sure sign that he is no paid teacher (23b9–c1, 31b5–c3; see 37c2–4, 38b1–4).

Because he is ignorant, he has no doctrines to sell to his students. Hence, when his slanderers are asked what it is he teaches that makes him, as they say, 'a most abominable person who corrupts the youth' (23d1–2), they do not know, and to disguise their ignorance they employ the standard accusations that are used against all philosophers (23d2–7). But cannot a man with no doctrines teach? Indeed, is it not precisely a feature of Socrates' mission that he does have something of monumental importance to teach his fellow citizens, namely, that they are ignorant and, thinking they are not, they invest too much in what is of little importance, and too little in what is of great importance (29d7–30b6)? This is not so much a doctrine as an exhortation to be moral and to philosophize; Socrates is thus justified in imagining himself to be less a wise man after the usual fashion than a gadfly (30e5), who stings the body-politic by rousing, inducing, and reproaching words (30e7). Still, can exhortation not count as teaching, and can those goaded into action by such exhortations not be seen as affected by them? If so, cannot Socrates in this sense be convicted rightly of teaching, and thus possibly of corrupting those who are stirred by his exhortations?

Socrates considers this objection at 33a5, beginning, once again, with a flat denial that he was ever anyone's teacher (33a5–6). He does not deny that through his exhortations he has something to teach his fellow Athenians. What he denies is that he is a teacher in the damning sense. To be this, he seems to assume, he would have to be selective about those to whom he talked. Socrates, however, is utterly undiscriminating in his choice of audience: he will speak to young or old (33a7), rich or poor (33b1–2), and has never offered anything in private that he would not offer anyone else quite openly (33b6–8). People are free to listen, or to join in conversation with him or not, as they wish. Socrates demands nothing in return, and promises nothing in the way of instruction to those who converse with him. This is why he says that no one can hold him responsible for anything any of those who have talked with him have done. No evil they do derives from any doctrines they learned or heard from him (33b3–6).

But his conversations are never dull, and young people are especially amused to watch Socrates refute those who make false claims of wisdom (23c2–4; 33b9–c4). Some imitate Socrates and undertake to examine people themselves, and on their own find many who think they have some understanding, when in fact they have little or none (23c4–7; see 39c8–d3). The men refuted by Socrates are frequently roused to hatred (21d1, e1–5); those refuted by his youthful imitators become convinced that Socrates has corrupted the youth (23c7–d2). This, then, would appear to be the real source of the charge of corruption.

From the point of view of a traditional Athenian, Socrates' 'service to the god' might well appear to be corruption. Fifth-century Athens was filled with proud men, men whose culture was built around them.

This was not merely a male-dominated culture, it was a male-authoritarian culture. Adult males did not just rule the state; they ruled their households as well, and everyone living within. According to Aristotle, this was nature's own way of things (*Pol.* 1253b1–11, 1259a37–b17). Such men were loquacious, combative, and sensitive to shame, to the need to come off best in public confrontations. What would be the effect, within such a culture, of a man whose mission took him daily into public places to show how little actual wisdom anyone had? Socrates' mission had the effect of showing young people how little their fathers really knew about how to live, and how ill-supported their values and traditions were. And Socrates' youthful imitators did not passively accept their elders' authority; rather, they questioned it, and were amused by their ability to refute and confuse their elders on their most vital and cherished beliefs.

It is entirely possible in fact that some of Socrates' youthful listeners became convinced, by his ability to refute unreflectively held traditional values, that no such values could be supported, and were thus led into the profoundest moral nihilism. First encounters with critical philosophic reasoning often have this effect, even today. But inasmuch as Socrates held a number of moral and religious beliefs with strong conviction, and did so consistently with his philosophical methods and presuppositions, such nihilism can have been neither intended by him or a logical consquence of his arguments. Some of Socrates' young listeners probably got the wrong idea from his refutations; some of their elders certainly did. The results of Socrates' philosophy doubtless required many changes in what is commonly and uncritically held within tradition. But not all changes are destructive, despite the discomfort they might cause.

Yet surely Socrates was aware that not all of those who witnessed his conversations understood their fundamental motivations. Surely he had to realize that some of his audience enjoyed the negative aspect of his mission as a sport in its own right, without regard for its real goals or the profoundly moral and religious foundation upon which it was erected. What could he say against those who would accuse him of at least contributing to the young people's corruption by arming them with weapons against the common morality and leaving nothing in its place? Do the costs of the examined life, when it is undertaken collectively, outweigh the benefits? Is it not better to have all accept traditional values, even if they are somewhat confused?

Socrates does have a reply: he has been 'commanded to do this by the god, both by oracles and by dreams and in every way in which divinity has ever commanded a man to do anything' (33c4–7). It is an article of faith to Socrates that the god would command no evil. Piety provides the crucial premiss in his defense against those who would hold against him the fact that he has a following, and that some of its members might draw destructive and inappropriate conclusions from the destructive elements in Socrates' peculiar form of philosophical activism.

4.4.3 SOCRATES' WITNESSES: THE 'VICTIMS' THEMSELVES

Many of his contemporaries misunderstood Socrates. In all likelihood, some of this misunderstanding resulted from the use of sophistical arguments by some who were thought to have spent time with Socrates. Such arguments may well have—at least in the eyes of the untutored—borne a strong resemblance to the Socratic *elenchos*. But even if some of those who engaged in sophistries learned a certain amount of logic from listening to Socrates and turned it to immoral ends, Socrates could hardly be held responsible for their having done so. Nor could he be held responsible for those among the young who sincerely imitated his elenctic method, even though its results no doubt irritated those whose beliefs were shown to be inconsistent.

Although his confidence that his work is divinely sanctioned generates his belief that the use of the *elenchos* leads to morally therapeutic results, his actual experience with people confirms it. His final defense against the charge of corrupting the youth capitalizes on this experience. He invites testimony from those most likely to have been victims of his corruption, if such there has been: the young men who have spend a great deal of time watching and listening to him, and their fathers and brothers (33c8–34b5).[59]

Surely if someone like Aristophanes' Strepsiades had been present in court that day, Socrates' offer would have produced a witness against him. But no one, in Plato's or in Xenophon's version, stood up in court and claimed to have been misled in any way by Socrates, nor did anyone make that claim on behalf of kin. The alleged 'victims' of Socrates' corruption, it seems, were his staunchest defenders.

That the offer is not accepted should perhaps not surprise us in the

---

[59] See Section 2.4.5 and especially note 65 for other discussion of this feature of Socrates' defense.

case of those most directly victimized by Socrates' teaching: *ex hypothesi* they are corrupted (34b1-2). Perhaps even similar reasons can be found for the silence of the indirect 'victims', the fathers and brothers of these 'corrupted'. It would be difficult for proud men from traditionally close-knit and defensive Athenian families to get up in court and denounce one of their own family members as being ruined, even if doing so promised to assist in bringing the real culprit to justice.

But surely some families could be found in which members had been discredited in ways from which other members would be eager to disassociate themselves. Socrates' own proffered witnesses, then, are not as interesting as those he invites Meletus to produce (34a2-6). The only security Socrates can have in this invitation, as we argued in Section 2.4.5, is that in fact no specific individual case of corruption has been made explicit by the prosecutors in court, no doubt because the grounds for their prosecution derived instead from the general prejudice generated by the 'first' accusations. But that prejudice, the bias of those who carelessly mistook Socrates for a nature-philosopher or sophist, could not have arisen in the minds of those whom Socrates himself invites to speak against him. Those whom he himself invites are persons who knew the moral quality of his activities. Had his prosecutors got close enough to act as informed witnesses against him they would have seen what he actually did in his daily discussions, and hence that they had no grounds for accusing him. Unlike Jesus, Socrates was not betrayed by someone close to him. But it is clear that the prejudice involved was a powerful one, and that witnesses and specific cases of corruption were not needed for the conviction and condemnation Meletus and his supporters won without them.

4.5   The Conclusion of Socrates' Defense

4.5.1   THE PERORATION

Among the several features that Socrates' defense shares with standard fifth-century forensic oratory is the use of a peroration in which the speaker makes certain final remarks to the jury that are not strictly part of his argument. But although Socrates concludes his defense with a peroration, what he actually says is anything but conventional. Contrary to what must have been recommended by the oratorical theories of the period,[60] Socrates forgoes any attempt to summarize the main points of his defense. And in spite of their legality,[61] he will not employ any of the emotional displays (common at the conclusion of high-stakes trials) aimed at winning the compassion of the jury.[62] Instead, Socrates uses what little time is left to him to explain why his jurors will see none of the heart-rending performances they no doubt expected.

Socrates prefaces his reasons for refusing to beg for his release by telling the jury that he is fully aware that he is in the gravest of danger (34c6-7). They should not assume that arrogance has blinded him to be the personal losses conviction will bring. Quoting Homer, he says that he is only human, 'not born of oak or rock' (34d4-5).[63] And like any other man with a family, he is mindful of what conviction will do to those who are dependent on him. He tells the jury that he has a family that includes three sons, two of whom are still small children (34d2-7). Although he cannot allow these considerations to shape his defense, they weigh upon him none the less; accordingly, Socrates seeks to disabuse the jury of their assumption that only 'pridefulness or lack of respect' (34d9-e1) could keep him from begging for their mercy. He is not, he assures them, totally indifferent to their power to determine his fate.

4.5.2 WHY BEGGING FOR MERCY IS DISGRACEFUL

Socrates' first reason for refusing to manipulate the emotions of the jury is that to do so would bring disgrace to him, to the jury, and to the city as a whole. He tells the jury, 'in the light of (πρός) my reputa-

---

[60] In the *Phdr.* (267d3-6) Plato tells us that rhetoricians of the period agree that the appropriate end of a speech is a peroration and that it should consist of a summary of the main points made by the speaker. Aristotle (*Rh.* 1414b4-14) confirms Plato's view of the matter, although he adds that a peroration is unnecessary in a forensic speech when the speech is short and its main points can be remembered easily. For more on the use and aims of a peroration, see Kennedy, 56-61.

[61] As Burnet points out ((2), 144), Xenophon (*Mem.* 4.4.4) believed that such appeals were illegal. But if Socrates had thought so, he certainly would have cited their illegality as grounds for not making them. In any case, the use of such appeals was simply too common for them to have been illegal. (See next note.)

[62] For evidence that such emotional appeals were quite common, see Burnet (2), 144-5, esp. note on 34c3. In addition to the references he cites, see Ar. *Vesp.* 568-72.

[63] The line appears twice in Homer, first in the *Iliad*, 22.126, and again in the *Odyssey*, 19.163. Burnet ((2), note on 34d4) assumes that Socrates is alluding to the *Odyssey* passage, where Penelope says the line to Odysseus. But the line also appears in the *Iliad*, spoken by Hector to himself before he is slain by Achilles. Since both

tion (δόξα) and yours and that of the whole city, it does not seem to be right (καλόν) to do any of these things, given my age and my reputation (ὄνομα), whether it is correct or incorrect' (34e2-5). He immediately proceeds to explain just what reputation he has come to have. It is held, he says, that Socrates is superior (διαφέρειν) in some way to many men (34e5-35a1). But it is disgraceful, he goes on to say, for anyone who seems to be superior to other men with respect to wisdom or courage or any other virtue to try to win a favorable verdict by playing on the jury's sense of pity (35a1-3). Of course, he has often seen others (including, he assumes, some of the jurors now sitting in judgment of his case (see 34c7-8)) engage in such displays and these include some of those who are generally thought to be most superior with respect to virtue (35b1-3). But by acting as they do when on trial, he says, they bring disgrace to the city (35a7-8). Thus, because he himself has gained such a reputation, in his case a reputation for wisdom (see 34e5-35a1; 20c4-d9),[64] Socrates concludes that it would be disgraceful (αἰσχρός) for him to engage in such demanding tactics.

It is not surprising, given everything else we know about Socrates, that he finds attempts to appeal to the emotions of the jury disgraceful. What is perhaps surprising is that his explanation turns on the disgracefulness of such practices on the part of those who have merely a *reputation* for virtue. His investigations of other men have revealed that neither he nor they actually possess virtue, in spite of whatever reputations they may happen to have (see 21b1-22e5). As a result, he has reason to believe that the reputation any Athenian, including himself, has for 'superiority with respect to virtue' is, in fact, undeserved. Moreover, surely Socrates thinks such behavior is disgraceful even when it is practiced by those who are renowned for their villainy. Socrates' first explanation, then, raises two questions. First, why does he not simply say that such appeals to emotion are disgraceful *per se* and that for that reason alone neither he nor anyone else should ever engage in them? Secondly, why does he think that such appeals bring disgrace not only to the litigant who employs them but also to the jury and the city as a whole?

passages fit the context of Socrates' remark, it is impossible to tell to which he is referring or if he is referring to either passage in particular.

[64] It is of course part of the 'first' accusations that have long circlated in Athens that Socrates is a sophist who teaches his doctrines. Although he denies that the accusation is true, he does not deny that he regards actually 'having wisdom' as a most admirable thing (see 19c5-7, 20b9-c1).

The key to understanding Socrates' first explanation is to be found in his remark that 'any stranger might respond that the Athenians who are superior with respect to virtue, men whom they themselves judge worthy of offices and other honors, are no better than women' (35a8–b3). This, Socrates tells the jury, brings disgrace to the whole city (35a7–8; see 38a7–8). The point of this remark cannot be that such actions are disgraceful because they tarnish Athens' reputation, as if the loss of Athens' reputation for virtue is itself disgraceful. For Socrates, in order for something to be truly disgraceful, it must be an evil. Earlier he told the jury that from his examination of his fellow Athenians he had come to the realization that their concern for their reputations was utterly misplaced, because they have not first attained virtue (see 29d4–30a2). Although Socrates believes that a reputation for virtue could actually be a good, and hence that its loss could be an evil, its goodness is always contingent upon one's first having actually acquired virtue.[65] Consequently, since Socrates believes that no Athenians truly possess virtue, he cannot believe the loss of their reputation in the eyes of those who scoff at their shameless behavior in court is an evil. Hence, it cannot be the loss of their reputation for virtue that explains his condemnation of emotional appeals to the jury.

But if those who have a reputation for virtue act in vicious ways, witnesses might be led to believe that such actions are not vicious and shameful. We often judge the virtue of a person by the quality of his or her actions; but it is entirely likely, especially in ancient Athens, that inferences would proceed in the other direction: a person's actions would be judged by the reputation of the agent performing them. Hence, those with a reputation for virtue must especially avoid disgraceful action, for by engaging in such action they create a misleading impression about virtue.

Moreover, though Socrates specifically denies that he possesses the wisdom requisite for virtue, as we have argued,[66] he is convinced of the truth of a variety of propositions regarding the nature and value of virtue. One of these truths is that virtue provides its possessor with an absolute safeguard against wrongdoing, and thus, for Socrates, the virtuous man will never succumb to his passions and act in a manner contrary to what virtue requires.[67] So Socrates may also worry

[65] See Brickhouse and Smith (9), and Section 4.2.2, above.

[66] See Sections 2.6 and 3.2.

[67] This follows directly from the 'Socratic paradoxes' that virtue is knowledge and is sufficient for the pursuit of the good.

that when those who have a reputation for superiority with respect to virtue shamelessly appeal to the emotions of the jury, they foster in those who witness such disgraceful performances a different, but still importantly false belief about the value of virtue: such men may convince their audience that even the most virtuous persons sometimes act in a manner contrary to what is admirable and right.

Socrates believes that fostering false belief about virtue is itself disgraceful.[68] As a result, he would view pandering to the emotions of the jury by those who have a reputation for virtue as triply disgraceful: such behavior is disgraceful in itself, and men of reputation who engage in it either promote the false belief that such behavior is not disgraceful or else promote the false belief that virtue provides no absolute protection against the performance of immoral action. Thus, because Socrates himself has a reputation for superiority with respect to virtue, it would be especially disgraceful for him to stoop to the tactics Athenian juries have so often witnessed. In so far as all who witness such actions or hear about it from those present would take such actions as evidence for one or the other of a pair of importantly false beliefs, such actions would bring disgrace to him, to the jurors, and to his fellow citizens.

Socrates' second reason for refusing to grovel before the jury is considerably more straightforward: 'apart from the matter of reputation, it does not seem to me to be just (δίκαιος) to beg the juror or to be acquitted by begging, but only to instruct and to persuade. The juror does not sit here to grant favors about justice, but to give judgment about it' (35b9–c4). He immediately reminds them that the jurors' oath they have taken binds them not to do just as they please, but to 'judge according to the laws' (35c4–5). Were he to encourage them to disregard that oath and were they to do so, they would all become guilty of impiety (35c5–7).

As we argued above,[69] Socrates' commitments require that he honor all just legal institutions, and he no doubt believes that the duty Athenian jurors have sworn to carry out is just. But the nature of the oath they have taken requires not simply that they, as jurors, attempt to ensure that the trial ends in a just outcome, but that they seek a just outcome according to the laws of the city. It is for this reason that Socrates repeatedly reminds the jury that he says only what is true and

---

[68] See Chapter 1, note 153.

[69] See Sections 1.5.3, 3.3, and 4.3.5, above, where we argue that Socrates believes that he must honor all just laws and legal institutions.

that they must set aside their long-standing prejudice against him and listen only to the truth.[70] Only in this way can they *judge* the case before them as their oath requires. Were Socrates to appeal to the juror's sense of pity by parading his family before them, he might well succeed in bringing many of them to vote for his acquittal. But in spite of the legality of the various appeals to pity so often practiced, Socrates' commitment not to encourage the jurors to violate their oath requires that he forgo all such ploys, even if engaging in them would assuage the wrath of those who would otherwise vote for his condemnation out of anger for his refusal to adopt the manipulative tactics they themselves had used in court.

4.5.3 ASSESSING THE RISKS OF SOCRATES' PERORATION

It might be thought that Socrates' decision to explain his refusal to appeal to the emotion of the jury constitutes a telling counter-example to the principal thesis of our interpretation of the *Apology*, namely, that Socrates' speech is throughout a sincere and serious attempt to gain his release in a manner consistent with his principles. Although his principles clearly prohibit him from making any appeal to the sympathy of the jury for the reasons he gives, it might be objected that his decision to explain why he cannot act as other litigants so often do seems hardly calculated to gain acquittal. On the contrary, it might be argued, his decision to explain what his principles require seems best understood as a deliberate attempt actually to enrage at least some of the jurors. After all, Socrates' final remarks are directed at an unspecified number of jurors who, he assumes, have engaged in such shameful maneuvers when they themselves had been litigants (34b7–d1). He worries that when, by his refusal to stoop to such tactics, they feel ashamed by being forced to recall their own ignoble behavior, they will vote against him out of anger (34c7–d1). Although he expresses doubt that any of them would actually vote against him out of anger generated by such humiliation (34d1–2), he is nevertheless mindful of such a possibility (34c7–d1). By choosing so emphatically to underscore his moral superiority, rather than simply remaining silent or using his time to summarize his defense, Socrates appears to be risking the gratuitous alienation of at least some portion of the jury and, thereby, knowingly undermining his chances for acquittal. If so, it would seem reasonable to suppose that, at least at the

[70] See Section 1.5.3.

conclusion of his defense, Socrates is not seriously trying to win his release. Rather, one might conclude, it is far more likely that Socrates is at most indifferent to the jury's judgment of his activities and that he uses his final remarks to draw the sharpest contrast possible between his own moral superiority and the shameless cowardice of so many other defendants, including at least some of those now sitting in judgment of him.

This objection assumes that, if we are right, Socrates would never knowingly alienate the sympathies of any of his judges. But though we believe, of course, that sense can be made of the *Apology* only if Socrates is understood always to be guided by his principles, it does not follow that in seeking acquittal he must never say what he knows will in all probability anger at least some jurors and, therefore, make them less disposed to be persuaded of the justice of his case. There is no reason to suppose that all the jurors feel the same way about everything that Socrates tells them in his speech. Thus, it is possible that the only way Socrates can hope to maintain the openness of any of the jurors to the justice of his case is to say what he knows will alienate others. Where this is the case, regardless of the proportions of the division among the jurors, if Socrates seeks acquittal by a majority persuaded of the justice of his case the only rational course for him to take is to risk alienating some in order to preserve the openness of others. It falls to us, then, to show that this is precisely the situation Socrates faces at the conclusion of his defense.

First, although Socrates knows that by his failure to plead for mercy he may well antagonize at least some of the jurors, he also must be aware that were he to say nothing to explain his failure those same jurors might nevertheless be angry. As he suggests, some jurors might assume that his decision not to beg was based on either pridefulness or lack of respect (34d9–e1), and might do so, moreover, whether he explained his behavior or not. Thus, by choosing to explain why his principles prevent him from begging, instead of remaining silent or merely summing up the main points of his defense, he may not substantially increase the likelihood that his jurors will be offended.

Secondly, although the jury fully expects Socrates to make some sort of appeal to their sense of pity, it is not the case that they would regard such an appeal as in any way morally or legally appropriate. On the contrary, regardless of how many jurors would actually be swayed by the appearance of his wife and children, for example, it is clear that Socrates regards all the jurors, including even those who have done things of this sort themselves, as seeing any such attempt to manipulate them as shameful.[71] If Socrates, in order to get acquitted, were to choose not to explain his refusal to beg, as the objection we are considering implies, all the jurors, including those who have never practiced such shameful tactics, will assume that it is either pridefulness or contempt that prevents him. Thus, were Socrates to say nothing to explain his refusal he would not be assured of avoiding the anger of those who have acted disgracefully themselves and he would risk antagonizing the rest of the jury, since all might mistake his reason for refusing. But if, on the other hand, he explains why he must not grovel, by explaining why it is disgraceful and wrong, he may well mollify at least those jurors who have not acted shamefully themselves in court. Thus, given the choices available to him at this point in the trial, if Socrates wishes to be acquitted without having to violate his principles it is rational for him to do precisely what he does: he must, at the end of his defense speech, attempt to persuade the jury that only by not begging for their mercy can he avoid bringing disgrace to himself and to them.

Finally, although many jurors would no doubt have considered it disgraceful for Socrates to bring a weeping wife and infant children before them, they also know that such appeals have often proved effective in helping to gain a litigant a favorable verdict. By choosing to explain why he cannot act as the jury expects, therefore, Socrates forces the point that he will not accept acquittal at the cost of violating the dictates of his principles. But by so doing he also underscores what is perhaps the central feature of his defense of the philosophical life: regardless of the dangers he has faced, he has always acted from an unflinching commitment to what is right. By implication, then, he underscores the sincerity and straightforwardness of his defense as a whole, and reminds the jury of the principal tenets on which it was based, by once again exemplifying them, without offering the customary summary of them. If this is correct, far from being a gratuitous attack on those jurors who themselves had disgraced themselves when they were in court, the peroration to Socrates'

---

[71] To understand Socrates' point, it is important to notice that Socrates assumes that even those jurors who have engaged in attempts to sway a jury through appeals to pity recognize the shamefulness of their actions. He does not suppose that he must convince anyone of the disgracefulness of such actions. On the contrary, he assumes that they will become angry as they recall their disgraceful behavior when he refuses to do such things himself.

defense provides an ingenious conclusion that aims at disabusing all the jurors of any mistaken notion they may have regarding his reason for refusing to beg for their mercy. By offering the peroration he does, Socrates demonstrates his respect for them as jurors, for the city as a whole, and for himself.

5

5.1 SOCRATES' FINAL
TWO SPEECHES

5.1 The Effectiveness of Socrates' Speech

5.1.1 A FEW MORE WORDS ABOUT THE STYLE AND TONE OF SOCRATES' DEFENSE

In the foregoing chapters we have tried to explain why Socrates hoped his defense would succeed, and how the actual defense he presented was supposed to serve this end. Our argument has been that sense can be made of the *Apology* only if Socrates is seen as attempting to secure his acquittal in a manner consistent with his principles. To be sure, we can conceive of ways in which he could have made his release more likely; but to have done so would have required him to violate one or more of his deepest moral or religious convictions. These same convictions, none the less, did not prevent Socrates from undertaking a serious defense. On the contrary: he thought himself obliged to do so, and he fulfilled his obligation with dignity, elegance, and economy.

We cannot rest our case here, however, for we have not yet discussed a number of aspects of the defense speech itself that might be seen as gratuitously ironic or arrogant, in which Socrates appears needlessly to jeopardize his own chances for acquittal. There are, after all, numerous places in his speech where Socrates refers to outbursts from the jury, apparently outraged at what he says (20e4, 21a5, 27b5, 30c3). And what else could it be, one might ask, but haughty defiance that explains Socrates' refusal to call those who sit in judgment on him 'judges' (δικασταί/*dikastai*), and his insistence on calling them instead 'men' or 'men of Athens'?[1] And how else can we regard Socrates' often extreme claims that go considerably beyond a strict refutation of the charges against him, as for example when he tells the

---

[1] See, e.g., Brann, 1. C. Phillipson considers this issue on 356; T. West simply states that Socrates 'studiously avoided' calling the jurors 'judges' (66, n. 123); see also Burnet (2), note on 17a1.

jury that he pleads not for himself but for them, lest they destroy the 'gift' presented to the city by the god (30d5-e1)?

Such evidence is not as compelling as its proponents would have us believe, however. For example, the significance of the jury's boisterous interruptions has surely been exaggerated by those who have cited it as evidence for Socrates' having needlessly jeopardized his release. Of course, Socrates is not willing to pander to the jury (see 34b7-35d3, 38d3-e5), and he does at least say things that many jurors may not have wished to hear. But derisive outbursts were by no means an uncommon feature of Athenian trials,[2] and it is not unlikely that expressions of defiance or arrogance were regular features of Athenian defense speeches. Thus, the fact that Socrates is also interrupted hardly warrants the claim that he needlessly irritates the jury or must be guilty of wanton disregard for their judicial function.

Similarly, calling the jurors simply 'men' or 'men of Athens' hardly constitutes an offense against them. Such appellations are at worst quite neutral and are in any case not unheard of in this context.[3] Nor does Socrates' later shift to '*dikastai*' show that his earlier form of address was offensive. Since he believes that the function of a juror is to judge according to justice, it is not determined before the outcome of the case has been decided who of those sitting in judgment of him will actually perform their function. Moreover, the bland form of address Socrates uses could hardly have prompted the jury to condemn him, since he does not contrast it with what he considers the more honorific label until after his fate had been entirely determined. Had he sought to address the jury in a provocative way, Greek offers any number of forceful and vivid forms of address, all of which Socrates eschewed for the plain neutrality of 'men' or 'men of Athens'. On the face of it, then, it seems quite unlikely that Socrates' form of address had a significant impact on the jury, even if '*dikastai*' was the more usual

---

[2] See Burnet (2), note on 17d1. For an excellent discussion of the phenomenon, see Victor Bers, 'Dikastic *Thorubos*', in *Crux* (Festschrift for G. E. M. de Ste. Croix), *History of Political Thought* 6 (1985), P. A. Cartledge and F. D. Harvey, eds., 1-15. One who takes Socrates' references to the jury's outbursts in the *Apology* as signifying Socrates' defiance is Guardini, 31.

[3] See C. Phillipson, who cites similar modes of address by Andocides, Aischines Rhetor, and Deinarchus, and yet another variation by Isocrates (356). To this list it is fair to add Lysias, who in *Against Eratosthenes* does not address the jurors as 'judges' until after using the plainer 'men' three times; nor does he show any preference for the former form of address in subsequent remarks.

form of address—which, in any case, is hardly established with any certainty by the historical evidence.[4]

Still, our critics might complain that Socrates' speech is less effective than it could have been if, as we claim, he really had tried to do everything he could do, within his principles, to gain his acquittal. For all we know, Socrates might well have fared better had he limited his defense to the formal charges, pointing out that Meletus can produce no one who has been corrupted (as at 33c8-34b5), and professing his belief in the 'state divinities', perhaps with witnesses to corroborate this claim. Such a limited defense, however, would not have answered all of the suspicions aroused by the 'first accusers', whom Socrates considered more dangerous than Meletus and his supporters (18b1-4). In order to pursue his release (and thus the correct outcome of the case as well as the continuation of his mission), Socrates had to relieve the jurors of the prejudice these 'first' accusations had aroused against him, a prejudice that extended well beyond the narrow issues raised by the formal charges. Hence, he was required to tell them in the clearest way possible the full truth about his life and mission. In doing so, he reminded them repeatedly that though they may not have wished to hear what he had to say, it was also their duty not to be angered by those truths.

It is no doubt true that at least parts of the speech were taken by the jury to be arrogant boasting, and this may well have had the effect of strengthening the bias against Socrates. But from the fact that something is taken as arrogance, it does not follow that it is intended as such. Indeed, Socrates himself explicitly warned the jury against drawing such an inference (20e4-5, 37a2-5); for he was well aware that some of the truths he had to tell would probably be mistaken for bravado, and it was of great importance to him that he should not be misunderstood. Yet, even if he did not intend to anger the jury, the fact remains that he knew that what he said would have that effect. Why then, it might be asked, did he not offer a more restrained and

---

[4] Though Burnet ((2), note on 17d1), T. West (15), and Phillipson (356) claim that '*dikastai*' is the customary form of address, none offers evidence for this claim. Nor should we expect any such evidence to be historically compelling: since the cases we have to compare are so few, and the above examples (see note 3, above) show that Socrates' forms of address are not uncommon, even in successful defenses, any claim as to what the usual practice was is prohibitively speculative. A view similar to ours is expressed by Bonner (see 171-2). Maas speculates that Socrates did not call his jurors '*dikastai*' before the final speech because it would be a form of rhetorical flattery to use that form of address.

hence more effective defense, if he really did want the jury to release him?

Socrates was not willing to gain his release at the cost of violating his principles. He knew, for instance, that he damaged his chances for gaining acquittal by not adopting an obsequious posture of the sort often taken by defendants. But to do so, he says, would be wrong and disgraceful (34b7–35d8). Although he was completely convinced of his innocence, his commitment to just legal institutions demanded that he assist the jurors in discharging their legal responsibility by giving them as much of the relevant truth as possible upon which to base their judgment. So Socrates was not free to narrow the scope of his defense. He had to tell the jury everything he could about the divine nature of his mission and his unqualified commitments to philosophy and the acquisition of virtue. He therefore had to attempt to inform the jury fully in spite of the likelihood that some who heard such extraordinary truths would be angered by his apparent lack of humility before the power of the court.

In any case, nothing in the way we have understood his principles required Socrates to bow and scrape to the jury. Rather, we argue that his reverence for the law, commitment to truth and virtue, and divine mission required that he do his best to defend himself against the false allegations against him. But his principles also required that he do nothing shameful or that might in any way lend support to the falsehood that he was actually guilty. What the proponents of the views we have rejected must do, therefore, is not merely select instances where Socrates must have known that what he said would anger certain members of the jury, for even the most carefully literal and sincere defense would almost certainly have had this effect on more than one occasion. Those who wish to cite such anger as evidence for Socratic irony or arrogance must show first that the claims Socrates made that aroused such anger must not be taken as the simple and literal truth and, then, that the risk of such a departure from direct simple sincerity is compatible with his principles.

Finally, even if Socrates believed that what he had to say might cause some of the jurors to be outraged and, as a result, vote against him, nothing in his speech violates his commitment to encourage jurors to abide by their oath 'to judge to the laws', nothing he says is untrue or unjust, and nowhere does he violate his mission. He emphatically warned the jury not to be angered by the truth; and as we have argued, his principles required that he inform the jury in the most forceful and complete way about the nature of his activities. If some of the jurors voted against him out of anger or prejudice, the impiety and injustice were theirs, not his.

5.1.2 THE JURY'S VERDICT

It might be supposed that the jury's vote to convict is evidence against our account. If Socrates' defense was everything we say it was, why would the jury convict him anyway? In fact, however, we are inclined to see in the jury's vote still further evidence for our view. Plato tells us that the margin by which Socrates was convicted was remarklably narrow (*Ap.* 35e1–36a6). Of the multitude of jurors, very nearly a majority actually voted for his acquittal. Had only thirty additional jurors voted for Socrates he would have won the case. He even says that had he been given more time to speak, he would have secured his release (37a7–b1). The closeness of the vote, if indeed many of the jurors were already deeply prejudiced against him at the outset of the trial, undermines considerably the claim that Socrates' defense had the effect of infuriating any but those members of the jury already blindly hostile to him. Despite the 'outrages' Socrates is alleged to have committed in his speech, and despite the general sentiment against Socrates, and indeed against all intellectuals at that time in Athens, almost a majority found him innocent. Were we to believe that Socrates' defense had the unhappy effects it is so often portrayed as having had, we would have to believe what seems altogether implausible, that a majority (or at least something very near it) were either neutral or favorably disposed towards Socrates before he undertook to defend himself. If not, it is difficult to see how his behavior could possibly have been seen as offensive to very many of the jurors.

5.2 Socrates' Counter-penalty Proposal

5.2.1 THE FINAL 'OUTRAGE'?

Perhaps the most notorious evidence cited in favor of the view that Socrates gratuitously sacrifices his chances for release comes after his conviction: when called upon to offer a counter-penalty, Socrates first likens himself to a hero, saying he deserves state maintenance by being given free meals at the Prutaneion (36d5–37a1), then rejects any penalties that might have been seen as appropriate (37a2–38b1), and finally offers a fine (38b1–9) which scholars have characterized as so 'ridiculously small'[5] as to have 'incensed' the judges.[6]

Those inclined to the view that Socrates' fine was an outrage pro-pose three items as evidence for their interpretation. First, it is said that Socrates' moral scruples forbid him to offer any substantial counter-penalty, for to do so would be to lend support to the charges of which he had been wrongly convicted. Secondly, as we have said, many scholars have said that the amount of the fine Socrates comes to offer is so absurdly small as to have invited his judges' wrath. Finally, commentators point to evidence for supposing that the second vote—to select death rather than the fine Socrates offers—was even more decisive than the prior vote to convict him had been. This is taken as showing that Socrates' counter-penalty speech or ultimate offer further alienated the jury that had already found him guilty of the most serious crimes.

We shall argue against all three of the above points. (1) As we argued for the claims Socrates made in his defense speech, we believe his most important moral scruples would compel him to offer as substantial a penalty as he can. (2) We believe this is precisely what Socrates does, for, contrary to what many have said, the fine Socrates offers is a substantial sum of money. (3) Finally, we find the alleged shift in votes after Socrates' offer both historically dubious and, even if true, no evidence for the view it is so often said to support.

5.5.2 SOCRATES' MORAL COMMITMENTS AND THE OFFER OF A COUNTER-PENALTY

Two of the three main sources on Socrates' trial—those provided by Xenophon and Diogenes Laertius—support the view that Socrates was committed to making no reasonable counter-proposal to the penalty of death stipulated in the indictment. According to Xenophon, when called upon to offer a counter-penalty Socrates simply refused, explicitly on the grounds that he was innocent and thus deserved no penalty (*Ap.* 23). On Diogenes' account, Socrates first offered to pay one μνᾶ (*mna*) of silver, but later changed his offer to a request for state maintenance (2.42). Were we simply to accept

---

[5] Friedländer, vol. 1, 170.
[6] Burnet (1), 182. Others who share this view include Barrow, 10; Bury (1), 565, and (2) 393, 395; Oldfather (1), 288; Riddell, xix, and Zeller (2), 200.

either of these accounts, it would be reasonable to suppose that Socrates was indeed unwilling to offer a recognizable counter-penalty. But in Plato's account, Socrates at least makes an offer, and is supported in this offer by Plato himself, as well as by three other friends. Regardless of their views about the seriousness of Socrates' offer, most scholars are inclined to accept Plato's version of at least this aspect of the trial as the most dependable of the three. Xenophon was in Asia at the time of the trial, and Diogenes, who wrote more than six centuries later, explicitly bases his view upon conflicting accounts with no apparent regard for their various historical merits.

The problem, then, is this: can Socrates' position be formulated in such a way as to explain consistently (*a*) his unwavering conviction that he is innocent of any crime; (*b*) his moral scruple against lending credence to the guilty verdict of the jury, even in the face of death; (*c*) his unwillingness to propose other forms of punishment such as banishment; and (*d*) his willingness to propose a fine of thirty μναῖ (*mnai*)?

In answering this complex question, we must bear in mind three of Socrates' most basic beliefs. First, regardless of how the strength of this commitment is to be interpreted (about which see Section 3.3), Socrates is duty-bound to obey the laws of Athens respectfully. Secondly, it is clear that Socrates does not view death as the worst thing that can happen to him; the commission of injustice would be a far greater evil and harm (see *Ap.* 29a4–30d5). It would therefore be a mistake to think of him as wishing to avoid death at all costs. In fact, it is clear that he views a number of possible penalties as considerably worse fates than the death penalty proposed by Meletus (37b2–8). If we take seriously Socrates' professions in the *Apology* and elsewhere, we must suppose that he is not even convinced that death is an evil thing.[7] At the same time, we know that Socrates would refuse to consider as just anything that involved harming someone or trading harm for harm, evil for evil.[8] If he is to be consistent with his own moral principles in this regard, he cannot propose a penalty that would be an evil, or that would harm him, for were that penalty selected by the jury he would become a party to harming someone, namely himself. But the potential for harm to himself is not the gravest danger

---

[7] Of course, by the third speech (see 40a3–c3) Socrates seems to be convinced that death is not an evil thing. We believe there are special reasons why he can be confident of this by then, and discuss these in Section 5.4. For now, let it suffice to say we believe he has no such certainty earlier in the dialogue, as is shown by the more guarded remarks he makes in the earlier two speeches, at 29a4–b6 and 37b6–7.

[8] See Chapter 1, note 152, for references.

Socrates must consider. Should he propose some evil and harmful counter-penalty, Socrates would thereby encourage the jurors to bring the gravest of all harms upon themselves: the injustice that infects and corrupts the soul. Meletus' proposed penalty would then be preferable, since it is not clear to Socrates that death would involve being harmed. Therefore, any penalty he might propose must be at least no more likely to harm him than that proposed by Meletus. Only in this way may Socrates offer his jurors an option by which they can save themselves the terrible price of injustice.

Finally, Socrates believes that he has been instructed by the god to practice philosophy. He is thus morally bound (in virtue of piety) to do the god's bidding. Any penalty he proposes must thus be consistent with the following three moral obligations: (1) he must not disobey or show disrespect for any law or legal authority; (2) he must not harm himself or anyone else, or encourage or facilitate any such harm being done; and (3) he must not in any way volunteer to do anything that would require disobedience to the god.

The second obligation requires that Socrates should not endorse a false moral claim, for to do so would be unjust in itself, and could promote injustice in others. But a majority of those to whom he speaks have already shown that they are convinced that he is guilty of a most serious crime. Socrates is thus faced with a conflict. On the one hand, he cannot in any way lend credence to the idea that he is morally culpable for his service to the god, for that would be impious itself. On the other hand, he is legally guilty, in virtue of the decision of the jury. And now it is time for him to offer an alternative penalty. What should he do?

We might, *pace* Xenophon, wonder why Socrates would offer any alternative in such circumstances. Why should he not simply accept the one proposed by Meletus? After all, Socrates says that he is not convinced that death is an evil, so if he accepts the death penalty he would not necessarily be allowing anyone to be harmed. Moreover, in refusing to offer any alternatives he would in no way lend support to the jury's false judgment that he was guilty.

All three of the moral obligations mentioned above require that Socrates should not do this, however. We do not know the degree of legal obligation placed upon the defendant in such a trial procedure to offer a counter-penalty.[9] One might think intuitively that it is unlikely

---

[9] Fowler, in his introduction to the Loeb text, states that 'the rule was that the accused after conviction, should propose a counter-penalty' (64), but cites no textual evidence for his apparent belief that this was mandatory. None of the standard

the defendant would be legally constrained to offer an alternative, for it is difficult to imagine what the penalty for disobedience to such a legal constraint could be. After all, the defendant would already face a serious penalty (the one proposed by the prosecution) that he would automatically receive if he failed to offer an alternative.

Still, there is reason to suppose that Socrates felt a moral obligation to offer such a penalty, given his view of one's proper relation to the law. It is no more plausible, for example, to suppose that the law required him to offer a defense against the charges of Meletus and his supporters. None the less, at 19a6-7 Socrates shows that he feels an obligation to the law to offer a defense,[10] despite the fact that he is not at all sanguine about its chances of success, saying that 'the law must be obeyed and a defense must be made'. Similarly, we have independent reason to suppose that the law specified that, once convicted, the defendant should propose an alternative to the penalty proposed by the prosecution. We can assume this not only on the ground that the actual trial procedure stipulates that the jury must choose between the penalties proposed by the prosecution and the defendant,[11] but also (ironically) from the remarks made by Xenophon.

As we have said, according to Xenophon, when it was time for Socrates to offer a counter-penalty he refused to do so. The Greek word Xenophon uses for the legal obligation incurred by Socrates here is a form 'κελεύω', which can mean a variety of things. In military contexts, it means 'command', as it may in legal contexts as well. However, it may also mean simply 'bid', 'encourage', or even 'request'. Whatever its force in this context, Socrates is very clear in stipulating the degree to which any such legal 'request' or 'command' places him under at least a moral obligation to act accordingly: in the *Crito*, Socrates says 'in war and *in court* and everywhere, you must do whatever your state and fatherland commands (or requests—κελεύῃ), or persuade it as to what is naturally just' (51b8-c1). Having been directed to do so by the legal procedure, Socrates would feel morally obliged either to make such an offer or to persuade his country as to what is naturally just. As we shall subsequently argue, his second

---

sources on Greek law specify this either (see Harpokration s.v. ἀτίμητος ἀγὼν καὶ τιμητός; Gernet, 61-81; Harrison, vol. 2, 80-2; MacDowell (2), 253; Lipsius, 248-53; Otto Schulthess, *RE*, cols. 1251-5). Each of these relies for its information on one or more of five passages from Demosthenes (53.18, 53.26, 56.43, 58.70, 59.6), none of which provides a definitive answer to this question.

[10] See Section 2.2.3.   [11] See Chapter 1, note 82.

speech in the *Apology* represents an attempt to do both of these things.

Apart from whatever obligations Socrates felt to the law, however, there are yet other reasons why he finds it necessary to propose an alternative to Meletus' proposed penalty. Socrates is, again, also committed to avoiding harm to anyone, in so far as it is in his power. He is not certain that death will harm him, and, as such, it is preferable to the other possible penalties he considers and rejects; he explicitly says that these others will result in harm. But as the plea he made on the jurors' behalf at 30c2–31c3 (see Sections 4.1.1 and 4.1.2) shows, Socrates *is* worried that his death will harm his jurors. So if an alternative can be found to the death penalty that Socrates knows will not harm him or his jurors, he will have compelling reason to propose it. As we shall show, the choice Socrates makes is precisely of this character.

Finally, Socrates is committed to following the will of the god, which he clearly takes as directing him to practice philosophy in Athens. Though the jurors have found him guilty, *he must use every morally acceptable option he has to pursue the god's directive.* Were he merely to accept death, when another penalty would allow him to continue in his mission, he would have willfully failed to carry out his duty to the god. Since such an alternative is in fact available (indeed, the one Plato says Socrates finally proposes), it would follow from his obligation to the god that he must offer it as an option to the jurors.

5.2.3 FREE MEALS AT THE PRUTANEION

The above considerations also show why what Socrates ultimately proposes as a counter-penalty is the *only* alternative he can propose consistently with his moral principles. Some scholars are not convinced of this, for it is clear that Socrates himself believes that another 'penalty' would be appropriate for the 'crimes' he has committed. As he considers the position he is in, of having to make a counter-penalty offer though he thinks himself utterly blameless, Socrates first suggests that he would be most justly rewarded with the honor of free meals at the Prutaneion (36d1–37a1), the treatment reserved for Olympic heroes and other special state benefactors.[12] Some have

---

[12] For a discussion of the Prutaneion and its functions, see Stephen G. Miller, *The Prytaneion: Its Function and Architectural Form* (Berkeley, Los Angeles, and London, 1978), esp. ch. 1, 7–9.

taken this as a decisive sign that Socrates never intended to offer a serious alternative to the death penalty.[13] There are, however, a number of reasons to deny this, not the least of which is, as we have said, that Socrates' own moral scruples require him to offer a serious alternative, if such is possible. But in addition, though there may well be irony in Socrates' suggestion, this irony is neither gratuitous nor is it likely to have been seen by the jury, or intended by Socrates, as a mere outrage. For one thing, Socrates' suggestion is not a novel one, stemming as it undoubtedly did from a poem of Xenophanes (B2; see esp. line 8), a part of the Greeks' cultural and philosophical heritage of which the jurors would almost certainly be aware. Secondly, even if the jury had been offended by this suggestion, it does not follow that the offer he eventually makes is not a serious one; that one part of Socrates' speech is ironic does not in any way imply that the whole of it, or every other part of it, is equally ironic. Thirdly, Socrates' morals require him to reaffirm his own moral blamelessness, lest any serious penalty he might offer to pay be taken as an admission of guilt. Since he will offer to pay what we shall argue is a substantial fine, Socrates must take care first to reiterate that he is innocent of the charges of which he has been convicted. This point could, of course, have been made in a more moderate way. But there is at least some reason to suppose that Socrates would see a need for special emphasis here—after all, the majority of the people to whom he is speaking have shown that they are convinced of a number of gravely mistaken things about him and his pursuits.

At least one thing is certain about Socrates' discussion of state maintenance, though a number of scholars have nevertheless got it wrong. Socrates does not propose maintenance as the penalty to be considered by the jury, nor would his discussion of it be taken as such. Yet Fox, for example, says that 'Socrates proposed a counter-penalty which is a direct insult to the jury' and cites 36b3–37a1 as evidence.[14] Fox never even mentions the ultimate offer of a fine. Similarly, West says that '[t]he true counter-penalty was maintenance at the Prytaneum'.[15] Guthrie flatly states that '[Socrates'] counter-proposal was, therefore, that he should be granted free meals at the Prytaneum',[16] and Taylor says about maintenance that 'it should be

---

[13] See, e.g., A. E. Taylor (2), 166, who says that 'to propose any penalty whatever would amount to admitting guilt'.
[14] Fox, 231.   [15] T. West, 255.   [16] Guthrie (2), 64.

noted that, strictly speaking, this is the τίμησις which Socrates offers as an alternative to the death penalty demanded by the accusers'.[17] Both Guthrie and Taylor give the impression that they regard the subsequent offer of a fine as merely an afterthought to this, though Taylor seems to think that the later offer was an added irony. But what Socrates says shows that he does not actually offer maintenance as an alternative penalty. For one thing, there is not a bit of evidence that the Athenian law provided that a defendant could offer more than one alternative to the penalty proposed in the indictment. On the accounts offered by Fox, West, Guthrie, and Taylor, however, this would be exactly what Socrates does. Perhaps they were led to this conclusion by Socrates' final words on the subject of maintenance: 'This is what I offer, maintenance at the Prutaneion (τούτου τιμῶμαι, ἐν πρυτανείῳ σιτήσεως—37a1). But that this is not the actual offer is clear both from the fact that he procedes this 'offer' by stipulating that this is what he would offer were it the case that he must propose something he really deserves (εἰ οὖν δεῖ με κατὰ τὸ δίκαιον τῆς ἀξίας τιμᾶσθαι), which is plainly not the case, and from the fact that when he finally does make an offer he says twice, 'This is what I offer' (38b5 and 8), where 'this' refers to the fine. In this way, Socrates plays upon the double sense of 'deserves' that constitutes his conflict. Morally, he deserves heroic treatment, but according the the law he deserves a penalty. Maintenance is not his proposed penalty, therefore, because it is not an alternative offered for the crime for which he has been convicted.

5.2.4 THE OTHER OPTIONS

Since maintenance, the best result Socrates believes possible, will not do as a penalty of the sort he feels obliged to offer, Socrates must find something else to propose as a penalty. But what can be propose? He cannot propose penalties he knows to be evil, for that would bring harm to him and to his jurors. He therefore tells them that he cannot offer either imprisonment or a substantial fine with imprisonment until it be paid, for he knows these to be evils (37b7–c4). Since he has no money, the two are *de facto* the same penalty, leaving him a slave to those in authority (38c1–2). Socrates' freedom is vital to him, for without it he cannot pursue his mission; those most in need of his elenctic inquiries will hardly take care to visit him in prison to reply to

---

[17] A. E. Taylor (2), 166. This view is also expressed by Scott ((2), 436).

his questions. Similarly, though perhaps his jurors would be willing to choose it over the death penalty (37c5), banishment would solve nothing, for if his own countrymen will not allow him to continue his service to the god surely no others would permit him to continue his mission (37c4-e2).

Readers of the *Apology* may be puzzled by the quickness with which Socrates dismisses banishment as a possible counter-penalty. After all, he does say that even though he would soon be driven out of other cities, the youth in those other cities would listen to him (37d6-7). If, therefore, he is to do what he says he must do—comply with the wishes of the god and bring about 'the greatest good for men' (37e5-38a3)—why would he not choose exile? Would not Socrates be in the best position to comply with the god's wish, even if only marginally, by choosing to go from city to city philosophizing until he is forced to leave?

Had Socrates truly believed that the command of the god would best be served by his going into exile and attempting to philosophize with others, he would surely have had to offer banishment as his counter-penalty. Unless we are to find him guilty of impiety, then, we must conclude that he was convinced that his mission could not be carried out in exile. But was his conviction a sound one, or did he misjudge his potential to continue to exhort and examine people?

First, it is relatively easy to see how Socrates could feel so certain that no other city would tolerate him for long. There were, it is true, other cities that were willing to entertain philosophers, as for example the case of Anaxagoras shows (see D. L. 2.14-15); but as Plato discovered, a troublesome philosopher could quickly wear out his welcome (see (Ps.-) Plato, *Letters* III, VII). And Socrates was indeed a troublesome philosopher: as his difficulties with both factions in Athens had showed him (32a8-33a1), his mission was likely to stir up bad feeling against him no matter what form of government was in power. Since Athens under the democracy was widely known for the freedoms she afforded her citizens, and since Socrates' present predicament showed that even in democratic Athens his mission was not tolerated, he could be quite confident that its practice would be prohibited elsewhere—especially once it had been publicly branded as dangerous by the pluralistic and freedom-loving Athenians. Socrates does not spell all of this out to the jury, it is true; but he would hardly have to. Least of all would the proud and politically self-righteous democratic Athenians to whom he spoke need to be told of the superior liberality of their city.

Socrates says that in other cities he will have two choices: either he could refuse to talk with the youths of the city (in which case they would persuade the elders to drive him away), or he could go ahead and talk with the youth (in which case the elders would for their own sakes drive him away (37d6–e2)). He does not elaborate on precisely why his being driven from city to city so predictably would be a fate worse than death. Nor does he say that he could have no good effect whatever during his brief stays. But both of these consequences must be assured, if his passing over exile as counter-penalty is proper; more importantly, both consequences should be clear enough to the jurors who must choose a penalty, if his counter-penalty speech is to be effective in the way his principles require him to make it.

From what Socrates does say, it is clear that he could expect no tolerance in other cities. But since the youths of other cities will listen to him as long as he stays, might he not hope still to have some good effect on at least some one youth somewhere, and thus still have at least that slim ground for proposing exile?

A number of things would have to be true for this 'slim ground' to be sufficient ground for Socrates to propose exile. First, he must see the likelihood of the jury's accepting the fine he plans to offer instead of exile as being effectively nil. Plainly, if the jury could be persuaded to accept a fine, the good he can expect subsequently to do is considerable, for he could then return to the practice of his mission in Athens. But as we shall argue in Section 5.3.3, there was at least some reason for hoping the fine might be accepted. But even if this was only a feeble hope, Socrates must weigh it against what he plainly assesses a feeble hope that he might do someone somewhere some good in a brief visit to another state, as he travelled endlessly in exile. It is difficult to see how Socrates could weigh the two choices: for one— exile—the likelihood that the jury might choose it is substantial but the likelihood that he could accomplish much good if they did is quite small; for the other—the fine—the likelihood that the jury might choose it is quite small, but the likelihood that he could do good if they did accept it is quite substantial.

There is yet another aspect of exile that Socrates would surely have borne in mind in rejecting it as an appropriate counter-penalty. Socrates is convinced that his mission is of such paramount importance that he must practice it without regard for the troubles it brings him (23b7–c1; 28d6–10). But he is also convinced that the god does not neglect the good man (41d2). So Socrates can be confident that the practice of his mission, whatever troubles it may bring him, will never condemn him to a life of wretchedness. Regarding banishment, he tells the jury with obvious sarcasm, 'A fine life that would be for me if I went away, a man at my time of life, wandering from one city to another and being driven out' (37d4–6). It is clear that Socrates does not consider such a life as promising him even minimal happiness. By including exile in the category of penalties he *knows* to be evil (see 37b7–8), Socrates shows that he views exile as a fate worse than death, which, as he says, he does not know is an evil (29a4–b2; 37b5–7). Since the god in his goodness would never condemn him to such a life, Socrates can be confident that no significant good would come of his attempting to pursue it. Thus, even if Socrates is hopeless about continuing his mission, either by going into exile or by offering to pay a fine, he still has reason to reject going into exile. That would be an evil, whereas paying a fine would be no evil (38b2); hence, to offer to pay a fine in no way encourages the jurors to do him an evil and hence harm themselves, whereas to offer to go into exile is to encourage the jury to do something evil and harmful. Finally, offering a counter-penalty which he realizes the jury will in all likelihood reject, and subsequently being put to death, does not contribute to an outcome he knows will be evil. Seen in this light, his choice is clear: he must reject banishment. And as he deliberates on these options, Socrates has further evidence that his reasoning has led him to the right conclusion: in rejecting exile as an option, his *daimonion* does not sound the alarm that he has erred (see 40c1–3, and the discussion in Section 5.5 below).

There remains, however, still another option. At 37e3 Socrates tells the jury that he might simply 'be quiet and live peacefully'. This option would, we may assume, allow him to live with his family and enjoy the comforts of Athens. In that respect, then, abandoning his examinations of others would not present the evil that he would receive in exile. But what might be the most obvious and attractive alternative to the jury is to Socrates altogether impossible if he is to avoid an even greater evil of another sort. He cannot offer to stop his verbal testing of men, although it is precisely what aroused the ire of his accusers. To abandon philosophical discourse would be impious and would then make him deserving of the state's wrath. Were he to escape punishment by doing that for which he should be punished, he would commit the greatest possible evil and injustice of all (37e3–38a5; see 29b6–30a7, *Grg.* 472e4–7).

So there seems to remain but one option. Socrates tells the jury, 'If I had money, I would propose a fine as the penalty, as much as I could pay; for that would do me no harm' (38b1–2). But he is poor, and can offer only one *mna* of silver. His friends, however, offer to stand as sureties for his final offer of thirty times this amount. Only this alternative will satisfy each of Socrates' moral commitments; if he pays the fine, he will thereby obey the law by offering a recognizable counter-penalty, he will in no substantial way harm himself or anyone else,[18] and he will be free immediately to return to the streets of Athens to do the god's bidding.

5.3 The Fine

5.3.1 THE AMOUNT OF THE FINE

Though, as we have reconstructed his reasoning, Socrates was left with but one serious option in offering a counter-penalty to the jury, most commentators find what Socrates ultimately offers as in and of itself an affront to the jury and a certain sign that Socrates did not take seriously the idea of offering a counter-penalty. As we have noted, the scholarly literature is replete with comments as to the inadequacy of the fine Socrates offers. One finds Burnet, for example, calling Socrates' proposed fine 'an inconsiderable sum' that 'apparently incensed the judges'[19] and Friedländer assessing it as a 'ridiculously small fine'.[20] This claim is familiar enough.[21]

There is, however, ample reason to suppose that Socrates' proffered fine was not a trifling sum. A *mna* was the equivalent of one

---

[18] See Section 4.2.2.
[19] Burnet (1), 147. But see note 27, below.   [20] Friedländer, vol. 1, 170.
[21] See Barrow, 10; Bury, 565; Oldfather (1), 288. Similarly, Hackforth (ch. 6), though not explicitly espousing this view, seems to take it as obvious. A. E. Taylor (2) presents a more ambiguous case, for on the one hand he claims that 'Socrates did not, after conviction, secure his life by promising a moderate fine, as he clearly could have done'. Later, however, he seems to concede that the amount of the fine was substantial (166–7; see note 27, below). Against this view we find only Schanz, who believes that any fine Socrates offered would have been accepted, and thus concludes that the fine offer is Plato's own invention, designed to avoid later criticisms of him for not helping Socrates in his time of need ((1), 98–9).

hundred silver δραχμαί (*drachmai*), or six hundred ὀβολοί (*oboloi*), or one-sixtieth of a τάλαντον (*talanton*). In weight, it was 15 oz., 83¼ g.—nearly a pound of silver. One way we might attempt to determine the value of Socrates' offer is thus to determine what that quantity of silver is worth at current market prices.[22] That this way of assessing the value of Socrates' offer is typical can be seen from the various standard sources that provide such estimated conversions to modern amounts. Fowler, for example, in his 1914 introduction to the Loeb edition of the *Apology*,[23] cites the worth of 1000 *drachmai* as only £35, which would render one *mna* (the amount Socrates says he can pay by himself) as equivalent to only £3.50 and his ultimate offer of thirty *mnai* as a mere £105. Liddell and Scott tell us a *mna* would be the equivalent of £4 in 1871.[24] Lamb, in his 1857 translation of Böckh's *Staatshaushaltung*, estimates the value of a *mna* at roughly $16.00 (American).[25] More such estimates can be found.[26]

But this way of estimating the value of Socrates' fine is quite misleading. A more reasonable method of determining its value is to ascertain the purchasing power of thirty *mnai* of silver in Athens at the end of the fifth century.[27] We know, for example, that at this time one *mna* alone would have been sufficient to purchase a small herd of goats, or two oxen, or approximately thirty gallons of olive oil, or 120

[22] For contemporary estimates, look under 'Metals' in the financial pages of any newspaper carrying such information.

[23] Fowler, 64.

[24] H. J. Liddell and R. Scott, *Greek-English Lexicon*, abridged (Oxford, 1963), 449.

[25] We calculate this from the estimated worth of a *talanton* given in A. Lamb's translation of Augustus Böckh, *Staatshaushaltung der Athener (The Public Economy of the Athenians)*, 2nd ed;. vol. 1 (Boston, 1857), 20.

[26] See, e.g., Oskar Seyffert, *Dictionary of Classical Antiquities*, revised and edited by H. Nettleship and J. E. Sandys (New York, 1957), 393. All such estimates show how dramatically the price of silver has gone up in the last few decades.

[27] The few scholars who have suggested that the puchasing power of the fine may have been large have, nevertheless, in all other ways supported the consensus view, i.e. that his moral scruple against admitting guilt required Socrates to behave in an ironical or offensive way, and that the final offer of a fine, regardless of its size, was contemptuous. Most of these also explicitly endorse Diogenes Laertius' view that the vote to condemn Socrates to death was by a wider margin than the vote to convict him had been, and cite this as evidence for their portrayal of Socrates' offer as motivated primarily by irony and resistance to the court. Representative examples of such a view can be found in Burnet (2); Guthrie (1). vol. 3 and (2); A. E. Taylor (2) and (3), 119; and T. West. But though we agree with their observations about the purchasing power of the fine, our arguments show why we are critical of their agreement with the view that Socrates' offer was not a serious attempt to secure his release.

gallons of domestic wine.[28] Thirty *mnai* would have bought as many as six Syrian slaves or as many as four highly skilled Carian goldsmiths.[29] Such a sum could have ransomed thirty prisoners of war (Arist., *Eth. Nic.* 1134b22), or provided a 'handsome' dowry for a young bride of the wealthy class ((Ps.-)Plato, *Letter* XIII, 361e1-2).[30] Perhaps more striking still is the fact that only one *mna* was the equivalent of approximately one hundred days' wages for a skilled artisan, and thus thirty *mnai* would have been the equivalent of approximately eight-and-a-half years' wages.[31] Indeed, according to one estimate, perhaps only as few as 1,200 of Athens' citizens could have afforded to pay a fine of this size.[32] And we must remember that in 399 BC Athens was still suffering the grave economic consequences of the recently lost war. The popular thesis that Socrates' suggested fine was purely ironic or a calculated insult to the jury becomes a good deal less plausible once one considers the considerable purchasing power of the sum he finally offers.

A look at the penalties we find reported for similar cases, however, might appear to undercut the seriousness of Socrates' offer. Death or banishment were commonly assigned in cases of impiety. Plutarch tells us, for example, that Alcibiades was sentenced to death (in *absentia*) for profaning the Mysteries (Plut., *Alc.* 22). We are told that Diagoras fled Athens but was pursued by a bounty of one *talanton* (Diod. 13.6.7), and that Theodorus was condemned to death by

---

[28] See Frost, 58. Other works on Greek economics provide abundant evidence as to the high purchasing power of silver and corroborate these assessments, as well as providing a number of others. See Böckh (op. cit., see note 25, above), and Jones.

[29] Frost, 58.   [30] See also Burnet (2), note on 38d7.

[31] We compute this from the average daily wage of an artisan, one *drachma*, as recorded in the *IG* 1.2.373-4. Pay for public offices varied, but was often lower than this. According to Aristotle (*Ath. Pol.* 62.2), the nine archons received four *oboloi* a day; various other offices, a *drachma*. Aristophanes (*Ach.* 66, 90) says that ambassadors received more, 2 *drachmai*, though this is disputed by Westermann in *CP* 1910, 203-16, who thinks it more like 1½ *drachmai*. Perhaps the most highly paid officials were the taxiarchs, who according to Westerman (id. ib., 595-607) were paid as much as 3 *drachmai*. Other state services received considerably less compensation: council members received 5 *oboloi* a day by the fourth century (Arist., *Ath. Pol.* 62.2., scholia on Ar., *Vesp.* 88, 300), and the first to arrive at the Assembly (those comprising a quorum), received between 1 and 3 *oboloi* (the price apparently rose rapidly around the first part of the fourth century; see Arist., *Ath. Pol.* 41.3). Socrates' jurors received only 3 *oboloi* a day. At that rate, Socrates' offer is worth *seventeen* years of service. For a discussion, see M. M. Markle, 'Jury Pay and Assembly Pay at Athens', in *Crux* (for reference, see note 2, above), 265-97. Markle argues that 3 *oboloi* per day would be sufficient to allow its recipient to support his family.   [32] Jones, 85.

drinking hemlock (D. L. 2.101,116). Other defendants, however, were more lucky. According to Diogenes Laertius, Anaxagoras was sentenced to a fine of five *talanta* and banishment (2.12-14), whereas Stilpon (5.6) and Protagoras (9.52; Arist. fr. 67 Rose; Plut., *Nic.* 23.4) were simply banished. There are other cases recorded where banishment and the confiscation of all property were called for (Lys. 7.3, 25, 35, 41).

Against such extreme penalties, Socrates' offer to pay a fine of thirty *mnai* (one-half of a *talanton*) might still appear to be insignificant. But there are problems in evaluating these other extreme cases. For one thing, the authority of these reports is a matter of much controversy. Moreover, we do not know whether, or how often, the penalties involved in these cases were actually paid. We do not know, for example, whether penalties involving large sums of money were ever collected or were even intended to be collected. Since the terms of imprisonment could be extended until a fine was paid in full, the imposition of an extremely large fine would have served to ensure that the convict would never again be an Athenian citizen.[33] It may also have been the case that extremely high fines placed upon those who did not have the means to pay resulted in the confiscation of their property. Socrates is a poor man, and the extent of his wealth on at least one account is considerably lower than the thirty *mnai* he offers to pay: according to Xenophon (*Oec.* 2.3), Socrates' total worth was but five *mnai*. So if banishment, together with the confiscation of all property, is taken as a reasonable alternative to death (and banishment is ruled out by Socrates himself for the reasons stated above), then his offer to pay a fine of thirty *mnai* is not at all inappropriate. He does offer a considerably greater sum than he could raise from his own resources, and this might well have been intended to counter in the minds of the jurors the fact that he refuses to suggest banishment as a penalty.

Some might be tempted to dispute this suggestion by noting Socrates' own remark in the *Apology* that the price charged by Euenos the sophist was a bargain. At 20a2–c3, Socrates recounts his conversation with Callias concerning the amount charged by Euenos for an 'education in virtue' of Callias' two sons. According to Socrates, Callias claimed that Euenos' charge was five *mnai*. Socrates then says, 'I called Euenos a most enviable man (ἐμακάρισα) if he

---

[33] See Harrison, appendix G.

really has this craft and teaches it at such a reasonable rate' (20b9–c1). One might conclude from this that if Socrates thinks that five *mnai* is a modest sum, then his own later offer of a counter-penalty must not be as substantial as we say it is.

Of course, there may be several ways in which Socrates' assessment of Euenos' fee is ironical. First, as we have seen, Socrates values virtue above all else, and cares little for material wealth. If Euenos really could teach virtue, therefore, Socrates would think his service the most valuable possible, and worth every bit of five *mnai* and more! But Socrates knows that Euenos is not really wise in regard to virtue; if Euenos really was, the oracle would be a liar, for Euenos would be wiser than Socrates. So Euenos is a fraud, and his product is worthless at any price. Secondly, we know that at least some sophists charged extraordinary fees for their 'services'. Relative to these, Euenos' fraud is one of the least expensive. Socrates might have said that Euenos' charge was 'reasonable' even though it involved a large sum of money, for many of his kind charged much more for the same fraud (see *Hip. Ma.* 282b1–e8; *Cra.* 384b2–c1).[34]

Yet other evidence for our view of the fine can be given. First, it is worth noting that under Athenian law a penalty of ten *mnai* was assessed against prosecutors whose cases were so weak as to win less than one-fifth of the jurors' votes, presumably as a protection against legal harassment (*Ap.* 36a7–b2).[35] If Socrates' proposed penalty, worth three times this amount, was 'an inconsiderable sum', then Athens' protection against sycophancy was no protection at all. Secondly, the smallest coin of the period was the χαλκοῦς (*chalkous*), worth one-eighth of an *obolos* (or 1/4800 of a *mna*). If Socrates had wished to make a clearly ironic offer, he could have picked any of a number of far smaller sums than the one he did, in fractions of *oboloi* or other small coins. Instead, he tells the jurors that if he had money he would gladly pay the largest fine he could (38b1–2). This presents a problem for the view that the fine he does offer is purely ironical, for those who see it as such must now call Socrates' blunt claim at 38b1–2 a lie.

Finally, Socrates' friends encouraged him to raise the amount of the fine to *thirty times* what he says he can pay without their help. Though Socrates himself may have been a poor man, these friends were quite wealthy. It would certainly have been odd if Socrates' four

---

[34] See also Guthrie (4), 41–2.   [35] See MacDowell (2), 64.

wealthy friends, fearing that the fine Socrates could offer to pay on
his own would be too low, encouraged him to raise the amount only to
a level that would still be rejected out of hand by the jurors as clearly
insufficient. If Socrates was committed to ironically offering an insignificant sum of money as a fine, he would hardly have been convinced by his friends to raise the amount he could offer. Because
Socrates was willing to employ his friends' resources, and because a
concern to convince the jury to accept the fine was plainly his friends'
motive for making their resources available, we must suppose that
each of the parties who were willing to contribute to a fine of thirty
mnai saw that sum as a serious and substantial counter-penalty.[36]
Only thirty of those who had found him guilty would have to be convinced to accept the fine for it to have won Socrates' release. Nothing was
lacking in the amount of the fine he offered to prevent him from winning these few votes. Another explanation must be found for
Socrates' ultimate condemnation.

5.3.2   THE FINAL VOTE OF THE JURY

We know of course, that Socrates' counter-penalty proposal was rejected by a majority of the jury, and that he was thus condemned to
death, the penalty proposed by the prosecution. Diogenes Laertius
claims that the jury voted for Socrates' execution by a wider margin
than that by which they found him guilty (2.42), and this claim has
been accepted so completely by modern authorities that it is typically
reported as one of the facts of the trial without caution or comment.
No doubt this is partly due to there being no ancient author who
offers an explicitly contradictory account. But it is also likely that
Diogenes' account is seen as lending support to the consensus view of
Socrates' second speech, according to which he virtually compels his
jurors to condemn him by showing his complete disdain for their
judgment, and by offering them no real alternative to the death
penalty.

   We are deeply suspicious of Diogenes' assessment of the final vote,
especially since he is the *sole* source for it. As we have already said,[37]
his account of the trial is inconsistent with Plato's in a number of
ways, and in each particular instance of such inconsistency there ap-

---

[36] It is interesting that this aspect of Socrates' offer goes virtually without
comment in most accounts; A. E. Taylor (2) is the sole exception, but even he
continues to insist on the insufficiency of Socrates' final offer.

[37] See Chapter 1, note 88.

pears to be no reason to prefer his authority to Plato's. It is curious, therefore, that the same scholars who disregard Diogenes' account of the trial in so many other particulars accept his tale of the final vote so uncritically. In fact, there is a puzzle in even this much acceptance of Diogenes' account, for it requires that some of those who had found Socrates innocent on the first vote later condemned him to death. Such a change of heart would not be puzzling if we accepted the account of the counter-penalty with which it is paired: Diogenes writes that Socrates first proposed a fine of one *mna*, but subsequently withdrew this suggestion to propose state maintenance as his final offer. We might not find it surprising that some of those who found Socrates innocent were still unwilling to reward his activities as they would a hero's. Given that the jury must by law choose between the penalty proposed by the prosecution and that offered by the defendant, on Diogenes' account Socrates left sympathetic jurors with only two options: a penalty or one of the state's greatest rewards. Many of those who found him innocent of impiety would surely still have balked at giving him state maintenance, and, were that Socrates' actual offer, such an 'alternative' might well have caused the defection of otherwise sympathetic jurors.

But despite the enormous variety of opinion one finds regarding the trial itself and Plato as a reliable authority, we know of no scholar who positively prefers Diogenes' account of the counter-penalty to the one we find in Plato. But then the common acceptance of the alleged change in votes becomes problematic, for even if Socrates' proposed penalty were but a small fine, or part of his second speech ironic, as the consensus view holds, it is surely odd that those jurors who found him innocent would subsequently change sides on the second ballot. After all, it seems reasonable to construe a 'not guilty' vote as presuming that the defendant deserves to pay no penalty at all. And it is surely implausible to claim that those who found Socrates innocent would be inspired by his alleged irony in the second speech to reverse themselves and condemn him to death. The jurors in question, after all, had already heard Socrates compare himself to Homeric heroes (28b9-d5) and call himself the state's greatest benefactor (30a5-7), a 'gift from the god' (30d7-e1; 31a7-8), and had none the less been willing to set him free after his first speech. What capital offense had Socrates committed in the eyes of such jurors in the second speech?

There is, moreover, at least some suggestion in Plato that the same number of jurors voted for the death penalty as had found Socrates guilty in the first vote. In the third and final speech, Socrates separates the members of the jury into two groups, and tells each group something different. The first group is identified indifferently as 'those of you who voted for my death' (38c7–d2) and as 'you who voted against me' (39c1–2). The other group Socrates addresses as 'those of you who voted for acquittal' (39e1). But if we were to accept Diogenes' account there must be three groups, not two: those who voted against Socrates both times; those who found him innocent, but subsequently voted to execute him; and those who voted for him both times. Socrates' division of the jury into only two groups in Plato's version would make little sense if any of the jurors favorably disposed towards him on the first vote had later changed their minds, for what he has to say to either of the two groups he does address in his final remarks would not be suited to such jurors.

If we do not suppose that the alleged change in votes occurred, the fact that the jury did not accept Socrates' proposed fine is easily explained. Because Socrates had already promised, if set free, to continue to do the very thing for which he was brought before them and convicted, we can reasonably suppose that those jurors who found him guilty in the first vote would hardly have considered accepting his proposal. A majority in favor of the death penalty would thus be assured.[38]

5.3.3   A FINAL OBJECTION CONSIDERED

It might be objected, on something like the grounds just given, that Socrates would surely have known that his offer would not be accepted, and thus that the penalty he proposed to pay cannot count as a

---

[38] This observation, however, also provides the one line of reasoning by which sense might be made of Diogenes' claim that there was a massive turn against Socrates on the second vote (2.42). Socrates' promise to return to the practise of his mission could have been seen as presenting a serious practical problem to even sympathetic jurors. We can assume that if Socrates were set free after paying a fine, we would be back in court almost immediately, only this time the fact that he had already been convicted of impiety for his activities would make the verdict (and undoubtedly the penalty) a foregone conclusion. Thus, Socrates' offer to pay a substantial fine might not have been seen as a viable alternative even to those who did not believe he was guilty of impiety. It is worth noticing, however, that the amount of the fine he offered would have nothing to do with its unacceptability. A veritable fortune in fines, offered in the utmost humility, would still not have compensated for his steadfast commitment to practice philosophy if he were released.

serious one.[39] But no principle of interpretation requires us to view Socrates as a clairvoyant. For one thing, Socrates admits that he is surprised that the margin by which he lost the initial vote was so close (36a3–5). If he were so good at predicting the jury's decisions, he would not have been surprised by this one. And given the closeness of the initial vote, he might well have hoped that offering a substantial fine would find acceptance with at least thirty of those that had found him guilty, and thus with the majority he would need to have the fine accepted. It is entirely possible that a number of those who had voted against him were not at all eager to have him executed. And if Socrates did hold what turned out to be the false hope that the fine would be accepted, he was not alone in holding it: after all, surely the same hope is what motivated his friends to help him raise the amount of the fine he offered. Had they supposed the situation was hopeless, their offer would have been pointless and Socrates' acceptance of it puzzling. Why raise the amount, if it is obvious that a majority of the jurors would not accept it? We might well suppose, therefore, that Socrates and his friends thought the thirty-*mnai* fine had some chance of acceptance, even if everyone considered it a desperately small one.

But even if we were to suppose that Socrates knew his offer would be rejected, this does not prove that it was not a serious one. The same considerations hold for his offer to pay a fine as for his initial decision to undertake a defense; recall that he had the gravest doubts that his efforts in that undertaking would succeed (see Section 2.2). The fact that the penalty he proposes is not likely to be selected by the jury is no different in principle. Just as we suppose that his defense is a serious one, we should similarly suppose that his proposed penalty is precisely what he says it is: a serious offer of a substantial fine in lieu of his life. Unfortunately, the jury is unwilling to accept it. That the jury would not consider the offer seriously does not make the offer itself a flippant one; it only shows that a majority of the jury is hostile. And if the offer were not serious, we must suppose that Socrates would not have been willing to make it under circumstances where he supposed it

[39] See A. E. Taylor (2), who claims that the offer was 'made with the full certainty that the court . . . will reject it' (166), and Piérart, who says that since Socrates has promised to go on philosophizing, 'les juges n'ont pas le choix' (293). Panagiotou similarly claims that Socrates 'is proposing a penalty on the understanding that it is not a penalty at all' ((2), 48), since he stipulates that paying the fine will not harm him. We do not agree that proper penalties must harm their recipients, especially given Socrates' view that one must never harm anyone, even in return for harm.

might be accepted. But our arguments show that Socrates' own moral commitments compel him to make the offer he does, and to hope for his and the jury's sake that it is accepted. So Socrates' offer is serious, regardless of what we think he expected the jury to choose. In making the offer, he has done all that he can to fulfill his various moral duties. Thus, when he receives his sentence he is not disturbed by the thought that he has failed to do what was right, for he has scrupulously done all he can to obey the letter and spirit of the law, as he understands it, to prevent evil, and to serve the god.

No law or moral scruple required Socrates to offer a penalty that the jury would be likely to select. But this does not mean that Socrates' offer to pay a fine, or any part of the deliberations that led to his making such an offer, were purely ironical or calculated to insult the jury. Rather, Socrates' morals required him to offer the jury what was for him a meaningful and substantial alternative to the penalty urged by Meletus. This he did without committing a further injustice or compounding that which had already been done, and without abandoning his service to the god. To have failed to act as he did would have been either to add injustice to injustice or to have become guilty of the very crime for which he had been wrongly convicted. It is testimony to Socrates' philosophic wit that he was able to find an alternative where there seemed to be an inescapable injustice. But it is evidence for Socrates' dim view of the worldly affairs of men that such wit did not find a happy application in court.

5.4   Socrates' Final Speech: Part I (38c1–39d9)

5.4.1   HISTORICAL PROBLEMS AGAIN

Plato's *Apology* concludes with yet another speech, which Socrates is supposed to have delivered to the jury 'while the authorities are occupied' (39e2–3). Our knowledge of Athenian law provides no clue as to what could have occupied 'the authorities' so substantially after Socrates' condemnation as to permit Socrates the time and peace and quiet needed for him to address the jury. Neither do we know of any provision in the law that sets time aside for last words from the condemned man. It might be supposed, therefore, that the presence of the third speech in the *Apology* is itself sufficient to qualify Plato's portrayal of the trial as pure fiction, in which an interlude in the legal procedure is even invented from whole cloth so that his hero may be given a few noble lines.[40]

But just as nothing we know of Athenian trial procedure strictly provides Socrates with the opportunity to make a third speech, nothing we know strictly prevents his making it. We do not know, for example, whether the jury immediately rushed headlong from the courtroom after the second vote; we have no reason to suppose that Socrates would be borne off to prison the moment his sentence had been determined, or put under an order to be silent. So, as some scholars have noted,[41] there is nothing to prevent our supposing that Socrates' third speech was informally undertaken, without official provision, but without the impediment of legal prohibition either. In fact, there may even have been legal provision for a final speech, for all we know. It is, perhaps, a bit difficult to imagine an Athenian jury quietly and attentively listening to the final remarks of a man they have already convicted and sentenced to death, unless there was a legal restraint upon them to do so. But then nothing in Plato's account requires us to suppose that the jury was quiet or attentive. He asks us merely to suppose that Socrates made the speech, whether or not it was heard or attended to. At least this much is true: the idea that Socrates would have the opportunity to address the jury one last time did not strike contemporary Athenians as absurdly implausible. Even Xenophon, who begins his account of the trial with an expression of concern for accuracy (*Ap.* 1), and who scrupulously reports that his source is Hermogenes (*Ap* 2), provides Socrates with a few final words to the jury (*Ap.* 24-6). And though the appearance of a third speech in both Plato's and Xenophon's accounts is hardly decisive evidence for there actually having been such a speech, especially given the different reports of its content in the two accounts, we have no historical ground for faulting Plato's or Xenophon's authority in this instance, either. Like the rest of Plato's account of the trial, moreover, and quite apart from its historical accuracy, the last of the three speeches he attributes to Socrates contains much of interest.

---

[40] See, e.g., Festugière (130); Tovar (2), 378.

[41] See, e.g., Burnet (2), 161-2 (arguing against Wilamowitz and Schanz), and Bonner, 169-70.

5.4.2 SOCRATES' ADDRESS TO THOSE WHO CONVICTED HIM

The first of the two groups Socrates addresses in his final speech is composed of those who had voted against him. To these men, Socrates' words are unrelentingly harsh. He scorns them for foolishly trying to buy time by killing him off (38cl), when at his advanced age he would have died soon enough anyway (38c6-7), and he bewails the ammunition they have thereby given to the enemies of Athens, who will now say that the Athenians put a wise man to death (38c3).

His words to the hostile jurors also confirm the interpretation we offered of the defense itself. Socrates raises the possibility that his conviction and condemnation was caused by his inability to persuade a majority of the jury (38d3-5), a possibility he strenuously rejects. Instead, he says, his lack of recklessness and shamelessness, which such jurors required of his courtroom behavior, was to blame (38d6-8; see also *Grg.* 522c8-e1). On the one hand, his rough words to these jurors are plainly said with a passion inappropriate to one supposed all along to have invited and encouraged his own condemnation by a playful lack of attention to his own defense. Socrates' indignation is that of a man wrongly condemned against his will, and despite his having made valiant efforts to refute the prejudices against him. He reviles these jurors with a ferocity that shows how terrible and egregious he supposes their error to have been.

On the other hand, he says clearly that what led to his conviction was not just any failure of his to behave according to the jurors' expectations but his specific unwillingness to do the sorts of things he warned them he would not do (38d9-39a6; see 34b6-35d8), such as wailing and lamenting and begging for mercy. At least according to Socrates, then, it was neither irony nor arrogance that caused his condemnation; it was his insistence upon offering a defense designed to suit the law, justice, and piety, and not one whose purpose was to appeal irrelevantly to the emotions. The attempt to pitch his defense in this way certainly may have seemed to many to be 'big talk' (μεγαληγορία—see Xen. *Ap.* 1-2). But just because Socrates was too concerned with his principles to structure his defense in such a way as to mollify the most hostile members of the jury, there is no reason to convict him participating aggressively in his own condemnation. He offered the jury 'big talk' just so that they could, in his view, for at least once in their lives think big. But his 'big talk' was not mere boasting, for he was always careful to explain the moral foundations upon which his presentation rested. In the end, both Socrates and the jury failed. In his final assessment of his jurors' failure, Socrates shows how little real excuse he supposes they have for it. Surely he allows no room for the supposition that anything he did mitigates their failure by having in any morally relevant way expedited it. He did not shamelessly beg them for mercy, and they killed him for it.

5.5 Socrates' Final Speech: Part II (39e1–40c3)

5.5.1 'MY DIVINE SIGN DID NOT OPPOSE ME'

After rebuking those who voted against him, Socrates turns to the minority who voted for his acquittal and tells than an astonishing thing:

a wonderful thing has happened to me. For in all earlier times the unusual *daimonion* always opposed me quite frequently, even in little things, if I was about to do something wrong. But now, as you see for yourselves, this thing that might be believed and is generally recognized to be the greatest of evils happens to me; but my divine sign (τὸ τοῦ θεοῦ σημεῖον) did not oppose me either when I left home at dawn, or when I came here to the court, or at any time in my speech when I was about to say something. Yet in other speeches it stopped me right in the middle of what I was saying. But now, never in this affair, in any act or word, did it oppose me. What do I suppose is the explanation for this? I will tell you. It is likely that what has happened to me will turn out to be a good thing, and those of use who suppose death to be an evil must surely not be right. *A great proof of this has come to me, for it surely would not be that the usual sign would not oppose me unless I was about to do something good.* (40a3–c3)

Socrates, it seems, is convinced that the proposition that his death is not an evil is proved by the failure of his *daimonion* to oppose him in the actions that led to his condemnation to die. Yet only a few Stephanus pages earlier, the same man was saying:

For to fear death, gentlemen, is nothing other than to think one is wise when one is not; for it is to think one knows what one does not know. For all anyone knows death might even be the greatest of goods to man, but they fear it as if they knew it was the greatest of evils. But is this not the most disgraceful ignorance, supposing one knows what one does not know? (29a4–b2)

Again at 37b5-7, Socrates reminds the jurors yet again that he does not know whether death is a good or an evil thing. Though Socrates plainly believed all along that death is nothing to be feared (see for example 32d1-2), it is 'a wonderful thing' indeed for Socrates now to have a 'great proof' of his belief. Precisely how did this happen?

5.5.2   SOCRATES' 'GREAT PROOF'

Let us reconstruct the 'great proof'. As many have noted, the *daimonion* in Plato's accounts only opposes but never advises Socrates (31d2-4, 40c1-3, 41d5-6) and thus warns him away from evil without actively directing him towards the good;[42] in Xenophon, the *daimonion* gives positive advice as well (*Mem.* 1.1.4, 4.3.12, 4.8.1; *Ap.* 12). But even though here Plato's Socrates discovers something entirely new to him, and decidedly positive in substance, the *daimonion* conveys the message not through positive, but rather only through a lack of negative interference. And since this event is reported only by Plato, we should perhaps begin our reconstruction of Socrates' proof with the way Plato makes the *daimonion* function:

1. The *daimonion* communicates with Socrates only to warn him if he is about to do something wrong (εἴ τι μέλλοιμι μὴ ὀρθῶς πράξειν; 40a6).

From here we might supply the obvious addition,

2. But in this case, the *daimonion* did not communicate with Socrates.

and thus try to reach the 'wonderful conclusion',

3. Hence, Socrates is about to do something good (τι . . . ἀγαθὸν πράξειν; 40c3).

Plato is very consistent in asserting that something like (1) is the case, and Socrates in the *Apology* plainly derives the conclusion (3) at least in part from (2). But the 'proof' as it now stands is wholly inadequate, for the conclusion is in no way ensured by the premisses. First, notice that (1) needs further specification. It might be construed only as

1a. The *daimonion* only opposes Socrates when he is about to do something wrong.

---

[42] For other references to Socrates' *daimonion*, see Chapter 1, note 126.

Or it might mean something more powerful, namely,

1*b*. The *daimonion* always opposes Socrates when he is about to do something wrong.

The disadvantage of (1*a*) is obvious: it leaves the argument invalid, for it permits (2) to be consistent with the denial of (3): the present instance may be one of those in which the *daimonion* does not oppose him despite his being about to do or suffer something evil, a possibility that is left open by (1*a*).

(1*b*) gets us validly to (3) using only (2) as well, and so we might suppose that this is what Socrates had in mind as anchoring his 'great proof'. But (1*b*) is an extremely powerful principle, and some of its consequences should give us pause. For one thing, if (1*b*) were true, Socrates would thereby be provided with utter indemnity against doing evil (without warning). Having had access to his *daimonion* 'since childhood' (31d1), and since it opposes him 'even in little things' (40a5-6), Socrates can be assured that—so long as he has desisted from actions preceded or interrupted by daimonic alarms—he has never done anything that is even the least bit evil. (1*b*) also would appear to provide Socrates in virtue of his *daimonion* with an incredibly powerful access to moral truth—access that is never elsewhere suggested in the dialogues. All Socrates would ever need to do to discern that an action was a good or a bad one would be to decide which of the two he was inclined to do at that moment, and do it. If what he decided was wrong, he would be opposed by his *daimonion*. And if he is not opposed, since according to (1*b*) he would be opposed if ever he were about to do something wrong, he can conclude that what he is doing is not wrong. One might well wonder why Socrates would ever need to philosophize—and why he would continually profess moral ignorance—if he had such secure and easily obtained non-philosophical access to moral information. These consequences seem terribly implausible.[43]

But perhaps instead we have not done a good job in construing the argument, for it may be that we have missed the other premises that get us from (2) to (3) without being committed to anything as strong as (1*b*). Socrates' contrast between the 'very small matters' on which the *daimonion* opposed him so often in the past and what is common-

---

[43] In our earlier article on this topic (Brickhouse and Smith (2)), we none the less attributed premiss (1*b*) to Socrates. We now think that attribution is mistaken.

ly thought the greatest of evils, death, might provide the premises we need:

4. Since the *daimonion* would oppose Socrates even on minor matters, it would surely always oppose him if he were about to undertake an evil of great consequence.

5. If death is an evil it is an evil of great consequence.

From (4), (5), and (2), we can conclude that Socrates' death is no evil thing.

Now it may be that this is the argument he had in mind, but if so, it is no 'wonderful thing' that has happened to Socrates, for he has been convinced by a flawed argument. For one thing, unless we know a great deal more about the *daimonion*, (4) seems less than perfectly certain, at best. Why should we suppose that the *daimonion* discriminates between great and small evils in sounding its alarm? Could it not act in a somewhat more haphazard way? And if its motive is that it hates for Socrates to do an evil, why should our principle not be as strong as (1*b*)? After all, if there are evil actions it will tolerate, how can we be so certain that it would not tolerate an occasional great evil? Worse, (5) seems in no way secured, for though it may represent a commonly held belief, the fact that a belief is commonsensical cannot count as a warrant for holding that belief with any confidence, as Socrates himself argues. So it seems that we face a dilemma: either Socrates' argument is valid but not sound (for premiss (1*b*) is surely false), or it is simply invalid, for any interpretation of the argument that does not commit Socrates to (1*b*), it seems, fails to guarantee his conclusion.

There is another thing about Socrates' 'great proof' that might puzzle us. From his *daimonion*'s silence, Socrates concludes that death is no evil. But which sorts of evils does the *daimonion* warn Socrates of: evils he might *suffer* or evils he might *do*? In the passage we have quoted is seems clear that it is the latter, but if so, how does it follow from his *daimonion*'s silence—even given a premiss as strong as (1*b*)— that in death Socrates will *suffer* no evil, and hence that death must not be an evil thing?

In what follows we shall attempt to defend the validity of Socrates' argument without resorting to premisses that would render it absurd and unsound. It will follow from our interpretation that Socrates receives some substantial degree of protection against evil from his *daimonion*. It need not follow from this argument, however, that given his *daimonion* Socrates has no need to practice philosophy or concern himself that some one or more of his actions could be wrong. We admit that the solution we offer is not articulated explicitly in this text, but we can show that it makes the best sense of Socrates' argument and that it coheres well with other recognized Socratic principles.

5.5.3 DENYING ONE OF THE HORNS OF THE DILEMMA

As we have already discussed at various places in this book (see esp. Sections 2.6 and 3.2), Socrates' profession of ignorance may be found throughout the early dialogues, and forms the basis of his defense against the 'first' accusations. But on any conception of Socrates' claims at 40a3–c3, there are some moral truths to which he has direct and certain access, for no matter how we interpret the strength of the principle that allows Socrates to make the inference he does, the confidence with which he proclaims his conclusion is complete. But the same method of assurance is open to Socrates whenever the *daimonion* interferes. Even if it does not always oppose him in wrongful action, whenever it does oppose him he many be at least as assured of the wrongfulness of that action as he is of the conclusion he derives at 40a3–c3 on the basis of the *daimonion*'s lack of opposition. Hence, even if the *daimonion* never interfered with Socrates on a matter of such great importance, it has many times provided him with reason to have complete confidence in his judgments, at least when those judgments are the product of opposition by the *daimonion*. Whence, then, his profession of ignorance?

Now one might, at this point, be inclined to dismiss either the 'proof' at 40a3–c3[44] or the confession of ignorance[45] as less than utterly sincere. There seem to us, however, to be good reasons to take both quite seriously. First, the main element of the 'proof' is Socrates' *daimonion*, which at 31d2–3 he tells us he has had since childhood.

---

[44] See, e.g., T. West, 226, who sees Socrates' use of διαμυθολογῆσαι at 39e5 as a warning to 'his listeners not to take the rest of the speech too seriously'. West's view is tentatively supported by Roochnik (218-19). This, however, is simply a mistaken way to read the Greek, for the word means nothing subtle, but rather only 'to talk with one another'. As Burnet says, 'There is no suggestion of "myth" in the word' ((2), note on 39e5). Another who doubts the force of Socrates' proof appears to be Reginald Hackforth, who says nothing about the proof itself but none the less concludes that Socrates' views on the issue remain 'quite agnostic' ((2), 171), presumably (though not explicitly) on the basis of Socrates' final words to the jury. (But about this, see note 54, below). [45] See, e.g., Gulley, 62-74.

Because his belief in his *daimonion* was apparently notorious,[46] and because that belief appears to have contributed substantially to Socrates' being charged with introducing new divinities in the state,[47] we can be assured at least that his belief in his 'divine sign' was taken seriously both by him and by others. And though this passage in the *Apology* is the only place in Plato[48] where the non-interference of his *daimonion* is said to produce positive moral results, we see little point in Socrates' exploiting it insincerely at this stage of the trial. Why undertake to deceive or mislead those to whom he now speaks, the members of the jury who voted in his favor? Notice that the same effect could be gained, if he is supposed only to seek to calm and reassure them, by giving the additional reasons for deriving his 'wonderful' conclusion that he gives immediately following his daimonic 'proof'. Hence, bringing in the *daimonion* insincerely is at best unnecessary and at worst quite deceptive. Though Socrates may be less than Kantian in his commitment always to tell the truth, we must not suppose him to be given to gratuitous exaggeration or mendacity.

Even less should we be tempted to suspect the sincerity of his confession of ignorance, unless we are prepared gravely to undermine his integrity (see Section 2.6.2). As we said, his claim of ignorance is one of the principal features of his defense against the 'first' accusers. And since he vows that he will tell his jurors only the truth (17b4–5; 18a5–6, 20d5–6, 22b5–6, 28a6, 28d6, 32a8, 33c1–2), if his confession of ignorance is insincere he thereby violates his vow to the jurors repeatedly, and on an essential point. For these reasons, it seems preferable, if at all possible, to attempt to provide a constructive resolution to this paradox without convicting Socrates of deceiving his friends on the jury—those who voted for him after he assured them he was ignorant, those whose fears for him he seeks to allay with his 'great proof'.

5.5.4 A SUGGESTION BY BURNET

One constructive resolution to the dilemma may be teased out of John

---

[46] At *Ap*. 31c7–d4, Socrates tells the jury that they have heard him talk about his *daimonion* 'at many times in many places'. See also *Euthphr*. 3b5–6 and references in Chapter 1, note 126.

[47] See Section 1.4.4.2.

[48] Xenophon defends the silence of Socrates' *daimonion*, as showing that Socrates' condemnation was really for the best given his age, at *Mem*. 4.8.1.

Burnet's notes on *Apology* 40a4 and c3.[49] Burnet limits the information available to Socrates by reading 'εἴ τι μέλλοιμι μὴ ὀρθῶς
πράξειν' as 'if I were going to do something amiss, i.e. something
unlucky and not . . . wrong.' Similarly, he renders 'τι . . . ἀγαθὸν
πράξειν' as equivalent to 'εὖ πράξειν', which in his view concerns only the practical consequences of actions and does not carry moral
force. In this way, Burnet might attempt to resolve the paradox by
urging that what Socrates derives from his *daimonion* is of no particular moral relevance and thus provides him no access to the sorts of
truth of which he professes to be wholly ignorant, even if we allow
that (1*b*) is a premiss of Socrates' argument.

Burnet is surely right to recognize in Socrates' claim an essential element of consequentialism, according to which one does not 'do well'
unless the consequences of one's actions are good ones. Since good
consequences are thus a necessary condition of 'doing well', there is
no conceivable situation in which Socrates could 'do something good'
but none the less suffer a bad consequence as a result—to do
something good, on this view, is precisely to act in such a way as, all
things considered, to ensure good results.

Of course, each time one does 'something good' one only assures
that the results one achieves are good results, *all things considered*.
There may well be situations in life in which no truly wonderful results
are possible—indeed, most if not all of our choices are presumably of
this sort. In assessing how good a result Socrates expects his death to
be in this case, one would do well to note that he thinks, as he later
says, that it may be like an everlasting 'dreamless sleep' (40c5-e2),
and that, as he says in his final words to the jury, it is not certain that
in death he will be better off than his jurors (42a2-5). Thus, to do
well, that is, to act in such a way as to achieve the best possible consequences all things considered, is not necessarily to act in such a way as
to achieve the best imaginable outcome, physical necessity, the laws
of logic, and the limitations of mortality aside. So although Socrates
can be assured that his death will not count as an evil *relative to his
other real options*, a number of things might nevertheless be better
than being dead. Surely this must be true, or anyone—even a
god—would be better off dead. Relative to other (imaginable) goods,
then, death might still count as an evil.

---

[49] Burnet (2), 165-6. See also Woodhead (425) for an expression of the view we
attribute to Burnet.

But Socrates is not exaggerating when he says that 'a wonderful thing has happened'. He says that 'those . . . who suppose death to be an evil must surely not be right'. As we have said, these words cannot mean that death cannot, under any circumstances, be even a relative evil. But 'those . . . who suppose death to be an evil' do not have it in mind to compare death to, for example, the blessed state of the gods and find it relatively less desirable. 'Those . . . who suppose death to be an evil' believe that death is an absolutely bad consequence, that is, the sort of consequence of an action that would provide a decisive sign of the agent's having failed to do well. People who think of death in this way may even suppose that it is the most disastrous of bad consequences. To think that death is an evil, then, is to think that it could never be the product of *eu praxis*. But the silence of his *daimonion* has assured Socrates that he has done well. The result of his doing well is that he is going to die. Hence, death cannot be the sort of thing that must count as an absolutely bad consequence. So Socrates can conclude, given his *daimonion*'s silence, that 'those . . . who suppose death to be an evil'—that is, those who consider death to be an absolutely bad consequence—must be wrong.

Burnet is surely wrong, however, in making a distinction between doing 'something amiss' and doing something that is morally wrong. For one thing, it appears to rely on a distinction between morality and prudence that an eudaimonist like Socrates would almost certainly resist. The moral life, according to Socrates, is the most prudent life, once we see rightly wherein our greatest interest, the most complete possible achievement of *eudaimonia* (happiness, good fortune, well-being), lies. Hence, if the practical consequences to which Burnet refers have no place in Socrates' moral theory, it would appear that they have no place in Socrates' theory of motivation. Amoral prudence is, after all, plainly of no concern to the Socrates of the *Apology*, who is willing to give up everything to follow the god's command (23b7–c1, 28d10–29a4, 31b1–c3, 36b5–9), and who would resolutely eschew any mode of defense he found shameful, even if it could secure the release he believes he deserves (34b7–35d8, 38d3–39b8).

Secondly, even if Socratic philosophy did acknowledge Burnet's distinction between moral and practical consequences, given that the gods appear to Socrates to be thoroughly moral beings, it would be odd indeed if the *daimonion* saw fit only to warn him away from non-moral evils, but remained aloof and unconcerned when he was about to commit moral evils. Such a reservation, we think, would be unlikely enough to merit clearer stipulation by Socrates.

Finally, Burnet himself refers us to the *Phaedrus* (242b8), where the *daimonion* warns Socrates away from an act whose relevant danger lies in giving offense to the god. It is true, plainly, that such a course of action would be extremely imprudent, but it makes no sense to suppose that this imprudence is unconnected to or sensibly detachable from its impiety. Surely, then, this instance has a decidedly and essentially moral character. In fact, the one instance of a daimonic warning Socrates cites in the *Apology* is misconstrued by Burnet. At 31c7–d5 Socrates says that his *daimonion* prevented him from entering politics. Burnet rightly notes that Socrates understands this daimonic interference as seeking to keep him from getting into trouble in the state. But the point of this is clear in context: Socrates has a religious mission in Athens, the supreme moral value of which greatly outweighs any petty benefits his political activity might secure, and the pursuit of which would almost certainly be ended prematurely if he were more active politically. It is not the mere length of Socrates' life that is important, on this interpretation, but the success of his mission. The god's business, as Socrates says, always comes first. For these reasons, we find the view suggested by Burnet to be inadequate.

5.5.5 ARGUMENTS FROM DAIMONIC SILENCE

Let us return, then, to our problem: how can Socrates be so confident that his *daimonion*'s silence entails that he will suffer no evil in death, without appealing to an implausibly strong premiss such as (1*b*)? According to premiss (1*b*), Socrates could be assured that his *daimonion* would oppose *each and every* wrong action he might ever undertake. He conceives, as we have said, of wrong actions as those whose consequences are bad. Hence, if (1*b*) were true the *daimonion* would have to oppose *each and every* action that would lead Socrates to a bad consequence.

But all Socrates requires, for his argument at 40a3–c3 to work, is that his *daimonion* would surely oppose him *in cases such as this one*, if he were about to suffer something evil. So for the argument to work we do not need—as per (1*b*)—utterly to indemnify Socrates against evil; we need only to indemnify him in *cases such as this one*. If it is not, then, a categorical guarantee that Socrates enjoys, what might it be about this case that convinces him that he would surely have received the opposition of his *daimonion* if things were going wrong?

Some actions or activities, to state the obvious, are more complex than others. The decision, for example, to move one's family and household from one city to another involves a very complex variety of actions to enact fully. One does not simply move (as if even the moving part were simple). One first deliberates about the move, bringing into consideration as best as one can all the costs and benefits of doing so. One discusses the possibility with one's friends and family, takes advice on various logistical problems, and makes an innumerable number of subsidiary decisions—whether to entrust one's household to a moving company (which one?) or to attempt to move it all oneself (and how?); whether to drive to the new city (is a new car necessary?) or take another form of transportation (what sort?); what route or transportation company to choose; when to make the move, how to notify interested parties, and so on. On the basis of each of these subsidiary decisions, one undertakes a vast number of subsidiary actions—all with the consequence that one has done what may be described as one (vastly complex) action, moving one's home from one city to another.

On the other hand, some actions are relatively simple. One may have a number of considerations in mind as one considers going to the shop now or later to buy bread, for example—or even as one decides whether or not to buy the bread. But though each step in the process might be viewed as involving a subsidiary action, the entire process remains incalculably simpler than that involved in moving from city to city.

Socrates says that his *daimonion* has opposed him 'quite frequently, even in little things'. If his 'sign' is this active, Socrates has good reason to believe that the more opportunities he gives his *daimonion* to oppose him (by acting wrongly), the more likely it becomes that he will suffer opposition by his 'sign'. Even if his 'sign' would not oppose him *every* time he went wrong (as per (1*b*))—even if it could not be depended upon to oppose him *a majority of the time*—if Socrates commits enough errors, opposition by the *daimonion* becomes virtually assured. By saying that its intervention is 'quite frequent', however, Socrates seems to think that it would oppose him *most* of the time. On the one hand, if what Socrates sets out to do is something relatively simple—and wrong—it is likely that the *daimonion* would oppose him. But he could not be sure: *ex hypothesi*, sometimes it would not oppose him even when he was acting wrongly, and this might be just such a time. If, on the other hand, what Socrates set out to do required a vast number of subsidiary actions, each of which itself could be a candidate for daimonic opposition and each of which contributed a necessary link in a chain that was leading Socrates into evil, the likelihood of opposition at one or more of the steps approaches certainty. So Socrates might now and again make an error that is unopposed; but the likelihood that he could make a long series of errors (or, for that matter, a long series of actions whose net product was a vast error), is virtually zero. The more active his *daimonion* is, the less likely a long series of unopposed mistakes becomes. And since his *daimonion* would oppose him even in petty things, Socrates can be confident that no such series could go unopposed simply because its constituent actions involved errors too trivial for his *daimonion* to heed.

The case at hand has at least the necessary degree of complexity. Socrates was not opposed in going to the court on the day of the trial, or in telling the jurors all the many (sometimes quite controversial and risky) things he told them. He was not opposed as he considered and rejected a number of counter-penalties, or in offering the fine. If his *daimonion* was very active, even in small things, and since at other times it would stop him repeatedly even in the middle of a speech (40b3–4), Socrates has excellent inductive reason for supposing that the net result of all his actions is no evil, for his *daimonion* never opposed him in any of the many opportunities he had given it in doing the many things inexorably leading to his condemnation. Even if he cannot be certain (as per (1*b*)) that *each and every one* of his acts was right, the great complexity of what he did on the day of his trial provides him with inductive evidence of the rightness of the trial's outcome so overwhelmingly strong that Socrates deems that evidence a 'wonderful thing'.

Two additional points must be made. First, it follows from this account that, strictly speaking, Socrates still cannot be absolutely certain that the net product of his many actions is not an evil, for inductive evidence of the sort we have proposed always leaves some chance of error, however small. But given the great complexity of Socrates' series of actions, the extreme activity of the *daimonion*, and its frequent pettiness, the chance of error in this case seems vanishingly minute. Socrates is convinced of his conclusion, just as we would be in a case where our inductive evidence reduced the chance of alternative possibilities beyond the point of reasonable concern.

Secondly, it also follows that Socrates does have—in his *daimo-*

nion—a virtually certain sign of the moral (or practical) acceptability of complex series of actions that are left unopposed. Given the great frequency with which he suffers daimonic opposition, we may suppose that Socrates rarely experiences unopposed complex series of actions; perhaps this is part of what strikes Socrates as 'wonderful' about the present instance. But whenever Socrates does undertake so complex a series of actions and remains unopposed, he can be confident that its ultimate product is no evil thing. This does not mean that Socrates could use his *daimonion* as a test of the truth of any given moral proposition, however. For many moral propositions, acting upon them may not involve sufficiently complex series of actions to allow the inductive evidence of daimonic acquiescence to build to the point of removing any practical concern about error. Again, on this hypothesis the *daimonion* may allow some errors to pass unopposed; Socrates needs to pile up enough actions toward a given end to make their collective freedom from opposition count as rendering the eventual outcome clearly acceptable. If the number of actions in the pertinent series is too small, the likelihood that their product is wrong remains to great for confidence.

Of course, Socrates could repeat such series of actions again and again in an attempt to build up greater confidence. In order to derive something like a moral generalization for a given type of act-series, however, his repetitions would need to be quite numerous and well designed to provide tokens of that type in a wide variety of contexts. Otherwise, he could never be sure that the acceptability of the series he had performed was due to the correctness of the type, rather than the acceptability of those tokens (for some unknown reason) in the limited contexts in which he had performed them. For example, he might easily get the impression that it was entirely acceptable to throw spears when blindfolded if he was unopposed every time he ever undertook to do so, but only ever undertook to do so when no one else was in the vicinity and thus at risk of injury. It would be up to Socrates, however, to discern the nature of the various contexts that might involve factors material to assessing the value of the generalization. Needless to say, the process of testing in this way quickly becomes extremely complex, and it is not clear how Socrates could ever satisfy himself that he had found enough evidence of sufficient variety to make the appropriate generalization, even if throughout his many trials his *daimonion* never opposed him. It is not even clear that Socrates has any method for determining that what appear to be similar contexts are in fact relatively similar; there may be unknown material differences each time of which he was unaware. So even the repetitions he might attempt might, for all he would know, not be true repetitions.

It follows that Socrates could not use his *daimonion*'s lacks of opposition as a source of 'wonderful proofs' that individual actions were correctly performed; for all he would know, its acquiescence in any individual case would be one of the (however rare) examples of its non-opposition to an evil-producing action. And even if he attempted to repeat the action many times and none of the attempted repetitions were opposed, Socrates could not conclude that the act- (or act-series-) type was morally acceptable, for it would remain possible both that his attempt at repetition had failed (for reasons of which he was not aware) and that even if they succeeded in being proper repetitions, the repetitions had not been performed in all the pertinent contexts.

To gain a 'wonderful proof', then, Socrates would need to perform a long series of actions, each of which was unopposed. And then the only thing proved would be that *this* particular act-series-token had not resulted in anything evil. That limited result in this case is extremely reassuring to Socrates, for it means that the consequence of this particular series of actions—his condemnation—is nothing evil. This is indeed 'a wonderful thing', and he offers this reassurance to concerned jurors as something to allay their fears on his behalf. But as wonderful as it is, it is philosophically insignificant: it tells us nothing about the value of death in general; in fact, it tells us nothing general at all.

For any other series of actions of sufficient complexity, Socrates could be assured that the ultimate consequence was acceptable when the *daimonion* had made no opposition. But as we have argued, this fact does not recommend the use of the *daimonion* in deliberation, for its silence implies no sanction of any general proposition one might follow in deliberating. If Socrates, foreseeing the need to make some decision involving a long series of actions, elected not to deliberate but only to follow one of the possible paths, he could only be assured that if he was going gravely wrong his *daimonion* would eventually oppose him. And if it did not, he could be assured that things had turned out acceptably. Given his *daimonion*'s activity, however, such mindless trial and error would propel him into opposition with such frequency that he would likely get nowhere. This is why even he would recognize a need for principles by which to deliberate.

He could not derive such principles from his 'sign', moreover, and so even though he might occasionally find himself in possession of a 'great proof' for some morally significant specific truth, Socrates could not hope that he could employ his 'sign' in such a way as to obtain from its silence what others could only hope to achieve through philosophizing.

5.5.6 ARGUMENTS FROM DAIMONIC OPPOSITION

But what about cases in which Socrates' *daimonion* does oppose him? Does it not follow that, at least in these cases, Socrates can know that the principle on which he was acting is wrong? It might be true that the *daimonion* occasionally fails to oppose him when he errs; but he never suggests that it ever opposes him when he is *not* in error. And if so, does it not follow that—at least in those cases in which he is opposed—he can no longer claim to suffer from ignorance? At least now he knows that what he was doing is wrong. Accordingly, does he not now also know that he should do the opposite, and if so, in what sense is he ignorant?

We may begin by scrutinizing more carefully what sort of information Socrates may suppose he gets from his *daimonion*. Let us trace a generalized version of how a daimonic message might be given to Socrates.

1. Socrates, presented with the option either to do X or to fail to do X, elects to do X—which unbeknowst to him[50] is an evil or harmful thing to do.

2. Socrates' *daimonion*, at some time before Socrates has actually done X (that is, either before he begins to do X, or after he has begun but before he manages actually to complete X), intervenes, warning Socrates away from the completion of X.

3. So informed by his *daimonion*, Socrates desists from doing X,[51] and learns that he ought not to do X.

If this is the pattern of such daimonic interference, how can Socrates profess ignorance, for he knows at least that he ought not to do X?

---

[50] We shall soon take up the case where Socrates employs the *daimonion* purposefully to clarify a former alarm.

[51] We know of no case where Socrates receives a daimonic alarm but ignores it, or goes ahead and completes the action despite the warning. Hence, there is no reason to suppose that he learned of the advantages of following its prohibitions by trial and error.

It should be clear from this that if what Socrates gains at (3) is to count as wisdom, then no constructive resolution of the paradox we have raised will be possible, for Socrates will both have wisdom (as per (3)) and claim wholly to lack wisdom (as at 21b4–5; see Section 2.6). Taking our clue from this observation, then, in what remains we shall seek to deny that the epistemic results of (3) are what Socrates would call the wisdom he claims to lack.[52]

Notice that unless the daimonic message is itself unclear it cannot be that the positive or negative assessment of X is left undetermined. The message Socrates receives is assuredly truthful, given its divine source (see for example 21b6–7), and thus he can be fully confident that whatever he is being deterred from is evil or harmful. But precisely what is being prohibited in any given case may not be entirely plain, as Socrates may undertake to do a number of things at once. Of course, some refinement is possible, for if the referent of the daimonic warning were embedded in a more complex action or set of actions, Socrates could go through and carefully extract the elements of what he was about to do and see which element (or elements) was (or were) the offender(s) by trying them out and seeing which one(s) cause the daimonic alarm to sound. But unless we assume (1*b*), the *daimonion* might not warn Socrates *each time* he was about to do something wrongful.

And there would always be a certain imprecision in this, for even very simple actions are typically compounds of a variety of elements, each of which may be composed of yet more basic elements, and so on. Indeed, it seems absurd to suppose that there could be a legitimate instance of action that was in the relevant sense *atomic*. Even if we could analyze an action into its components, it is most unlikely that we could ever perform atomic actions atomically, that is, uncompounded with other actions. Thus, even if Socrates were the sort of philosopher to concern himself with the sorts of practical and

---

[52] At 20d4–9, Socrates allows that he has a kind of wisdom, which he calls 'human wisdom' (ἀνθρωπίνη σοφία), in contrast to the sort of wisdom, which he calls 'greater than human', claimed by the Sophists. But since he also denies that he has any understanding, it appears that any wisdom Socrates has must be embodied either in his recognition of his own ignorance or in his ability to refute those who claim to have the wisdom they lack, an ability which still does not bestow any positive understanding in the subject-matter of his refutations (23a3–b4). But this wisdom, which Socrates says is 'of little or no value' (23a7), is not the sort Socrates claims to lack. Rather, it is the substantial, positive sort in which he, and indeed all humans, are 'worth nothing' (23b3–4).

theoretical issues involved in such a conceptual analysis (which he most certainly was not), there is good reason to believe he could never isolate with certainty the offending from the inoffensive elements of the actions that prompted his daimonic alarm to sound. Hence, even if he could solve all the theoretical intricacies of analyzing the elements of his actions, a certain imprecision in what he learns at stage (3) is sure to remain: he will not know precisely what aspect(s) or element(s) of his action is (are) the reason(s) for the alarm. Of course, this imprecision does not nullify Socrates' ability to judge confidently that the act (compound) from which his *daimonion* deters him is in some way or ways evil or harmful.

But the above imprecision is not the only thing lacking in what Socrates learns when his *daimonion* gives its warning. Though Socrates may confidently conclude that *this token* of the act (compound) he was about to undertake was evil or harmful, he is left wholly without information as to whether the problem is in the act (compound) type, or just in this token of it. That is, he can infer only that it would be wrong to do such a thing *now*; he does not know whether or not it would be acceptable for him to try again at some other time. Since the *daimonion* only warns him not to do the thing in question *at the time in question* and *in the circumstances in question*, it may not be anything in the act itself that is the problem. For all Socrates knows, the problem derives from some anomaly in the immediate context or environment in which the act is to be performed, an anomaly Socrates may never encounter again. Hence, it is not enough that he should be able to analyze his actions down to their atoms, as it were, if he is to recognize fully the evil or harm of which his *daimonion* warns him; he must also be able to recognize all of the relevant circumstantial context of the act in question, for the wrong may not reside in the act itself but rather in its (perhaps quite unique) effects on that environment.

And we have not yet exhausted what is missing from the information Socrates gets from any given daimonic alarm. Suppose that Socrates could somehow discern both the precise element (or elements) of the act in question relevant to the evil or harm of which he is warned, and suppose also that he is able to recognize what a___ ts of the environment of the act (if any) are relevant to the wi_ _ess of this particular act-token. Socrates still, however, may not u_ rstand what it is about that element (or elements) that makes it (or the___ wrong in this context. One may know that speeding bullets do the killing in a shooting, and also that Jones's standing in front of one's gun is what makes the current environment a bad one in which to shoot one's gun; but one may still not understand how or why speeding bullets kill people.

But perhaps the most important gap of all in Socrates' understanding can be seen in the fact that nowhere in Plato's early dialogues do we find him claiming to have any of the answers to his 'τί ἐστί' questions: 'what is (a given) virtue?' Certainly, if he did, he could not truthfully claim to have no wisdom great or small, especially given his conception of what constitutes the greatest things (see 22d3-4, 22d6-8, 29d7-30a2, 30a7-b6), and thus in what understanding the greatest wisdom would consist. Though he might know that the act-token he was about to undertake is evil or harmful (the *daimonion* tells him this much), he could not understand *why* it is so, for he does not understand what it is to be evil or harmful. Socrates, then, would at least have to have the answer to one or more of his 'τί ἐστί' questions to understand why any given wrongful act was wrongful.

So when the *daimonion* warns him away from an action, there are at least four significant gaps in Socrates' state of cognition: (*a*) Socrates does not know precisely in which aspect or aspects of the act (type or token), if any, the wrongness lies; (*b*) Socrates does not know which aspect or aspects of the environment of this act (token), if any, contribute to the wrongness of this act (token); (*c*) Socrates does not know what it is about the elements of the act (type or token) and environment that make this act (token) wrong; and perhaps most importantly, (*d*) Socrates does not understand what it is for a thing to be good or evil, beneficial or harmful.

5.5.7 DAIMONIC INTERFERENCE AND WISDOM

Once we notice how little information Socrates gets from a daimonic alarm, we can see why Socrates could never be made wise by his *daimonion's* alarms. The problem with them is not fallibility but uninformativeness. After all, when the *daimonion* tells Socrates that he should desist from what he is about to do, he can be completely certain that he must not continue what he was about to do. But this information tells him nothing about what it is that is wrong, when it is wrong, why it is wrong, and what it is to be wrong. The god does not lie to Socrates, but does manage to tell him next to nothing through the *daimonion*. What Socrates gets from his sign, therefore, is virtually worthless for the pursuit of the sorts of truth Socrates seeks philosophically—truth that explains and defines, and which thus can be applied to the judgments and deliberations required for the achievement of the truly good life for men.

In the *Apology* and elsewhere, Socrates shows that he believes that wisdom consists in understanding, and, as we have said (see Section 3.2.3), there are men in Athens who have some wisdom, involving understanding of 'many and fine things' (22d2), the craftsmen who are wise in their crafts. Indeed, this is the only case of wisdom that Socrates grants to others, obscured though it is by their folly in thinking that they understand other more important things when they do not (22d4–e5). Socrates' superiority in wisdom does not derive from his having more understanding, for he explicitly disallows that (21d5–6, 22e1–5).

If we look at what the craftsmen have that Socrates lacks, however, we confirm our impression that his *daimonion* can never provide Socrates with the wisdom he seeks. The craftsman has a τέχνη; that is, he has the ability to produce goods or services by the application of practical skills, knowledge of generalizable procedures, and of materials and protocols, and so on. His *daimonion* does not afford Socrates any comparable ability, for even if it allows Socrates to produce good actions, it only does so *ad hoc*. Each daimonic alarm, since it comes without explanation of any kind, affords no ground for judging cases other than the one it governs, and it gives only the least possible adequate ground for judging that one. Of course, Socrates could attempt to generate a great body of data from attempting actions that trigger his divine monitor, but the explanation of its alarms will always be his alone to generate, quite fallibly and without any creative assistance from divination.[53] Hence, generalizations or propositional claims based upon the behavior of his *daimonion* are highly inferential and go well beyond what he actually gets from any of its alarms. Since Socrates disclaims wisdom of any kind, then, we may suppose that he does not believe that he can derive moral expertise from his *daimonion* with anything like the same skill and assurance that craftsmen, in his view, have in the practice of their crafts.

But now we may return at last to the unique claim Socrates makes

---

[53] That Socrates believes in other forms of divination is clear not only from his account of the oracle to Chairephon but also from the 'oracles and dreams' to which he refers at *Ap*. 33c4–7 (see Section 2.6.4 and notes).

at 40a3–c3, for here he derives his assurance from the fact that his *daimonion did not* sound an alarm. He concludes that his going off to die, which would be considered by many to be the worst possible thing that could happen to him, is really something good. It is true that in deriving this conclusion Socrates shows a great degree of confidence on an issue about which he had no ground for conviction one way or the other. Previously, he did not know whether death would be an evil or not, and now he is convinced it will not be, for him at least. But as we have argued in Section 5.5.5 above, daimonic silence provides Socrates with no access to wisdom either. Our view of what Socrates would suppose constitutes wisdom, if correct, allows us to deny that he would count his 'great proof' or even actual daimonic alarms as affording Socrates access to the wisdom he claims to lack. This is clear if we analyze what is still missing from Socrates' state of information even given the *daimonion's* silence.

(*a*) Even though Socrates has excellent reason for supposing that the product of his actions leading up to and during the trial is not an evil thing, he still does not understand what it is about this product, or the environment in which it was derived, that makes it permissible or good, since he has no confident theory of moral goodness (or permissibility), or for that matter of death. At best, then, Socrates has gathered a number of actions (all of the relevant ones of his own) that could serve as possible data for a theory of morally permissible or good action, but he cannot even be confident of any given one of them that it really is permissible or good. And since, according to our argument, Socrates' conception of wisdom requires at least that it derive from confident (or certain) and highly (or completely) justified generally and practically applicable theories, the new stockpile of data Socrates has gathered would not constitute wisdom even if the value of each of its elements *were* certain.

(*b*) Socrates may conclude that his own death will not be an evil thing, but he cannot conclude that anyone else's would not be evil, for the silence of the *daimonion* entails nothing general. Socrates' proffered interpretation (at 40c3–41d5) of why his death will not be an evil is, of course, more generally applicable, but this is Socrates' own interpretation, one that is in no way guaranteed by the *daimonion* or its silence.[54] Hence, Socrates has got from the *daimonion* only a very

---

[54] In fact, Socrates' interpretation contains two quite different and quite separable accounts. The first imagines only two conceptions of the afterlife and concludes that both are preferable to life (40c4–41c8). Socrates calls this

likely instance of non-evil (or goodness), which does not constitute what he would recognize as wisdom.

5.5.8 A FEW CONCLUDING REMARKS ABOUT SOCRATES' 'GREAT PROOF'

We have attempted to offer a way in which Socrates' confession of ignorance and his 'great proof' at 40a3–c3 are both sincerely claimed, and compatible. The motive for our argument is at least in part an uneasiness with the suggestion that Socrates (or Plato) would knowingly create an inconsistency, or speak insincerely about either issue. Perhaps a more liberal conception of Socratic honesty would permit a less elaborate resolution to this problem than the one we have offered, but we would defend our resolution at least this far: it is consistent with what we know of Socratic philosophy as Plato reports it, and does no violence to good sense.

One final problem with Socrates' 'great proof', however, we shall not undertake to resolve, namely, Socrates' apparent commitment to the equivalence of 'good' and 'not evil'. Socrates' *daimonion* warns him only when he is about to do something evil. From his *daimonion*'s silence, in this case as we have interpreted it, he may thus conclude that what he has done—and what he is about to suffer—is not evil. But Socrates concludes that he is bound for 'something good'. We see nothing in Socrates' 'great proof' that warrants this substitution, and we believe that there are good philosophical grounds for resisting it. We do not see in this, however, any reason to suppose that Socrates is insincere in the claims he makes at 40a3–c3, for it is a common feature of Socratic arguments to see opposites as exhaustive alternatives. It is true, of course, that one can find passages in which he avoids this mistake, as for example at *Gorgias* 467e1–468a6. But even there it turns out that the neutral things are pursued, if pursued,

---

interpretation a 'hope' (ἐλπίς—40c4), which would seem to disqualify it as anything certain. The second says that his death is a good because it is better for Socrates to die now and be freed from troubles (41d3–6), which does not imply anything about what follows death except that it will be better for Socrates than he could expect if he kept on living. This is quite compatible with the general scepticism with which the dialogue concludes (42a2–5). But Socrates' final remark in no way vitiates the conclusion that for Socrates death will be a good thing; relative to whatever else is possible for him, death will be a blessing. Of course, it is quite compatible with this that those to whom Socrates speaks are better off living; the troubles Socrates escapes by dying might not be in prospect for those to whom Socrates speaks. We shall have more to say on these issues in the next sections.

only for the sake of the good. Unless, then, Socrates always has reason to assume that the domain of discourse is in each case limited to those things that have either the quality in question or its opposite, the one fallacy we find in the 'great proof' of *Apology* 40a3–c3 is not unusual in Socratic arguments.[55]

5.6   Socrates' Final Speech: Part III (40c4–42a5)

5.6.1   SOCRATES ON DEATH AND THE AFTERLIFE

At 40c4, Socrates undertakes to explain why he thinks his death will be no evil. It is interesting to note the similarity between this and the one other passage in which Socrates' *daimonion* had been a part of his arguments. At 31c7–d5, Socrates says that his *daimonion* had opposed his participating in politics, and he immediately goes on to give his reasons for supposing such to be good. So it is here: after telling his jurors of his 'great proof', he goes on immediately to tell them why he supposes the *daimonion*'s lack of opposition was good. Surely, as he says in his 'great proof', it must be that his death will be a good thing.

But what is it about death that could make it a good thing? Socrates' speculations that follow are not presented with anything like dogmatic conviction, nor does he anywhere say that the two alternatives he imagines are the only possible ones. The entire discourse has the feel of a statement of the alternatives he believes are most commonly accepted, and all he seeks to do in this discussion is to show how both may be counted a gain for him. Nowhere does Socrates state that he has undertaken a study of the varieties of opinion about death and the afterlife or independent research into the question himself, and nothing he says should encourage us to assume that the two alternatives he outlines exhaust, in his view, all the possibilities.[56] They serve the purpose of exploring with those

[55] Ehnmark ((2), 19) also notes the fallacy involved in the inference from 'not evil' to 'good', calling it 'an inference in no wise logically satisfying'. But Ehnmark attributes the fallacy to the fact that 'logic has to suffer in religious beliefs' (ibid.).

[56] Roochnik sees Socrates' remarks here as a complicated piece of rhetoric which is designed to look like an argument, but which, if it were an argument, would be logically faulty (213). On Roochnik's view, Socrates cannot honestly mean what he says about death, for if he did he would violate his earlier complaint (at 29a4–6) about others who supposed they knew what they did not (214). Since he takes the real nature of Socrates' remarks to be persuasive rhetoric, Roochnik is not bothered

who have proved to be his friends two options (perhaps among
many), one of which might well be true, and that is enough for
Socrates.[57] Again, his assurance that his death is no evil does not
come from his consideration of these options, but rather from what
he calls his 'great proof'. Socrates credits the speculations that
follow the 'great proof' as providing only 'much hope' (40c4).

The first of the two possibilities Socrates considers is that death
might be 'to be nothing, so that the dead have no perception of
anything' (40c5-7). If this is what it is to be dead, Socrates says it
would be a 'wonderful gain' (40d1-2). In comparison with the other
nights and days of one's life, one would count few times more pleasant
than a night passed in dreamless sleep. Even the Great King (of
Persia), for whom the number of pleasant days and nights is
presumably unsurpassed, would find this to be true (40d2-e2).

It has been averred that this is a specious argument, on the ground
that what makes a dreamless sleep pleasant is only the refreshed feeling one has when one wakes up from it, for without perception
(αἴσϑησις) there can be no pleasure (ἡδονή).[58] In addition to our
earlier reservations against even calling Socrates' considerations
here 'arguments', two things count against such an objection. First,
as we have said, it is typical for Socrates to view opposites as
exhausting the possible options in a given issue. In this case, his
inference obviously has this character. Even if a dreamless sleep can-

---

by the fact that what he takes Socrates to be doing would have the effect of deceiving at least some of the jurors who are favorably disposed towards Socrates.
Ehnmark's much earlier discussion of these two passages (in his (1), see esp. 115),
seems to us to make better sense. Another who questions the alternatives Socrates
offers in the third speech is Armleder, who accuses Socrates of making 'a careless
philosophical argument' (46) and insists that 'He is not to be taken literally as
meaning that death is either a profound sleep, or that in death the soul migrates
from this world to another' (46). Armleder's objections are answered to our
satisfaction by Hoerber (1).

[57] One option Socrates never mentions is that later endorsed by Plato in the *Phd.*,
Phdr., *Rep.* X, and *Laws*, namely, that the soul transmigrates after death into other
living things, including animals as well as humans. Yet surely Socrates was aware of
such a view and its Pythagorean roots by the time he was brought to trial. Given the
nature and tone of his remarks here, however, and the great likelihood that none of
his jurors held the Pythagorean view, nothing requires Socrates to consider such an
option in offering his jurors 'much hope'. (Socrates' silence on this point also
suggests that Plato had not yet become convinced of this view, though it is possible
that he suppressed mention of it for the purposes of a more accurate representation
of Socrates, who did not believe it.)

[58] Again, by Roochnik (214). See also Anastaplo (1), 27.

not strictly be said to be positively pleasant, it may be said at least to be untroubled and without pain. If it is presumed that all that is required to count as pleasant is that a state should not qualify as troubled or painful, then a dreamless sleep counts as pleasant. Secondly, Socrates does not assert dogmatically that senselessness is pleasant; he says only that it is pleasant *by comparison to the experiences typically involved in normal life*. The sense of his remark is plainly that the experiences typically involved in normal life make them less desirable than senselessness. So we do not have to suppose that in order for Socrates' 'argument' to work, we must assume death somehow to involve the actual sensation of pleasure. We merely have to accept his contention that senselessness is preferable to the troubles and pains we typically suffer in life. Socrates' employment of a night spent in dreamless sleep is designed to provide a model for what death would be like on this hypothesis: a night of dreamless sleep stretched to eternity. *Not* to wake up from such a sleep is what Socrates calls a gain (40e2–3). No doubt, not everyone would share Socrates' very negative assessment of the typical enjoyments of daily life, but surely his point here cannot be dismissed simply as 'intrinsically senseless'.[59]

The other alternative Socrates considers is that it is, 'according to the tales that are told, a kind of change and migration of the soul from this to another place' (40c7–9). There has been some discussion as to whether or not this alternative represents what was actually the common opinion about the afterlife in Athens at the time.[60] But it seems to us that common Athenian religious opinion is impossible to reconstruct with any degree of confidence. Reading Homer and the tragic poets might help, for example, but there is no reason to suppose that any given author can be seen as an index of common sentiment. And Socrates' second option about the afterlife is neither so detailed nor so plainly divergent from stories about the afterlife we see elsewhere to convince us that there is anything suspicious in his reckoning the version he offers as 'κατὰ τὰ λεγόμενα' (according to the tales that are told).[61] Again, we must

---

[59] Roochnik, 215.   [60] See, e.g., Ehnmark (1), 116.

[61] It is noteworthy how many times Socrates qualifies the account of the soul's migration by saying things like 'if this is true' (see 41a8, 41c6–7) and by reminding his jurors that its source is 'the tales that are told' (see 40c7, 40e5–6, 41a3, 41c6–7). If Socrates' account was supposed to do more than reassure the jurors, and rather to convince them, his heavily qualified rhetoric would be inexplicable.

remember that Socrates considers his remarks at this point as being like a chat between friends (40a1), and we do not find any sense in supposing that Socrates would obfuscate or dither in such a setting.

But there is also nothing about this passage or the event it represents that should require us to demand a thoroughly accurate portrayal of contemporary religion. We would have no reason to discount Socrates' sincerity if we found exaggeration or peculiarity within it. Socrates is reassuring those jurors whom he supposes might be concerned for him, and if he takes certain liberties with the (varieties of) opinion one might have found in Athens concerning the afterlife, it is only because he seeks to show that, as far as he is concerned, the jurors have no particular reason for anxiety on his behalf. After all, as he has already told them, no one really knows what the afterlife is like, if there is one, and hence the pretty version he offers of the idea that souls migrate elsewhere at death has just as much claim to likelihood as any grimmer tale that might be told. To deny the validity of Socrates' optimistic version would be to claim the very sort of knowledge he says that all lack. Of course, the jurors might still worry that other less desirable possibilities have not been ruled out by Socrates' discussion, and nothing Socrates says in the third speech masquerades as an argument to the effect that such possibilities are impossible. But the 'great proof' serves, at least to him and to those jurors who accept the value of Socrates' *daimonion*, as assurance that whatever death is, it is no evil thing for Socrates. The rest, including Socrates' account of what the migration of the soul to another place might be like, offers only 'much hope' (40c4).

In fact, there is special reason to deny that Socrates wishes to do anything more than offer a bit of reassurance in this discussion. Those who fear death, as he has already said, are guilty of 'the most disgraceful ignorance' (29b1-2).[62] But the reason their condition is so disgraceful is that in fearing death they act as if they know what they do not know (29a4-b1). But surely anyone who left the court after Socrates' third speech with dogmatic conviction that death was a good thing would be no less disgracefully ignorant, being confident that they knew what they did not know, than those who feared death as if it were the greatest evil. Though commentators seeking a Socratic argument as to why his death is a good thing might wish for

---

[62] Socrates' elsewhere calls the fear of death 'irrational and cowardly' (*Grg.* 522e2).

something more powerful, Socrates himself would be the last person on earth to seek to try to seduce the friendly jurors into 'the most disgraceful ignorance'. He does wish to remind them that they have no particular reason to grieve for him, and even have some reason for hope on his behalf.

Socrates' actual account of what the migration of the soul might be like makes no pretense of logical precision; indeed, it is at best discontinuous, though not inconsistent. He first imagines that upon arrival in the next world, having left the world where people claim to be judges, one is asked to be judged by 'those who are really judges, who are said to sit in judgment there' (40e7–41a3).[63] Surely this would be no slight benefit (41a5).

Socrates next imagines that in the next world he will be able to meet Orpheus, Musaeus, Hesiod, and Homer, and says he would be willing to die many times if such were what is in store for him (41a6–8). And if in the afterlife he should be able to meet and compare what had happened to him with the sufferings of Palamedes or Aias, son of Telemon, or any of the others who had been killed according to an unjust trial, he would not find it unpleasant (41a8–b5). But the greatest thing of all (41b5), an 'irresistible happiness' (41c3–4), would be to be able to continue his philosophical examination of people in the next world. The next world, after all, would be populated with the greatest people who had ever lived—men like Agamemnon, Odysseus, and Sisyphus (41b8–c1), as well as countless others, both men and women (41c1–2).[64] And in the afterlife, one would not be killed for engaging in philosophy, for the residents of Hades are immortal (41c4–6).

The hope such stories offer Socrates' judges is, of course, predicated upon the likelihood that there is some truth in them, and, as we have said, nothing in what Socrates says to them offers any guarantee of such. Nor are the reasons he offers for looking forward to death generally applicable: Socrates may have nothing to fear from such judges as Minos and Rhadamanthus, but some of his jurors might be more anxious; Socrates might find enjoyment in compar-

---

[63] Socrates lists the likely candidates as Minos, Rhadamanthus, Aiakos, and Triptolemos (41a3–4). The same list, minus Triptolemos, is suggested at *Grg.* 523e8–524a1. Since we do not suppose Socrates' discussion in either place to be an assertion of dogmatic convictions, we see no ground for concern in the discrepancy between the two accounts.

[64] Discussions of the various people Socrates selects in this section of the third speech as those with whom he would most like to speak in the afterlife may be found in Anastaplo ((1), 20–6) and in Brenk.

ing his lot with Palamedes and Aias, but his jurors may not share Socrates' interest, or feel they have anything important in common with Palamedes or Aias; Socrates might enjoy cross-examining Odysseus and Sisyphus, but his jurors might prefer a different way of spending eternity. So the entire focus of Socrates' rendering of 'the tales that are told' of the afterlife is personal; the account he offers shows why he has reason for 'much hope', and why his friends on the jury might reasonably be inclined to share that hope with him. Naturally, if the afterlife is anything like what Socrates imagines, his jurors will find much in it to their liking as well. But that is not the point of Socrates' friendly chat with his judges at the end of the *Apology*.

5.6.2 'NO EVIL COMES TO A GOOD MAN EITHER IN LIFE OR AT THE END OF IT'

Socrates has been telling his jurors why they should not worry that something evil has happened to him. At the beginning of the final paragraph of the *Apology* he adds yet another reason as to why they should not be worried on his behalf, as well as why they themselves should be hopeful about death: 'no evil comes to a good man either in life or at the end of it, and his affairs are not neglected by God' (41d1-2). In a surprisingly confident way, Socrates says of this principle that it is the truth (41c9).

In Section 4.2, we argued that Socrates' claim, at 30c8-d1, that neither Meletus nor Anytus could harm him should be read as presupposing the limitation that the form of harm in question was the harm to his soul that would result from ignorance and vice. We noted in that section that an unqualified reading of Socrates' claim would bring it into unnecessary conflict with a variety of other passages in which Socrates explicitly refers to harms that might be suffered by a virtuous man, even to the degree of leaving him wretched and better off dead!

But at the conclusion of 4.2.3, we also noted that this passage at 41d1-2 is typically cited, along with the earlier one, as one of the strongest pieces of evidence for attributing the sufficiency of virtue doctrine to Socrates,[65] an attribution we dispute. We are now in a

---

[65] See, e.g., Burnyeat (3), 230; Grote (2), 243; Irwin, 100; Vlastos's review of Irwin in the *TLS* 24 Feb. 1978, 230-1.

position to show why we believe that this passage may be read in precisely the same way as we read the earlier passage.

The first thing to notice in this regard is that immediately after making the statement Socrates goes on to say, 'but this is clear to me, that it is better for me to die and be released from troubles' (41d2-4). He reminds the jury, as per his 'great proof' at 40a3-c3, that his confidence that it is indeed better for him to die derives from the fact that his *daimonion* did not oppose him either before or during the trial (41d5-6). What is significant here is that Socrates has no confidence about just what will happen at death. It may be that his soul will migrate to Hades where he will be allowed to examine and question the people there; but it may only be that death will be a 'dreamless sleep' for all eternity. Thus, his final words, directed to those jurors who voted for his acquittal, are significant. 'But the time has come to go. I go to die and you to live; which of us goes to a better thing is clear to none but the god' (42a4-5).

At the very conclusion of the *Apology*, then, Socrates believes that although he will be better off dead, he is not convinced that his is the better lot. As his final words show, those members of the jury who voted for his acquittal may be better off alive than he is dead. If we are to make sense of these passages, Socrates must believe at the conclusion of his trial that even if death is complete extinction, he will be better off dead than continuing to live on, burdened with the 'troubles' from which oblivion would be a relief. The problem for the standard reading of the passage, thus, comes to this: when Socrates makes his pronouncement at 41d2-5 that no evil can come to a good man in life or in death, unless he is guilty of contradicting himself within the briefest of passages, he cannot be asserting that moral goodness provides a complete indemnity from the harms that make life no longer worth living.

In seeking an alternative reading of the passage that will avoid such obvious contradiction with Socrates' own assessment that his life is no longer worth living, we would do well to notice that 'the good man' cannot be made to suffer evil either in life or in a continued existence after death, if there is life after death. So although he cannot be certain what happens at death, he does think it is a possibility that the person will migrate to Hades. But what is a *person*; precisely what would migrate to Hades? Surely he does not believe that an ensouled *body* will migrate (see *Grg.* 524b2-4).

Because the soul is the only thing that is common to both 'life' and continued existence after the death of the body, and because the possession of a good soul is the only thing that makes a man a good man, Socrates must be referring to the soul as that which cannot be made to suffer evil if it possesses moral goodness.

Although nowhere in the *Apology* does he explicitly say so, elsewhere Socrates maintains that vice is the only thing that can harm the soul.[66] And since he also believes that once virtue is acquired is can never be lost,[67] it is perhaps tempting to think that when he claims that 'no evil comes to a good man' he means that nothing can harm the soul that has attained virtue. Although Socrates is no doubt prepared to defend such a view, it is none the less doubtful that at 41d1-2 he means to equate 'good man' with 'one who possesses moral virtue'. Unless we are prepared to deny either Socrates' sincerity in his numerous disclaimers of wisdom or his identification of wisdom with virtue, we must conclude that Socrates does not regard himself as possessing virtue. Yet, as we have discussed in Section 4.1.4, he does consider himself the moral superior of his fellow citizens. Convinced as he plainly is of both the rightness of his activities and that he has never acted unjustly, his speech to those jurors who voted for his acquittal, and indeed his argument that he has been an enormous benefactor of the city, make little sense unless Socrates is convinced that he is a good man. Thus, because he must be referring to the soul at 41d1-2, Socrates appears to be claiming that no evil comes to a good soul, even if that soul lacks the understanding of what virtue is, and hence fails to possess virtue itself.

One final difficulty remains, however. Thus far we have argued that in order to make sense of the Socratic claim that 'no evil comes to a good man', he must be understood to be relying upon the following: (1) the soul is that which cannot be harmed in life or death if it is good, (2) a soul may aptly be called 'good' if it either possesses (*a*) virtue or (*b*) the kind of Socratic humility that keeps one free of the confident ignorance and injustice of which Socrates

---

[66] In the *Grg.* Socrates indicates that men have three sorts of things that count as their possessions: souls, bodies, and material goods. Disease and poverty are the harmful conditions of bodies and material possessions respectively, whereas vice is the harmful condition of the soul (447c2-4). See *Cri.* 47e6-48a1.

[67] This plainly follows from the Socratic paradoxes to which we have already referred: virtue is wisdom and wisdom, once acquired, will never result in vice.

accuses his fellow Athenians, and yet which does not constitute the understanding requisite for full virtue. Further, we have supposed that (3) Socrates regards his soul to be good only in sense (*b*). But it might be objected that even if one grants all three points, it is simply false that no evil can come to a soul possessing only goodness in sense (*b*). It is true that Socrates is completely convinced that his activities are virtuous because they have been ordained by the god himself. And given his faith in his *daimonion*, he can have the additional reassurance that few, if any, of his individual actions have been wrong. Hence nothing could make him abandon his belief that his life has been blameless. Yet surely others could be good in sense (*b*). His fellow Socratics, for example, who share his moral principles and his conviction that salvation comes through philosophy, but who lack understanding of virtue, are certainly also morally superior to other Athenians.[68] None the less, so long as they lack the necessary epistemic warrants for their views, however correct those views may turn out to be, they will always be subject to dissuasion by means of clever and persuasive, but mistaken, considerations.[69] If so a soul made good only through Socratic humility may fall prey to harm after all. So, it might be supposed, because Socrates announces at 41d1-2 that 'no evil somes to a good man', he cannot be referring to those whose souls are good in sense (*b*).

This objection would be telling if at 41d1-2 Socrates is necessarily maintaining that a 'good man' is somehow forever indemnified against ever coming to hold a single false belief about virtue. But the claim 'no evil comes to a good man' is ambiguous. On the one hand, it may mean that the possession of goodness *always* protects the soul from any evil whatever. But this plainly conflicts with Socrates' beliefs that one may be called 'good' even if one lacks full virtue and that only understanding is always stable in the face of counter-arguments and attempts at non-rational forms of persuasion. The alternative, however, is a significantly weaker claim. Socrates may simply be saying that *in so far as* one's soul is good, it is not subject to evil in either life or in death. Thus, in so far as they sustain goodness in their souls, his jurors can be assured that their souls will suffer no evil, and this is true both in life and in death.

Finally, if one assigns the stronger meaning to claim that 'no

---

[68] That there are other philosophers who share Socrates' commitments is made plain at *Cri.* 46b1-50a3, esp. 49a4-b6.

[69] For the instability of belief, see, e.g., *Euthphr.* 11b6-8, and *La.* 194b1-4.

evil comes to a good man', Socrates would have to admit that the kind of good men he was referring to would not have to practice philosophy. Because, on the stronger interpretation, a good man could be confident that his soul is absolutely protected from ever suffering any evil, he would have no reason to continue to submit his beliefs to elenctic scrutiny—a good man in this sense would have understanding and so would not need inquiry. But it is clear that Socrates regards himself as a good man, and although his commitment to carry out the wish of the god will never permit him to abandon the practice of philosophy, he also believes that the elenctic testing of his own beliefs profits him—indeed, without it his life would not be worth living (see 38a1-6). Thus, even though his own soul has been good throughout his life, since as far as he knows it has never been stained with injustice, he does not think that it was at any time absolutely secure from being harmed. What protection he gave it came from the continued examination of his beliefs. He must have believed, then, that only *in so far as* his soul is good (the weaker meaning of 41d1-2) it could not suffer evil.[70]

It is not insignificant that Socrates' claim that 'no evil comes to a good man' is directed at those jurors who voted for his acquittal and whom he now regards as 'φίλοι' (friends (40a1)). Socrates cannot be confident that they are good men. But, unlike his prosecutors and those jurors who voted to condemn him, Socrates now has reason to believe that his 'friends' are persuaded that philosophy should not be suppressed. Nevertheless, they may not comprehend its full value to the soul. Like their fellow citizens, they no doubt still labor under the 'pretense of wisdom' that death is always something to be feared, believing that there is nothing they can do to make their souls escape the terrible fate that awaits them at death (see 28b3-9 and esp. 29a4-b2). He says that he wishes to speak with those jurors who voted for his acquittal in the first place to tell them of his new-found conviction, derived from his *daimonion*, that 'those of us who think death is an evil are mistaken' (40b4-5). And he prefaces his remark regarding the protection against harm provided by goodness by telling those jurors 'you ought to be hopeful (εὐέλπιδας) regarding death and to be mindful of this one truth . . .' (41c8-9). The one truth of which they ought to be mindful is that 'no evil comes to a good man either in life or at the end of it'. Like his

---

[70] A similar conclusion is reached by Cornford (1), 308.

earlier plea that it is in the jurors' interest to vote for his acquittal, Socrates proclaims this truth for their benefit. Because they believe that death is always something to be feared, they fail to see what Socrates has come to realize. As long as one's soul is good, not even death can harm it. Socrates makes this his final plea on their behalf, knowing that unless they see the protection goodness provides they may not devote themselves to becoming good and to the philosophical examination becoming good requires. So, once again, Socrates is acting as Athens' 'divine gift', whose service to the god is to make men better.

5.6.3 SHARING SOCRATES' MISSION

Socrates concludes his final address with a prophecy to the jurors who condemned him:

I say to you, O you who have killed me, that punishment will come to you right after my death, far more harsh, by Zeus, than the death to which you have condemned me. For now you did this believing that you would be released from having to give an account of your lives, but I say that you will find the result to be quite the opposite. Those who will examine you will be more numerous, whom I now restrained but you did not notice it. And they will be harsher, being younger, and you will be even more irritated. For if you believe that by killing people you will prevent anyone from reproaching you for not living rightly, you do not think rightly. For such a release is neither at all possible nor good; rather, the best and easiest release is not to restrict others, but to make oneself as good as possible. With this prophecy to you who condemned me, I go away. (39c3–d9)

As a part of his reassurance to those jurors who voted for him, Socrates says that he is not angry with either the other jurors, who voted against him, or his accusers; for it is clear, he says, that what has come to pass is a good thing. But he reminds all who listen that it was not for the sake of anything good that he was condemned or accused; rather, it was out of a desire to injure him, and that desire he continues to find blameworthy. These men continue to think that he was a trouble-maker, and, in view of this, Socrates makes a last request of them:

When my sons grow up, take your revenge, gentlemen, by harassing them in the way that I have harassed you. If they should seem to you to care for money or something else rather than for virtue, and think of themselves as being what they are not, reproach them, as I have you, as not caring for what they should and for thinking they are something when they are worthless. If you should do this, both I and my sons shall have received just things from you. (41e2–42a2)

So it appears that despite his death Socrates' mission in Athens will not come to an end. Those who sought to end it will have failed because, according to Socrates' prophecy, younger and more aggressive men will carry it on, though perhaps without seeing it, as Socrates has, as a religious mission. Even those who sought to end it can continue it, by reproaching and harassing Socrates' sons as Socrates has reproached and harassed his fellow Athenians. Indeed, as he allowed at 23c2–7, some of the young men who have accompanied Socrates have already begun imitating him and discovering that many people who think they are wise about the greatest things are in fact wise about little or nothing.

Socrates is convinced, as he is famous for saying, that the unexamined life is not worth living (38a5–6). His very last words to his jurors show that he is not convinced that those to whom he speaks are fated to live worthless lives as soon as he is gone. But this requires that at least some of them will continue to lead *examined* lives, for otherwise Socrates could be entirely confident that his passing would utterly condemn his jurors to lives that are not worth living. In each of these passages, then, Socrates shows that, as important as his mission in Athens has been, his fellow Athenians are not totally without hope despite its imminent end. The sense of this cannot be that somehow the effects of Socrates' mission can and will be derived in some other way; the sense must be that others will secure, as Socrates himself has been foremost in securing, a continuing examination of their own and others' lives.

Of course, it is most unlikely that the jurors and accusers whom Socrates implores to 'harass' his sons will do so in the relevant way, thinking as they do that such activities are impious and wrongful. But we need not suppose, from the patent unlikelihood that his last wish will be granted him, that the wish itself is insincere. Far from it; for, as we have shown Socrates views the kind of 'harassment' he has undertaken to be the best thing that can happen to anyone, and thinks that those who do such 'harassing' bestow thereby the greatest benefit their 'victims' can receive. Though it is clear that he cannot really hope that his accusers and opposing jurors will actually undertake to grant him his final wish, there is every reason to suppose that he would feel deeply indebted to them, on behalf of his sons, if perchance they did. If there is irony in Socrates' request, therefore, it does not undercut the literal sense of what he says.

We have argued elsewhere that, whatever sense is to be made of Socrates' philosophical method, it must allow that method and its service within his mission to be shared and even undertaken by others.[71] Socrates' own sense of his mission may be unique. He is, perhaps, the only one devoted to practicing it as an act of piety; it would indeed be pious for others to pursue philosophical examination as well,[72] but those who do pursue it may do so only out of amusement or purely intellectual interest. Still, even Socrates avoids saying that his mission was given to him uniquely; his final analysis of the meaning of the oracle to Chairephon is that the god 'is not speaking of Socrates, but rather uses my name and makes me an example, as if he was saying, "this one of you, O Athenians, is wisest who, like Socrates, recognizes that he is really of no worth as regards wisdom" ' (23a8–b4). Only a few Stephanus lines later Socrates first mentions the young men who imitate his service to the god. Socrates does not suggest that his young imitators suppose they engage thereby in a religious mission; but neither does he suggest that in imitating him they somehow fall significantly short of obtaining the same results Socrates himself obtains. We conclude that, as regards his mission, though only Socrates may have seen himself as having been 'commanded to do this by the god, both by oracles and by dreams and in every way in which divinity has ever commanded a man to do anything' (33c4–7), nothing he does cannot be done by others, and, indeed, nothing he does will cease to be done in Athens after his death. Neither his exhortations, therefore, nor his examinations of others, nor even the beneficial products of these, are unique to Socrates himself. If they were, his death would be a horrific evil, for nevermore would the benefits he bestowed upon Athens be available.

But surely Socrates must not be so naïve as to suppose that just anyone can make the sorts of complicated logical and intuitive moves necessary to practice a creative and successful elenctic examination of another's views. Often in the early dialogues, Socrates' 'harassing' in-

---

[71] See our (11), 194–5. Other texts also suggest that Socrates believes that others can do what he does. See. e.g., *Grg.* 457e3–458b1; 487e1–488b1.

[72] It would appear to follow from Socrates' view of the oracle and the proper response to it that he would take anyone who undertook his pursuits in Athens as acting piously. For discussions of the connection between Socrates' conception of the connection between piety and the practice of philosophy, see D. Anderson; Heidel (1), 174; McPherran (1), and (2), 306–9; C. C. W. Taylor, 113–18.

volves the most subtle and brilliant reasoning, which it would be foolish to suppose that anyone at all could have performed. Man's salvation, he is convinced, is in living the examined life. So to share Socrates' mission and thus to achieve the piety, justice, and moderation required to protect oneself from evil, must one be as logically incisive, ingenious, and intellectually subtle as Socrates? Does goodness—such as is possible for men who lack full understanding of vitrue—require intellectual brilliance? Are all dull-wits condemned to lives worse than death?[73]

We think not. On Socrates' account, it is true that only the examined life is worth living for men. It does not follow from this, however, that only he who plays *Socrates*' part in the elenctic process leads an examined life. Socrates' interlocutors also benefit from being examined, provided that they enter into philosophical discussion with a willingness to correct their beliefs in the light of inconsistencies that are called to their attention during the elenctic process and, hence, as long as they say what they truly believe.[74] A right-minded person who wishes to be questioned will have the best chance of keeping himself right-minded by engaging in dialogue with all who hold out the promise of working the *elenchos* upon him, and by never supposing that anyone is an ultimate authority. The failure of one elenctic argument to demonstrate an inconsistency in one's views would thus not lead one into a false and dangerous sense of moral confidence. So long as one engaged regularly in philosophy, one would soon enough find flaws in one's beliefs under attack and beyond defense. So those who are intellectually incapable of employing the *elenchos* to examine themselves and others may still actively submit to elenctic examination by people who *are* capable of doing so. Thus, so long as some live who are capable of performing elenctic examination, all can lead 'examined lives'. Some qualified elenctic practitioners—other than

---

[73] Our attention was called to the special problem of Socrates' exhortation to all to philosophize, given the obvious fact that not all are intellectually capable of doing much in the way of testing themselves and others via the *elenchos*, by Mark McPherran, who (in his (1)) offers an interesting account of what Socrates could mean by his exhortation. The following discussion owes a great deal to McPherran's analysis. Other interesting accounts of Socrates' exhortation are offered by Anastaplo ((1), 19-20) and Scolnicov, who see a need to examine others so that one may succeed in knowing oneself (Anastaplo), or knowing anything at all (Scolnicov). Neither Anastaplo nor Scolnicov explicitly considers the case of one who is intellectually incapable of examining others effectively.

[74] See *Grg.* 500b5-c1; *Rep.* I 346a3-4, 350e1-5: *Cri.* 49c11-d5; *Prt.* 331c4-d1; see also Gregory Vlastos's discussion of this rule in his (9), 35-8.

Socrates himself—lived even during Socrates' life, as his remarks at 23c2-7 and his prophecy at 39c3-d9 show. Perhaps none of these were as talented as Socrates was. It seems they were all younger and harsher than the master himself. Nevertheless, he implied that qualified elenctic practitioners will survive his death.

All of this is not, however, in any way to deny the gravity of Athens' loss in Socrates' death. Though there may remain others who can bestow upon the Athenians the good bestowed by Socrates, 'god's gift' is lost to them. As we have said, Socrates viewed his jurors to be at grave risk in judging his case, that they 'not err utterly regarding this gift of the god by voting against me' (30d7-e1). But as we have also argued, the essence of Socrates' concern for the jurors at this point was that they not be convinced of the evil of supposing that what he does is impious and corrupting. The error he fears they will make is not that they will rid themselves of the only hope they have to be examined properly; the error is that they will stain their souls and damage themselves through vice. Of course, it is true that the loss of Socrates is no smaller matter, for as 'god's gift' he is especially talented in examining people; but also he is the only one likely to be found willing to give his entire life over to performing such examinations, oblivious to poverty, the enmity of others, and the neglect of all the rest of his personal and civic life. It will not be easy for Athens to find another like Socrates (31a2), it is true; but it is the degree of his devotion to the task that is unique, not his ability to perform it at all. Others can do it, as 23c2-7 shows; and others will continue to do it after his death, as 39c3-d9 shows.

In condemning Socrates to death, therefore, the Athenians lost their most devoted examiner of lives, but not their only competent one. But this was the least of the losses they suffered, on Socrates' view, for he saw himself as replaceable and in fact certain to be replaced, if only in a somewhat fragmented way. Far greater was the harm the Athenians brought upon themselves, according to Socrates, by convicting themselves of shameful ignorance and vice, in thinking themselves wise enough not to need the goading of their gadfly's stinging, and in believing that in the pain of elenctic stings was to be found moral wrong and corruption. Socrates had always berated his fellow Athenians for thinking this way; and he never relented, even in his very last words to the jurors.

BIBLIOGRAPHY

A truly exhaustive bibliography on work pertinent to the study of Plato's *Apology* would be a research tool of enormous value, but would involve far greater resources in time and skill than we have. The following is but an approximation of such an opus, which we hope, in the absence of a comprehensive bibliography, will be of use to scholars wishing to pursue further study.

Any bibliographer must make a variety of judgments, and those we have made will almost certainly fail to be perfectly consistent or fully defensible. We have attempted to include all those materials of which we knew that we thought might be of interest to scholars working on the *Apology*. But there are a few noteworthy exceptions to this general strategy. (1) We have not tried to include a broad sampling of works on other Apologies of Socrates, such as those by Xenophon or Libanius. Our entries on such topics reflect only those that held special interest, one way or another, to us. We have tried to give a reasonably extensive sample of works on 'The Socrates Problem', however, which would naturally emphasize other sources on Socrates. (2) We have included translations of Plato's *Apology* only when such translations were accompanied by some substantial scholarly apparatus, such as notes or commentary. We do not pretend even to approach a complete listing of such works, however. (3) The decision to include work not directly related to the interpretation of Plato's *Apology* reflects our judgment of what might illuminate our subject, and nothing more. Other scholars reviewing such works might well find them useless in their own research, and be chagrined to find that other works they find crucial to be missing. This may only reflect ignorance or an oversight on our part, but it may also reflect our prejudices. (4) We have made no particular effort to include works from the nineteenth century or before, unless there is some reason to suppose that access to such work would be possible without inordinate difficulty for contemporary scholars. (5) Works in languages other than English are no doubt more incompletely represented than those in our native language. This reflects partly our degree of access to such materials and partly our inability to read a number of the languages in which Socratic studies have been published. We elected to include items in such languages when we knew of them because scholars who can read them might find them useful. Works in English not included in the following bibliography are almost certainly items of whose existence, or else of whose relevance, we were simply not aware. We make no pretense, however, of having read all the items in this bibliography.

We have arranged the bibliography in two parts. Part I is a listing of other bibliographies scholars might find useful in filling in the gaps in ours. We have tried to note the nature of each entry in this list, and we have made extensive use of a number of them in our own research and in preparing the following bibliography. Each of the purely bibliographical entries in Part I includes references to other bibliographies, many of which we have not included here. The most complete list of such bibliographies is given in *L'Année Philologique* (see Marouzeau, Part I). Part II is a listing of works of interpretation or at least involving some substantive contribution that might be material to the understanding of Plato's *Apology*. This section includes translations that make some scholarly contribution, scholarship focused on Plato's *Apology* (including suggestions about emendations to the text), and other works relevant to the study of Plato's *Apology*. We have not undertaken to place these into separate categories, or to add a critical apparatus by which to explain the relevance we suppose each entry to hold. In most cases, happily, such will be apparent from the titles of the works, but in other cases readers may have to discover this from finding references to the work in question in our text or notes (see the author's name in our index), or possibly by finding the work listed and reviewing it for themselves. Not all of the entries in Part II are cited in our five chapters; it was not possible for us to locate, read, and cite each of them. As a result, some may be included that are of little or no actual value to the study of Plato's *Apology*; indeed, we found some of those we did locate and read to be of marginal value at best, but elected to include them anyway, as possibly of more substantial interest to other scholars. Some of the entries in Part I refer the reader to entries in Part II of the bibliography. This signifies that such entries are not merely bibliographical works but refer to works of scholarship whose bibliographies we recommend. The abbreviations we have employed follow those in *L'Année Philologique* (see Marouzeau, Part I), as amended by McKirahan (see listing in Part I). Abbreviations we have used that cannot be found in McKirahan are either those of *L'Anneé Philologique* that are not included in McKirahan's list, or, in a few cases, ones we have had to invent ourselves. All abbreviations are listed in our Index of Periodicals and Abbreviations.

In the event that our book should come out in another edition, we solicit information from our readers as to the inadequacies of the following bibliography.

Part I: Useful Bibliographies for Socratic Scholarship

Brisson, Luc. 'Platon 1958-1975.' *Lustrum* 20 (1977), 5-304. A very thorough Plato bibliography, helpfully cross-indexed.

Cherniss, Harold. 'Plato 1950–1957.' *Lustrum* 1959, 5–308, and 1960, 321–648. Reasonably thorough critical bibliography on Platonic scholarship that includes work from earlier years as well.

Deschoux, M. *Comprendre Platon: Un siècle de bibliographie platonicienne de langue française (1880–1980)*. Paris, 1981. A fine extensive work on French scholarship on Plato.

Foucaud, F. *Ensayo bibliográfico de las obras de Platón y Aristóteles y de los escritos sobre estos mismos filósofos*. Cordoba, 1936. Discussion of a number of works on Plato and Aristotle.

Friedländer, Paul (see entry for Friedländer, vol. 2, in Part II of this bibliography). Bibliography and notes for his chapters are combined; useful for work on Plato's dialogues, listed separately by dialogue.

Gigon, O. *Bibliographische Einführungen in das Stadium der Philosophie 12: Platon*. Bern, 1950. General Plato bibliography.

Guthrie, W. K. C. (see entries for Guthrie (1) and (2) in Part II of this bibliography). (1) gives a good general Plato bibliography; (2) offers a bibliography for Socrates.

Irwin, T. H. (see entry for Irwin in Part II of this bibliography). Good selected bibliography on Plato scholarship, divided into topics.

La France, Y. 'Les Études platoniciennes: Contribution canadienne (1970–77).' *Philosophiques* 4 (1977), 51–37. Review of Canadian works on Plato with a bibliography for Canadian work on Plato for 1960–76.

Lineback, Richard H. *et al.*, eds. *The Philosophers' Index* 1–22 (1967–88), s.v. *Apology*, Plato, Socrates. A reasonably comprehensive annual listing of work in philosophy, especially for work in English.

_____ *The Philosophers' Index: A Retrospective Index to US Publications from 1940*. 3 vols. Bowling Green, 1978. s.v. Plato, Socrates. See above.

de Magalhães-Vilhena, V. (see de Magalhães-Vilhena (1) and (2), below). (1) includes an extensive 100-page bibliography on Socrates, Plato, and the Socratics (as well as some other materials); (2) adds a few entries to the first, and provides an excellent bibliography of ancient testimonia on Socrates.

Manasse, E. M. 'Bücher über Platon.' *PhilosRdschau* Sonderheft I and II. Tübingen, 1957 and 1961. I gives a critical review of work in German; II gives one for work in English.

Marouzeau, J., Ernst, Juliette, *et al. L'Année Philologique* 1–57 (1928–88), s.v. Plato Philosophus, Socrates Philosophus. Annual bibliographies covering the years 1924–86. Most bibliographers begin here, though works in philosophy journals are frequently not listed.

McKirahan, Richard D., Jr. *Plato and Socrates: A Comprehensive Bibliography (1958-1973)*. New York and London, 1978. A very thorough and useful bibliography, with separate sections on Plato and Socrates, as well as on each of Plato's works.

Rosenmeyer, T. G. 'Platonic Scholarship, 1945-1955.' *CW* 1957, 173-82, 185-96, 197-201, 209-11. Excellent bibliography of Plato scholarship, helpfully cross-indexed.

Part II: Selected Bibiliography with Special Emphasis on Plato's Apology

Adam, Adela Marion. (1) *The Apology of Socrates*. Cambridge, 1914.

____ (2) 'Socrates *Quantum mutatus ab illo.*' *CQ* 12 (1918), 121-39.

Adam, J. *Platonis Apologia Socratis*. 11th ed. Cambridge, 1936.

Adkins, A. W. H. (1) 'Clouds, Mysteries, Socrates and Plato.' *Antichthon* 4 (1970), 13-24.

____ (2) *Merit and Responsibility*. Chicago and London, 1960.

____ (3) *Moral Values and Political Behaviour in Ancient Greece*. New York, 1972.

Adorno. F. *Introduzione a Socrate*. Bari, 1970.

Afan, Ruhi M. *Zoraster's Influence on Anaxagoras, the Greek Tragedians and Socrates*. New York, 1969.

Akarsu, B. 'Socrates' Conception of Virtue' (in Turkish). *FelsefeArk* 13 (1962), 57-73.

Alarco, L. F. *Sócrates y Jesus ante la muerte, I: Sócrates*. Lima, 1972.

Alastos, Doros. *Socrates Trial: Drama Reconstruction*. London, 1966.

Alexander, W. H. 'Nor Any Other Man Either.' *TRSC* 39 (1946), 1-29.

Allen, R. E. (1) 'Irony and Rhetoric in Plato's *Apology.*' *Paideia* (Buffalo) 5: *Special Plato Issue* (1976), 32-42.

____ (2) 'Law and Justice in Plato's *Crito.*' *JPh* 69 (1972), 557-67.

____ (3) *Socrates and Legal Obligation*. Minneapolis, 1980.

____ (4) *Plato's Euthyphro and the Early Theory of Forms*. New York, 1970.

____ (5) 'The Trial of Socrates: A Study in the Morality of the Criminal Process.' In Martin L. Friedland, ed. *Courts and Trials: A Multi-Disciplinary Approach*. Toronto and Buffalo, 1975, 3-21.

Alsberg, Mas. *Der Prozess des Sokrates im Lichte moderner Jurisprudenz und Psychologie*. Mannheim, Berlin, Leipzig, 1928.

Alsina, J. 'Socrates, Platón y la verdad.' *BIEH* 1 (1967), 39-43.

Anastaplo, George. (1) 'Human Being and Citizen: A Beginning to the Study of Plato's *Apology of Socrates*.' In G. Anastaplo, *Essays on Virtue, Freedom, and the Common Good*. Chicago, 1975, 8-29, 233-46.

———— (2) 'Citizen and Human Being: Thoreau, Socrates, and Civil Disobedience.' In the same collection as Anastaplo (1), above. 203-13, 313-16.

Anderson, Daniel E. 'Socrates' Concept of Piety.' *JHPh* 5 (1967), 1-13.

Anderson, J. K. *Xenophon*. New York, 1974.

Anderson, Maxwell. *Barefoot in Athens*. New York, 1951.

Andrée, G. 'Der Aufbau und die literarische Bedentung der Platonischen Apologie.' Dissertation, University of Freiburg, 1923.

Andrewes, Antony. 'The Arginousai Trial.' *Phoenix* 28 (1974), 112-22.

Anselmet, Raymond, A. 'Socrates and the *Clouds*: Shaftesbury and a Socratic Tradition.' *JHI* 39 (1978), 171-82.

Argyle, A. W. 'Χρησμολόγοι and Μάντεις.' *CR* 20 (1970), 139.

Armleder, P. J. 'Death in Plato's *Apology*.' *CB* 42 (1966), 46.

Arnim, H. von *Platons Jugenddialoge*. Leipzig and Berlin, 1914.

Ast, G. A. *Platons Leben und Schriften*. Leipzig, 1916.

Attenhofer, A. 'Sokrates.' *Roschers Monatshefte* (1931), 418-24.

Aubenque, P. 'La conversion socratique.' *ÉPh* (1970), 159-66.

Austin, Scott. 'The Paradox of Socratic Ignorance (How to Know that You Don't Know).' *PhilTop* 15 (1987).

Baker, W. W. 'An Apologetic for Xenophon's *Memorabilia*.' *CJ* 12 (1916-17), 293-309.

Ballard, E. G. *Socratic Ignorance: An Essay on Platonic Self-knowledge*. The Hague, 1965.

Banfi, Antonio. *Socrate*. 2nd ed. Milan, 1944.

Banu, I. 'Critical Appreciation of the Socratic Moment in the History of Greek Philosophy' (in Rumanian with Russian and French summaries). *StudClas* 2 (1960), 99-125.

Barchi, Mario. *Socrates: La vita e il pensiero*. Spoleto, 1959.

Barker, Andrew. 'Why Did Socrates Refuse to Escape?' *Phronesis* 22 (1977), 13-28.

Barker, Ernest. *Greek Political Theory: Plato and His Predecessors*. 4th ed. New York, 1951.

Barnes, Jonathan. 'Socrates and the Jury, Part II.' *PAS*, supp. 54 (1980), 193-206.

Barrow, Robin. *Plato and Education*. Boston and London, 1976.

Barzin, M. 'Sur les neuées d'Aristophane.' *BAB* 54 (1968), 378-88.

Bassett, S. E. 'Note on αἰνίττεσθαι: Plato *Apology* 27A, 21B.' *CR* 42 (1928), 58.

Bastide, G. *Le moment historique de Socrate*. Paris, 1939.

Baumann, E. D. (1) 'Het daimonion semeion van Sokrates.' *Tijdschr. voor Wijsbegeerte* 31 (1938), 256-65.

_____ (2) 'De leerjaren van Sokrates.' *DNGids* 53 (1938), 145-59.

Beamer, E. M. 'The Socratic Image in Plato.' Dissertation Syracuse University, 1972.

Beatty, Joseph. 'Thinking and Moral Considerations: Socrates and Arendt's Eichmann.' *JVI* 10 (1976) 266-78.

Beckman, James. *The Religious Dimension of Socrates' Thought*. Waterloo, 1979.

Belaval, Y. 'Socrate'. In B. Parain, ed. *Histoire de la Philosophie I. Encyclopédie de la Pléiade* 26. Paris 1969, 451-63.

Berns, Lawrence. 'Socratic and Non-Socratic Philosophy. A Note on Xenophon's *Memorabilia* 1:1:13 and 14.' *RMeta* 28 (1974), 85-8.

Benson, Hugh H. (1) 'A Note on Eristic and the Socratic Elenchus' JHPh (forthcoming).

_____ (2) 'The Problem of the Elenchos Reconsidered.' *AncPhil* (forthcoming).

Bertmann, Martin A. 'Socrates' Defense of Civil Obedience.' *StudGen* 24 (1971), 576-82.

Bertram, Heinrich. *Platons Verteidigungsrede des Sokrates und Kriton*. Gotha, 1903.

Betz, Joseph. 'Dewey and Socrates.' *Transactions of the Pierce Society* 16 (1980), 329-56.

Beversluis, John. 'Socratic Definition.' *APQ* 11 (1974), 331-6.

Bicknell, Peter J. 'Sokrates' Mistress Xanthippe.' *Apeiron* 8 (1974), 1-5.

Birnbaum, W. *Sokrates: Urbild abendländischen Denkens, Persönlichkeit und Geschichte* 81. Göttingen, 1973.

Birt, T. *Sokrates der Athener*. Leipzig, 1918.

Blackie, John S. *Four Phases of Morals: Socrates, Aristotle, Christianity, Utilitarianism*. New York, 1892.

Blakeney, E. H. *The Apology of Socrates*. London, 1929.

Blank, David. 'Socrates vs. Sophists on Payment for Teaching.' *CA* 4 (1985), 1-49.

Blasucci, S. (1) 'Aspetti costruttivi dell'ironia socratica.' *MiscFranc* 67 (1967), 38–77.

—— (2) 'L'ironia di Socrate.' *MiscFranc* 63 (1963), 429–66.

—— (3) *L'ironia in Socrate e in Platone*. Trani, 1969.

—— (4) 'La sapienza di Socrate.' *MiscFranc* 70 (1970), 329–47.

—— (5) *Socrate: Saggio sugli aspetti costruttivi dell'ironia*. Milan, 1972.

Bleckly, Henry. *Socrates and the Athenians: An Apology*. London, 1884.

Blits. J. H. 'The Holy and the Human: An Interpretation of Plato's *Euthyphro*.' *Apeiron* 14 (1980), 19–40.

Blum, A. F. *Socrates: The Original and Its Images*. London and Boston, 1978.

Blumenthal, H. 'Meletus the Accuser of Andocides and Meletus the Accuser of Socrates: One Man or Two?' *Philologus* 117 (1973), 169–78.

Boder, W. *Die sokratische Ironie in den platonischen Frühdialogen. Studien zur antiken Philosophie* 3. Amsterdam, 1973.

Boehme, R. *Von Sokrates zur Ideenlehre, Beobachtungen zur Chronologie des platonischen Frühwerke*. Bern, 1959.

Bonfante, L. and Raditsa, L. 'Socrates' Defense and His Audience.' *BASP* 15 (1978), 17–23.

Bonnard, A. *Socrate selon Platon, Textes choisis et présentés*. Lausanne, 1945.

Bonner, Robert J. (1) *Evidence in Athenian Courts*. Reprint, New York, 1979.

—— (2) 'The Legal Setting of Plato's *Apology*.' *CPh* 3 (1908), 169–77.

—— and Smith, Gertrude. *The Administration of Justice from Homer to Aristotle*. Vol. 2. Chicago, 1930 (reprint, New York, 1968).

Börtzler, F. 'Das wahre Gesicht des Sokrates.' *NJW* 6 (1925), 709–17.

Brança Miranda, M. de. 'O mensagem de Sócrates aos nossos dias.' *Vozes* 55 (1961), 81–7.

Brandwood, Leonard. (1) *A Word Index to Plato*. Leeds, 1976.

—— (2) 'The Dating of Plato's Works by the Stylistic Method: A Historical and Critical Survey.' Dissertation, University of London, 1958.

Brann, Eva. 'The Offense of Socrates: A Re-reading of Plato's *Apology*.' *Interpretation* 7 (1978), 1–21.

Brenk, F. E. 'Interesting Bedfellows at the End of the *Apology*.' *CB* 51 (1975), 44–6.

Brickhouse, Thomas C., and Smith, Nicholas D. (1) 'Irony, Arrogance and Sincerity in Plato's *Apology*.' In E. Kelly, 29–46.

____ (2) ' "The Divine Sign Did Not Oppose Me:" A Problem in Plato's *Apology.' CanJP* 16 (1986), 511-26.

____ (3) 'The Formal Charges against Socrates.' *JHPh* 23 (1985), 457-81.

____ (4) 'The Origin of Socrates' Mission.' *JHI* 44 (1983), 657-66.

____ (5) 'The Paradox of Socratic Ignorance in Plato's *Apology.' HPQ* 1 (1984), 125-31.

____ (6) 'Socrates and Obedience to the Law.' *Apeiron* 18 (1984), 10-18.

____ (7) 'Socrates' Evil Associates and the Motivation for his Trial and Condemnation.' In J. Cleary, vol. 3 (1987).

____ (8) 'Socrates' First Remarks to the Jury in Plato's *Apology of Socrates.' CJ* 81 (1986), 289-98.

____ (9) 'Socrates on Goods, Virtue, and Happiness.' *OSAP* 5 (1987), 1-27.

____ (10) 'Socrates' Proposed Penalty in Plato's *Apology.'* AGPh 64 (1982), 1-18.

____ (11) 'Vlastos on the Elenchus.' *OSAP* 2 (1984), 185-95.

Brock, E. 'Sokrates und die Altphilologie.' *ArchivPhilos* 3 (1949), 316-23.

Brulé, P. E. *La philosophie morale de Socrate.* Ottawa, 1946.

Brumbaugh, Robert S. (1) 'Plato and Socrates.' In *Plato for the Modern Age.* Westport, Connecticut, 1979. 29-50.

____ (2) 'Socrates: The Search for the Self.' In *The Philosophers of Greece.* Albany, 1981. 123-32.

Brun, Jean. *Socrate.* 4th ed. Paris, 1969. (An English translation by Douglas Scott is available: *Socrates,* New York, 1978.)

Brunelli, Valeria Benetti. *Il pensiero educativo della Grecia.* Rome, 1939.

Brunner, C. 'Sokrates: Der erste freie Mann.' *Zeit* 22 (1967), 10.

Bruns, Ivo. *Das literarische Porträt der Griechen.* Berlin, 1896.

Brunt, N. 'De socratische vergissing.' *ANTP* 55 (1962-3), 189-99.

Burge, E. L. 'The Irony of Socrates.' *Antichthon* 3 (1969), 5-17.

Burnet, John. (1) *Greek Philosophy: Thales to Plato.* London, 1914.

____ (2) *Plato's Euthyphro, Apology of Socrates, and Crito.* Oxford, 1924.

____ (3) 'Socrates.' In *Encyclopaedia of Religion and Ethics.* vol. xi. New York, n.d. 665-72.

____ (4)'The Socratic Doctrine of the Soul.' *PBA* 7 (1916), 235-60.

Burnouf, D. 'Le crime politique de Socrate: L'opposition à l'idéologie nationale.' *RPP* 13 (1958), 355-8.

Burnyeat, Miles. (1) 'Examples in Epistemology: Socrates, Theaetetus, and G. E. Moore.' *Philosophy* 52 (1977), 381-98.

Burnyeat, Miles. (2) 'Socrates and the Jury' *PAS* supp. 54 (1980), 235-60.

_____ (3) 'Virtues in Action.' In Vlastos (6), 209-34.

Bury, J. B. (1) *A History of Greece.* New York, 1962.

_____ (2) 'The Life and Death of Socrates.' *Cambridge Ancient History* 3rd ed. (1940) vol. 5, ch. 13.4, 386-97.

_____ (3) 'The Trial of Socrates.' *RPAA*, 1926.

Busse, Adolf, *Sokrates.* Berlin, 1914.

Buttrey, T. V. 'Plato's *Apology* 23c and the Anger of the Catechized.' *LCM* 6 (1981), 51-3.

Caird, Edward. *The Evolution of Theology in the Greek Philosophers.* Glasgow, 1904 (reprint, New York, 1968).

Calder, William M. III. (1) 'Plato's *Apology of Socrates:* A Speech for the Defense.' *BUJ* 20 (1972), 42-7.

_____ (2) 'Socrates at Amphipolis (*Apology* 28e).' *Phronesis* 6 (1961), 83-5.

Callot, E. *La doctrine de Socrate.* Paris, 1970.

Calogero, C. (1) 'Gorgias and the Socratic Principle *Nemo sua sponte peccat.*' *JHS* 77 (1957), 12-17.

_____ (2) 'Il messaggio di Socrate.' *Cultura* 4 (1966), 289-301.

Calvert, Brian. 'Plato's *Crito* and Richard Kraut.' In S. Panagiotou. (ed.) *Justice, Law and Method in Plato and Aristotle.* Edmonton, 1987. 17-33.

Camarero, A. *Sócrates y las creencias demónicas griegas.* Cuad. del Sur, Bahiá Blanca, Brazil, 1968.

Camelli, G. *Apologia di Socrate.* Naples, 1932.

Canilli, A. 'Attualità dei sofisti e di Socrate.' *Acme* 24 (1971), 47-70.

Capizzi, A. (1) 'Il problema socratico.' *Sophia* 25 (1957), 199-207.

_____ (2) 'La testimonianza platonica: Contributa alla ricerca di una determinazione dell'elemento socratico nei dialoghi.' *RassFilos* 6 (1957), 205-21, 301-37.

_____ (3) *Socrate e i personaggi filosofi in Platone.* Rome, 1969.

Cappelletti, A. S. 'Arquelao, maestro de Sócrates.' *RFil* 9 (1960), 79-96.

Caprariis, V. de. (1) 'Per una interpretazione di Socrate.' *PP* 2 (1947), 168-88.

_____ (2) 'Umanismo e politica di Socrate.' *PP* 8 (1953), 264-302.

Caramella, S. 'La secolarizzazione nel pensiero di Socrate.' *IncCult* 4 (1971), 319-32.

Carbonara, C. *La filosofia greca: Socrate, i socratici minori.* 2nd ed. Naples, 1965.

Casini, N. (1) 'Il processo di Socrate.' *Iura* 8 (1957), 101-20.

____ (2) 'In margine al processo di Socrate.' *Iura* 10 (1959), 114-17.

____ (3) *Platone: L'Apologia di Socrate.* Florence, 1957.

Celotti, T. *L'Eutifrone, L'Apologia di Socrate, Il Critone.* Palermo, 1971.

Chambry, É. *Apologie de Socrate. Criton. Phédon.* Paris, 1966.

Chroust, Anton-Hermann. (1) 'Socrates: A Source Problem.' *NSchol* 19 (1945), 48-72.

____ (2) 'Socrates in the Light of Aristotle's Testimony.' *NSchol* 26 (1952), 327-66.

____ (3) *Socrates, Man and Myth.* South Bend, Indiana, 1957.

____ (4) 'Xenophon, Polycrates, and the Indictment of Socrates.' *C&M* 16 (1955), 1-77.

Ciholas, P. 'Socrates, Maker of New Gods.' *CB* 57 (1981), 17-20.

Cilento, V. 'Il dèmone.' *PP* 3 (1948), 213-27.

Classen, C. J. *Sprachliche Deutung als Triebkraft platonischen und sokratischen Philosophieren.* Munchen, 1959.

Clay, Diskin. 'Socrates' Mulishness and Heroism.' *Phronesis* 17 (1972), 53-60.

Cleary, John (ed.). *Proceedings of the Boston Area Colloquium in Ancient Philosophy.* Vols. 1 (1985), 2 (1986), and 3 (1987). Lanham, New York and London.

Cohen, Cynthia B. 'The Trial of Socrates and Joseph K.' *PhilLit* 4 (1980), 212-28.

Cohen, Maurice. 'Confucius and Socrates.' *The Journal of Chinese Philosophy* 3 (1976), 159-68.

Cohen, S. Marc. 'Socrates on the Definition of Piety: *Euthyphro* 10a-11b.' *JHPh* 9 (1971), reprinted in Vlastos (6), 158-76.

Colbert, James G., Jr. 'El intelectualismo etico de Sócrates.' *AnuFilos* 6 (1973), 11-28.

Collin, P. *Apologie de Socrate.* 5th ed. Liège, 1959.

Colson, Darrel D. 'On Appealing to Athenian Law to Justify Socrates' Disobedience.' *Apeiron* 19 (1985), 133-51.

Congleton, Ann. 'Two Kinds of Lawlessness: Plato's *Crito*.' *PolitTheor* 2 (1974), 432-66.

Cooper, Lane. *Plato on the Trial and Death of Socrates: Euthyphro, Apology, Crito, Phaedo.* Ithaca, 1941.

Cornford, Francis M. (1) 'The Athenian Philosophical Schools, I: The Philosophy of Socrates.' *Cambridge Ancient History.* Cambridge, 1933. Vol. 6, 302-9.

—— (2) *Before and after Socrates.* Cambridge, 1932.

Costa, V. *Apologia di Socrate.* Palermo, 1965.

Cotton, Gerard. *Socrate.* Brussels, 1944.

Coulter, C. 'The Tragic Structure of Plato's *Apology.*' *PhQ* 12 (1933), 137-43, and abstract, *TAPhA* 62 (1931), xxv-xxvi.

Coulter, James Albert. 'The Relation of the *Apology of Socrates* to Gorgias' *Defense of Palamedes* and Plato's Defense of Gorgianic Rhetoric.' *HSPh* (1964), 269-303.

Cremona, A. 'Filosofia del diritto e filosofia morale in Socrate.' *RIFD* 35 (1958), 101-4.

Cresson, André. *Socrate, sa vie, son oeuvre, avec un exposé de sa philosophie.* 3rd ed. Paris, 1962.

Crombie, I. M. *An Examination of Plato's Doctrines.* 2 vols. London, 1962.

Cromey, R. D. 'Sokrates' Myrto.' *GB* 9 (1980), 57-67.

Cron, Christian. (1) *Causae Socraticae.* Augsburg, 1857.

—— (2) *Platons Verteidigungsrede des Sokrates und Kriton.* Leipzig, 1868. (A translation into English with revisions was published as *Plato's Apology and Crito,* by Louis Dyer, Boston, 1895.)

Cross, R. Nicol. *Socrates: The Man and His Mission.* London, 1914 (reprint, Freeport, New York, 1970).

Daniel, James and Polansky, Ronald. 'The Tale of the Delphic Oracle in Plato's *Apology.*' *AncWorld* 2 (1979), 83-5.

Dannhauser, Werner. *Nietzsche's View of Socrates.* Ithaca, New York, 1974.

Daros, J. 'Plato and his Relationship with Socrates.' *Athena* 24 (1963), 60-1.

Davar, Firoze. *Socrates and Christ.* Ahmedabad, India, 1972.

Davies, C. 'Socrates.' *HT* 20 (1970), 799-805.

Davies, J. K. (1) *Athenian Propertied Families: 600-300 BC.* Oxford, 1971.

—— (2) *Democracy and Classical Greece.* Stanford, 1983.

Dawson, Miles M. *The Ethics of Socrates.* New York, 1974.

Decharme, P. *La Critique des traditions réligieuses chez les Grecs des origines aux temps de Plutarque.* Paris, 1904.

Delatte, A. 'La figure de Socrate dans l'*Apologie* de Platon.' *BAB* 36 (1950), 213–26.

Delcourt, M. *L'oracle de Delphes*. Paris, 1955.

Deman, T. (1) *Le témoignage d'Aristote sur Socrate*. Paris, 1942.

——— (2) *Socrate et Jésus*. Paris, 1944.

Dembitzer, Z. 'Ad Platonis Apologiam Socrates p. 32B.' *Eos* 30 (1927), 173–5.

Dénes, T. 'Socrate et la valeur de la pédagogie.' *BAGB* (1969), 201–7.

Derenne, Eudore. *Les Procès d'impiété intentés aux philosophes à Athènes au Vme et au IVme siècles avant J.-C.* Liège and Paris, 1930 (reprint, New York, 1976).

Dickoff, J. and James, P. 'Socrates: Still a Folk Hero for Education?' *PPES* 26 (1970), 193–219.

Diels, H. and Kranz, W. *Der Fragmente der Vorsokratiker*. 6th ed. Berlin, 1952.

Diès, A. *Autour de Platon*. 2 vols, Paris, 1927.

Dihle, A. *Studien zur griechischer Biographie*. Göttingen, 1956.

Di Lorenzo, Raymond. 'The Critique of Socrates in Cicero's *De Oratore*: Ornatus and the Nature of Wisdom.' *PhilRhet* 11 (1978), 247–61.

Dixit, R. D. 'Socrates on Civil Disobedience.' *IndPQ* 8 (1980), 91–8.

Dodds, E. R. *The Greeks and the Irrational*. Berkeley and Los Angeles, 1951.

Doerrie, H. 'Xanthippe, die Gattin des Sokrates.' *RE* 9 A2, 1335–42.

Doering, August. *Die Lehre des Sokrates als sociales Reform-system*. Munich, 1895.

Dorter, Kenneth. 'Socrates on Life, Death and Suicide.' *Laval Theologie et Philosophie* 32 (1976), 23–41.

Dover, K. J. (1) (ed.) *Aristophanes' The Clouds*. Oxford, 1968.

——— (2) 'Freedom of the Intellectual in Greek Society.' *Talanta* 7 (1975), 24–54.

——— (3) *Greek Popular Morality in the Time of Plato and Aristotle*. Berkeley and Los Angeles, 1974.

——— (4) 'Socrates in the Clouds.' In Vlastos (6), 50–77.

Drachmann, A. *Atheism in Pagan Antiquity*. London, 1922.

Dreisbach, Donald F. 'Agreement and Obligation in the *Crito*.' *NSchol* 52 (1978), 168–86.

Drengson, A. R. 'The Virtue of Socratic Ignorance.' *APhQ* 18 (1981), 237-42.

Drexler, H. 'Gedanken über den Sokrates der platonischen *Apologie*.' *Emerita* 29 (1961), 177-201.

Dubs, H. H. 'The Socratic Problem.' *PhR* 36 (1927), 287-306.

Duff, R. A. 'Socrates' Suicide?' *PAS* 83 (1982-3), 35-48.

Ducan, P. 'Socrates and Plato.' *Philosophy* 15 (1940), 339-62.

Dupré, R. 'Socrate.' *BAGB* (1948), 77-90.

Dupreél, E. *La légende Socratique et les sources de Platon*. Brussels, 1922.

Durant, Will. 'Socrates.' In *The Life of Greece*. New York, 364-73.

Durić, M. N. 'Materijalni principi sokratove etike.' *LMS* 383 (1959), 172-6.

Düring, I. (1) 'Socrates' Valedictory Words to his Judges.' *Eranos* 44 (1946), 90-104.

_____ (2) *Sokrates' försvarstai*. Vol. 3. *Komm*. Lund, 1967.

Dybikowski, J. 'Socrates, Obedience, and the Law: Plato's *Crito*.' Dialogue 13 (1974), 519-35.

_____ (2) 'Was Socrates as Reasonable as Professor Vlastos?' *YR* 44 (1974), 293-6.

Dyer, Louis. *Plato: Apology of Socrates and Crito, with extracts from the Phaedo and Symposium, and from Xenophon's Memorabilia*. Rev. by Thomas D. Seymour. Waltham Mass., 1908.

Eckstein, F. *Apologie, Kriton und die Rahmenpartie des Phaidon*. Frankfurt, 1951.

Edelstein, *Xenophontisches und platonisches Bild des Sokrates*. Berlin, 1935.

Edmunds, Lowell. 'Aristophanes' Socrates.' In J. Cleary, vol. 1 (1985), 209-30.

Eggers Lan, Conrado. *Apología de Sócrates*. Buenos Aires, 1971.

Ehnmark, E. (1) 'Socrates and the Immortality of the Soul.' *Eranos* 44 (1946), 105-22.

_____ (2) 'Some Remarks on the Idea of Immortality in Greek Religion.' *Eranos* 46 (1948), 1-21.

Ehrenberg, Victor. (1) *From Solon to Socrates*. 2nd ed. London, 1973.

_____ (2) *The People of Aristophanes*. 3rd ed. New York, 1962.

Eibl, H. *Delphi und Sokrates: Eine Deutung für unsere Zeit*. Salsberg, 1949.

Eisner, Robert. 'Socrates as Hero.' *PhilLit* 6 (1982), 106-18.

Eitrem, S. *Sokrates*. Oslo, 1952.

Elias, Julius A. ' "Socratic" vs. "Platonic" Dialectic.' *JHPh* 6 (1968), 205-16.

Elmore, J. 'Note on the Episode of the Delphic Oracle in Plato's *Apology*.' *TAPhA* 38 (1907), xxxiii-xxxiv.

Engler, F. 'Sokrates.' *ELeb* 12 (1963), 25-6.

Erasmus, S. 'Richterzahl und Stimmenverhältnesse im Sokratesprozess.' *Gymnasium* 71 (1964), 40-2.

Erbse, H. (1) 'Sokrates und die Frauen.' *Gymnasium* 73 (1966), 201-20.

_____ (2) 'Zur Entstehungszeit von Platons *Apologie des Sokrates*.' *RhM* 118 (1975), 22-47.

Euben, J. Peter. 'Philosophy and Politics in Plato's *Crito*.' *PolitTheor* 6 (1978), 149-72.

Faggella, M. *Eutifrone, Apologia, Critone, Fedone*. Naples, 1935.

Fahr, Wilhelm. *Theous Nomizein*. New York, 1969, esp. 131-57.

Farias, D. 'Vigiliae platonicae: Il tema del sonno e del sogno nell'*Apologia*.' *RFNeo* 53 (1961), 314-19.

Farrell, Daniel M. 'Illegal Actions, Universal Maxims, and the Duty to Obey the Law: The Case for Civil Authority in the *Crito*.' *PolitTheor* 6 (1978), 173-89.

Feaver, Douglas and Hare, John. 'The *Apology* as an Inverted Parody of Rhetoric.' *Arethusa* 14 (1981), 205-16.

Feibleman, James. *Religious Platonism*. London, 1959.

Fenelon, Francois de Salignac. 'Socrates.' In *Great Men and Famous Women*. Vol. 2. New York, 1894. 38-43.

Ferejohn, Michael T. (1) 'Socratic Thought-Experiments and the Unity of Virtue Paradox.' *Phronesis* 29 (1984), 105-22.

_____ (2) 'The Unity of Virtue and the Objects of Socratic Inquiry.' *JHP* 20 (1982), 1-21.

Ferguson, A. S. 'The Impiety of Socrates.' *CQ* 7 (1913), 157-75.

Ferguson, John. (1) 'An Athenian Remainder Sale.' *CPh* 65 (1970), 173.

_____ (2) 'On the Date of Socrates' Conversion.' *Eranos* 62 (1964), 70-3.

Fernández Galiano, M. *Defensa de Sócrates*. Madrid, 1945.

Festugière, A.-J. *Socrate*. Paris, 1977.

Field, G. C. (1) *Plato and His Contemporaries: A Study in Fourth Century Life and Thought*. 2nd ed. London, 1948.

_____ (2) 'Socrates.' In *The Oxford Classical Dictionary*. Oxford, 1953. 845-6.

Field, G. C. (3) *Socrates and Plato*. London, 1913.

_____ (4) 'Socrates and Plato in the Post-Aristotelian Tradition.' *CQ* 18 (1924), 127-36.

Finley, Moses I. 'Socrates and Athens.' In Finley, M. I. *Aspects of Antiquity*. London and New York, 1972, 60-73.

Fischer, J. L. (1) *Sokrates nelegendárni*. Prague, 1965.

_____ (2) *The Case of Socrates*. Trans. I. Lewitová. Prague, 1969.

Fitton, J. W. 'That Was No Lady, That Was . . .' *CQ* NS 20 (1970), 56-66.

Flagg, Isaac. *Plato, The Apology and Crito*. New York, Cincinnati, and Chicago, 1907.

Fontenrose, Joseph. *The Delphic Oracle*. Berkeley, Los Angeles, and London, 1978.

Forbes, John Thomas. *Socrates*. Edinburgh, 1905.

Forchhammer, Peter Wilhelm. *Die Athener und Sokrates: Die Gesetzlichen und der Revolutionär*. Berlin, 1837.

Foss, O. 'Vem var Sokrates?' *NT* 29 (1953), 112-19.

Fouillée, Alfred Jules Émile. *La Philosophie de Socrate*. 2 vols. Paris, 1874.

Foulk, Gary F. 'Socrates' Argument for Not Escaping in the *Crito*.' Personalist 55 (1974), 356-9.

Fowler, Harold North. *Plato I. Euthyphro. Apology. Crito. Phaedo. Phaedrus*. Trans. with introductions (Loeb Classical Library). Cambridge, Mass. and London, 1914.

Fox, Marvin. 'The Trials of Socrates: An Interpretation of the First Tetralogy.' *ArchivPhilos* 6 (1956), 226-61.

Fraine, J. de. 'Rhetorische gemeenplaatsen in de voorrede de *Apologia Socratis*.' *Philol. Stud.* (Louvain, 1942), 87-94.

Frese, R. 'Die "aristophanische Anklage" in Platons *Apologie*.' *Philologus* 81 (NF 35) (1926), 377-91.

Friedländer, Paul. *Plato*. Trans. H. Meyerhoff. 3 vols. New York. 1958, 1964/5, 1969.

Friere, António. 'Sócrates No Pensamento Grego.' *RPortFil* 37 (1981), 133-77.

Frost, Frank. *Greek Society*. Lexington, Mass., Toronto, and London, 1971.

Fukishima, T. *Apology, Crito, Phaedo* (in Japanese). Tokyo, 1972.

Gadamer, Hans-Georg. 'Religion and Religiosity in Socrates.' In J. Cleary, vol. 1 (1985), 53-75.

Galli, Gallo. (1) 'L'Apologia di Socrate.' *Paideia* (Arona) 2 (1947), 273-92.

_____ (2) *Socrate ed alcuni dialoghi platonici.* Torino, 1958. Galli (1) is revised in 81-109 of Galli (2).

García Bacca, J. D. *Eutifrón, Apología, Critón* Mexico City, 1965.

García Calvo, A. *Platón, diálogos Socráticos.* Salvat and Madrid, 1972.

García Yaguee, F. *Defensa de Sócrates.* 2nd ed. Madrid, 1966.

Garcia-Máynez, Eduardo. 'Tesis del *Critón* sobre el dener de obediencia a las leyes del estado y a las sentencias de sus jueces.' *Dianoia* 20 (1974), 10-22.

Gavin, William (1) 'A Note on Socrates and "The Law" in the *Crito.*' *Aitia* 7 (1979), 26-8.

_____ (2) 'Death: Acceptance or Denial: The Case of Socrates Re-examined.' *Religious Humanism* (1977), 134-9.

Geach, Peter. 'Plato's *Euthyphro*: An Analysis and Commentary.' *Monist* 50 (1966), 369-82.

Gelzer, T. 'Aristophanes und sein Sokrates.' *MH* (1956), 65-93.

Gernet, Louis. *Droit et Société dans la Grèce Ancienne.* Paris, 1955.

Giannantoni, Gabriele. (1) *Che cosa ha veramente detto Socrate.* Rome, 1971.

_____ (2) 'La pritania di Socrate nel 406 a.C.' *RSF* (1962), 3-25.

Giannini, H. (1) *Sócrates o el oráculo de Delfos.* Santiago, 1971.

_____ (2) 'Un mito acerca de la historia de Sócrates.' *AUChile* 124 (1966), 88-101.

Gigon, Olof. (1) *Les grands problèmes de la philosophie antique.* Paris, 1961.

_____ (2) *Socrates: Sein Bild in Dichtung und Geschichte,* 2nd ed. Bern, 1979.

Gill, Christopher. 'The Death of Socrates.' *CQ* NS 23 (1973), 25-8.

Girsberger, Karl Ernst. *Sokrates von Athen: Eine Studie.* Graz, 1935.

Glucker, J. 'De poetico quodam apud Platonem fragmento.' *SCI* 1 (1974), 1-2.

Gnizio, F. P. 'Il demone di Socrate e il suo messaggio.' *ALGP* 14-16 (1977-9), 219-313.

Godley, A. L. *Socrates and the Athenian Society in his Day.* London, 1896.

Gomez Robledo, A. *Sócrates y el socratismo.* Mexico City, 1966.

Gomperz, Theodor. (1) 'Die Anklage gegen Sokrates in ihrer Bedeutung für die Sokratesforschung.' *NJA* 53 (1924), 129-74.

_____ (2) *Greek Thinkers.* 2 vols, New York, 1905.

_____ (3) 'Sokrates' Haltung vor seinen Richtern.' *WS* 54 (1936), 32-43.

Gomperz, Theodor. (4) *Sophistik und Rhetorik.* Leipzig, 1912.

Gontar, David P. 'The Problem of the Formal Charges in Plato's *Apology.' TSPh* 27 (1978), 89-101.

Gooch, Paul W. 'Socrates: Devious or Divine?' *G&R* 32 (1985), 32-41.

Gordon, R. M. 'Socratic Definitions and "Moral Neturality".' *JPh* 61 (1964), 433-50.

Gosling, J. C. B. *Plato.* London and Boston, 1973.

Greene, W. C. (ed.). *Scholia Platonica.* Haverford, 1938, 4-7, 419-23.

Grote, George. (1) *A History of Greece.* 10 vols. London, 1888.

_____ (2) *Plato and the Other Companions of Socrates.* 3 vols. London. 1875.

Grube, G. M. A. *The Trial and Death of Socrates.* Indianapolis, 1975.

Guardini, Roman. *The Death of Socrates.* Trans. Basil Wrighton. New York, 1948.

Guéry, L. 'Un soldat nommé Socrate.' *RevFacCathOuest* 2 (1961), 16-26.

Guilhamet, Leon. 'Socrates and Post-Socratic Satire.' *JHI* 46 (1985), 3-12.

Gulley, Norman. *The Philosophy of Socrates.* New York, 1968.

Gundert, H. 'Platon und das Daimonion des Sokrates.' *Gymnasium* 61 (1954), 513-31.

Gustarelli, A. *Socrate e Platone.* Milan, 1953.

Guthrie, W. K. C. (1) *A History of Greek Philosophy.* 5 vols. London, 1962, 1965, 1969, 1975. (The following entries (2) and (4) are reprinted with some changes and additions from vol. 3.)

_____ (2) *Socrates.* Cambridge, 1971.

_____ (3) *Socrates and Plato* (The John Macrossan Memorial Lecture, University of Queensland). Brisbane, 1958.

_____ (4) *The Sophists.* Cambridge, 1971.

Hack, R. K. *God in Greek Philosophy to the Time of Socrates.* New York, 1970 (reprint of 1931 ed.).

Hackforth, R. M. (1) 'The *Apology* of Plato.' *JHS* 55 (1935), 83-4.

_____ (2) *The Composition of Plato's Apology.* Cambridge, 1933.

_____ (3) 'A Corner of the Socrates Problem.' *PCPhS* 148-50 (1931), 2-3.

_____ (4) 'Great Thinkers I: Socrates.' *Philosophy* 8 (1933), 259-72.

Haden, James. (1) 'On Plato's Inconclusiveness.' *CJ* 64 (1969), 219-24.

_____ (2) 'On Socrates with Reference to Gregory Vlastos.' *RMeta* 33 (1979), 371-89.

_____ (3) 'Socratic Ignorance.' In Kelly, 17-28.

Hadot, P. 'La figure de Socrate.' *Eranos-Jb* 43 (1974 (1977)), 51-90.

Hahn, L. C. G. 'Het denkmoment "Sokrates". ' *Dialoog* 2 (1961-2), 114-24.

Hansen, Mogens Herman. 'Hvorfor Henrettede Athenerne Sokrates?' *MT* 40-3 (1980), 55-82.

Harrison, A. W. R. *The Law of Athens.* 2 vols. Oxford, 1971.

Hart, Richard E. 'Socrates on Trial.' In Kelly, 143-50.

Hartmann, O. J. 'Sokrates, Vater des Abendlandes, Revolutionär des Geistes und Märtyrer seines Auftrags.' *Kommenden* 21 (1967), 16–18.

Hathaway, Ronald F. 'Law and the Moral Paradox in Plato's *Apology*.' *JHPh* 8 (1970), 127-42.

Hatzfeld, J. 'Socrate au Procès des Arginuses.' *RÉA* 42 (1940), 165-71.

Havelock, Eric. (1) 'The Evidence for the Teaching of Socrates.' *TAPhA* 65 (1934), 282-95.

_____ (2) 'The Socratic Self as it is Parodied in Aristophanes' *Clouds. YClS* 22 (1972), 1-18.

_____ (3) 'Why was Socrates Tried?' in M. White, ed. *Studies in Honor of Gilbert Norwood. Phoenix* supplementary vol. 1. Toronto, 1952. 95-109.

Hawtrey, R. S. W. 'Socrates and the Acquisition of Knowledge.' *Antichthon* 6 (1972), 1-9.

Hayashi, T. 'A Problem of Human Development in Socrates' (in Japanese). *TUEA* 9 (1962).

Heidel, W. A. (1) 'On Plato's *Euthyphro*.' *TAPhA* 31 (1900), 164-81.

_____ (2) Review of Busse *AJPh* 36 (1915), 332-8.

Helm, James J. *Plato, Apology: Text and Grammatical Commentary.* Chicago, 1981.

Helms, P. *Sofisterne, Sokrates og de ensidige Sokratiske Retninger.* Copenhagen, 1929.

Henry, Maureen D. 'Socratic Piety and the Power of Reason.' In Kelly, 95-105.

Hiestand, Max. *Das Sokratische Nichtwissen in Platons ersten Dialogen: Eine Untersuchung über die Anfänge Platons.* Zurich, 1923.

Higgins, W. E. 'Socrates.' In *Xenophon the Athenian.* Albany, 1977. 21-43.

Hignett, C. A. *A History of the Athenian Constitution.* Oxford, 1952.

Hildebrandt, Kurt. *Platon.* Berlin, 1933.

Hoerber, Robert G. (1) 'Note on Plato, *Apologia* XLII.' *CB* 42 (1966), 92.

Hoerber, Robert G. (2) 'Plato's *Euthyphro.*' *Phronesis* 3 (1958), 95-107.

Holter-Bechtolsheim, H. 'Sokratesskildringen i Platons *Apologi.*' *Forehandlinger paa det 8. Nord. Filologmöde* (1935), 105-7.

Horneffer, E. (1) *Der junge Plato* I: *Sokrates und die Apologie.* Giessen, 1922.

_____ (2) *Platon gegen Sokrates.* Leipzig, 1904.

Houlgate, L. D. 'Virtue is Knowledge.' *Monist* 54 (1970), 142-53.

Howison, George Holmes. 'The Philosophical Principles, Theoretical and Practical, Expressed and Implied in Plato's *Apology.*' *UCPUB* 3 (1889).

Hübscher, Arthur. *Sokrates.* Frankfurt, 1950.

Humbert, Jean. (1) *Polycrates, l'accusation de Socrates et le Gorgias.* Paris, 1930.

_____ (2) *Socrate et les petits socratiques.* Paris, 1967.

Hyde, Walter Woodburn. 'Atheism among the Greeks.' Abstract in *TAPhA* 76 (1945), xxxiv-xxxv.

Imhof, M. 'Sokrates und Archelaos. Zum I. Sokratesbrief.' *MH* 39 (1982), 71-81.

Inatomi, E. (1) *Eros and Death in Socrates* (in Japanese). Tokyo, 1973.

_____ (2) *The Educational Dialectic of Socrates* (in Japanese). Tokyo, 1973.

Infantino, S. S. 'The Vindication of Socrates and the Prevention of Skepticism in the Young.' Dissertation, University of Chicago, 1975.

Irmscher, J. *Sokrates: Versuch einer Biographie.* Leipzig, 1982.

Irwin, Terence H. *Plato's Moral Theory.* Oxford, 1977.

Jackson, B. Darrell. 'The Prayers of Socrates.' *Phronesis* 16 (1971), 14-37.

Jackson, H. 'The *Daimonion* of Socrates.' *JP* 5 (1874), 232-47.

Jaeger, Werner. (1) *Paideia.* Vol. 2. Oxford, 1944.

_____ (2) *The Theology of the Early Greeks.* Oxford, 1947.

Jäkel, Werner, and Erasmus, Siegfried. *Lehrerkommentar zu Platons Apologie.* Stuttgart, 1962.

Jambet, C. *Apologie de Platon.* Paris, 1976.

James, Gene. 'Socrates on Civil Disobedience and Rebellion.' *SoJP* 11 (1973), 119-27.

Jannucci, M. 'I primi germi della dialettica platonica nell'*Apologia* e nel *Critone.*' *Pensiero* 20 (1975), 201-21.

Jensen, P. J. *Sokrates.* Copenhagen, 1969.

Jones, A. M. H. *Athenian Democracy.* Oxford, 1957.

Jordan, James N. 'Socrates' Wisdom' and Kant's Virtue.' *SWJP* 4 (1973), 7-23.

Jowett, Benjamin, 'Introduction of Plato's *Apology of Socrates*.' *The Collected Dialogues of Plato*. Trans. B. Jowett. New York and London, 1892.

Juliá V. 'El metódo socrático.' *CuadFilos* 12 (1972), 63-7.

Kagawa, K. 'A Background of Plato's *Apology*' (in Japanese). *JCS* 2 (1954), 47-50.

Kahn, Charles. 'Did Plato Write Socratic Dialogues?' *CQ* NS 31 (1981), 305-20.

Kaku, A. 'Virtue and Wisdom in Socrates.' (in Japanese). *RLHirosake* 2.4 (1966).

Kalinka, E. 'Das Nichtwissen des Sokrates.' *WS* 50 (1932), 36-46.

Kamlah, W. 'Sokrates und die Paideia.' *ArchivPhilos* 3 (1949), 277-315.

Karavites, P. 'Socrates in the *Clouds*.' *CB* 50 (1973-4), 65-9.

Katsimanis, Kyriakos S. 'Messages delphiques et Socratisme.' *Philosophia* (Athens) 4 (1974), 155-67.

Kaufmann, George. 'Socrates and Christ.' *HSPh* (1951).

Kaufmann, Walter. 'Nietzsche's Admiration for Socrates.' In *Nietzsche: Philosopher, Psychologist, Antichrist*. New York, 1968. 391-411.

Keaney, John J. 'Plato's *Apology* 32c8-d3.' *CQ* NS 30 (1980), 296-8.

Kelly, D. A. 'Conditions for Legal Obligation.' *SWJP* 4 (1973), 43-56.

Kelly, Eugene (ed.). *New Essays on Socrates*. Lanham, New York, London, 1984.

Kemper, H. 'Platons *Apologie* in heutiger Sicht.' *Anregung* 13 (1967), 107-11.

Kendall, W. 'The People versus Socrates Revisited.' *ModA* 3 (1958), 98-111.

Kennedy, George. *The Art of Persuasion in Ancient Athens*. Princeton, 1963.

Kerferd, G. B. *The Sophistic Movement*. Cambridge, 1981.

Keseling, P. 'Sophokles' *Antigone* in Platons *Apologie des Sokrates*.' *PhW* (1936), 141-3.

Kessidi, F. K. (ed.). (1) *Plato and his Epoch* (in Russian). Moscow, 1979.

———— (2) *Socrates* (in Russian). Moscow, 1976.

Kesters, H. *Kérygmes de Socrate: Essai sur la formation du message socratique*. Louvain, 1965.

Kidd, I. G. 'Socrates.' *The Encyclopedia of Philosophy.* Vol. 7. Ed. Paul Edwards *et al.*, London and New York, 1967.

Kierkegaard, S. *The Concept of Irony, with Constant Reference to Socrates.* Trans., intro., and notes by L. M. Capel. London, 1966.

Kirk, G. S., Raven, J. E., and Schofield, M. *The Presocratic Philosophers.* 2nd ed. Cambridge, 1983.

Klages, L. 'Das Problem des Sokrates.' *AGMath* 10 (1927), 103-11.

Kleve, K. 'Anti-Dover or Socrates in *The Clouds.*' *SO* 58 (1983), 23-37.

Klosko, George. (1) 'Criteria for Fallacy and Sophistry for Use in the Analysis of Platonic Dialogues.' *CQ* NS 33 (1983), 363-74.

_____ (2) *The Development of Plato's Political Theory.* New York and London, 1986.

_____ (3) 'Plato's Utopianism: The Political Content of the Early Dialogues.' *RPol* 45 (1983), 483-509.

_____ (4) 'Socrates on Goods and Happiness.' Forthcoming in *HPQ.*

Kostman, James. 'Socrates' Self-betrayal and the "Contradiction" between the *Apology* and *Crito.*' In Kelly, 107-30.

Kralik, Richard. *Sokrates: Nach den Überlieferungen seiner Schule.* Wien, 1899.

Kraus, René. *The Private and Public Life of Socrates.* (Trans. Barrows Mussey). New York, 1940.

Kraut, Richard (1) 'Comments on Gregory Vlastos, "The Socratic Elenchus".' *OSAP* 1 (1983), 59-70.

_____ (2) 'Plato's *Apology* and *Crito*: Two Recent Studies.' *Ethics* 91 (1980), 651-64.

_____ (3) *Socrates and the State.* Princeton, 1983.

Krentz, Peter. *The Thirty at Athens.* Ithaca, 1982.

Krokiewicz, A. *Sokrates.* Warsaw, 1958.

Kronska, I. *Sokrates,* Warsaw, 1968.

Krueger, G. 'Das Prooemium von Platons *Apologie.*' *AU* 9 (1966), 29-34.

Kube, Jörg. *TECHNE und ARETE: Sophistisches und platonisches Tugendwissen.* Berlin, 1969.

Kuhn, Helmut. (1) *Sokrates. Versuch über den Ursprung der Metaphysik.* Munich, 1959. (Also, (2), article by the same title in *NRdschau* 70 (1959), 328-51.)

Labriola, Antonia. (1) *La dottrina de Socrate secondo Senofonte Platone ed Aristotele.* 4th ed. Milan, 1947.

_____ (2) *Socrate.* 4th ed. (a cura di Benedetto Croce). Bari, 1947.

Lacey, A. R. 'Our Knowledge of Socrates.' In Vlastos (6), 22–49.

Laguna, T. de. 'Interpretation of the *Apology.*' *PhR* 18 (1909), 157–75.

Landmann, Michel. 'Socrates as a Precursor of Phenomenology.' *Ph&PhenR* 2 (1941–2), 15ff.

Landormy, P. *Socrate.* Paris, 1933.

Lang, Mabel. *Socrates in the Agora.* Princeton, 1978.

Lasaulx, E. von. *Des Sokrates Leben, Lehre und Tod.* Stuttgart, 1958.

Lechner, K. 'Sokrates im Staatsdienst.' *Hochland* 63 (1971), 567–79.

Leider, K. *Sokrates.* Hamburg, 1970.

Leitz, A. 'Gerechtigkeit und Gesetz bei Plato und Xenophon.' *AU* 12 (1969), 104–21.

Leonard, William Ellery. *Socrates: Master of Life.* Chicago, 1915.

Lesher, James H. 'Socrates' Disavowal of Knowledge.' *JHPh* 25 (1987), 275–88.

Leskey, Albin. *A History of Greek Literature.* Trans. J. Willis and C. de Heer. New York, 1966.

Lesses, Glenn. 'Is Socrates an Instrumentalist?' *PhilosTop* 13 (1985), 165–74.

Levi, P. 'Sokrates und sein Prozess.' *N&S* (1929), 141–71.

Levin, Richard. *The Question of Socrates.* New York, 1961.

Lewes, George Henry. 'Socrates.' In *The Biographical History of Philosophy.* Vol. 1. New York, 1883. 122–48.

Librizzi, Carmelo. (1) *La morale di Socrate.* Naples, 1954.

_____ (2) *Socrates o l'educatore.* 2nd ed. Rome, 1965.

Lichtenstein, E. 'Sokrates, das Bild des Erziehers.' *PädagRdsch* 16 (1962), 339–45.

Lipsius, J. H. *Das attische Recht und Rechtsverfahren.* Leipzig, 1905–15.

Livingstone, R. W. *Portrait of Socrates, Being the Apology, Crito and Phaedo of Plato.* Oxford, 1938.

Llamazon, Benjamin S. 'Philosophy in the University: Athena or Socrates.' *Thomist* 40 (1976), 635–64.

Loening, Thomas Clark. 'The Reconciliation Agreement of 403/402 BC in Athens: Its Content and Applications.' Dissertation, Brown University, 1981.

Lofberg, J. O. 'The Trial of Socrates.' *CJ* 23 (1928), 601–9.

Lombardo, G. *Apologia di Socrate.* Florence, 1934.

Lombardo, Joseph. 'Husserl's Method in Phenomenology and the Socratic Method of Teaching.' *Aitia* 8 (1980), 10-16.

López Castellón, E. 'Cuestiones sobre antropología ética socrática.' *EstFilos* 20 (1971), 335-56.

Lord, Louis E. *Aristophanes: His Plays and His Influence.* New York, 1963.

Louis, Sabine. (1) 'Ein Versuch zur Lösung des "Sokratischen Problems".' *Philosophia* (Athens) 7 (1977), 241-65.

———— (2) 'Sokrates: Ein Porträt.' *Conceptus* 14 (1980), 58-67.

Lüthje, H. 'Sokrates und die religiöse Entwicklung der Menschheit.' *Christengemeinschaft* 33 (1961), 25-7.

Luschnat, O. 'Fortschrittsdenken und Vollendungsstreben im Hellenismus.' *TheolV* 5 (1954-8), 88-110.

Lutoslawski, Wincenty. *The Origin and Growth of Plato's Logic.* London, New York, and Bombay, 1897.

Maas, P. 'How Socrates Addressed the Jury.' *CR* 53 (1939), 58-9.

MacDowell, Douglas M. (1) *Andokides on the Mysteries.* Oxford, 1962.

———— (2) *The Law in Classical Athens.* Ithaca, 1978.

MacKenzie, Mary Margaret. *Plato on Punishment.* Berkeley, Los Angeles, London, 1981.

MacNaghten, R. E. 'Socrates and the *Daimonion.*' *CR* 28 (1914), 185-9.

Magalhães-Vilhena. V. de. (1) 'La pensée et l'action: Socrate et la politique platonicienne.' *IL* 6 (1954), 108-13, 147-51.

———— (2) *Le problème de Socrate: Le Socrate historique et le Socrate de Platon.* Paris, 1952.

———— (3) *Socrate et la légende platonicienne.* Paris, 1952.

Maier, Heinrich. (1) *Sokrates: Sein Werke und seine geschichtliche Stellung.* Tübingen, 1913. (Italian trans. (2) *Socrate. La sua opera e il suo posto nella storia.* By G. Sanna. 2 vols. Florence, 1943-4.)

Majoli, Luigi. *Il processo di Socrate.* Naples, 1933.

Manasse, E. M. 'A Thematic Interpretation of Plato's *Apology* and *Crito.*' *Ph&PhenR* 40 (1980), 393-400.

Manetti, Giannozzo. *Vita Socratis et Senecae* (ed. Alfonso de Petris). Florence, 1979.

Marasco, G. 'I processi d'empietà nella democrazia ateniense.' *A&R* 21 (1976), 113-31.

Marcel, R. ' "Saint" Socrate, patron de l'humanisme.' *RIPh* 15 (1951), 135-43.

Maritain, J. 'Socrate et la philosophie morale.' In *Mélanges offerts à Étienne Gilson*. Toronto and Paris, 1959. 389–402.

Marrasso, A. *Apologia de Sócrates*. Buenos Aires, 1938.

Martano, G. 'L'*Apologia di Socrate* nella genesi della dialettica platonnica.' In R. Franchini, ed. *Scritti in onore di Nicola Petruzzellis*. Naples, 1981. 255–60.

Martin, G. 'Socrates: On The Interpretation of his Ignorance' (trans. R. D. S. Hartman). In J. W. Davies, ed. *Value and Valuation: Axiological Studies in Honor of Robert S. Hartman*. Knoxville, 1972. 107–13.

Martin, Rex. 'Socrates and Obedience to the Law.' *RMeta* 24 (1970), 21–38.

Martin, V. 'Le problème du Socrate historique.' *RThPh* 67 (1935), 217–42.

Masaracchia, A. (1) *Apologia di Socrate*. Torino, 1971.

_____ (2) 'Senso e problemi dell'*Apologia* platonica.' *Helikon* 4 (1964), 111–52.

May, J. R. 'Class Ideology as Philosophy: Philosophy and Politics in Plato's *Apology, Gorgias,* and *Republic*.' Dissertation, Boston College, 1976.

Mazon, P. 'Meletos accusateur de Socrate.' *RÉA* 44 (1942), 187.

Mazzantini, C. 'Intorno all'immortalità dell'anima umana nella filosofia platonica.' *Athenaeum* NS 18 (1940), 244–60.

McLaughlin, Robert J. 'Socrates on Political Disobedience: A Reply to Gary Young.' *Phronesis* 21 (1976), 185–97.

McPherran, Mark. (1) 'Socrates and the Duty to Philosophize.' *SoJP* 24 (1986), 541–60.

_____ (2) 'Socratic Piety in the *Euthyphro*.' *JHPh* 23 (1985), 283–309.

Menzel. A. 'Untersuchungen zum Sokratesprozess.' In *Hellenika: Gesammelte Kleine Schriften*. Baden and Wien, 1938. (Reprinted from *SAWW* 145 (1903), 1 ff.)

Meridor, Ra'anana, and Ullman, Lisa. 'Plato's *Apology* 24a6–b1.' *AJPh* 99 (1978), 36.

Metzger, A. 'Die sokratische Todessehnsucht.' *Merkur* 15 (1961), 301–28.

Meunier, M. *La légende de Socrate*. Paris, 1965.

Meyer, Thomas. *Platons Apologie*. Stuttgart, 1962.

Meyerhoff, H. 'From Socrates to Plato.' In K. H. Wolff *et al.*, eds. *The Critical Spirit: Essays in Honor of Herbert Marcuse*. Boston, 1967. 189–201.

Miller, John F. III. 'The Socratic Meaning of Piety.' *SoJP* 9 (1971), 141–9.

Miller, Stephen G. *The Prytaneion: Its Function and Architectural Form.* Berkeley, Los Angeles, and London, 1978.

Mills, Dorothy. 'Socrates.' In *The Book of Ancient Greeks.* New York, 1965. 361-78.

Miniarczyk, Marek. 'Wer galt im Altertum als Atheist?' *Philologus* 128 (1984), 157-83.

Mirgeler, A. *Sokrates.* Hellerau, 1926.

Mitchison, Naomi, and Crossman, R. H. S. *Socrates.* London, 1937.

Moline, Jon. *Plato's Theory of Understanding.* Madison, 1981.

Momeyer, Richard W. 'Socrates on Obedience and Disobedience to the Law.' *PResArch* 8 (1982), No. 1458.

Mondolfo, R. *Sócrates.* 6th ed. Buenos Aires, 1969.

Montenegro. A, 'El tradicionalismo político de Sócrates.' *REPolít.* 49 (1953 no. 72), 37-64.

Montgomery, John Dickey (ed.). *The State versus Socrates: A Case Study in Civic Freedom.* Boston, 1954.

Montuori, Mario. (1) 'La filosofia socratica e il problema delle fonti.' *NRS* 37 (1953), 363-73.

_____ (2) 'Nota sull'oracolo a Cherefonte.' *QUCC* 39 (1982), 113-18.

_____ (3) *Socrate dal mito alla storia.* 2nd ed. Athens, 1967.

_____ (4) 'Socrate filosofia e politica.' *GCFI* 1 (1970), 87-99.

_____ (5) *Socrates, Physiology of a Myth.* Trans. J. M. P. Langdale and M. Langdale. Amsterdam, 1981.

_____ (6) 'Socrate tra Nuvole prime e Nuvole seconde.' *AAN* 77 (1966).

Moravcsik, Julius. 'Understanding and Knowledge in Plato's Philosophy.' *NHPh* 15-16 (1976), 53-69.

Moreau, J. (1) 'L'ironia socratica.' *CV* 14 (1959), 404-11.

_____ (2) 'Socrate, son milieu historique, son actualite.' *BAGB* (1951), 19-38.

Mori, T. 'Wisdom and Τέχνη: On Socratic 'Επιστήμη' (in Japanese). *FUHJ* 4.2 (1972).

Morichere, Barnard. 'Sur la méconnaisance de Socrate.' *RMM* 76 (1971), 441-7.

Morr, J. *Die Entstehung der platonischen 'Apologie'.* Reichenberg, 1929.

Mossé, C. *Athens in Decline: 404-86 BC.* Trans. J. Stewart. London, 1973.

Mountjoy, P. T., and Smith, N. W. 'A Reply to Thornton's "Socrates and the History of Psychology". ' *JHBS* 7 (1971), 183-6.

Mueller, G. 'Another Approach to Socrates.' *IJE* 43 (1932-3), 429-39.

Mueller, W. G. 'Bidrag til forståelsen af den sokratiske etik.' *MT* 17 (1971), 44-7.

Mulgan, R. G. 'Socrates and Authority.' *G&R* 19 (1972), 208-12.

Müller, Emil Heinrich Otto. *Sokrates geschildert vor seinen Schülern*. 2 vols. Leipzig, 1911.

Munding, H. 'Sophia und Meinungsbildung zu *Apol*. 21b-23b.' *AU* 12 (1969), 51-61.

Murai, M. *Philosophy and Education in Socrates* (in Japanese). Tamagawa, 1972.

Murphie, Jeffrie. 'The Socratic Theory of Legal Fidelity.' In P. Weiner and J. Fisher, eds. *Violence and Aggression in the History of Ideas*. New Brunswick, 1974. 15-33.

Murray, Gilbert. *A History of Greek Literature*. London, 1897.

Nadler, S. 'Probability and Truth in the *Apology*.' *PhilLit* 9 (1985), 198-201.

Nagasaka, T. 'Socratic Doubt' (in Japanese). *Methodos* 1 (1968).

Nakamura, K. (1) 'On the Mission of Socrates in Plato's *Apology* 36c5-d1'. (in Japanese). *HiroshimaUS* 19 (1967).

_____ (2) 'Plato's Basic Thought: Something Common to Socrates and Plato as Seen in Socrates' Mission in the *Apology* and the so-called Socrates' Biographical Account in *Phaedo* 95e-102a' (in Japanese). *HUDLB* 19 (1971).

Natali, G. *Socrate nel giudizio dei padri apologisti*. Ascoli, 1912.

Navia, Luis E. (1) 'A Certain Man Named Socrates.' In N. Capaldi, et al. (eds.) *An Invitation to Philosophy*. Buffalo, 1981. 35-56.

_____ (2) 'A Reappraisal of Xenophon's *Apology*.' In Kelly 47-65.

_____ (3) 'The Philosophical Impulse: The Case of Socrates.' In E. Kelly and L. E. Navia (eds.) *The Fundamental Questions*. Dubugne, Iowa, 1981. 1-57.

_____ (4) *Socrates: The Man and His Philosophy*. Lanham, New York, London, 1985.

_____ (5) *Socratic Testimonies*. Lanham, New York, London, 1987.

Nazzaro, A. V. 'Il Γνῶθι σαυτόν nell'epistemologia filoniana.' *AFLN* 12 (1969-70), 49-86.

Nebel, G. *Sokrates*. Stuttgart, 1969.

Negri, F. *Difensa di Socrate*. Casale, 1930.

Nehamas, Alexander. 'Socratic Intellectualism.' In J. Cleary, vol. 2 (1986), 275-316.

Nemes, Z. 'On Socrates' Public and Political Attitude.' *ACD* 14 (1978), 19–22.

Nersesīantš, Vladik Sumbatovich. *Socrates* (In Russian). Moscow, 1977.

Nestle, W. *Griechische Studien*. Stuttgart, 1948.

Neumann, Frederick. *Über das Lachen und Studien über den platonischen Sokrates*. The Hague, 1971.

Neumann, Harry. (1) 'The Philosophy of Individualism: An Interpretation of Thucydides.' *JHPh* 7 (1969), 237–46.

―――― (2) 'Plato's *Defense of Socrates:* An Interpretation of Ancient and Modern Sophistry.' *LibEd* 56 (1970), 458–75.

―――― (3) 'Socrates and the Tragedy of Athens.' *SocRes* 35 (1968), 426–44.

―――― (4) 'Socrates in Plato and Aristophanes.' *AJPh* 90 (1969), 201–14.

Nicoll, W. S. M. 'Some Manuscripts of Plato's *Apologia Socratis*.' *CQ* NS 16 (1966), 170–7.

Nilsson, M. P. *Greek Piety*. Oxford, 1948.

Nissen, P. 'Gudomlig uppenbarelse och mänsklig logik.' *Eranos* 36 (1938), 99–107.

Nohl, H. *Sokrates und der Ethik*. Leipzig, 1904.

Norvin, W. *Sokrates*. Copenhagen, 1933.

Notopoulos, J. A. 'Socrates and the Sun.' *CJ* 37 (1941–2), 260–74.

Noussan-Lettry, Louis. *Apología de Sócrates*. 3rd ed. Buenos Aires, 1973.

―――― (2) 'El interrogatorio de Meleto, inversión, hypérbole y parodia de la relación juridico-positiva.' *EClás* 14 (1970), 297–310.

―――― (3) 'Νομίζειν Θεούς. Platón, *Apología* 35c4–d7.' *REC* 10 (1966), 26–36.

―――― (4) 'El núcleo especulativo de la *Apología* platónica: *Apología* 20c–23c.' *Philosophia* (Argent) 29 (1964), 20–49.

―――― (5) 'El redescubrimiento del texto de la *Apología* platónica en la investigación contemporánea.' *CuadFilos* 4 (1963), 47–59.

―――― (6) 'El segundo discurso de la *Apología* platónica: Incidencia textual de observaciones de Hegel.' *Philosophia* (Argent) 38 (1972), 5–17.

―――― (7) 'Sobre diferencia Hermaneuticay Lenguaje.' *CuadFilos* 13 (1973), 11–22.

―――― (8) *Spekulatives Denken in Platons Frühschriften Apologie und Kriton*. Freiburg/Munich, 1974.

―――― (9) 'Das Verhältnis der Texte als Sache philosophlegeschichtlicher Hermaneutik: Zu Platons *Apologie* und *Kriton*.' *ZPhF* 25 (1971), 523–34.

Nussbaum, G. (1) 'Socrates' Educational Method in the *Apology*.' Abstract in *PCA* 55 (1958), 22.

_____ (2) 'Some Problems in Plato's *Apology*.' *Orpheus* 8 (1961), 53–64.

Nussbaum, Martha. (1) 'Aristophanes and Socrates on Learning Practical Wisdom.' *YClS* vol. 26: *Aristophanes: Essays in Interpretations*, ed. J. Henderson (Cambridge, 1980), 43–97.

_____ (2) 'Commentary on Edmunds.' In J. Cleary, vol. 1 (1985), 231–40. (See Edmunds, above.)

O'Brien, M. J. *The Socratic Paradoxes and the Greek Mind*. Chapel Hill, 1967.

Oggioni, E. *Socrate e Platone, Scienze filosofiche*. Bologna, 1963.

Ojoade, J. O. 'Socrates: Was He Really a Sophist?' *Phrontisterion* 5 (1967), 48–61.

Oldfather, W. A. (1) 'Mr. Shaw and Socrates.' *CJ* 15 (1919–20), 436–7.

_____ (2) 'Socrates in Court.' *CW* 31 (1938), 203–11.

Organ, Troy. 'The Excellence of Socrates.' *Darshana* 17 (1977), 27–34.

Osborn, Edward B. *Socrates and his Friends*. London, 1929.

O'Sullivan, J. N. 'On Plato *Apology* 23c–d.' *AJPh* 97 (1976), 114–16.

Overman, C. A. 'Plato's *Apology*: A Literary Approach.' Dissertation, Brown University, 1976.

Paisse, J. M. (1) 'De la sagesse socratique.' *BAGB* (1971), 353–67.

_____ (2) 'La critique, source de sagesse.' *BAGB* (1973), 519–28.

Panagiotou, Spiro. (1) 'Justified Disobedience in the *Crito*?' In S. Panagiotou (ed.) *Justice, Law and Method in Plato and Aristotle*. Edmonton, 1987. 35–50.

_____ (2) 'Socrates' "Defiance" in the *Apology*.' *Apeiron* 21 (1987), 39–61.

Pannwitz, Rudolf. *Gilgamesch-Sokrates: Titanentum und Humanismus*. Stuttgart, 1966.

Papp, J. 'Platon Apologiá jának törtenetisége.' Dissertation, Szeged, 1933.

Parke, H. W. 'Chaerephon's Inquiry about Socrates.' *CPh* 56 (1961), 249–50.

_____ , and Wormell, D. E. W. *The Delphic Oracle*. 2 vols. Oxford, 1956.

Patocka, J. 'Remarques sur le problème de Socrate.' *RPhilos* (1949), 186–213.

Patzer, A. 'Resignation vor dem historischen Sokrates.' In A. von Patzer, ed. *Apophoreta für Uvo Hölscher zum 60. Geburtstag*. Bonn, 1975, 145–56.

Payne, Thomas. 'The *Crito* as a Mythological Mime.' *Interpretation* 11 (1983), 1-24.

Petander, Karl. *Sokrates: Personlighetstankens förkunnare.* Stockholm, 1959.

Peterman, John E. 'The Socratic Suicide.' In Kelly, 3-13.

Petrie, R. 'Aristophanes and Socrates.' *Mind* 20 (1911), 507-20.

Pfleiderer, Edmund. *Sokrates, Plato und ihre Schüler.* Tübingen, 1896.

Philippson, R. (1) 'Sokrates' Dialektik in Aristophanes' *Wolken.*' *RhM* 75 (1932), 30-8.

——— (2) 'Sokrates: Eine Gedenkfeier.' *HG* (1932), 2-14.

Phillipson, Coleman. *The Trial of Socrates.* London, 1928.

Piat, C. *Socrate.* Paris, 1900.

Picht. G. 'Die Ironie des Sokrates.' In H. W. Wolff, ed. *Probleme biblischer Theologie: Gerhard von Rad zum 70. Geburtstag.* Munich, 1971, 383-401.

Piérart, Marcel. 'Le second discours de Socrate à ses juges, Platon, *Apologie*, 35e-38b.' *LÉC* 40 (1972), 288-93.

Platis, E. N. Οἱ Κατήγοροι τοῦ Σωκράτη: Φιλολογικὰ Μελέτη. Athens, 1980.

Plescia, Joseph. *The Oath and Perjury in Ancient Athens.* Tallahassee, 1970.

Plochmann, George Kimball. 'Socrates, the Stranger from Elea, and some Others.' *CPh* 49 (1954), 223-31.

Pöhlmann, Robert von. *Sokrates und sein Volk: Beitrag zur Geschichte der Lehrfreiheit.* Munich and Leipzig, 1899.

Popper, Karl. *The Open Society and its Enemies*: Vol. 1, *The Spell of Plato.* 5th ed. rev. Princeton, 1966.

Prosch, Harry. 'Towards an Ethics of Civil Disobedience.' *Ethics* 77 (1967), 176-92.

Pucci, P. (1) 'Notes critiques sur l'*Apologie* de Platon.' *RPh* 37 (1963), 255-7.

——— (2) 'Σοφία nell'*Apologia* platonica.' *Maia* 13 (1961), 317-29.

Pusey, Nathan Marsh. 'Alcibiades and τὸ φιλόπολι.' *HSPh* 51 (1940), 215-31.

Quandt, Kenneth. 'Socratic Consolation: Rhetoric and Philosophy in Plato's *Crito.*' *PhilRhet* 15 (1982), 238-56.

Rabbow, P. *Paidagogia: Die Grundlegung der abendländischen Erziehungskunst in der Sokratik.* Ed. E. Pfeiffer. Göttingen, 1960.

Rabinowitz, W. G. 'Platonic Piety: An Essay towards the Solution of an Enigma.' *Phronesis* 3 (1958), 108-20.

Radermacher, L. *Weinen und Lachen Studien über antikes Lebensgefühl.* Vienna, 1947.

Radermacher, L. *Weinen und Lachen Studien über antikes Lebensgefühl.*

Ramello, P. 'Due testimoni del processo contro Socrates: Platone e Senofonte.' *AFGL* 1 (1980), 35-40.

Randall, John Herman. 'The Historical and the Platonic Socrates.' In *Plato: Dramatist of the Life of Reason.* New York, 1970. 93-102.

Raoss, M. 'Ai margini del processo di Socrate.' *Seconda miscellanea greca e romana.* Studi pubbl. dall' Ist. ital. per la storia antica 19. Rome, 1968. 47-291.

Rapaport, A. 'Ad Platonis *Apologiam* 32b.' *Eos* (1925), 12.

Raskin, H. D. *Sophists, Socrates, and Cynics.* London, 1983.

Raubitschek, A. E. (1) 'Damon.' *C&M* 16 (1955), 78-83.

_____ (2) 'Prokrisis *(Apologie* 35a7-b2).' In P. von Steinmetz, ed. *Politeia und Res Publica: Beiträge zum Verständnis von Politik, Recht un Staat in der Antike, dem Andenken Rudolf Starks gewidmet. Palingenesia, Monogr. und Texte zur klass. Altertumswiss* 4. Wiesbaden, 1969. 89-90.

Raven, J. E. *Plato's Thought in the Making.* Cambridge, 1975.

Raschini, M. A. *Interpretazioni socratiche.* Milan, 1970.

Re, M. C. del. (1) 'Il processo di Socrate e la sua problematica nella critica moderna.' *A&R* 6 (1961), 83-94.

_____ (2) 'L'estremo voto di Socrate.' *Sophia* 25 (1957), 290-4.

Redfield, James. 'A Lecture on Plato's *Apology.*' *JGenEd* 15 (1963), 93-108.

Reinach, J. 'A proposito di il processo di Socrate di N. Casini.' *Iura* 9 (1958), 121-2.

Renouvier, Charles. *Manuel de Philosophie ancienne.* 2 vols. Paris, 1844.

Ribbing, Sigurd. *Sokratische Studien.* Uppsala, 1870.

Ricci, M. *Socrate, padre dei nihilismo. Struttura logica e significato teoretico del discorso socratico.* L'Aquila, 1971.

Riddell, James. *The Apology of Socrates.* Reprint, New York, 1973.

Ritter, Constantine. (1) *Platon.* Vol. 1. Munich, 1910.

_____ (2) *Sokrates.* Tübingen, 1931.

Robberechts, L. 'Périclès et Socrate.' *RevNouv* 44 (1966), 270-85.

Roberts, J. W. *City of Sokrates*. London, Boston, Melbourne, and Henley, 1984.

Robin, Léon. (1) *Platon*. Paris, 1935.

___ (2) 'Sur une hypothése récente relative a Socrate.' *RÉG* 29 (1916), 129–65.

Robinson, Richard. *Plato's Earlier Dialectic*. Oxford, 1953.

Rogers, Arthur Kenyon. 'The Ethics of Socrates.' *PhR* 34 (1925), 117–44.

___ (2) *The Socratic Problem*. New York, 1933.

Rohatyn, Dennis A. 'The *Euthyphro* as Tragedy: A Brief Sketch.' *Dialogos* 9 (1973), 147–51.

Rolland, de Renéville J. *'Criton* on de l'obeissance.' *RMM* 71 (1966), 36–53.

Roochnik, David L. *'Apology* 40c4–41e7: Is Death Really a Gain?' *CJ 80* (1985), 212–20.

Rosen, Frederick. (1) 'Obligation and Friendship in Plato's *Crito*.' *Polit-Theor* 1 (1973), 307–16.

___ (2) 'Piety and Justice in Plato's *Euthyphro*.' *Philosophy* 43 (1968), 105–16.

Ross, Donald A. 'Socrates.' In *The McGraw Hill Encyclopedia of World Biography*. Vol. 10. New York, 1973. 115–18.

Ross, W. D. 'The Problem of Socrates.' *PCA*, 1933, 7–24.

Rossetti, L. (1) 'Alla ricerca dei logoi sokratikoi perduti I, II–III.' *RSC* 22 (1974), 424–38, and 23 (1975) 87–9, 361–81.

___ (2) 'La questione socratica. Un problema malposto.' *RSF* 38 (1983), 3–24.

___ (3) 'Platone biografo di Socrate: Un riesame.' *Proteus* 4 (1973), 63–101.

___ (4) 'Recenti sviluppi detta questione socratica.' *Proteus* 2 (1971), 161–87.

___ (5) 'Socrate e il ruolo della dissimulazione nel processo educativo.' *PedVit* 1 (1974–5), 41–59.

Rudberg, G. (1) Der platonische Sokrates.' *SO* 7 (1928), 1–24.

___ (2) *Platon*. Lund, 1943.

___ (3) 'Sokrateslärjungen Platon.' *Theoria* 1 (1935), 193–202.

___ (4) 'Sokrates' Reden.' *SO* 24 (1945), 8–15.

Rumpf, H. 'Die sokratische Prüfung: Beobachtungen an platonischen Frühdialogen.' *ZPäd* 13 (1967), 325–45.

Ruscitti, R. *Socrate*. Vicenza, 1969.

Ryle, Gilbert. *Plato's Progress*. Cambridge, 1966.

Sakisaka, Y. 'A Certain Doubt in the *Apology*' (in Japanese). *SK* 11 (1972).

Salguero, C. A. 'An Inquiry Concerning Socrates' Trial.' *Athena* 25 (1964), 13–14, 17.

Salvador de Lima, P. H. 'O julgamento de Sócrates. *Verbum* 18 (1961) 149–68.

Samson, B. 'Der Prozess des Sokrates.' In *Aktuelle Probleme aus dem Gesellschaftsrecht und anderen Rechtsgebieten: Festschrift für Walter Schmidt zum 70. Geburtstag am 18. Dezember 1959*. Berlin, 1960. 354–88.

Sanmartí, F. 'El espíritu filosófico de la época socrática.' *Esp* 3 (1954), 13–25.

Sandvoss, E. (1) 'Asebie und Atheismus im klassischen Zeitalter der griechischen Polis. *Saeculum* 19 (1968), 312–29.

_____ (2) *Sokrates und Nietzsche*. Leiden, 1966.

Santas, Gerasimos X. (1) 'The Socratic Fallacy.' *JHPh* 10 (1972), 127–41.

_____ (2) *Socrates: Philosophy in Plato's Early Dialogues*. London and Boston, 1979.

Sarri, Francesco. (1) 'Isocrate come testimone di messaggio Socratico.' *RFNeo* 66 (1974), 40–58.

_____ (2) 'Rilettura delle "Nuvole" di Aristofane come fonte per la conoscenza di Socrate.' *RFNeo* 65 (1973), 532–50.

Saunders, A. N. W. *Greek Political Oratory*. Harmondsworth (Middlesex) and New York, 1970.

Saunders, S. A. 'Studies in Plato's Style in the First Tetralogy.' Dissertation University of Iowa, 1974.

Saupe, W. 'Platon in neuer Sicht: Das Wesen der sokratischen Ironie und Bedeutung für die Soziolpädagogik und Sozialethik unserer Zeit.' *WZPot* 13 (1969), 451–5.

Sauvage, Micheline, and Sauvage, Marie. *Socrates and the Human Conscience* (trans. Patrick Hepburne-Scott). New York and London, 1960.

Schanz, Martin. (1) *Ausgewählte Dialogue Platons*. Vol. 3, *Apologie*. Leipzig, 1893.

Schanz, Martin. (2) 'Socrates als vermeintlicher Dichter: Ein Beitrag zur Erklärung des Phaidon.' *Hermes* 29 (1894), 597–603.

Schmalenbach, H. 'Macht und Recht: Platons Absage an die Politik.' *Natur und Geist: Festschrift für F. Medicus*. Zurich, 1946. 183 ff.

Schmalzriedt, E. 'Sokrates.' In *Enzykl. Die Grossen der Weltgesch.* Vol. 1. Zurich, 1971.

Schopenhauer, Arthur. 'Socrates.' In *Fragments of the History. Selected Works of Arthur Schopenhauer.* Trans. E. B. Bax. London, 1909. 45–52.

Schrempf, Christof. *Sokrates, seine Persönlichkeit und sein Glaube.* Stuttgart, 1955.

Sciacca, M. F. (1) 'El demonio de Sócrates.' *Nación* 9 July 1961, 4a secc.

_____ (2) *Studi sulla filosofia antica.* Milano, 1971. 'Socrate.' 207–24; 'Il significato e i limiti dell'ironia di Socrate.' 225–34.

Scolnicov, Samuel. 'The True Political Man: Socrates on Knowledge and Politics.' In John Agresto and Peter Riesenberg, eds. *The Humanist as Citizen.* National Humanities Center, 1981. 16–24.

Scott, John A. (1) 'The Athenians and the Condemnation of Socrates.' *CJ* 22 (1926–7), 677–8.

_____ (2) 'Why Meletus Demanded the Death Penalty.' *CJ* 15 (1919–20), 436–7.

Seeskin, Kenneth. (1) *Dialogue and Discovery: A Study in Socratic Method.* Albany, 1987.

_____ (2) 'Is the *Apology of Socrates* a Parody?' *PhilLit* 6 (1982), 94–105.

_____ (3) 'Reply to Nadler.' *PhilLit* 9 (1985), 201–2.

Seibert, C. 'Der Prozess des Sokrates.' *MDR* 20 (1966), 295.

Senter, Nell W. 'Socrates, Rhetoric, and Civil Disobedience.' *SWPStud* 1 (1976), 50–6.

Sesonske, Alexander. 'To Make the Weaker Argument the Stronger.' *JHPh* 6 (1968), 217–31.

Shero, L. R. (1) '*Apology* 26D–E and the Writings of Anaxagoras.' *CW* 35 (1941–2), 219–20.

_____ (2) 'Plato's *Apology* and Xenophon's *Apology*.' *CW* 20 (1927), 107–11.

Shikano, H. 'A Portrait of Socrates' (in Japanese). *HSOsakaMedSch* 3 (1972).

Shorey, Paul. (1) 'Plato: *Apology* 27E' *CPh* 23 (1928), 68–70.

_____ (2) 'The Question of the Socratic Element in Plato.' *Proceedings of the Sixth International Congress of Philosophy.* New York, 1927. 316–23.

_____ (3) *What Plato Said.* Chicago, 1933.

Siden, D. 'Did Plato Write Dialogues before the Death of Socrates?' *Apeiron* 14 (1980), 15-18.

Silverberg, R. *Sócrates*. Mexico City, 1967.

Skard, E. 'Zu Platons *Apologie* 23B.' *SO* 24 (1945), 151-3.

Skemp, J. B. (1) *Plato. G&R* suppl. *New Surveys in the Classics* 10 (1976).

_____ (2) 'Plato's Account of Divinity.' *DUJ* 29 (1967-8), 26-33.

Skorpen, E. R. 'Socrates on Piety.' *Humanist* 22 (1962), 184-5.

Skousgaard, Stephen. 'Genuine Speech vs. Chatter: A Socratic Problematic.' *Kinesis* 6 (1974), 87-94.

Smith, Nicholas D. 'Socrates.' Forthcoming in *The Dictionary of Literary Biography*. Columbia, South Carolina, 1988.

Sorel, G. *Le procès de Socrate: Examen critique des Thèses socratiques.* Paris, 1889.

Spear, O. and Ramat-Gan, 'Sokrates: Wort und Verantwortung.' *Universitas* 23 (1968), 745-52.

Speigel, Nathan. *Socrates: His Life and Thought* (in Hebrew). Jerusalem, 1979.

Spiegelberg, H. *The Socratic Enigma*. New York, 1964.

Spranger, E. 'Sokrates.' *Ant* 7 (1931), 271-8.

Stazzone, V. *Apologia de Socrate*. Brescia, 1959.

Stefanini, L. *Platone*. 2 vols. 2nd ed. Padova, 1942.

Steffen, V. 'Czy instnial Sokrates pieknyi mlody?' *Eos* 40 (1939), 13-22.

Steinen, H. von den. 'Sokrates und Platon.' *NRdschau* 64 (1953), 248-75.

Stenzel, J. 'Sokrates (Philosoph).' *RE* 2. Reihe, v. Halbb. (1927), 811-90.

Stephens, James Whyte. 'Socrates on the Rule of Law.' *HPQ* 2 (1985), 3-10.

Stern, V. 'Sokrates.' *Altertum* 3 (1957), 195-205.

Stock, St G. *The Apology of Plato*. Oxford, 1890 (reprint 1953).

Stokes, Michael. *Plato's Socratic Conversations*. Baltimore, 1987.

Stone, I. F. *The Trial of Socrates*. Boston, 1987.

Strauss, Barry S. *Athens after the Peloponnesian War: Class Faction, and Policy, 403-386 BC*. Ithaca, NY, 1987.

Strauss, Leo. (1) 'On Plato's *Apology of Socrates* and *Crito*.' In *Essays in Honor of Jacob Klein*. Annapolis, Md., 1976, 155-70.

_____ (2) *Socrates and Aristophanes*. New York, 1966.

Strycker, É. de. (1) 'La structure litéraire de l'*Apologie de Socrate*.' Abstract in *RBPh* 39 (1961), 174.

Stryrker, E. de (2) 'Les temoignages historiques sur Socrate.' *Mélanges Grégoire* 2 (*Annuuire de l'Institut de Philologie et d'Histoire orientales et slaves* 10 1950), 199–230.

_____ (3) 'The Oracle Given to Chaerephon about Socrates.' In J. Mansfield and L. M. de Rijk, eds. *Kephalaion: Studies in Greek Philosophy and its Continuation Offered to C. J. Vogel*. Assen, 1975. 39–49.

_____ (4) 'The Unity of Knowledge and Love in Socrates' Conception of Virtue.' *IPQ* 6 (1966), 428–44.

Studniczka, F. *Ein neues Bild des Sokrates*. Leipzig, 1926.

Sweeney, Leo. 'A. E. Taylor on Socrates and Plato.' *SWJP* 8 (1977), 79–99.

Tagle, M. A. 'Sócrates y el escepticimo.' *RevUNC* 3 (1962), 141–50.

Tanaka, M. *Collected Works III: The Sophists, Socrates and Others* (in Japanese). Tokyo, 1969.

Tarozzi, G. *Socrate*. Rome, 1932.

Tarrant, Dorothy. (1) 'The Pseudo-Platonic Socrates.' *CQ* 32 (1938), 167–73.

Tatakis, V. N. Ὁ Σωκράτης: ἡ ζωή του, ἡ διδασκαλία του. Athens, 1970.

Tate, J. (1) 'Greek for Atheism.' *CR* 50 (1936), 3–5.

_____ (2) 'More Greek for Atheism.' *CR* 51 (1937), 3–6.

_____ (3) 'Plato, Socrates and the Myths.' *CQ* 30 (1936), 142–5.

_____ (4) 'Reply to Professor A. E. Taylor.' *CQ* 27 (1933), 159–61.

_____ (5) 'Socrates and the Myths.' *CQ* 27 (1933), 74–80.

Taylor, A. E. (1) 'Plato's Biography of Socrates.' *PBA*, 28 March, 1917.

_____ (2) *Plato: The Man and His Work*. London, 1960.

_____ (3) *Socrates*. Garden City, 1953.

_____ (4) 'Socrates.' In *Encyclopaedia Britannica* vol. 20 (1957). 915–20.

_____ (5) 'Socrates and the Myths.' *CQ* 27 (1933), 158–9.

_____ (6) *Varia Socratica*. Oxford, 1911.

_____ (7) *What Plato Said*. Chicago, 1933.

Taylor, C. C. W. 'The End of the *Euthyphro*.' *Phronesis* 27 (1982), 109–18.

Taylor, J. H. 'Virtue and Wealth according to Socrates (*Apology* 30b).' *CB* 49 (1973), 49–52.

Tejera, Victorino. 'Ideology and Literature: Xenophon's *Defense of Socrates* and Plato's *Apology*.' In Kelly, 151–9.

Teloh, Henry. (1) 'The Importance of Interlocutors' Characters in Plato's Early Dialogues.' In J. Cleary, vol. 2 (1986), 25–38.

_____ (2) *Socratic Education in Plato's Early Dialogues*. Notre Dame, Ind. 1986.

Teraoka, H. 'Daimon in Socrates' (in Japanese). *MisakaWCB* 3 (*Misaka Junior College Bulletin* 15) 1970.

Thirlwall, C. *The History of Greece*. 8 vols. London; esp. 'On the Trial of Socrates', appendix 7 to vol. 4, 1847. 526-62.

Thornton, H. 'Socrates and the History of Psychology.' *JHBS* 5 (1969), 326-39.

Toole, H. (1) 'Αἱ ἱστορικαὶ χρονολογίαι ἐν τῷ βίῳ τοῦ Σωκράτους' *EEAth* 24 (1973-4), 372-82.

_____ (2) ' 'Η ἱστορικότης τῆς Πλατωνικῆς 'Απολογίας.' *EEAth* 24 (1973-4), 383-96.

_____ (3) 'The Social Status of Socrates as Inferred from his Military Service and other Information' (in Greek). *Platon* 27 (1975), 147-52.

_____ (4) 'Socrates: Was he a Mystical and Superstitious Person?' (in Greek). *Athena* 75 (1974-5), 318-34.

Tovar, Antonio. (1) 'Sobre la teoría politica de Sócrates y Platón.' *EClás* 9 (1965 n. 44), 69-75, followed by discussion with Rodriguez Adrados *et al.*, 79-103.

_____ (2) *Vida de Sócrates*. 3rd ed. Madrid, 1966. (Our citations are to French translation, *Socrate: sa vie et son temps,* 2nd ed. by H. E. del Medico, Paris, 1954.)

Toynbee, Arnold. 'The Search for a Prophet: Socrates and Jesus.' In Montgomery, 203-21.

Troilo, S. *Apologia di Socrate*. Naples, 1936.

Turlington, Bayly. *Socrates: The Father of Western Philosophy*. New York, 1969.

Turner, Frank M. 'Socrates and the Sophists.' In Frank M. Turner, *The Greek Heritage in Victorian Britain*. New Haven and London, 1981. 264-321.

Turolla, E. 'Una prima crisi spirituale di Platone riflessa nell'*Apologia*.' *A&R* 5 (1937), 102-18.

Tyler, W. S. *Plato's Apology and Crito*. New York and London, 1860.

Urwick, E. J. 'The Quest of Socrates.' *Sunrise* 8 (1959), 264-8.

Valaori, I. 'Socrate: Invatatura, acuzarea si moartea.' *RCl* (1934-5), 1-12.

Valgimigli, Manara. *Platone, Apologia di Socrate*. Bari, 1929.

Vandiest, J. 'Proces van Sokrates.' *Dialoog* 3 (1962-3), 46-66.

Van Dijk, I. *Socrates*. 2nd ed. Haarlem, 1942.

Vatai, Frank Leslie. *Intellectuals in Politics in the Greek World*. London, Sydney, Dover, 1984.

Verdenius, W. J. 'De socratische methode.' *Hermeneus* 25 (1953), 3–8.

Versényi, Lazlo. (1) *Holiness and Justice: An Interpretation of Plato's Euthyphro*. Lanham, New York, and London, 1982.

_____ (2) *Socratic Humanism*. New Haven and London, 1963.

Vessalio, A. *Diálogos socráticos*. Mexico City, 1963.

Vicaire, Paul. 'Platon et la divination.' *RÉG* 83 (1970), 333–50.

Vives, J. 'De la intransigencia socrático a la intolerencia platónica.' In Δώρῳ σὺν ὀλίγῳ. *Homenatge a Josep Alsina*. Present. de Bejarano, V., dir Miralles, C. Barcelona, 1969.

Vlastos, Gregory. (1) 'Editor's Introduction to Plato's *Protagoras*.' *Protagoras* trans. M. Ostwald. Indianapolis, 1976, vii–lvi.

_____ (2) 'Happiness and Virtue in Socrates' Moral Theory.' *PCPhS* NS 30 (1984), 181–213.

_____ (3) 'The Historical Socrates and Athenian Democracy.' *PolitTheor* 2 (1983), 495–516.

_____ (4) 'Introduction: The Paradox of Socrates.' In Vlastos (6), 1–21.

_____ (5) 'On the Socrates Story.' *PolitTheor* 7 (1979), 253–4.

_____ (6) (ed.) *The Philosophy of Socrates*. Garden City, 1971.

_____ (7) 'Socrates' Disavowal of Knowledge.' *PhilosQ* 35 (1985), 1–31.

_____ (8) 'Socrates on Obedience and Disobedience.' *YR* 42 (1974), 517–34.

_____ (9) 'The Socratic Elenchus.' *OSAP* 1 (1983), 27–58.

_____ (10) 'Socratic Knowledge and Platonic Pessimism.' *PhR* 66 (1957), 226–38.

_____ (11) 'Socratic Irony.' *CQ* NS 37 (1987), 79–96.

_____ (12) 'What did Socrates Understand by his "What is F?" Question.' In G. Vlastos, *Platonic Studies*. 2nd ed. Princeton, 1981.

Vloemans, A. *Socrates*. The Hague, 1963.

Vogel, Cornelia J. de. (1) 'The Present State of the Socrates Problem.' *Phronesis* 1 (1955), 26–35.

_____ (2) 'Une nouvelle interprétation du problème socratique.' *Mnemosyne* (1951), 30–9.

_____ (3) 'Who was Socrates?' *JHPh* 1 (1963), 143–61.

Voigtländer, Hans-Dieter. 'Zu Platons *Apologie* 22A6/8.' *Hermes* 91 (1963), 120–3.

Vries, G. J. de. 'Novellistic Traits in Socratic Literature.' *Mnemosyne* 16 (1963), 35–42.

Wade, F. C. 'In Defense of Socrates.' *RMeta* 25 (1971), 311-25.

Walton, Richard E. 'Socrates' Alleged Suicide.' *JVI* 14 (1980), 287-300.

Watson, Walter. 'The Voice of God.' In Kelly, 173-9.

Weber, Franz J. von (ed.) *Platons Apologie des Sokrates.* Paderborn, 1971.

Weber, M. F. 'An Immanent Interpretation of Five Platonic Dialogues: *Apology, Crito, Phaedo, Timaeus,* and *Laws* X.' Dissertation Catholic University of America, 1968.

Wenz, P. S. 'Socrates on Civil Disobedience: The *Apology* and the *Crito.*' *TWA* 61 (1973), 103-16.

West, Elinor J. 'Plato and Socrates: The Men and Their Methods.' In Kelly, 131-6.

West, T. G. *Plato's Apology of Socrates.* Ithaca and London, 1979.

Weston, A. H. 'The Question of Plato's *Euthyphro.*' *CB* 27 (1951), 57-8.

Wiggers, Gustav F. *A Life of Socrates.* London, 1840.

Wilamowitz-Möllendorff, Ulrich von. *Platon* vol. 1. Berlin, 1920.

Willim, Albert. *Platon. Apologie de Socrate.* 4th ed. Liège, 1951.

Winspear, A. D. and Silverberg, T. *Who Was Socrates?* New York, 1960.

Witwicki, W. *Eutyfron, Obrona Sokratesa, Kriton.* Warsaw, 1958.

Wohlgemuth, L. 'Die Lehre des historischen Sokrates: Versuch einer Rekonstruktion.' *OPhW* 2 (1927), 10-42.

Wolff, Edwin. *Platons Apologie.* Berlin, 1929 (reprint, Berlin, 1979).

Wolgensinger, F. H. *Platons Apologie des Sokrates und andere zeitgenössische Texte.* Zürich, 1945.

Woloszyn, S. 'Socratic Philosophy and its Role in the History of Education' (in Polish). E. Frydman and I. Kaltenberg, eds. In *Problemy kultury i wychowania Zbiór studiów.* Warsaw, 1963.

Wood, Ellen Meiksins, and Wood, Neal. *Class Ideology and Ancient Political Theory: Socrates, Plato, and Aristotle in Social Context.* New York, 1978.

Woodbury, Leonard. (1) 'Socrates and Archelaus.' *Phoenix* 25 (1971), 299-309.

____ (2) 'Socrates and the Daughter of Aristides.' *Phoenix* 27 (1973), 7-25.

Woodhead, M. D. 'The Daimonion of Socrates.' *CPh* 35 (1940), 425-6.

Woodruff, Paul. *Plato, the Hippias Major.* Indianapolis, 1982.

Woozley, A. D. (1) *Law and Obedience: The Arguments of Plato's Crito.* Chapel Hill, 1979.

____ (2) 'Socrates on Disobeying the Law.' In Vlastos (6), 299-318.

Wotke, F. 'Die Berufsauffassung des Sokrates.' *OPhW* 6 (1934), 7-10.

Wundt, M. 'Sokrates.' *Pädagog. Lexikon* 4 (1931), 625-33.

Yaffe, M. D. 'Civil Disobedience and the Opinion of the Many: Plato's *Crito*.' *ModS* 54 (1976-7), 123-36.

Young, Gary. 'Socrates on Obedience and Disobedience.' *Phronesis* 14 (1974), 1-29.

Zeller, Eduard. (1) *Phil. d. Gr.* vol. 1. Leipzig, 1922 (reprint, 1963).

____ (2) *Socrates and the Socratic Schools*. Trans. O. J. Reichel. London, 1877.

Zimmerman, Johannes. *Platon. Apologie. Erläuterungen*. Paderborn, 1953.

Zimmerman, Michael E. 'Socratic Ignorance and Authenticity.' *TSPh* 29 (1980), 133-50.

Zinn, Howard. *Disobedience and Democracy*. New York, 1968.

Zubiri, Xavier. *Sócrates y la sabiduria Griega*. Madrid, 1940.

Zuccante, G. (1) *Intorno alle fonti della dottrina di Socrate*. Pavia, 1902.

____ (2) *Socrate. Fonti. Ambiente. Vita. Dottrina*. Milan, 1905.

Zürcher, J. *Das Corpus Academicum in neuer Auffassung dargestellt*, Paderborn, 1954.

LIST OF PERIODICALS
AND ABBREVIATIONS

A&R	*Atene e Roma*
AAN	*Atti dell'Accademia di Scienze morali e politiche della Società nazionale de Scienze, Lettere ed Arti di Napoli*
AC	*L'Antiquité Classique*
ACD	*Acta Classica Universitatis Scientiarum Debreceniensis*
Acme	*Acme*
AFGL	*Appunti di Filologia Greco–Latina*
AFLN	*Annali della Facolta di Lettere e Filosofia della Universita di Napoli*
AGMath	*Archiv für Geschichte der Mathematik*
AGPh	*Archiv für Geschichte der Philosophie*
Aitia	*Aitia*
AJPh	*American Journal of Philology*
ALGP	*Annali del Liceo Classio G. Garibaldi di Palermo*
Altertum	*Altertum*
AncPhil	*Ancient Philosophy*
AncWorld	*Ancient World*
Anregung	*Anregung*
Ant	*Die Antike: Zeitschrift für Kunst und Kultur der Altertumswissenschaft*
Antichthon	*Antichthon*
ANTP	*Algemeen Nederlands Tijdschrift voor Wijsbegeerte en Psychologie*
Apeiron	*Apeiron*
APQ	*American Philosophical Quarterly*
ArchivPhilos	*Archiv für Philosophie*
Arethusa	*Arethusa*
Atheneum	*Atheneum*
Athena	*Athena* (Athens)
AU	*Der altsprachliche Unterricht*
AUChile	*Anales de la Universidad de Chile*
BAB	*Bulletin de la Classe des Lettres de l'Académie Royale de Belgique*
BAGB	*Bulletin de l'Association Guillaume Budé*

BASP	*Bulletin of the American Society of Papyrologists*
BIEH	*Boletín del Instituto de Estudios Helénicos*
BUJ	*Boston University Journal*
C&M	*Classica et Mediaevalia*
CA	*Classical Antiquity*
CanJP	*Canadian Journal of Philosophy*
CB	*Classical Bulletin*
Christengemeinschaft	*Die Christengemeinschaft*
CJ	*Classical Journal*
CPh	*Classical Philology*
CQ	*Classical Quarterly*
CR	*Classical Review*
CuadFilos	*Cuadernos de Filosofía*
Cultura	*La Cultura*
CV	*Citta di Vita* (Rome)
CW	*Classical Weekly* (later, *Classical World*)
Darshana	*Darshana International*
Dialogos	*Dialogos*
Dialogue	*Dialogue* (Canada)
Dialoog	*Dialoog* (Antwerp)
Dianoia	*Dianoia*
DNGids	*De Nieuwe Gids*
DUJ	*Durham University Journal* (England)
EClás	*Estudios Clásicos* (Madrid)
EEAth	Ἐπιστημονικὴ Ἐπετηρὶς τῆς φιλοσοφικῆς Σχολῆς τοῦ Πανεπιστημίου Ἀθηνῶν
ELeb	*Das Edle Leben*
Emerita	*Emerita*
Eos	*Eos*
ÉPh	*Études Philosophiques*
Eranos	*Eranos*
Eranos-Jb	*Eranos-Jahrbuch*
Esp	*Espíritu*
EstFilos	*Estudios Filosoficos* (Spain)
Ethics	*Ethics*
FelsefeArk	*Felsefe Arkivi* (Istanbul)
FUHJ	*Fukuoka Univ. Humanities Journal*
G&R	*Greece and Rome*
GB	*Grazer Beitrage*
GCFI	*Giornale critico della Filosofia Italiana*
Gymnasium	*Gymnasium*
Helikon	*Helikon*

Hermeneus	*Hermeneus*
Hermes	*Hermes*
HG	*Humanistisches Gymnasium*
HiroshimaUS	*Hiroshima University Studies, Literature Department: Philosophy*
Hochland	*Hochland*
HPQ	*History of Philosophy Quarterly*
HSOsakaMedSch	*Humanity Studies* (Osaka Medical School)
HSPh	*Harvard Studies in Classical Philology*
HT	*History Today*
HUDLB	*Hokkaido University Department of Literature Bulletin*
Humanist	*The Humanist*
IJE	*International Journal of Ethics*
IL	*L'Information Litteraire*
IncCult	*Incontri Culturali*
IndPQ	*Indian Philosophical Quarterly*
Interpretation	*Interpretation*
IPQ	*International Philosophical Quarterly*
Iura	*Iura*
JCS	*Journal of Classical Studies* (Japan)
JGenEd	*Journal of General Education*
JHBS	*Journal of the History of the Behavioral Sciences*
JHI	*Journal of the History of Ideas*
JHPh	*Journal of the History of Philosophy*
JHS	*Journal of Hellenic Studies*
JP	*Journal of Philology*
JPh	*Journal of Philosophy*
JVI	*Journal of Value Inquiry*
Kinesis	*Kinesis*
Kommenden	*Die Kommenden: Eine unabhangige Zeitschrift für geistige und soziale Erneuerung*
LCM	*Liverpool Classical Monthly*
LÉC	*Les Études Classiques*
LibEd	*Liberal Education*
LMS	*Letopis Matice Srpske* (Novi Sad)
Lustrum	*Lustrum*
Maia	*Maia*
MDR	*Monatschrift für Deutsches Recht*
Merkur	*Merkur*
Methodos	*Methodos: Studies in Classical Philosophy* (Kyoto University Department of Literature)

MH	*Museum Helveticum*
Mind	*Mind*
MisakaWCB	*Misaka Women's College Bulletin*
MiscFranc	*Miscellanea Francescana*
Mnemosyne	*Mnemosyne*
ModA	*Modern Age*
ModS	*Modern Schoolman*
Monist	*Monist*
MT	*Museum Tusculanum* (Copenhagen)
N&S	*Nord & Süd*
Nación	*Le Nación* (Buenos Aires newspaper)
NHPh	*Neue Hefte für Philosophie*
NJA	*Neue Jahrbucher für die Klassische Altertum*
NJW	*Neue Jahrbucher für Wissenschaft und Jugendbildung*
NRdschau	*Neue Rundschau*
NRS	*Nuovo Rivista Storica*
NSchol	*New Scholasticism*
NT	*Nordisk Tidskrift*
OPhW	*Opuscula Philologica*
Orpheus	*Orpheus*
OSAP	*Oxford Studies in Ancient Philosophy*
PädagRdsch	*Pädagogische Rundschau*
Paideia (Arona)	*Paideia* (Arona)
Paideia (Buffalo)	*Paideia* (Buffalo)
PAS	*Proceedings of the Aristotelian Society*
PBA	*Proceedings of the British Academy*
PCA	*Proceedings of the Classical Association*
PCPhS	*Proceedings of the Cambridge Philological Society*
PedVit	*Pedagogia e Vita*
Pensiero	*Pensiero*
Personalist	*Personalist*
Ph&PhenR	*Philosophy and Phenomenological Research*
PhilLit	*Philosophy and Literature*
Philologus	*Philologus*
Philosophia (Argent)	*Philosophia* (Argentina)
Philosophia (Athens)	*Philosophia* (Athens)
Philosophiques	*Philosophiques*
Philosophy	*Philosophy*
PhilosQ	*Philosophical Quarterly*
PhiloRdschau	*Philosophische Rundschau*
PhilTop	*Philosophical Topics*

PhilRhet	*Philosophy and Rhetoric*
Phoenix	*Phoenix*
PhQ	*Philological Quarterly*
PhR	*Philosophical Review*
Phronesis	*Phronesis*
Phrontisterion	*Phrontisterion*
PhW	*Philologische Wochenschrift*
Platon	Πλατῶν
PolitTheor	*Political Theory*
PP	*La Parola del Passato*
PPES	*Proceedings of the Philosophy of Education Society*
PResArch	*Philosophy Research Archives*
Proteus	*Proteus*
QUCC	*Quaderni Urbinati di Cultura Classica*
RassFilos	*Rassegna di Filosofia*
RCl	*Revista Clásica (Orpheus–Favonicus)* (Bucharest)
RE	*Pauly–Wissowa, Real Encyclopedia der Classichen Altertumswissenschaft*
RÉA	*Revue des Études Anciennes*
REC	*Revista de Estudios Clásicos* (Mendoza)
RÉG	*Revue des Études Greques*
REPolít	*Revista de Estudios Políticos* (Madrid)
RevFacCathOuest	*Revue des Facultes Catholiques de l'Ouest*
RevNouv	*La Revue Nouvelle* (Tournai)
RevUNC	*Revista de la Universidad Nacional de Cordoba*
RFNeo	*Revista di Filosofia Neoscholastica*
RFil	*Revista de Filosofia* (La Plata)
RhM	*Rheinisches Museum für Philologie*
RIFD	*Revista Internazionale de Filosofia del Diritto*
RIPh	*Revue Internationale de Philosophie*
RLHirosake	*Review of Literature* (Hirosaki University)
RMeta	*Review of Metaphysics*
RMM	*Revue de Metaphysique et de Morale*
RPAA	*Rationalist Press Association Annual*
RPh	*Revue de Philologie*
RPhilos	*Revue Philosophique (de la France et de l'Étranger)*
RPol	*Review of Politics*
RPortFil	*Revista Portuguesa de Filosofia*
RPP	*Revue de Psychologie des Peuples*
RSC	*Revista di Studi Classici*

RSF	*Revista critica di Storia della Filosofia*
RThPh	*Revue de Theologie et de Philosophie*
Saeculum	*Saeculum*
SAWW	*Sitzungsberichte der Osterreichischen Akademie der Wissenschaft in Wien*
SCI	*Scripta Classica Israelica*
SK	*Seishin Kagaku* (Japan University)
SO	*Symbolae Osloenses*
SocRes	*Social Research*
SoJP	*Southern Journal of Philosophy*
Sophia	*Sophia*
StudGen	*Studium Generale*
Sunrise	*Sunrise* (Pasadena, California)
SWJP	*Southwestern Journal of Philosophy*
SWPStud	*Southwest Philosophical Studies*
Talanta	*Talanta*
TAPhA	*Transactions of the American Philological Association*
TheolV	*Theologia Viatorum: Jahrbuch der Kirchliche Hochschule, Berlin*
Theoria	*Theoria*
TLS	*Times Literary Supplement*
TRSC	*Transactions of the Royal Society of Canada*
TSPh	*Tulane Studies in Philosophy*
TUEA	*Tohoku University (Sendai) Education Annual*
TWA	*Transactions of the Wisconsin Academy of Sciences, Arts and Letters*
UCPUB	*University of California Philosophical Union Bulletin*
Universitas	*Universitas*
Verbum	*Verbum* (Rio de Janeiro)
Vozes	*Vozes* (Petropolis)
WS	*Wiener Studien*
WZPot	*Wissenschaftliche Zeitschrift der Pädagogische Hochschule Potsdam*
YClS	*Yale Classical Studies*
YR	*Yale Review*
Zeit	*Das Zeit. Wochenzeitung für Politik, Wirtschaft, Handel und Kultur*
ZPäd	*Zeitschrift für Pädagogik*
ZPhF	*Zeitschrift für philosophische Forschung*

GENERAL INDEX

INDEX OF PASSAGES

Titles of spurious or doubtful works are bracketed.

Printed in the United Kingdom
by Lightning Source UK Ltd.
103267UKS00002B/13